THE FOUNDATIONS OF
SOCIAL ANTHROPOLOGY

The
Foundations
of
Social Anthropology

by

S. F. NADEL

Professor of Anthropology, Australian National University

LONDON: COHEN & WEST

And, as the science of man is the only solid foundation for the other sciences, so, the only solid foundation we can give to this science itself must be laid on experience and observation.

HUME: *A Treatise of Human Nature*

The new tinge to modern minds is a vehement and passionate interest in the relation of general principles to irreducible and stubborn facts.

WHITEHEAD: *Science and the Modern World*

To this we now add, as a helpful analogy provided it is not pressed too far, that conscious purpose is the 'matter' and chance the 'empty space' of the objective world. In the physical universe matter occupies only a small region compared with the empty space; but, rightly or wrongly, we look on it as the most significant part. In the same way we look on consciousness as the significant part of the objective universe, though it appears to occur only in isolated centres in a background of chaos.

EDDINGTON: *The Philosophy of Physical Science*

COPYRIGHT

FIRST PUBLISHED JANUARY 1951
SECOND IMPRESSION FEBRUARY 1953
THIRD IMPRESSION 1958
FOURTH IMPRESSION 1963
FIFTH IMPRESSION 1969

SBN 7100 1880 0

PRINTED IN GREAT BRITAIN BY
LOWE AND BRYDONE (PRINTERS) LTD., LONDON, N.W.10

Preface

This book is not a Textbook on Social Anthropology. It does not attempt to summarize either the knowledge we possess of primitive societies or the advances we have made in their study. At least, such a summary is incidental to the main theme of the book, which is concerned, rather, with the logical premises that underlie our knowledge of societies (whether they be primitive or otherwise) and with the prerequisites, conceptual and technical, of any enquiry meant to lead to this knowledge. If the clumsily informative titles of earlier scholars were still in fashion I might have called my book 'Prolegomena to the Study of Society: being an Enquiry into the Nature of Sociological Knowledge'. As it is, I speak simply of 'Foundations'.

This book, then, is about *Method*. But I trust that it does not thereby qualify for Poincaré's cynical comment: 'Nearly every sociological thesis proposes a new method which, however, its author is careful not to apply, so that sociology is the science with the greatest number of methods and the least results.'[1] The methods here analyzed are constantly applied—by others as well as myself. Also, they have produced results, to which the literature of anthropology amply testifies. In a different sense, however, there is some lack of agreement between anthropological method and practice. For much that is fundamental in the method of social anthropology has been applied tacitly as well as unguardedly, without full awareness of all that it implies. Indeed, judged from this viewpoint, it seems true to say that anthropology has been concerned too much with results, and too little with thinking about method. I have attempted to 'think about method'; and here my task has often resolved itself into bringing into the open what other anthropologists have left unexpressed, rendering tacit methods explicit, and exhibiting their full import. Much of what I shall have to say will thus be a restatement of things well known. Yet I felt that they needed restatement, both in explicit terms and in some new

[1] Henri Poincaré, *Science and Method*, pp. 19–20.

A*

v

order capable of standing on its own, that is, in the form of a system. Scientific progress rests in large measure on such a re-ordering of 'things known'; which is my justification.

Restatement involves, inevitably, the choice of new words or the revision of familiar ones. In this book, therefore, considerable space will be devoted to linguistic and terminological issues. I do not think that an apology is needed. That all sciences operate with words is a truism; that our science also deals with a subject matter in great part made up of words, I hope to show. Nor will it be denied that the linguistic usage in our discipline is greatly in need of reform and that we have let its diversity and arbitrariness grow too far. It is in a sense a task of conscience to cut back this growth. Yet I would overrate neither the promise nor the urgency of this task. Even sciences more mature and more rigorous than ours have not fully unified their vocabulary.[1] Nor can diversity and arbitrari-ness of usage be avoided entirely. In some ways, and at some stage of our enquiries, we all act like Humpty Dumpty and make words mean what we like. And if I am here trying a little to correct this failing in others, I may well be guilty of it myself.

Finally, I have ranged more widely over the field of knowledge than is customary in books on social anthropology. Yet my concern with philosophy, natural science, or logic, and my broad treatment of psychology should not be judged far-fetched or unwarranted. If anthropology is ready to claim a place among the sciences, as I believe it is, that place needs to be defined; and this definition can in turn be given only in terms of the relationships linking the Study of Man with the whole universe of scientific knowledge.

Whether I happened to be dealing with anthropological pro-blems in the narrow sense or with these more far-flung issues, I could not but follow the paths which others have shown. As regards the scholars whose ideas guided my enquiry, their names will ap-pear throughout the book and their influence be visible at every step. But let me state at once my greatest indebtedness. It is, in the field of sociology, to the work of Max Weber and Talcott Parsons; in anthropology, to Malinowski and Radcliffe-Brown; and in psychology, to Wolfgang Köhler, Karl Koffka, and Kurt Lewin.

[1] Let me quote this passage from Whitehead: 'Logic is, by far, that branch of philosophy best systematized with the aid of a stable technical language.' Yet 'there is considerable variation in the usages of (crucial) terms among logicians' (*Adventures of Ideas*, p. 294).

But I must not forget another influence, as decisive and fruitful—that of my own students, who listened to many of my ideas in the course of lectures and whose criticisms and questions have helped to shape such answers as I am able to give.

S. F. N.

University of Durham
November 1949

Contents

CHAPTER		PAGE
I	PROLEGOMENA: WHY ANTHROPOLOGY?	
	1 The Approach to Primitive Society	2
	2 Anthropology, Sociology, and History	8
	3 The Bridge of Understanding	17
II	THE AIMS OF SOCIAL ANTHROPOLOGY	
	1 Facts and Theory	20
	2 Anthropology divided	25
	3 Premises of Observation	28
III	OBSERVATION AND DESCRIPTION	
	1 The Use of Informants	35
	2 The Use of Language	39
	3 The Personal Equation	48
IV	PSYCHOLOGY IN OBSERVATION	
	1 The Problem	56
	2 Behaviourism	57
	3 The Alter Ego	64
	4 Motives behind Behaviour	68
	5 Nomenclature	72
V	THE MATERIAL OF OBSERVATION	
	1 The Nexus of Behaviour	75
	2 Social Dimensions	78
	3 Action Autonomous	87
	4 Grouping Autonomous	90
	5 The Individual	91
	6 Pointer Relations	98
	7 Note on Change and Evolution	100
VI	INSTITUTIONS	
	1 Problems of Definition	107
	2 Standardization	111
	3 Institution and Group	118

CHAPTER   PAGE

4 Aim Contents — 123
5 On Classification — 129
6 Interaction of Institutions — 136
7 Residual Categories — 142

VII GROUPINGS
1 Definitions — 145
2 Recruitment — 151
3 Groups and Institutions — 156
4 Cohesion and Endurance — 165
5 Internal Order — 169
6 External Order — 176
7 Society as a Whole — 183
8 Residual Categories — 188

VIII EXPLANATION
1 Anthropology and Natural Science — 191
2 Explanation and Common Sense — 194
3 Explanation and Analysis — 199
4 Causality — 207
5 The Hierarchy of Sciences — 209
6 Conclusions — 219

IX EXPERIMENTAL ANTHROPOLOGY
1 The Comparative Method — 222
2 Technique — 229
3 The Limitations of the Method — 237
4 The Nature of Sociological Laws — 246

X EXPERIMENTAL ANTHROPOLOGY (continued)
1 The Categories of Social Understanding — 256
2 Logical Consistency — 258
3 Purpose — 265
4 Causality — 276
5 Rules of Application — 279

XI PSYCHOLOGICAL EXPLANATIONS: MENTAL ENERGY
1 Preliminaries — 289
2 Social Psychology — 290
3 Object and Function Language — 294
4 Mental Energy — 298

CHAPTER   PAGE

    5 The Dynamic Properties of Mental Events   302
    6 Psychological Linkage   313
    7 Energy in Explanation   323

XII PSYCHOLOGICAL   EXPLANATIONS: ACTION
       POTENTIALS
    1 Instincts and Pseudo-Instincts   328
    2 Generic Action Potentials   333
       (i) Pleasure—Displeasure   337
       (ii) Equilibrium—Tension   340
       (iii) Conformity—Shame   348
    3 The Limits of Psychological Understanding   354
    4 Drives and Rationality   363

XIII FUNCTION AND PATTERN
    1 The Function Concept   368
    2 Integration and Survival   371
    3 The Totality of Culture   380
    4 Pattern Formations   385
    5 Configurations   395
       (i) Purpose—Ethos   395
       (ii) Purpose—Eidos   398
       (iii) Ethos—Eidos   401
    6 Conclusions: Culture and Personality   402

  BIBLIOGRAPHY   409

  INDEX   415

CHAPTER I

Prolegomena : Why Anthropology?

W hen discussing methods and first principles in social anthropology the devotees of this branch of learning rarely omit some reference, of more or less apologetic nature, to the youth of their discipline. In his posthumously published essay on *A Scientific Theory of Culture* the late Professor Malinowski attempted what was, to him, a final synthesis, a self-reliant system, of anthropological knowledge; yet even there you will find that inevitable apologetic opening:

'Anthropology, as the science of man at large, as the most comprehensive discipline in humanism without portfolio, was the last to come. It had to peg out its claims as to scope, subject matter, and method as best it could. It absorbed what was left over and even had to encroach on some older preserves. . . .'[1]

There seem to be good grounds for such becoming modesty of youth. As a field of interest, where observations appear worth making and discoveries worth recording, social anthropology is little more than a hundred years old. As an attempt to systematize observation it is much younger, having only in the last few decades emerged as a separate branch of enquiry from other disciplines, similarly concerned with man and society—biology, psychology, human geography, or comparative and universal history. Nor perhaps is the distinctness of social anthropology even now unequivocally defined; it is not yet a redundant task to draw the dividing line between social anthropology on the one hand and, say, ethnology and cultural history on the other.

All of which goes to say that the concepts of social anthropology must still be fluid, its technique tentative, and its generalizations controversial. Yet there is no reason for being too apologetic, and the plea of youth may easily be overstated. At least, such a plea could not account for all that is tentative and uncertain in the

[1] B. Malinowski (1944), p. 3.

anthropologist's approach. For if the concepts of social anthropology are fluid and its techniques often tentative, this is due also to the nature of its material, that is, to that most fluid and manifold reality—human existence and behaviour in all its forms and in all climes and regions. If even the scope of social anthropology needs defining, this reflects the complexity of the phenomena upon whose various aspects so many sciences direct their interests. Thus, if apologize we must, let us plead the magnitude of our task and ambition no less than our late arrival among the sciences of man.

1. The Approach to Primitive Society

The scope of any science is to obtain and extend knowledge. In social anthropology as it is commonly understood we attempt to extend our knowledge of man and society to 'primitive' communities, 'simpler peoples', or 'preliterate societies'. If anyone is here tempted to ask why we should wish to do so, several answers can probably be given. Whatever they are, they will only paraphrase the same fact—that we *are* extending our study of society in this sense, as we are everywhere and constantly extending the orbit of knowledge over new fields. Knowledge is no doubt its own reward, though this is merely a trite rationalization of something that is simply given. As in all other disciplines, practical considerations— here the interests of missionaries, colonial administrators, and the like—have now and then produced an additional stimulus. But the primary reason is both more compelling and less utilitarian. It lies in the nature of science, which suffers no *terra incognita*. If an anthropologist asks naïvely why, if we are only interested in studying society writ large, we should turn to primitive cultures rather than to our own civilization 'which we know a million times better . . . and where we have abundant and adequate data',[1] the answer is simply that our own society is not the only one, and its phenomena not the same as those found, or apt to be found, in primitive society.

The further question, why we study society at all, I would much sooner leave unanswered lest it involve us in the futile argument about the respective claims of 'pure' and 'applied' science. Any kind of knowledge, once it is obtained, is there to be used or applied: 'True science is *par excellence* such knowledge *as hath a tendency to use*.'[2] Thus, our urge or desire to go on expanding our

[1] P. Radin (1933), p. 52.   [2] L. Hogben (1938), p. 27.

knowledge does not contradict that other desire, to apply knowledge to practical problems; nor yet need those who pursue knowledge keep aloof from any attempts at putting it to use; on the contrary, I shall later defend precisely this view. Yet as I have suggested, the utilitarian motive does not exhaust the impulse behind
social enquiry. And if it is said that 'the only valid distinction
between pure and applied research . . . lies between enquiries concerned with issues which *may eventually* and issues which *already
do* arise in the social practice of mankind',[1] I would object to the
word 'only' in the sentence (while agreeing with everything else).
For surely there is a world of difference between an enquiry whose
eventual application does not at the time concern the enquirer and
one at once assessed against practical issues. The wish to do things,
to bring about some desired change, as it presupposes knowledge,
so it may well stimulate and guide scientific enquiry. Yet equally,
that wish will often grow out of enquiries and knowledge that have
pressed on by their own impetus. Finally, any application of knowledge also means its testing and verification, that is, once more an
expansion of the realm of known things. And nothing more can usefully be said.

To return to our narrower province of social enquiry. The conventional limitation of social anthropology to the study of 'primitive
peoples' is no longer strictly true. But we may disregard this for
the moment. It is clear, however, that 'primitive', 'simpler', or
'preliterate', represent essentially relative concepts, implying some
comparison between the field of social anthropology and our own
culture and society; which latter field is studied by two other disciplines, history and sociology. The comparison further implies a
yardstick—of evolution, growth, or complexity. Does, then,
anthropology start where history and sociology leave off, or perhaps end where these begin? Does it extend the scope of social
enquiry over a field which, since it is deficient in certain qualities of
complexity or certain achievements of evolution, is closed to
sociology and history?

Considering this question only from the viewpoint of technique
and method, this appears to be the case. One such deficiency is
fully familiar, namely, the absence of documentary evidence.
Whatever the definition of history, it is concerned with past events.
The methods of social history (or of historically-minded sociology)

[1] Op. cit., p. 28.

imply the existence of written records, from which the past can be described and reconstructed. I said 'social history'; to avoid mis-understandings, let me make it clear that I mean the kind of history that has been written by Mommsen or Rostovtseff, Trevelyan or Vinogradoff. Admittedly, there is also archæology, which reconstructs a past undocumented by records and written evidence. But this form of digging-up the past is both one-sided and indefinite. It may reveal styles of art, the spread of technology, the siting of cities, perhaps forms of worship: as to regularities of social behaviour, forms of group organization, norms or beliefs, even the precise use to which the surviving artefacts were put, it remains largely silent. Archæology by itself is not and never can be *social* history. At best, archæology is suggestive of social history—a social history which cannot be written from these sources only. Moreover, the time perspective for archæological discoveries is measured in centuries or millenia; you cannot link generation with generation or produce precisely timed antecedents for concrete subsequent events.

In the study of primitive civilizations a history of archæological nature is possible and has been attempted. The German *Kultur-kreis* theory is such a history without historical records, based, though not on the excavation of strata, yet on the interpretation of the obtaining cultural diversity in terms of past sequences of strata. American Diffusionism, of more restricted scope but much greater precision, equally extracts from the observable distribution of cultural items evidence as to their past sequence and migration. These are legitimate pursuits: but they are not yet history as I here understand it. Whether or not these reconstructions overstate the influence of 'borrowing' in cultural growth we need not examine. Even if the diffusion of cultural items is unequivocally demon-strated, it offers no understanding of the past beyond the implied suggestion, however strong, that there must have been reasons, apart from occasions, for the acts of 'borrowing'—that the latter filled a pre-existing need or matched the outlook and mood of the society in question. These are constructions *ex post facto* and, essentially, plausible assumptions as to the social situation at the time. In other words, they presuppose a social history but do not, by themselves, produce it.[1]

---

[1] The facts of diffusion have, however, a relevant negative implication, namely, that the society examined existed, at some period, without this or that

A second deficiency in the study of primitive civilization is perhaps to-day not as readily admitted. Sociology as well as history presuppose a certain familiarity of the observer with the nature of the data he studies; both disciplines imply that certain commonly used categories are immediately applicable, and that the probabilities and consequences of actions are either readily understood or deducible with self-evidence from the general background of experience. New items discovered in history, or new problems examined by sociology, fall into place against this background of an experience which is common to observer and observed. This is not true of primitive society, which is unfamiliar and often strange (though it has become old-fashioned to admit this).[1] In any event, there is no background of common experience uniting observer and observed: items do not fall readily into place, and probabilities cannot be calculated with self-evidence. Social categories must be evolved *ad hoc*; they cannot be simply taken for granted.

This strangeness of primitive cultures, their separation from our civilization, were strongly felt by the early anthropologists. Sir Henry Maine, when discussing primitive law, notes that 'the phenomena which early societies present us with are not easy at first to understand. . . . It is a difficulty arising from their strangeness. . . . One does not readily get over the surprise which they occasion when looked at from a modern point of view.'[2] Morgan, speaking of primitive religion, is willing to admit 'that it may never receive a perfectly satisfactory explanation', since all 'primitive religions are grotesque and to some extent unintelligible'.[3] Obviously, this unfamiliarity diminishes as knowledge progresses. Thus we have grown much more optimistic, and much less ready to admit intellectual defeat. To-day the tendency is to emphasize, not the strangeness of primitive society, but its akinness to our own. Often, indeed, observers seem animated by the desire to demonstrate how, after all, man is the same everywhere. Whether this identity of human civilization might not be prematurely stated, or stated for levels of abstraction too general to be of much value, we

---

cultural item. This relevance of diffusion for social enquiry belongs to the order of limiting and background factors of which we shall speak presently (see below, p. 13).

[1] Kroeber still speaks of the 'institutions strange in flavour' to which anthropology 'turned its attention' (1923, p. 2).

[2] Sir Henry Maine (1888), pp. 119–220.

[3] Lewis Morgan (1877), p. 5.

may for the moment disregard. The fact remains that even such a general identity must be extracted from cultural material strikingly different from that with which historians and sociologists normally deal. If, in primitive man, we discover our cousin, we do so after having penetrated many layers of disguise.

The social anthropologist, then, examines societies 'without history', and cultures of an 'exotic' nature. Under this twofold set of conditions his technique and method evolved. Lack of adequate records necessitates a study concerned with the present rather than the past, with things visible rather than extractable. It means fieldwork, not work in archives and libraries, and concern with day-to-day events rather than with long-range processes. The unfamiliarity of the cultural make-up necessitates prolonged study, and study of an intimate nature, in which the strangeness is overcome by something like an intellectual assimilation. It also entails great comprehensiveness, since in the unfamiliar context nothing can be taken for granted and the relevance or irrelevance of particular facts is not immediately visible. Add to this the practical limitations of fieldwork. This intimate and intensive study is carried out in a society to which one must travel, and where one can stay only for a limited period; also, it is carried out among a people where even verbal communication presents a problem, so that the study of the native language may have to precede the study of culture and social life. All this means restriction in range. The anthropologists thus tended to become the biographers of single societies; often they chose small groups, where the intensive studies could be more adequately applied; always they had to exclude, or to use merely in an approximate fashion, that most valuable tool of modern sociology—statistics.

If the anthropologist thus became an explorer as well as a recorder, both a pathfinder and cartographer, this has fashioned his whole outlook. Finding no ready-made categories into which his 'strange' data would self-evidently fit, he has to work out his own categories, even his own terminology. He must search for his own First Principles where sociology or history merely apply or extend established principles. He asks new questions where the other students of society merely look for answers to customary questions. The peculiarities and restrictions of anthropological study thus also turned into advantages of method; for here were born a more searching spirit of enquiry and a viewpoint unbiased by convention and prejudice. Apology for shortcomings may justifiably give way to pride in new achievements.

Yet, as has been mentioned, it is no longer true to describe anthropology as being concerned only with 'primitive' and 'preliterate' societies, 'without history'. To-day anthropological research has been extended to West Africa, China, Indonesia and India, that is, to societies which are certainly not without written history, which are only partly preliterate, and 'primitive' or 'simple' only in a very inaccurate sense. Nor does the attribute 'exotic' apply any longer. The subject matter of anthropological enquiry is 'exotic' only for the anthropologist from the West who seeks knowledge (or perhaps intellectually refined adventure) in the study of the indigenous societies of Africa, Oceania, South America, and so forth. This is clearly not true of the Chinese or Indian anthropologists who have recently begun to investigate their own cultures; while the Western anthropologist who chooses for his field native life in colonial cities or regions exemplifying the encroachment of Western civilization meets at least with some familiar aspects. Furthermore, certain studies, still styled as anthropological, have also been carried out in Europe and America, among communities belonging fully to our own civilization. Indeed, many of us think that here we have a new and promising field for anthropological enquiry.

There is sense in calling even these researches anthropological: for they still remain true to that searching spirit of enquiry which evolved in the study of simpler and preliterate peoples. We treat a familiar culture as though it were a strange one, without historical background. We consciously choose this approach so that we may view the culture from a new angle and throw into relief features obscured by other forms of study. Again, we concentrate upon observation rather than extraction, upon intensive analysis rather than wide-range surveys, hoping to discover things which the conventional sociological research would omit and historical documents fail to record.

Let us not drive this parallel too far. To ignore advanced sociological techniques—of surveys and statistical enquiry—where they can be applied is obviously shortsighted; to shut out history where its facts are available for use, unjustifiable. Study a civilization with a long and documented history without paying attention to it, and you will misconstrue your facts; study a complex society by intimate observation only, discarding the help which wide-range sociological enquiry can offer, and you will arrive at disconnected data—picturesque, perhaps, but of limited value.

All this is obvious enough. But it appears to assign to the social anthropologist a new, and not very impressive, role. From the pioneer of a new study of society he seems to have become a 'failed' sociologist or an anti-historian *malgré lui*. He is, in fact, neither—though he is sometimes hailed, or pitied, as one or the other. He is a sociologist who turned to new fields and, forced by the nature of his material, had to develop new methods. This has its advantages as well as shortcomings; anthropology certainly opened up a vast range of new facts not otherwise approachable. Perhaps, too, the advantages outweigh the shortcomings: but here I am speaking as an anthropologist, and thus as an interested party. However this may be, the aims of the sociologist and anthropologist are the same, though the two disciplines differ in technique and method.

The relation between history and social anthropology is of a different kind; here the aims differ, though the methods of the historian also serve the anthropologist and may often be indispensable. But let me explain this more fully.

2. ANTHROPOLOGY, SOCIOLOGY, AND HISTORY

We have spoken of sociology and history as though the scope and interest of these disciplines were unequivocally defined. This is far from the truth. There are the sociologists who, like Simmel, Max Weber, Talcott Parsons, von Wiese or Sorokin, concentrate on theoretical problems and on 'pure' sociology. They examine the structure of society in the abstract; they are preoccupied with questions of methodology and logic, and aim at formulating basic principles and categories of social existence. Then there are the more earth-bound sociologists of social surveys and field studies, pursuing research into practical social problems—criminality, social classes, community organization. There are, too, the social philosophers, concerned with problems of values and ethics and the whence and whither of human civilization: men like Spencer, Hobhouse, Westermarck, Durkheim. Nor must the historically-minded sociologists (or sociologically-minded historians) be forgotten.

All these lines of research are aspects rather than rigid branches of the study of society, between which divisions are fluid. Sociology is, fundamentally, a synoptic science. The social anthropologist, by virtue of his calling, is even more fully committed to such a synoptic view. His is Terence's motto—*Nihil humani a me alienum puto*. Economics, religion, kinship, law, art—they all fall within his purview. Like the practical sociologist, the anthropologist is primarily a fieldworker; yet having to search for his own First Principles (as I put it), he rubs shoulders with the theoretical sociologist; and anthropologists are as ready as social philosophers to plumb the depths of the 'whence and whither of civilization'. The over-ambition of youthfulness? Perhaps; but surely also the breadth of view of those sailing uncharted seas.

As regards the relationship of anthropology and history, I would hold that the social anthropologist is not a historian. But what kind of historian is he not? History seems to be very much as history does, and historians do all sorts of things. It is mainly the philosophers (or philosophically-minded historians) who lay down rigidly what history is and can do, or what it is not and can never do—and one such proposition we shall presently discuss. The practical students of history may not hold themselves bound by such pronouncements. Whether that makes them bad historians is open to doubt, though it makes them a different kind of historian. But clearly, all historians, of whatever persuasion, share one characteristic that distinguishes them from the sociologist and anthropologist. All historians study events and actions 'in the past'.[1] This is not as clear-cut a distinction as it might seem. To begin with, where does the past begin, or an 'ordinary' past turn into a 'historical' one—a year ago, or ten, fifty, a hundred years ago? Moreover, when an anthropologist writes a book on a tribe he studied fifteen years ago, does this make him a historian? Obviously not, unless his aim of study has altered with the lapse of time; for the anthropologist would still describe and examine his tribe as though it existed here and now. Nor, conversely, does the historian turn into a sociologist merely because he writes about present-day England or France. The difference, then, lies in the *aspect* under which these scholars approach their data. The historian deals with events under the aspect of the past and with the emphasis on all discoverable connections with the past, while the anthropo-

[1] R. G. Collingwood (1946), p. 213.

logist deals with his facts under the aspect of the present and with the emphasis on connections valid here and now.

This diversity of aspects goes further. It is more fully explored in the philosophical formulations referred to before. Mostly, they are concerned with separating History from Science. And here the weight of evidence seems to be that the historian views events or sequences of events under the aspect of their uniqueness and individuality; and that historical examination fulfils itself in completely ascertaining and describing such events in their context of time and place (whether the events be physical or mental).[1] 'For the historian there is no difference between discovering what happened and discovering why it happened.'[2] Conversely, in the kind of enquiry which is not historical but *scientific* we view events under the aspect of their repetitiveness and regularity, regardless of time and place, and use the observation of the individual and particular for the formulation of universally valid laws. To paraphrase Collingwood, the scientist examines 'what happened' on particular occasions so as to be able to state in general terms why, or how, things happen.

This definition of the scope of history is not strictly accurate. Complete ascertainment and description is an illusion: always there is selection, and hence the assumption of relevance.[3] And relevance here means the capacity of events to have consequences, that is, their causal efficacy (Ed. Meyer). Even the context of time and place can be demonstrated only on the grounds of some anterior knowledge as to connections likely to be relevant. In 'completely' describing Caesar's death historians will hardly embark upon the examination of the musical style obtaining in Rome at the time; of the organization of the metal workers whose product killed Caesar; or of the sex life of Brutus and his associates. To put it more cautiously, the historian will not do so unless he has good reason to consider these facts relevant in a causal sense. The assumption of relevance which is behind the selection and ordering of historical data comes from general regularities known to govern human action or the sequence of physical events. The narrow causal nexus which the historian demonstrates when he connects particular

---

[1] See Ed. Meyer (1902); H. Rickert (1910); R. G. Collingwood (1946), pp. 176–7; M. Mandelbaum (1939); J. Wisdom (1934), pp. 9–10.

[2] R. G. Collingwood, ibid.

[3] Of the selectiveness imposed upon the historian by the fortuitous preservation of records we need not speak. See A. J. Toynbee (1935), vol. I, p. 7.

events with each other is always an instance of a wider, universally valid, causality, such as the scientist aims at (and the historian is aware of). In any statement on particular events and their sequence general, 'scientific', laws are thus implicit, much as we shall later see theoretical insight of a general nature to intrude upon 'pure' observation and description.[1] Yet for one thing, these general regularities are mostly so general and well known that they can be taken for granted and tacitly implied. Thus it is at once convincing if the historian connects Caesar's death with the political antagonism rather than with the musical style of the day. And for another, the general regularities belong to the background of historical statements. Even if the wider causality implicit in the historian's statements is sufficiently novel or specific to warrant special mention (for example, if he were to make Brutus's sex life responsible for Caesar's murder), it is only adduced with the aim of accounting for a particular sequence of events. The general regularities, whatever they are—psychological mechanisms, the laws of physical causality, or merely the unanalyzed probability that such-and-such events have such-and-such consequences—are, for the historian, background factors. And it is their relegation to the background which makes history history, and not science, and which allows us to speak of history (if somewhat loosely) as of a 'narrative concerned with particular series of events'.[2]

Let me then rephrase my assertion that anthropology is not history. It is not history in the sense here understood; rather does the aim of anthropology correspond to that of science. The fact remains, however, that various scholars, though on the whole sharing this view of the nature of history, are reluctant to admit the claim of social anthropology to be more than history or something different. They would argue that anthropology has no choice; it *must* be history, or at least, it cannot have the best of two worlds.

This seems an unconvincing argument; more exactly, there are two such arguments. The first is a defeatist one, and merely expresses grave doubts as to whether anthropology will ever discover scientific 'laws'.[3] This sort of reasoning has little weight and can be

[1] The historian 'cannot provide his explanation of particular facts without the scientist's (universal and generic) laws'. J. Wisdom (1934), pp. 9–10.

[2] M. Mandelbaum (1939), p. 13.

[3] See, for example, F. Boas (1928), pp. 211, 235–6, or R. Lowie (1937), pp. 222, 224–5. For my part, Professor Radcliffe-Brown has said about all there is to say on this point: '. . . There are some ethnologists or anthropologists who hold that

dealt with later. The second argument holds that, as social anthropology is dealing with historically determined facts, it must be
either history or nothing.[1] Now, 'historically determined' may
merely mean that the facts considered by social anthropology exist
in time and space—in fixed time and space; or it may also mean
that these facts are the outcome of unique ('historical') sequences
of events. It seems to me that arguments of this kind beg the
question; it surely remains to be seen whether or not regularities or
'laws' can be discovered behind the fixedness in time and place and
behind the apparently unique provenance of social phenomena. As
we shall see, there are limits to our discovery of social or cultural
'laws'; but they only circumscribe the compass within which
anthropology can be 'science', and do not negate this possibility.
Generally speaking, no branch of learning is defined by the nature of
the data it examines alone, for example, by their unique location in
time and space; if this were the case, geology, astronomy, and in
great part biology would be historical disciplines, incapable of
yielding scientific laws. What distinguishes different disciplines is
as much the *aspect* under which observations are made and the *aim*
with which the data of observation are analyzed and interpreted—
though certain kinds of data may prove intractable in this respect.
But of this enough has been said for the moment.

We must, however, examine a different question, namely, that
of the manner in which the anthropologist should use such historical evidence as may come his way. In this event, it seems to me,
the anthropologist reverses the relationship between particular
events and general regularities which is typical of history, that is,
he treats historical happenings as background factors. The historical happenings which come to his knowledge play such a part
in two ways. First, the past may throw open a range of events
beyond those directly observable and so add to the instances in
which 'laws' or regularities might be discerned. Undoubtedly,
however, the available historical evidence on primitive societies

it is not possible, or at least not profitable, to apply to social phenomena the
theoretical methods of natural science. For these persons social anthropology, as
I have defined it, is something that does not, and never will exist' (1940), p. 2.

[1] This sort of reasoning underlies Radin's outlook as well as that of other
anthropologists, such as Kroeber or Boas. E.g.—'The whole problem (of culture)
appears to be a historical one'; for 'each cultural group has its own unique
history' (F. Boas, 1920, pp. 311, 317). A defence of this view has also come from
the philosopher's camp; see below, p. 193.

will not very often be sufficiently full and coherent to be useful. Secondly, and more importantly, historical events also set limits to the range of discoverable regularities. They do so inasmuch as they are bound to time and place, and prove to be unique and not repetitive, that is, inasmuch as they are not susceptible to a treatment other than historical. Historical facts of this 'intractable' kind, then, introduce into our search for regularities the irreducible factor of *accident*.

Think of the victorious invasion of one group by another, which results in a sharp class division between the alien ruling class and the indigenous subject group; of the threat from better equipped hostile neighbours which forces a dispersed community to band together in closely packed settlements; of immigrations which lead to pressure on the land and a particular type of land tenure; or of an epidemic decimating the population and so causing its labour organization or kinship system to operate in a new way. All these are 'extraneous' accidents, beyond the control of the group whose culture we are examining. But equally, the unique events may arise within that group—in the form of a new law or course of action imposed by a powerful chief; in the form of a new dance or ritual accepted on the authority of an inspired priest; or in the form of some new cultural fact reaching the group through 'borrowing' or 'diffusion' and being voluntarily adopted. It is a trite thing to say that the past is the father of the present; but to understand that the past may constitute a background of events simply given and irreducible, is to adopt a critical attitude of great importance. In the simplest case, this knowledge of the past will guide and correct our understanding of any present state of affairs. I shall not, for example, theorize about processes of internal social differentiation, which elsewhere might adequately explain a class structure, if I know about the historical invasion; I shall not interpret the concentrated type of settlement in terms of some law of 'social density' if I know that it evolved in self-defence; I shall not regard the appearance of a particular style of art as an instance of some law of evolution or of some autonomous psychological mechanism if I am aware that diffusion had been at work, and so forth. But in a more far-reaching sense the historical facts cancel the very understanding we are after. Here are just-so happenings, beyond which we cannot go, if we are concerned with the repetitiveness and regularity of social phenomena.

B

Perhaps no event is wholly unique, and no accident quite irreducible to some regularity. All I intend to say is that historical
events of the kind here quoted are unique and accidental in those
respects in which they are relevant for my study of this or that
society. The connection between invasion and class stratification,
or between pressure on land and certain economic adjustments, is
probably repetitive throughout a wide range of societies, primitive
or civilized; but the fact that these social laws (rather than others)
have been brought into play in the society I wish to understand, is a
unique event, which I can only record. The concentration of a
population in large settlements has social consequences which I
can understand in terms of repetitive regularities; but the impetus
which set these processes in motion is simply given. When in any
society a leader arises who changes its mode of life, or when a
group adopts this or that cultural item from outside, I can legitimately search for some pre-existing readiness, that is, for a state of
affairs which, on the grounds of general knowledge, would be
likely to lead to some such results as actually happened; yet that
the readiness was matched there and then by a suitable occasion is,
once more, accident.

Let me say in parenthesis that all these 'unique events' might
also happen under our eyes, and not only in the past of cultures and
societies; of this we shall speak in a later context. Here we are concerned only with events in the past, which, being as it were closed
chapters, *res gestae*, and having had their particular consequences,
exemplify more typically the just-so happenings which limit our
search for regularities. Now it is true that the fragmentary historical
evidence on primitive societies will often present us with events
only apparently disconnected and unique. But it does not altogether account for the intrusion of accident. Certain scholars seem
reluctant to accept this status of accident in anthropological
enquiry. It has been said that 'applied to the development of
cultures, the convenient phrase "historical accident" is only a screen
for ignorance; a magic word to lull curiosity'.[1] Which seems to
mean that, if we only had sufficient knowledge of the facts involved in the 'development of cultures', there would be no need to
speak of accidents. This argument is misleading, if not fallacious.
What counts is not the fortuitous possession of knowledge, but the
relevant bearing of this knowledge on the kind of problems we see

[1] R. Linton (1947), p. x.

ourselves. When we speak of accident we do not necessarily mean events which are unintelligible in the terms of *any* known regular connection between facts; we may only mean that the events in question cannot be defined in the terms of such regular connections as we are concerned with.[1] When a person breaks a leg on an icy road, and the circumstances are known, the event can be wholly accounted for in the terms of physical and physiological laws; yet if the problem we are concerned with is the biography of this individual, this event remains an accident nonetheless. The historical accident is of this nature, and will not be spirited away even by the fullest knowledge we might possess of the past of primitive (or other) societies.

I might, for instance, be able to trace the invasion in our previous example to pressure on the land in the home of the invaders, which forced them to emigrate; and the pressure on the land to yet other immigrations; and these to some climatic event, say, desiccation, in the region from which the immigrants have come. Some such processes were probably responsible for the wave of migrations and invasions which led to the foundation of several of the West African conquest States.[2] Or again, I might link the diffusion of a messianic visionary cult among certain tribes with the 'despondency and hope' animating them at the time; and I might trace this psychological trait to the destruction of the economic and political safety which the groups suffered through the coming of the White Man;[3] and this fact again, to the emigrations from Europe, and further, to political and economic conditions in Europe, and so on, *ad infinitum*. How far we can in fact proceed in this fashion we need not discuss. However this may be, these are clearly causal chains such as the historian might construct; and each link in these chains implies that knowledge of some generally valid regularity of which we have spoken. Yet these causal chains have no relevance for the problem with which we are concerned. Our problem is to understand a state of affairs that happens to be the final consequence of a chain of events, namely, the fact that this or that society has a class structure or a visionary cult, and to

---

[1] I am not considering situations where we face an irreducible uncertainty of this kind, since this would involve us in the philosophical controversy about indeterminacy. I shall have to say a few words on this later (see p. 193).

[2] S. F. Nadel (1942), p. 75.

[3] The example I have in mind is the spreading of the Ghost Dance among the North American Plains Indians. See A. Goldenweiser (1937), p. 486.

understand this fact in such a fashion that the particular case can be expressed in the terms of a general law. Now, in the first example the events leading up to the invasion, which in turn leads to the class structure, occur outside the society we consider; they create the state of affairs we wish to understand but are not of it. The knowledge of the regularities involved in these extraneous events is not the kind of knowledge we are after; hence from our point of view the events remain 'unique events' and accidents. In the second example, we must ask whether the processes apparently responsible for the adoption of the visionary cult in such-and-such societies are still operative, that is, still sustain the state of affairs we wish to understand. In so far as these processes have ceased to operate and only left their end-result (now sustained by some other processes), they add no relevant knowledge, or are relevant only as just-so happenings. In other words, these causal chains show that cultural facts whose presence (continued presence) in a particular social context we wish to understand have not dropped from the sky but had an intelligible occasion; but within our framework of reference that occasion is as intractable as though it had dropped from the sky.

From this point of view, incidentally, we can readily dispose of the search for origins, which has proved such a bane for the growth of a scientific anthropology. To some extent, of course, a search for origins which is purely speculative and unsupported by genuine historical evidence can be dismissed out of hand.[1] But even if it were more adequately supported, it must still pass the test of relevance here outlined; and by this test any 'origin' which is only just that and does not account for the continued presence and operation of the cultural fact in question is ruled out as irrelevant or, at best, as relevant only in the sense of an historical accident.

Somewhere, then, we draw a line of relevance through the historical evidence, however complete it may be, and say that beyond this, the knowledge is not our kind of knowledge. The line of relevance is dictated by interest and self-imposed scope or, if you like, by curiosity. There is, inevitably, some arbitrariness in this—the same degree of arbitrariness which also separates the interests of different disciplines and is behind the writing of

[1] Social Anthropology, conceived of as a science, 'rejects all attempts at conjecturing the origin of an institution where there is no information based on reliable historical records' (A. R. Radcliffe-Brown, 1931, p. 17).

histories rather than History. There are, too, considerations of a practical kind, since life is after all short, and one cannot attempt to do everything. But equally, the line of relevance bears on a more fundamental fact, namely, that our subject matter—culture and society—has definite boundaries. Of this we shall speak more fully in a later context. Within his self-imposed orbit, then, the student of society treats historical facts as 'unique' and admits 'accidents', though within a wider or different orbit both uniqueness and accident may well disappear.

One final comment. I have stated before that in speaking of history I mean social history, and not the vague, one-sided reconstructions which archæology and quasi-archæology can offer. It will have become clear also that by history I do not merely mean time perspective. Time perspective belongs to everything social (as it belongs to almost everything that fills our universe). Institutions and groupings stretch back in time; kinship genealogies trace descent through past generations; laws have their precedents, and political systems and religions the weight of long standing. But these facts do not cause us to adopt a specifically historical viewpoint. They correspond to another aspect of social phenomena, visible wherever they are visible, namely, continuity. And this stands apart from the main concern of history, which is with the *uniqueness* and *distinctiveness* of events in the past.

3. THE BRIDGE OF UNDERSTANDING

Perhaps we should, in conclusion, consider a criticism which the layman sometimes voices (and the anthropologist sometimes invites), namely, that much in social anthropology is in the nature of art rather than science; that anthropological fieldwork is akin to the sympathetic, intuitive understanding, say, of the novelist rather than to the cold, 'objective' analysis of the scientist. If such remarks are meant to characterize the aims of social anthropology, they can be rebutted without much ado. But if they are applied to aspects of field technique, the criticism is not so easily refuted.

I have spoken before of the need, in anthropological fieldwork, to achieve 'something like an intellectual assimilation' to the unfamiliar culture. Malinowski, the pioneer of modern fieldwork, speaks thus of this aspect of anthropological study: 'It may be given to us for a moment to enter into the soul of the savage and through his eyes to look at the outer world and feel ourselves what it must feel to him to be himself.'[1]

Much in this process of 'empathy' can be reduced to simple empirical facts. Complete knowledge and ready use of the vernacular; long sojourn in the community; and, above all, the cumulative effect of the constant enquiries into everything that is observed—all these build up a familiarity with the native society which, in more poetic language, one might call 'entering into the soul of the savage'. When you find yourself making jokes at which the people laugh (no mean achievement, this); when you have mastered their ways of linking concepts and adducing proof; or when you can predict with fair accuracy what X will do and feel in such-and-such a situation, you have accomplished an adequate 'assimilation'.

When the jokes are made at you and you are expected (and known) to react in the proper manner, and when you yourself have become enmeshed in the rules of predictable behaviour valid in the society, you may be said to have accomplished assimilation *summa cum laude*. I can think of several such peaks in my own fieldwork. Once, in Nupe country, I was granted a tribal rank; and when a Nupe man addressing me a few days later used, not my new rank, but the honorific title reserved for distinguished white men, he was severely rebuffed by others for this solecism. An old Nupe diviner and magic expert insisted on my accepting a charm to protect me from witchcraft (since my enquiries into this sinister subject must have exposed me to the revenge of the witches). And the same man prepared a magic draught for my wife to make her have children (since our state of childlessness at the time accorded ill with my high position in the tribe).

Whether so complete an absorption into the native life is necessary or of special value is a moot point. It is, in any event, not consciously aimed at, but only an incidental result. Indeed, it has its dangers. For absorption in the native society means having a fixed place in it, which, like all social positions, implies limitation of outlook. As a rank-holder, bound by etiquette and status, features of social life on lower levels may be closed to you; as an adopted member of a kin group, you may learn of kin obligations and rivalries from one view point only. Detachment thus has its advantages.[2]

---

[1] B. Malinowski (1932), p. 517.

[2] I have dealt with this point more fully in my essay on 'Interview Technique in Anthropological Fieldwork'. See F. C. Bartlett (1939), pp. 326–7.

Nor clearly does 'absorption' alone make an anthropologist. However, the ideal balance between the two, and the ideal measure of 'intellectual assimilation', can hardly be arrived at by abstract argument.

Not everyone will be equally capable of attaining this ideal. That not everybody is a linguist or can spend sufficient time in the field —these contingencies we may for the moment disregard. I am thinking of factors which, with all facilities given, might yet render fullest 'assimilation' difficult. There are those who observe unfamiliar facts with ease and accuracy, and those who do not. Some have, and others have not, the intangible faculty of thinking with another person's mind and seeing through his eyes. Call it empathy if you like: something of this faculty must be present in the good field anthropologist.

But something of this faculty must be given to all students of human conduct. It is a vocational qualification, just as some faculty of intuition is indispensable to the creative scientist. This does not make the scientist a mystic, or the anthropologist, in his field, a novelist. It merely means that, without imagination, scientific thought is barren. But here arise only the sparks of comprehension, not the steady light of scientific understanding. The brilliance of one will add to the strength of the other. The brilliance might equally deflect attention; the impressionist anthropologist is no safer than the unimaginative one. Once more the safe balance cannot be worked out on paper. Yet systematic understanding has its rules; imagination can be guided by method, and insight stimulated by the ordered formulation of problems. To this aim, of outlining methods and formulating problems, this book is devoted.

CHAPTER II

The Aims of Social Anthropology

I. FACTS AND THEORY

Like all empirical disciplines social anthropology rests upon statements on observation—not just any statements, but relevant ones: relevant, naturally, as regards the kind of thing we are interested in; and relevant also as regards the use we wish to make of our observations. The·former relevance follows from the nature of our enquiry, which is concerned with social and cultural phenomena and not, for example, with physical and physiological ones. The second relevance is defined by the two aims with which social (like any other) enquiry may be carried out—the aim of description, or of explanation. This distinction somewhat over-simplifies the position and will have to be re-examined later on; but let it pass for the moment. Description presents things or events as though they were immediate data of observation;[1] it presents them, further, as 'just-so' existing, and existing in a particular form. Explanation works upon the immediate data and presents them as already elaborated; it adds meaning to 'just-so' existence, that is, it subsumes the particular under a general order. Full scientific insight is insight into an order of things, and full scientific knowledge, knowledge of general validity. Science, then, implies explanation. Social anthropology is a science only to the extent to which it can explain.

The observations upon which it rests take the form of *field research*; the descriptive approach in anthropology constitutes the field of *Ethnography*. For the explanatory approach we have no convenient separate name, though certain scholars would speak of 'Comparative Sociology' to denote this concern with knowledge of

---

[1] This qualification is necessary since we also describe things or events which we have not ourselves observed or which we observe only indirectly, e.g. through existing descriptive records. Ideally, description is the presentation of immediate data of observation.

general validity.[1] This term, however, refers essentially to the technique involved; and since we consider social anthropology to be a science in virtue of its explanatory approach, we may simply equate the two.

This, incidentally, is the nomenclature current in this country. American and continental scholars also speak of Ethnology in the sense in which we use the term Social Anthropology. But it seems useful to reserve the former term for the study of primitive cultures from an historical and diffusionist viewpoint, a usage which has been suggested by Professor Radcliffe-Brown. Certain American anthropologists prefer to speak of 'cultural' rather than 'social' anthropology.[2] Recently a new term has been suggested, 'culturology', meant to indicate even more precisely our subject matter, which is held to be the autonomous, 'extra-somatic' and 'super-psychological' reality of culture, and the explanation of human behaviour in the terms of that reality.[3] Actually, neither 'social' nor 'cultural' anthropology defines our subject matter satisfactorily; as I hope to show, it is essentially two-dimensional, being always both 'cultural' and 'social'. But for this very reason I mistrust the exclusive concern with culture. Though I do not wish either to deny the 'reality' of culture or to reduce it to somatic or psychological factors, I cannot accept as final the precept that human behaviour must be explained in terms of culture. For it ignores the complexity of the process of scientific explanation, whether of human behaviour or anything else. And if we took this precept at its face value we should be led into meaningless tautologies—such as that people behave in a certain way (which means, exhibit a certain culture trait) because their culture makes them do so. But of all this we shall treat more fully at a later stage.

Ethnography and social anthropology are clearly complementary. The first is the raw material for the second. The two are facts and theory, a multitude of statements on particular observations and their explanatory synthesis.[4] Explanations, of course, differ widely in scope and can be undertaken on very different levels. But

---

[1] See A. R. Radcliffe-Brown (1931). See also below, p. 227.

[2] E.g. R. H. Lowie (1936), R. Linton (1946), M. J. Herskovits (1948).

[3] Leslie A. White (1947 a and b).

[4] This juxtaposition is sometimes phrased differently, referring to the distinction between 'descriptive' and 'analytical' approach. But analysis is only a preliminary process—the breaking-up that precedes ordering. Analysis is explanatory only in that it permits of subsequent synthesis.

whether the explanation is of narrow range and still relatively close to the immediate data of observation, or produces some widely embracing theory, it is always a statement embodying order and synthesis. Always, too, explanation can only evolve with data furnished by observation and description, as these in turn are stimulated and guided by the theoretical synthesis.

Nor is this cross-fertilization ever at rest. Theories are constantly being tested against new facts, often re-defined and sometimes abandoned. There are, of course, good theories and bad—theories which account or do not account for the range of facts observed at any time. There are, too, T. H. Huxley's 'beautiful' theories, tragically murdered by an 'ugly little fact'. But the best and most beautiful theory can only account for what is known or observable by existing techniques; and even theories subsequently proved inadequate have added to knowledge or posed problems from which wider knowledge eventually sprang. Thus theories change with observed facts, and observation of facts changes into, and with, theories. The circle of description and explanation, of what Whitehead calls 'assemblage' and 'systematization', is of the very essence of science.[1]

All this is commonplace. But in the perspective of time this circle may appear broken up into two separate arcs, one more important and fundamental than the other. At various stages observation and description have been pronounced to be the primary task of science, while preoccupation with theory was relegated to a nebulous 'later'. Said Francis Bacon: 'We must bring men to particulars and their regular series and order, and they must for a while renounce their notions, and begin to form an acquaintance with things.'[2] And three hundred years later the German physicist Kirchoff preached 'description, and nothing but description'. These warnings, though undoubtedly salutary at the time, are one-sided and ultimately misleading. Preoccupation with observing and describing (or with what is taken to be purely observing and describing) is sterile: 'The history of science shows beyond doubt that the vital factor in the growth of any science is not the Baconian passive observation but the active questioning of nature which is furthered by the multiplication of hypotheses as hypotheses.'[3]

[1] A. N. Whitehead (1938), p. 2.
[2] *Novum Organum*, Book I, Aphorism XXXVI.
[3] Morris Cohen (1946), p. 5.

The temptation, however, to take the opposite view is great, and greatest in a young science like anthropology which, one feels, must put first things first; and facts clearly come before theories. Lowie, a great defender of facts before theory, quotes with approval this passage from the book of a great scientist: 'To the scientist who always detects new features in every major solution of a problem systematizing and schematizing always appears premature, and he gladly leaves it to the more practised philosopher.'[1] But Lowie omits to mention that to the man who wrote this we also owe a comprehensive theory of knowledge. It is, then, perhaps not superfluous to argue again the fallacy of any such antithesis of facts and theory, be it in science in general or in anthropology in particular. We may go even further, and say that any antithesis of the two is fallacious. Theory, systematization, enter at crucial points into the assemblage of facts. The two spring from the same roots, and the assemblage already partakes of systematization.

For it is doubtful if there is much sense in regarding 'assemblage' as the primary, and 'systematization' as a subsequent phase in scientific enquiry. No science starts with random assembling and with the collection of facts for their own sake. Science starts with problems, that is, with the question why such and such facts occur in a given context or in a given conjunction. Science begins with the desire to understand—to see things in a systematic order (whether the desire is acknowledged or not). Description is a first step towards the realization of this desire. Equally (since we move in a circle), description is, at any given moment, also a second step already presupposing some preceding effort at synthesis. Observation and description imply classification—a first ordering of the field of phenomena and a first assessment of relevance. This 'ordering' comes from several sources: from general experiences previously gained by the observer; from the organization of our mind, which lays some 'ordering' into the very act of observation; and from the self-evident categories of common sense. All these combine to make classification appear 'merely as an indication of characteristics already there'.[2] But in scientific enquiry this 'ordering' is, in much greater measure, derived from the examination and synthesis of earlier knowledge of the specific kind aimed at in the enquiry. Here classification reflects, above all, 'the current

[1] Ernst Mach, *Erkenntnis und Irrtum*, quoted from R. Lowie (1937), p. 152.
[2] A. N. Whitehead (1919), p. 32.

character of importance',[1] and only some previous effort at synthesis can vouchsafe this currency. Classification and relevance are thus a precipitate of explanation and already of the stuff on which theories are made; yet without their guidance we should little know what to observe and how to describe.

If I see A hand over a certain commodity to B, every phase of the transaction is factual evidence and nothing more; but if I distinguish between this transaction and other similar ones, calling one 'economic' and the other a 'gift', I am operating with categories of classification reflecting wide comparison, inference, selection by relevance and, ultimately, theory. If I describe biographically the behaviour of some individual, I am strictly factual; but if I divide his life span into childhood, adolescence, adulthood, instead of into periods based on the varying number of meals eaten or hours spent in sleep, indeed if I divide the continuous flow of life at all into phases which have a beginning and an end, I classify, select, abstract, interpret.

Facts are safer than theory and more solid than explanation, as observation is safer and more solid than thinking about observation. Where one ends and the other begins is a problem over which philosophers have worried for more than two thousand years. As regards the wide range of fragmentary experience which common sense is adequate to handle, the intrusion of theory into factual observation can be disregarded by all save philosophers. When facts are collected into classes or broken up into components for the purpose of deliberate enquiry, this intrusion, though it may be unwitting, demands recognition. 'Facts' always exist as the outcome of a classifying attack—upon what? One is tempted to say—upon the given continuum of phenomena. Yet even in naïve observation this continuum appears already structured, though this structuring is often ambiguous and fortuitous. Naïve observation is heightened to scientific observation through selecting from the ambiguous and through re-ordering the fortuitous. Scientific observation means a re-structuring of the structured. When we, as scientists, speak of 'only facts' we mean a product of omission, selection, and inference. Here indeed 'matter-of-fact' is nothing but 'an abstraction'.[2]

Observation and description, then, though standing apart from explanation, absorb the principles of order which are its first-

[1] A. N. Whitehead (1938), p. 22.   [2] op. cit., p. 25.

fruits. 'Pure' observation or description is merely observation and description where this order is tacitly implied and taken for granted. The desire for explanation, the desire to see things firmly and finally ordered, may outrun observation. But equally, we may take the implicit order for granted too long or too easily. In preaching facts rather than theory scientists have often rebelled against theories divorced from observation; this is what Bacon meant and others before and after him. But often this attitude merely expressed reluctance to render theories explicit, to submit them to new scrutiny, or to abandon the safety of common sense—itself a storehouse of tacit assumptions and obsolete theories.[1] Periods or schools of fact-worship as against preoccupation with theory there have been and probably always will be. In the human sciences, and thus in social anthropology, they are essentially the periods and schools of common sense triumphant.[2]

2. ANTHROPOLOGY DIVIDED

The comparison of the growth of social anthropology with tha of natural science needs correction. In natural science synthesis (or reluctance to embark upon it) and observation (that is, experiment) usually go together. In phases of 'fact-finding' the scientist—any scientist—is content to be only an observer; when theoretical insight is pressed farther, he will be at once observer and theorist. The nature of anthropological study tended to turn the interplay of factual observation and theoretical synthesis into a division of labour rather than into an alternation of phases or schools of thought. In the early periods of anthropological research, at least, such a division of labour was sharply pronounced. It coincided largely with the practical division between work in the field and scholarly pursuits in study and library. Travellers, missionaries, doctors, colonial administrators, were the assiduous collectors of facts; the anthropologist at home worked them into theories. The first edition of *Notes and Queries of Anthropology* (1874) professed

[1] 'To venture upon productive thought without . . . an explicit theory is to abandon oneself to the doctrines derived from one's grandfather' (A. N. Whitehead, 1933, p. 286).

[2] P. Radin, a sanguine anti-theorist, will tell you that tangible results of importance can always be obtained 'if enough factual material has been collected in the right manner' (1933, p. 31). Surely the proviso 'in the right manner' is the crux; as here stated, it would seem to be merely a matter of common sense.

the aim 'to enable those who are not anthropologists themselves to supply information which is wanted for the scientific study of anthropology at home'. The first theorists in anthropology either did not travel at all or only to a very limited extent, not proportionate to the field they covered in their researches.[1] Moreover, the theoretical enquiries were often inspired by interests and problems derived from fields extraneous to social enquiry in the strict sense of the word—Darwinism and the theory of evolution, comparative jurisprudence, the history of ethics or religion, or, lately, psychology and psychoanalysis. Thus the theoretical studies came to be overweighted in this sense or that, and the writers were apt to seize upon observed facts as mere illustrations for their theories. Withal, descriptive and theoretical research tended to proceed by separate paths, each carried on by its own momentum. The theoretical studies, self-centred upon their various interests, offered incidental summaries of ethnographical data rather than a true synthesis and a progressive solution of the problems thrown up by field research; while ethnography, though it extended widely over groups and regions, developed with little common focus.

Of the fundamental change which turned anthropology from an aspect of evolution and a chapter of Universal History into a branch of Durkheim's study of 'things social', the historians of our discipline may tell. We are concerned with another, equally fundamental change, which went hand in hand with the former— the end of the division of labour between observer and theorist. Several reasons appear to be responsible for this change. It is natural that the observer who discovered the inadequacy of theories produced by others should be tempted to evolve better ones himself. But partly the scholars in the forefront of modern anthropology *wish* to explain and not merely to describe. The mass of descriptive material already accumulated certainly makes mere additions to it seem somewhat irrelevant. There is, no doubt, a personal factor at work also; while the spirit of the times, the greater preoccupation to-day with social problems and difficulties, must further stimulate this more searching form of enquiry.

The modern enquirer, then, is ethnographer and social anthropologist in one. The identity may only be one of person—the

[1] This aspect of early anthropology is illustrated in A. I. Richards, *The Development of Fieldwork Methods in Social Anthropology* (see F. C. Bartlett, 1939, Chap. XII, and R. H. Lowie, 1937, Chap. VIII).

anthropologist using his own field material as well as that of others
to arrive at comprehensive theories of primitive society. Radcliffe-
Brown, Benedict, Linton are examples. Or the study of a single
society may be shot through and through with discussions of a
theoretical order and generalizations bearing on society at large—
as in the writings of Malinowski, Margaret Mead, Evans-Pritchard,
and others.

This change in the anthropologist's outlook is not a panacea. The
latter approach especially harbours the danger of premature
generalizations and insufficient verification. There should, perhaps, be more patient waiting for comparative examination and
synthesis. But too patient waiting renders research sterile and turns
the 'assemblage' of facts into a welter. There is no escaping the
dilemma. The fast multiplying discoveries, as they furnish material
for the theoretical synthesis, so they may tempt us to postpone it.
Certain ethnographers indeed shrink from the synthesis; Lowie
speaks of Boas's 'deliberate aversion to systematization'.[1] While
others, who compose their field studies in a spirit of theoretical
enquiry, will yet feel at one with Pavlov when he says: 'How could
I halt for any comprehensive conception to systematize the results
when each day new experiments and observations brought us
additional facts?'[2]

Thus much in the wealth of ethnographical data is still raw
material, or raw material insufficiently refined; much still awaits
that fuller synthesis which will alone lead to valid generalizations
on primitive culture and society. We are, perhaps, now truly bound
to move from an era of 'assemblage' to one of 'systematization'.
Whether this task should be shouldered by field researchers turned
theorists or by a new school of theoretical anthropologists I cannot
decide. I feel that the former is more desirable; that anthropology
has abandoned its earlier division of labour with good reason; and
that the observer is best able to handle the problems thrown up by
his research. But I may be biased. The opposite solution has in
fact been attempted with considerable success by Chapple and
Coon, in whose book on Anthropology you will find this passage:
'the anthropological fieldworker, on whose findings we are dependent for our information. . . .'[3]

[1] (1937), p. 152.
[2] (1928), p. 42 (Quoted from Bertrand Russell, 1931, p. 56).
[3] Chapple and Coon (1942), p. 282.

3. PREMISES OF OBSERVATION

It is now time to ask: What do we observe, and how do we, as anthropologists, observe and describe?

We observe behaviour of man in the group—the behaviour of individuals towards each other and in respect of each other. The last part of the sentence is important. For only in the simplest cases do we observe direct interaction and mutual response: A acts, and B or C, or both, respond in a certain way. In more complex situations the interaction is intermediate and indirect: A acts in a certain way because B has acted in such-and-such a way in the past, or because C may act in this fashion in the future. Moreover, B may be dead at the time, and B or C personally unknown to A. What remains, then, is co-adaptation of behaviour (Radcliffe-Brown's 'co-aptation') or, simply, co-activity.

Such intermediate interactions may occur simply through one actor remembering or anticipating the behaviour of another. But the linkage may be more intermediate still, resting on something that is not itself behaviour but only a token of it. This token may lie in any material object created by behaviour, that is, in behaviour materialized—such as the tool I use and to the design of which I shall adapt my motions, or the house in which I live in a manner compatible with its size or layout. Or the token may lie in a sign or symbol, that is, in behaviour abstracted and referred to—by means of speech, writing, or some other sign system. Speaking and writing are of course themselves forms of behaviour; but they provoke the appropriate response not merely through being performed, but through bearing their reference and signifying some other behaviour, past or future. Ultimately, signs and symbols can be effective without the behaviour that produces them being actually performed at the time; this would be true of the ideas current in a society, its norms, beliefs, in short, its ideological elements.

I would thus include ideas and their symbolic representations in the category of co-activity. Indeed, no other solution is possible. An idea not communicated is beyond examination; once it is communicated (by means of some comprehensible sign or symbol), it becomes at least potentially action provoking action. Nor can symbols of whatever kind—from crude signs to language, from pragmatic models to works of art—ever be imagined away from the interplay of behaviour; for they are both the products of action and the starting points of new action, on the part of those who perceive and comprehend the symbol. Conversely, co-activity implies communication, and this in turn the use of signs or symbols. Let me here disregard the more precise distinction between the two and merely say that the kind of co-activity that goes with social existence implies the capacity of the actors to refer to absent objects, persons, or events, and to handle situations by means of such references. We cannot conceive of social behaviour that would at any moment require the actual presence of the things it becomes concerned with. And it is the essence of signs and symbols that they enable us to dispense with this requirement; for whatever else they are, they are 'substitutes', capable of 'initiating' a particular behaviour in the absence of the stimuli normally producing it.[1]

Anthropologists are fond of saying that man alone has produced symbols. This may be true, though it is irrelevant for a discussion not concerned with comparing man with animals.[2] But it is both true and relevant that the use of symbols is inseparable from man's social existence, and that 'communicational' facts (which means signs or symbols) exist 'where the behaviours of men are in society'.[3]

Is there any behaviour of man which is not 'in society'? The (somewhat conventional) phraseology we used before, when we spoke of 'man in the group', seems to suggest that there is such behaviour. But since man does not exist without the group (omitting Robinson Crusoes, 'wolf-children,' and other dubious anomalies), this addition would seem to be either misleading or redundant. It is, however, not quite that. The qualification has meaning in that it distinguishes between forms of acting and behaving which are part of the existence of the group and those which, though occurring in the group, are not of it. The distinction is essentially one between recurrent and unique behaviour. The forms of behaviour, then, with which we are primarily concerned are recurrent, regular, coherent, and predictable. The subject matter of our enquiry is *standardized behaviour patterns*; their integrated totality is *culture*.

[1] Charles Morris (1946), pp. 6, 10. This is an abbreviation of a much fuller and much more complicated statement. Cf. also J. Dewey (1938), p. 52—Symbols make ordered reasoning possible 'without any of the existences to which symbols apply being actually present'.

[2] Also, the truth of this assertion would depend on the precise definition of symbols as against signs.

[3] A. F. Bentley (1935), p. 346,

c

This does not mean that we do not also observe and occasionally describe incoherent, diffuse, unique, and unpredictable behaviour. But when we find behaviour that is all these things, we attempt to relate it to some established standardized pattern or at least to view it against such a background. Completely unstandardized behaviour belongs to the fringes of the social field: it is capable of description, but must elude the grasp of anthropological enquiry and understanding. The study of such behaviour may have to be relegated to the disciplines which deal with the unique behaviour of individuals—history, biography (historical or psychological), and psycho-pathology.

A final condition defining our subject matter is not easy to formulate. It is roughly expressed in the verbal distinction between *action* and *behaviour*. By behaviour we mean motor events which simply happen in individuals (or organisms); by action, such events if they are intended to have consequences, that is, to effect some change in the environment (human or material) of the actors or in the relations between the two. Action implies intention, plan, some direction of aim, while behaviour can be unintentional, involuntary, and accidental. A person making motions in his dream, an accidental suicide, the excited gestures of a hysteric—all these are forms of behaviour and, considered only as such, sociologically meaningless. But such a sharp verbal distinction is perhaps merely a play upon words; nor has it ever to my knowledge been consistently applied.[1] Our subject matter, then, is action, or behaviour that is aim-controlled. This statement needs to be qualified; for behaviour, though not itself intentional and aim-controlled, may form part of aim-controlled activity: the raving of a hysteric may have religious significance; dreams, related to others and interpreted, may become incentives for specific action; an accidental suicide may alter the social status of the family in which it occurred. Our proposition must therefore be reformulated as follows: Behaviour is sociologically relevant only if it is aim-controlled or enters into aim-controlled action patterns; in other words, if the behaviour can be expressed in terms of a *task*.

---

[1] Talcott Parsons's work is an exception. For this scholar the subject matter of social enquiry is action, and its basic element, the 'unit-act'. The fundamental aspect of unit-acts is that they imply an 'end'—'a future state of affairs to which the action is oriented'. (See 1937, pp. 44 *et passim*.)

The task embodies the aim as part of its inner organization, the aim constituting the implicit content or quality of the action. Though this is always true, it is doubtful if any task-like behaviour patterns exist which have only this implicit aim, that is, fulfil themselves in simply being executed. Approximations, however, do occur. They are exemplified in actions whose very performance offers some satisfaction or enjoyment of a physiological or psychological kind, such as a dance, the pleasurable movements of craftsmanship, or certain forms of dramatization in which the mimic representation of some subject is all the actors aim at. More often, however, the aims of actions point beyond the immediate performance to an end-result, to a distinct 'future state of affairs', which the completed action is intended to bring about, be it another action, a physical event, or a mental state. Thus a man will till the soil so that crops may grow on it and afterwards be available for consumption or exchange; or he will behave in a certain way so that his behaviour should be approved or judged fitting by existing norms and values; or finally, he may choose a certain course of action because its completion will satisfy him emotionally, for example, enable him to triumph over a rival. The three instances I have chosen exemplify the main types of end-results which occur in task-like behaviour, and hence three distinct (though overlapping) categories of action. In each the implicit and immediate aim of behaviour points to a more explicit proximate aim, realized in the end-result. According to the different nature of these proximate aims and end-results we can name the three categories of action: firstly, purposive-rational actions, in which the end-result is a means to a further end-result; secondly, value-orientated actions, in which the end-result conforms to an approved or valued state of affairs; and thirdly, in Max Weber's terms, affectually orientated actions, in which the end-result is a psychological (emotional) state of the actor.[1]

We need not pursue this further. Nor need we concern ourselves with certain new problems which here arise, such as the possibility

---

[1] This whole outline follows closely Weber's classification of social actions. Max Weber introduces a further category, that of traditional action, in which people behave in a certain way 'through the habituation of long practice'. In my view traditional behaviour is either a weaker replica of value-orientated behaviour (if acting in accordance with tradition is understood to be a 'good' way of acting), or merely automatic habitual behaviour, which has no aim-direction at all. (See Max Weber, 1947, p. 105).

of proximate aims miscarrying, and of end-results for various reasons failing to correspond to the aimed-at 'future state of affairs'. All these questions will become important later, when we shall discuss the nexus between behaviour patterns or behaviour patterns and events. For the present we are considering sociologically relevant behaviour in general and need emphasize only that such behaviour always implies an aim—whatever its bearing upon more or less remote end-results.

The identification of sociologically relevant behaviour with task-like actions to some extent follows from the two characteristics previously stated—that social behaviour is behaviour of individuals in respect of each other, and that social behaviour is recurrent, regular, and standardized. It seems worthwhile, however, to show the precise extent of this implication, since it bears on a fundamental postulate of social enquiry.

When we conceive of certain behaviour patterns as 'co-adaptive' and as recurrent or standardized, we mostly tacitly assume that they express aims—that they are intended to be whatever they are. This seems elementary; if I see people regularly celebrating funerals, or growing corn, or having wrestling matches, then surely I assume that they want to have funerals or grow corn or engage in wrestling. But often students of anthropology seem reluctant to say so openly. They are quite prepared to look for ulterior aims or even for the ultimate social purpose in such activities; or they readily name basic organic needs and drives as the motivating force behind social action. But the reference to aims, as it were, in the middle region, between ultimate social purpose and animal drive, is viewed with suspicion; it seems to introduce an unwarranted explanatory element, as it also introduces the difficult and nowadays unfashionable category of consciousness.

Let me state, first of all, that 'aim' and 'task' in the sense here used are not explanatory principles. They still belong fully to the order of descriptive facts, representing an attribute of the observed data without which these would not be what they are—data of social behaviour. Furthermore, task and aim indeed mean purpose, and so consciousness, and having introduced these concepts I will not baulk the issue. Following a behaviourist cue, I might try to explain the difficulty away by saying that all that I really admit is regularity and recurrence of behaviour; that in speaking of 'aims' I merely use a term conveniently summarizing such behaviour. This subterfuge would not do, even if I meant to use it. For even in regular, recurrent forms of behaviour it is still necessary to distinguish those which are aim-controlled from others which are not. It is clearly not so that in every instance of regularly occurring behaviour the individuals concerned desire it to occur thus regularly. Think of road accidents, birth-rate (including the prerequisite behaviour), or perhaps suicides—which all exhibit statistical recurrence and regularity. There are aims somewhere in these recurrent patterns of behaviour; but here the aims, that is, the anticipations of results, and the end-results stand apart. The end-results by themselves, recurrent though they are, are sociologically meaningless. At least, they remain so unless the patterns of behaviour can be seen as 'actions' and 'tasks', and linked with consciously had aims. When sociologists examine these patterns of behaviour, as distinct from surveyors, statisticians, biologists, or perhaps behaviourist psychologists, they examine them for the aim-directions and the interplay of aims they involve.

But let me add that I do not mean to imply that conscious purpose is behind every part-task or part-action and is always present in explicit and exhaustive form, so that every item of behaviour will appear to follow from a clearly controlling aim. Items of behaviour may be habitual and automatic or, as behaviourists would say, 'conditioned'; the aim may merely be that of acting in a certain customary way, without a conscious motive bearing on the action itself. But for us there must be, somewhere in the task pattern, consciousness, and somewhere in its activation, purpose. Without these two factors there can be no social understanding; more precisely, there can be no material susceptible of such understanding.

I have stated this as a postulate, and such it is. If it seems to imply that, in the very first step of observation, we have to move beyond the 'objective' data into the obscure realm of 'subjective' motivations, I shall later attempt to show that this step is far from being so dubious or dangerous as it is often made out to be. Here I would stress that it is inevitable.[1] The concept of the 'task' will prove crucial throughout our discussion. It had to be introduced so early

---

[1] Cf. Talcott Parsons: It is a 'cardinal point' in the study of social action that it has a 'subjective aspect'. The 'frame of reference' with which we approach action is 'subjective'—it deals with things 'as they appear from the point of view of the actor' (1937, pp. 26, 46).

since even the first, preliminary definition of our subject matter is impossible without it. This, I think, the examples have shown. If students of society avoid this or similar concepts for their apparent dangers, they merely conceal the difficulties instead of facing them.

At this point it is convenient to divide our approach and to deal separately with the material of observation and description, and with these techniques themselves. The two, of course, condition one another, the material of observation depending on available techniques as much as the latter depend on the nature of the things one wishes to observe and describe. It is commonplace for any treatise in an experimental discipline to preface the analysis proper with a statement on the experimental arrangement and instruments used. Anthropology is not in this sense an experimental science, and the anthropologist does not use instruments in the strict sense of the word. But his working conditions are such as to justify a similar preface. Perhaps 'justify' is even too weak a word; Malinowski, would have said 'necessitate' and 'demand'.[1]

[1] B. Malinowski (1932), pp. 2–3.

CHAPTER III

Observation and Description

This chapter is not intended to be a full and detailed account of anthropological field methods. Nor yet is it limited to these, but treats also of certain problems of presentation. In either case the emphasis will be on matters which bear closely on the nature of anthropological data and so on the mutual determination (and limitation) of technique and material. Here four points seem to stand out: (1) the use of informants in anthropological observation; (2) the use of language in observation and description; (3) the effect of the observer's 'personal equation'; and (4) the extension of observation beyond tangible behaviour to mental processes (the last point requiring treatment in a separate chapter).

1. THE USE OF INFORMANTS

In any observation we refer, ultimately, to sensory data—to what we perceive with our senses, what we see, hear, touch, feel. In the natural sciences we use instruments, more sensitive than some of our senses; they observe for us; they register the facts in such a fashion that we need apply our senses only to the reading of the instruments, that is, within a range where our sensitiveness is adequate. Anthropologists, alas, have no instruments, though they do use means to record what they should observe only inadequately. These means are the verbal statements of informants. Though through their use we can extend the limits of immediate observation, this substitute is unhappily not more reliable or sensitive, rather on the contrary; for it entails several sources of error which it is often difficult to neutralize.

I regard, then, the use of informants as additional to direct observation. For a wide range of social behaviour this must be so. The execution of productive tasks or technological processes; the behaviour of individuals towards each other, say, in the family group; the physical layout of settlements; or the performance of ceremonials—these are instances of occasions when direct observation cannot be replaced. But when contrasting direct observation with the more indirect approach through informants, we should more precisely speak of informants specially selected and, as it were, appointed. For some form of verbal information is bound up with every act of observing social behaviour. The persons acting in a certain way are often also chance-informants on their way of acting, whatever it may be—a technological process, an economic transaction, a religious observance, or a family gathering. If it is not from the actors themselves that we elicit such running commentary, it will be from someone else who has the requisite knowledge. These are assistants in observation, not yet 'recorders' replacing it.

As regards the latter, their role is sometimes exaggerated. Certain American anthropologists, trained in the reconstruction of cultures which exist only in memory, consider enquiry through 'recorders' the predominant and even exclusive form of anthropological observation. One document, prepared by one informant, is said to give you the picture of a whole culture.[1] Such documents, it is claimed, are for the anthropologist what archives are for the historian. This is sheer informant-worship. Verbal or recorded information is preeminent in the sphere of culture where behaviour itself crystallizes in the form of verbal statements—in myths, tradition or folklore, and in the formulation of beliefs and norms. Beyond that, working through 'appointed' informants is an auxiliary operation, and sometimes a control, but never the sole or main line of attack.

That this auxiliary operation is unavoidable, I have stated. There is wide agreement nowadays that the fieldworker should spend a considerable period in the society he studies, at least one full year, so that all normal events should fall within his purview. But even a year's stay might not enable him to observe, say, a triennial ritual. Even during a prolonged stay certain events may never occur—the death and crowning of a chief, a breach of exogamous rules or incest tabus, or instances illustrating every aspect of the working of a legal system. Limitations in time have their corollary in limitations in space. The wider the area of study and the greater the variety of culture, the more fully must the fieldworker rely on indirect observation.

[1] P. Radin (1933), pp. 115–9.

Certain of these shortcomings can be avoided if teamwork replaces the conventional single-handed anthropological investigation. Perhaps we may leave this point until later. But even the most efficient team cannot do without informants; informants, and the sources of error entailed in using them, will always be with us.

The sources of error are most pronounced when we aim at historical information and at the explanation of things and actions observed. Radcliffe-Brown, Malinowski, and many others have emphasized that we must not expect correct answers when questioning the people about the reason for or the meaning of some cultural activity. But their answers are not altogether without value; though they are sources of error in one sense, in another they are themselves significant social facts, data in their own right, and so sources of knowledge. For verbal information on social action is of course itself action, and may be as standardized. Often such information is produced in specific contexts—in the transmission of tribal lore to the younger generation, in controversies over the exact nature of a law, or in the conventionalized interpretation of myths and ceremonials. When the context of an enquiry approximates to these conventional contexts, the informant, in explaining this or that cultural feature, will offer the standardized version, a statement expressing the notions of his society. When he explains why his people do a certain thing or avoid doing another he may make much of the emotional reactions ('it is pleasant'—'it is hateful') or talk in pseudo-historical language. To be sure, these explanations only vouchsafe habitual sentiments and an ideologically distorted 'history'. Yet as such, they are an object of study in themselves; they demonstrate the bias of the society towards utilizing a certain emotional appeal or rationalizing the present by reference to the past. In other words, we have here conventionalized truths, and hence a particular kind of evidence for our understanding of the society.

Even when we do not touch upon interpretation, and when the informant's desire to produce accurate, unbiased data need not be doubted, he would yet tend to produce a norm, the blueprint of his culture and society, the 'should-be' rather than the 'is'. One must not be confused with the other, though both are important. For if one gives the accepted rules of social behaviour, the other defines their validity in practice. If such information bears upon the past, the discrepancy will be much greater. There is the selective nature of memory to be reckoned with. Stories about a golden age, when everything was much better (and more 'normal') than it is nowadays, form part, not only of legends, but of many would-be realistic accounts of the past.

Every informant, finally, is a member of his society, and so a 'social person', with a limited scope of action in the society and a limited range of insight into its arrangement and working. What he remembers will reflect what he saw and knew; the accuracy of his descriptions and explanations will vary with his age, status, or sex. Older people have seen more of society than younger; they also know more of its inside working. Take the novice in an initiation rite, who can only describe the appearance of ghosts while the older men, better informed if not wiser, will know that the 'ghosts' are dressed-up tribesmen. On the other hand, older men would be able to describe the activities, say, in a young men's age set association, only from memory, since they would not be involved in its activities at the time. The old men in a Nuba tribe could give me no information on the preparations, then in full swing, for certain age set dances: 'these are affairs of the young', they said.

In stratified societies, the range of insight is more or less rigidly restricted by status. Those who belong to the lower class will not observe, or observe adequately, happenings in the upper class. The *élite*, the ruling group governing a society, will of necessity have a more extensive range of insight; but it may be biased by their own class consciousness and aloofness. Often have I been told by Nupe noblemen that some religious cult of the peasants was merely a ridiculous and nonsensical practice, not worth recording. Where my exalted informants *did* recall it, their description was full of misunderstandings and distortions. Need we go so far afield for our examples? Not so long ago it was common to hear from members of our own upper classes that the unemployed were merely persons too lazy to work.

Men usually have a wider insight into their society than women, since in most groups the men supervise the household, are in some measure responsible for their family, and generally guide group life. But even here there are limits and the pitfalls of unconscious bias. Men may know all about cooking recipes or a mother's technique with her baby; but most Nupe men I met knew nothing about the intricacies of female trading, and in the Sudan most Arab men proved very inaccurate informers on so important a tribal practice as female circumcision.

Once more the 'bias' in the description becomes for us an object of study in itself. It defines the scatter of common knowledge about social institutions through the society, and the degree to which such a scatter is adequate or necessary for their effective operation. Inasmuch as these forms of bias are also sources of error, they can be checked and controlled by various means—by the judicious choice of informants from various walks of life; by a judiciously concrete technique of questioning; by the collection of several complementary statements and of numerous case studies; above all, by ascertaining the 'bias' which must follow from the general organization of the society.[1]

2. THE USE OF LANGUAGE

Anthropologists of whatever persuasion are to-day widely agreed that field research should be carried out in the vernacular. The pitfalls of inaccurate translation, leading to inaccurate understanding, can only in this manner be adequately overcome. I am aware that at least one anthropologist of repute holds that working through interpreters is, for all ordinary fieldwork purposes, as adequate as working through the indigenous language; in fact, proficiency in the indigenous language is considered a superfluous achievement, unnecessarily burdening the mind, pandering to one's vanity, and deflecting attention from the real task.[2]

I do not think that Dr. Mead's extreme view will find many supporters. For my part, I consider that it misses certain essential aspects of language, which it seems worthwhile to examine more fully. For this view rests on the twofold assumption that, for the anthropologist, language is nothing but a 'tool', and that languages in general are such perfect and uniform tools of discourse that they can be translated into each other, phrase by phrase, without loss of precision. Neither assumption holds. Language is undoubtedly one of our 'tools' to get at facts; but among these facts is, again,

---

[1] For the technique of questioning see B. Malinowski (1932), pp. 12–13, and my discussion, 'Interview Technique in Social Anthropology', in F. C. Bartlett (1939), Chap. XIII.

[2] Margaret Mead (1939).

language—not only the statements made to us by informants (specially selected or otherwise), but the statements made by the people among themselves, in contexts we observe, and as part of these contexts.

Social behaviour, needless to say, is in large measure linguistic behaviour, whether we think of orders, instructions or other communications which initiate behaviour, or of statements about behaviour and the things behaviour is concerned with, as in moral and other judgments, in the naming of events, relationships, or activities, and in accounts of the world surrounding the people. In a sense, then, the anthropologist's position is unique. His subject matter is in great part made up of language; and the only way he has of presenting it is once more by means of language (*his* language). Translation, therefore, there must be. The question is whether the anthropologist should also be the translator or take his translation second-hand. You may say this will depend on the efficiency of the interpreter. Now, we need not concern ourselves with the gross errors which might arise when an interpreter is insufficiently familiar with our language, or poorly educated, or estranged from his culture, perhaps because of the very qualifications which make him useful to us. I do not know whether the 'ideal' interpreter exists; but let us assume he does and is in every respect the wish-fulfilment of the anthropologist.

Can we then say that, through his translation, we shall grasp all that is said, the sense or significance of phrases, and shall only miss out how it is said, that is, the precise, particular choice of expressions? Dr. Mead seems to have some such distinction in mind when she considers the knowledge of the vernacular to be unimportant in strictly anthropological enquiry and important only when the enquirer is concerned with the 'psychological' implications of speech and language. Such a distinction cannot be maintained. The meaning of 'what' is said is entailed in 'how' it is said. For, with few exceptions, words have no unique, unvarying, one-to-one relationship with the things they signify.[1] Rather, the same word may be applicable to different situations and mean different things, as in turn the same thing may be called by different names. This latitude in the meaning of words and their choice in a particular context add more or less relevantly to the import of what they are

---

[1] Such exceptions are proper names or specific technical terms such as *tetrahedron* or *drosophila melanogastes*.

meant to convey there and then; the *mot juste* in one context is such because of what it may signify in others. And it cannot be presumed that the latitude in the meaning of words and the chances of choice are the same in different languages.

Here we are, of course, referring to the oft-quoted difficulties of precise translation, which experts find formidable even if it is from one familiar language to another. We popularly speak of the 'associations' which the words have for those speaking a particular language and evoke in their minds, and which are lost in translation; so that words apparently equivalent in two languages would yet lead thought and imagination along divergent paths. I am not thinking of the difficulties entailed in the translation of poetry, oratory, and the like, where the emotional overtones of words (if I may use this vague phrase) play so important a part. Let us think rather of prosaic statements where, however, precision is important, such as in legal or scientific language. There is no need to quote examples; translations of legal or scientific works are full of alternative phrases, of annotations to make clearer the meaning of particular words, or of literal quotations to short-circuit such discursive renderings, all of which testify to the difficulties of the task. In other words, they testify to the absence of precise equivalents in the different vocabularies, so that more or less successful approximations are all we can hope to find and produce.

The position in social enquiry is much the same. The lack of precise equivalents may of course merely mean that the particular social fact (institution, relationship, etc.) referred to in the language from which we translate is absent in the culture into whose language we translate. The Roman *pater familias* simply does not exist in modern English society, the ordained 'priest' in Mohammedan countries, or the Russian soviets in Western Europe. This point we may for the moment disregard and concern ourselves only with things, activities, and so forth, which are common to the cultures whose languages we must reconcile. Still the task retains most of its difficulties. We must still search for accurate equivalents where none may offer; we must still reckon with the diverse 'associations' of similar words in different languages. Expressed more concretely, we shall meet with only roughly equivalent words, which yet have a somewhat different currency in the different languages, being used in a different series of situations and hence with a different 'latitude of meaning'. Whatever the degree of equivalence we

ultimately achieve, it will depend on our knowledge of this currency of words. One example for many: In every primitive society
there will be a word X (or several such words) expressing the
opprobrium in which a certain act is held, say, incest. We must
clearly aim at assessing the precise weight of the term, since it
stands for an important moral judgment, and in some fashion
render it in our language. Now any of the following words might
be applicable: horrible, disgusting, vile, disgraceful, shameful, sinful, criminal, improper, 'not done'. Each has a more or less definite
connotation in our language, that is, is capable of being used in
certain situations but not in others. Which is the 'right' translation
for X in the given situation will depend on all the other situations
in which it may (or may not) legitimately be used—whether it is
used also for common legal offences (thus meaning 'unlawful'), or
for acts amounting to sacrilege ('sinful'), or for things physically
repugnant ('vile', 'disgusting'). The 'right' translation, then,
is derived from the comparison, not of words, not even of contexts, but of the whole semantic arrangement of the languages.
And the same is true of a whole range of other words which we have
to use at every step, namely, words in which the people express their
attitudes to things and their motives for acting in a given fashion,
as when they speak of 'loving' or 'hating', of 'fear', 'trust', 'obedience', and so forth.

Let me stress that, even so, we may arrive only at approximate
equivalents. Attitudes and motives are of course expressed, not
only in language, but also in behaviour (which we judge by criteria
to be discussed later). And the name which we should consider
adequate to describe the behaviour might well fail to accord with
the currency of the indigenous word. The people using the word X
to denote both the quality of incest and that of, say, common
offences may exhibit a marked repugnance for offenders of the
former but not of the latter kind, in which case we simply have
nothing that quite corresponds to X. To convey the nature of the
diverse reactions we should have to ignore the given nomenclature; and to convey this, we should have to obliterate the divergence in behaviour. The Nupe, for example, have the same
word, *leifi*, for all kinds of offences, including those which, judging
by the reactions of the people, correspond to 'sins' (as we should
call them); in Arabic you can call things that are physically repugnant, evil, and shameful, by the same name, *shen*; in French you

can only 'hate' enemies and the like, while in English you can hate enemies as well as unpleasant food. Which clearly does not mean that the situations and objects so uniformly named are not distinguished in fact, that is, differently reacted to.

Now, I am not suggesting that there is no way out of this difficulty. Whether we preserve the nomenclature or decide to disregard it, we can correct the inaccuracy entailed by means of a more discursive phraseology or by suitable annotations or comments— the usual method of conscientious translators. Indeed, the people themselves may, by similar means, adapt their nomenclature to different occasions, for example, narrow down the latitude of a word by means of suitable adjectives and other amplifying or qualifying remarks. But the latitude of meaning remains; and there is the need for adapting it. Whichever way we look at it, one language will employ two words when another employs one, or some circuitous phraseology where the other can choose brief expressions. There remains, in other words, an irreducible difference in the semantic economy of the different languages. And this brings me to another point. For this difference in semantic economy is as such a source of important information not obtainable by any other means; so that we must have this knowledge also, whatever the requirements of a successful translation (or, for that matter, the capacities of the 'ideal' interpreter).

Languages, in brief, are symbol systems, and words the unit symbols, that is, they stand for something, refer to it, signify it. More precisely, words are *made* to refer and signify, in virtue of some underlying consensus and given rules of operation. So that anyone handling words in accordance with the rules will make others who are familiar with them (i.e. speak that language) aware of whatever the words signify, whether the effect stops at the mere awareness or extends to some appropriate response in behaviour. The things signified by words, it would seem, can be objects, persons, events, activities, states of affairs, and relations between each or any of these.[1] Yet it is at least inexact (if not meaningless) to

---

[1] As we are primarily concerned with the 'semantic economy' of languages we may disregard certain aspects of words which seem immaterial in this context. Thus I am not considering the 'formal' parts of language (conjunctions, prepositions, 'quantifiers', etc.) which 'have not themselves any reference' but only indicate certain cognitive operations to be performed with the references of other words (see K. Britton, 1939, pp. 114–15). Nor am I considering the specifically pragmatic use of language, in which the word-sign or symbol may be

say that words refer directly to objects, events, and so forth. Rather do they refer to the way in which objects and events are perceived, manipulated, reacted to, and generally thought about. If we call an object (concretely) a *book* instead of something else, we state 'a set of traits' which the object, or any of its class, 'should have if it is to be' a book,[1] and which are apprehended by a series of perceptions and manipulations—seeing the shape of the object, testing the nature of its material, verifying that it contains print (since otherwise it would be a 'notebook'), assessing its size (since too small an object of this kind would be a 'pamphlet'), and so forth. And if we call a book (now speaking abstractly) *prose* instead of something else, we state certain characters which it must have. to be an instance of that state of affairs, and which are ascertained by prescribed procedures ('operations', as logicians would say)—the sort of procedures which made M. Jourdain suddenly realize that he had been speaking prose all his life without knowing it. Generally speaking, any word is a *shorthand* for some such sets of traits or characters, and stands for a *cognitive summary* of numerous such ways of experiencing objects, events, or states of affairs.

It is clear that this shorthand of words does not bring together only a coherent series of ways of experiencing—coherent in that they all combine in demonstrating the nature of one class of objects, events, or states of affairs. Numerous words also bring together experiences which seem to be of palpably diverse order, as when the same name 'blood' is given both to the physical substance (which we can see to be red, feel to be sticky, discover to flow in the human body, or can analyze chemically) and to close kinship (which we verify through observing behaviour or through tracing genealogies). Here we usually distinguish between the literal and metaphorical use of words. But both still fall within one 'cognitive summary'; though it no longer implies a unitary entity built up from different traits, it yet implies the awareness of some unity in the different entities. More precisely, the common name implies a relationship of affinity imputed to the different entities and conceived of as sufficiently important to warrant the single shorthand.

---

reduced to a mere 'signal' for behaviour. I shall finally disregard the conventional (but in reality very difficult) distinction between 'concrete' and 'abstract' words, which may in fact depend only on the context in which a particular word is used (see J. Dewey, 1938, p. 351).

[1] J. Dewey (1938), p. 355.

Again, the linguistic grouping-together stands for a distinct way of 'thinking about' things, events, and so forth.

Perhaps we should emphasize that this argument is not affected by examples, which can readily be quoted, of some apparent discrepancy between the naming of phenomena and other evidence on how the speakers 'think about' them. Obviously, people who have one word both for physical ugliness and moral depravity will yet react differently towards the two; and people who use different words for the death of humans and of animals, or for 'shade' and 'shadow', will yet show in other ways that they understand the physical phenomenon common to both. But we are not maintaining that the naming of phenomena indicates the *only* relationship that is recognized between them; we take the naming to indicate only that *some* relationship (out of many) is recognized and understood to be relevant. If we denied this, we should be affirming that nomenclatures are random and fortuitous—which is absurd, in spite of a few instances to the contrary (e.g. homonyms). Admittedly, in any given speech situation these wide 'summaries' are reduced to a narrower reference, appropriate there and then, which narrowing down is effected both by the linguistic context and the material situation in which the words occur. Furthermore, the routine of linguistic usage may obscure the speaker's awareness of the conceptual connections extending beyond the given context— though this would vary with the speaker's intellect, interests, and education. Yet the study of changes in the currency of words, of the extension of pristine meanings and the invention of new words, offers ample evidence of this awareness unobscured.

Nor are all these facts only 'psychologically' important, falling outside our field of interest. Inasmuch as the 'summaries' laid into words rest on current notions as to relevant connections between things, they reflect the knowledge valid in a culture, its interests, values, and norms. The linguistic usage of a people, and equally the verbal reports on its culture (such as the anthropologist elicits), are thus themselves instances of the working of the culture—if we can read the evidence.

If in a primitive language the same word is used for 'real' marriage and for a nominal or temporary union of man and woman, it is a significant indication of the width of the concept and so of the evaluation of these modes of behaving. Social status and the membership of groups are rendered visible by the diacritical use of names (if I may anticipate a term to be introduced later), whose every application will indicate whether a particular person 'belongs' or does not 'belong'; to trace the repetitive or varied use of these names is thus to trace the social framework. If a people uses the term 'gift' both for transactions between persons and for offerings to deities, the linguistic identification reveals a significant feature in their attitude to the supernatural. In the widespread use of the same word for the physical substance 'blood', for close kinship, for the gravity of crimes ('shedding of blood'), and for their moral or social consequences (when people speak of 'blood revenge', or of 'blood' being between the kin of assailant and victim), the embracing meaning stands for a distinct conceptual nexus, mystic, but strongly effective as a motive for action. And this is no less true of the technical language of economics, where the usage of such words as 'wealth', 'poverty', 'sale', 'price', once more indicates the current notions as to the 'relevant connections between things'.

To say it again, all these facts are there, within the anthropologist's reach, 'if he can read the evidence'. And this is accessible only through a full knowledge of the indigenous language. The 'virtuosity' of the linguist-anthropologist, which Dr. Mead regards as misplaced ambition, is only the fullest preparation for his task. But ideals are often impossible. Not every anthropologist has the gifts of a linguist, nor will he always have sufficient time at his disposal to acquire a complete knowledge of the indigenous language.[1] It might be argued that no anthropologist should be forced to work with insufficient time at his command. But anthropologists are not always their own masters; besides, the desire to investigate several groups (for example, for reasons of comparison) is often great, while one's lifetime is unhappily short. Thus we must make concessions and admit the need for compromise. There seem to be three 'second best' solutions. One is the collaboration with a linguist who has the required expert knowledge of the language. The second, the acquisition of a stock of relevant vernacular concepts for use in the anthropological enquiry; but this solution, I

---

[1] If I may quote from personal experience, I used Nupe exclusively after six months' study, and spoke it fluently after nine. Though Nupe language is rendered difficult by its tones and rich vocabulary, it has a simple grammar; I was, besides, fortunate in being able to use an excellent printed grammar and dictionary. It took me six months to master a Nuba language, which has no tones, a simple grammar and vocabulary, but is unrecorded.

feel, can only work in an enquiry of limited scope. Thirdly, there is the use of a *lingua franca* or of an indigenous language spoken by several tribes in addition to their own. My own experience may serve as an example.

When I worked as Government Anthropologist in the Nuba Mountains, among ten small tribes most of which spoke different languages, my aspirations to linguistic proficiency had to be shelved. But I restricted the range of my enquiry; also, I studied one of the Nuba languages, which was understood in a number of the tribes, while in others I used the form of Arabic which the Nuba themselves have adopted almost as a *lingua franca*. The use of an indigenous language widely understood entails many fewer pitfalls than that of an alien tongue. In the first place, the bilingual individuals are not strangers or outcasts, nor cultural hybrids alienated from their community. Moreover, the languages themselves will often be closely akin both in structure and semantic principles. This does obviously not apply to a *lingua franca* such as Arabic. But its long use (for two generations now) by some of the Nuba tribes has turned it almost into a new dialect, more congenial to their needs of expression. Here as in similar situations of enduring contact, equivalents of meaning have been evolved by the people themselves in a gradual process. These equivalents have not to be discovered on the spur of the moment, and in new, unprecedented contexts, as would be the case when a strange language is used. Pitfalls and errors will remain, but they are of lesser weight since the gap which the translation has to bridge has itself been narrowed.

Let me, in conclusion, return to a point made earlier in this discussion. As language is a tool of observation, so it is one of description. What we observe we must report, and this is only possible through language. Obviously, too, our reports, if they are to be of value, must be communicable; the verbal statement in which I describe what I saw must have a precise meaning for others. Science is based on communicable not on private experiences, and here linguistic precision is the first condition. Now this postulate to some extent conflicts with the aim of rendering full justice to the peculiarity of indigenous concepts, many of which, as we know, refer to modes of behaviour, relationships, and the like, which simply do not occur in our own culture. It is not surprising, therefore, that in anthropology certain vernacular words have become tacitly accepted as untranslatable—such as *mana, tabu, totem, potlach*. The results have not been too happy. Never sharply defined in a neutral language, the concepts so expressed have tended to assume a different meaning in different contexts. Moreover, the expedient is threatening to grow into a habit, and it is by no means rare to find anthropological accounts so full of vernacular terms that a glossary is needed to understand them. Yet clearly, carried too far, the use of vernacular words in description must lead to statements which are no longer communicable.

The question of communicability does not end with the pros and cons of the use of vernacular terms. Great variety in the way in which identical descriptive terms are used by different anthropologists is equally confusing, and equally obstructs the progress of our science. This, unhappily, is the case to-day. Anthropology has expanded so fast and its work grown so dispersed, embracing such widely different cultures, that its terminology is on the point of losing all identity. Soon an anthropological Council of Nicaea will be needed to save the unity of the science from terminological schisms. But of all this we spoke before.

3. The Personal Equation

If there is a danger of anthropology becoming a 'private' science (a contradiction in terms), the reason lies deeper than in its confused phraseology. Where the human being is the only 'instrument' of observation, the observer's 'personal equation' must be all-pervading; and where the data observed are once more human data, the observer's personality might easily override the best intentions of objectivity. In the final interpretation of the data some such bias is probably inevitable. It might be argued that, as long as interpretative and descriptive statements are kept distinct, no harm is done; on the contrary, the personal viewpoints and the varying philosophies which different students of society may bring to their material would all enrich the science of man. Yet in so far as it is also true that even the observation of facts already entails omission, selection, and emphasis, that is, a first, inevitable interpretation, the observer's personality cannot be permitted such latitude.

The remedy seems clear: if such subjectivity is unavoidable, it can at least be brought into the open. Which means that the reasoning underlying observation and description must be clearly formulated, its premises explicitly stated, and its operations shown step by step. Inevitably, it must be reasoning within a *system*; for the final ordering of facts, which is the aim of science, cannot arise from an 'assemblage' which is itself unordered. This book aims at precisely this. Its reasoning might not fit other viewpoints or philosophies; nor would I claim always to be right where others are wrong. Indeed, the question of being right or wrong does not arise; rather is it a question of adequacy—adequacy to the facts for which, by this or any other conceptual system, we have to account. All I would claim is to have attempted such a system, consistently constructed (so far as lay in my ability) and, above all, explicitly stated. The greatest risk of mishandling scientific problems lies, not in the different viewpoints and philosophies or perhaps in the divergent personalities of the scientists, but in the inexplicit statement of the assumptions and concepts with which they operate. For in this manner their findings preclude the crucial test of adequacy and become neither truths nor falsehoods, but intractable pseudo-truths. Let me here quote the statement of a philosopher, extreme though it is. Scientific thought is full of 'logical and scientific myths'; these are not *wrong*; they are 'unguarded' in the sense that their 'truth is limited by unexpressed presuppositions'.[1]

This is only one way of escaping from the dilemma. Even with his system of concepts and categories clarified, the anthropological observer remains under the influence of his personality. He cannot but see with his eyes, hear with his ears, and unconsciously respond to a context emotionally weighted with the emotional side of his nature. In natural science the effects of the personal equation have long been known; since it affects observation mainly through the varying accuracy of sense perception, it can be tested and controlled with little difficulty. If a similar viewpoint were applied in anthropology, it would mean a careful selection, based on thorough psychological examination, of the anthropologist before he is sent to the field.

There is nothing paradoxical or ludicrous in such a view. What is paradoxical is that it has not long since been adopted or demanded more pressingly. Radin (with whose views I rarely agree) has spoken in strong terms about the complete disregard among anthropologists of this vital aspect of their science.[2] He has not, to my knowledge, advocated anything stronger than careful selection.

[1] A. N. Whitehead (1938), p. 15.   [2] P. Radin (1933), p. 110.

But I have also heard the suggestion that all prospective field-workers should be psychoanalysed. I am not certain whether this rather special form of personality-examination is the most useful one, but some form of psychological testing seems imperative. It need not be regarded as a basis for selection only. It will offer, to the fieldworker himself, the necessary knowledge of his 'personal equation'. Perhaps training in psychology would prove adequate, and this too has been advocated.[1] By such means the anthropologist will more readily appreciate his unconscious bias and will be enabled to guard against the pull of forces he has learned to evaluate.

Here I am speaking from personal experience. My experience as psychologist has taught me to evaluate the 'pull' of my own mind —towards schematic representation, a synthesizing rather than enumerating memory, towards over-readiness in discovering 'meaning' and meaningful connections. In consequence I have consciously tried to guard against it. Painstakingly detailed and repeated observations; a method of questioning and checking in which I postulated the opposite of what I was ready to assume; a plan of enquiry in which diverse items were combined at all stages; and great emphasis on quantitative evidence—such were my weapons. Weapons of one kind or other there must be; if they are already familiar to all anthropologists, so much the better.

Let me briefly turn to a related subject, touched upon before, namely, teamwork in anthropological field research. In a different sense this method, too, is a means of overcoming the limitations of the personality. One person cannot be in two places at once; and one person cannot know everything. In the field study of wide-spread groups and complex civilizations the old technique of single-handed observation becomes 'sadly inadequate. Even dis-regarding the well-nigh encyclopædic knowledge which the anthropologist would have to possess to cope adequately with language, economics, kinship, political and religious systems, art, technology, and so forth, where these exist in any degree of complexity, there still remain the sufficiently formidable obstacles of space and time. Whether Dr. Mead's optimistic statement that 'a trained student can master the fundamental structure of a primitive society in a few months' was ever true I will not decide;[2] obviously this depends on what is meant by 'master' and 'fundamental

[1] F. C. Bartlett (1937), pp. 416–8.   [2] Margaret Mead (1929), p. 8.

structure'. That it is untrue for the study of societies of any size or complexity should be self-evident.

The solution, then, is specialization or teamwork or both. No anthropologist would dream of claiming that, merely through being an anthropologist, he could also study primitive music. But the position as regards, say, economics is really closely similar; and where anthropologists include among their aims a psychological investigation of the group they study (whatever they may mean by 'psychological'), their competence is equally questionable. Unless this is realized, anthropological encyclopædism is bound to become amateurish, and the over-ambition of the individual fieldworker bound to lead to incomplete studies.

Teamwork in anthropology has hardly yet started. Exponents of a young science, pioneers of a synoptic discipline, anthropologists are excusably individualistic. To each his field, explored by him, means an intensely personal adventure, almost a personal possession. Anthropologists may also feel, as my friends Evans-Pritchard and Fortes have once put it, that the 'passing through a single mind' of the fieldwork data adds something peculiarly valuable to our kind of study. Yet once more we must face the issue that science cannot, in any respect, be 'private'.

In conclusion, we must touch upon one particular aspect of the 'personal philosophy' of anthropologists, namely upon the ethical values and the humanitarian ideals they bring to their research. Being human beings, they cannot be without either; and being students of society, they cannot fail to be stirred by the issues of this kind which are raised in any history and in any society. The question thus arises how far they may, or should, express this philosophy in their work. For the anthropologist this question will tend to have a more specific bearing since he is at least traditionally concerned with 'primitive' societies, which to-day he finds almost everywhere exposed to the impact of Western civilization. This impact is always one of values and ideals. Where, then, do we stand —among the onlookers or the partisans?

In turning to this aspect of anthropology we are, of course, going beyond the scope of this chapter, which is devoted to problems of technique; yet the problem I have in mind is most conveniently included in a section dealing with the 'personal equation'. Nor perhaps is it quite correct to speak here simply of 'personal' equations or philosophies. To be sure, anthropologists have their political and ethical creeds, and so belong to this or that camp of social philosophers. Yet on certain basic issues we are all in accord. We are heirs to the same traditions of thought; we hold the same views on the relationship between 'primitive' and 'advanced' peoples and share the same moral convictions as to the manner in which the backward races should be treated. We all agree that our own civilization must not ride roughshod over their traditional culture, as we also agree that respect for it must not be turned into a fetish or an excuse for barring these peoples from all change and advance. We may regret the disappearance of primitive cultures, whose study can teach us so much, and we are aware of the threat to their stability from rapid and radical changes; yet no one would dream of defending the perpetuation of a state of ignorance and superstition, of beliefs in witchcraft, of inadequate nutrition and production, or of a cruel and iniquitous law. Now, to hold all these views is one thing; to plan precisely how they should be put into effect or to criticize such plans and policies, quite another. In the former case we can remain onlookers, 'pure scientists'; in the latter, we clearly weigh one set of values against another—the gratifications of traditional life against all that is meant by 'progress'—and pass judgment; we must, in some measure, become partisans. It is on this issue, above all, that anthropologists are divided and voice once more their 'personal philosophy'.

While certain anthropologists would remain aloof from these practical questions, others consider it their right and duty to 'apply' anthropology in practice. I count myself among the latter.[1] But I would hold that this is no true alternative. More precisely, the antithesis between a 'pure' anthropology and one openly committed to value judgments is a false antithesis. One might defend aloofness from practical issues on a number of grounds. One might argue that any science will best develop when it need not orient itself on interests of practical import; one might argue further that, in the case of anthropology, the scientist cannot hope to change policy even if his researches demonstrated its wrongness; there is, too, the grave moral responsibility he must shoulder when aiming to influence decisions that bear on 'the lives of men'.[2] Valid though these arguments are, they seem to me to miss the mark. In the

---

[1] The whole issue has been admirably summarized in Edwin W. Smith (1946), Chap. 4.

[2] These and similar points are raised by R. W. Firth (1938), pp. 195–7.

main, they are arguments of expediency; but it needs a more fundamental reason to defend the aloofness of our discipline. Nor is this reason unfamiliar; for it is often claimed that science, of any kind, must aim at the 'objective' analysis of 'facts' and hence bar all value judgments, that is, all statements on what is 'better' or 'worse', 'right' or 'wrong', in a human or moral sense. Rash and crude judgments of this kind must obviously be avoided; equally it is possible to avoid them. Yet in a more subtle sense value judgments must enter into every social enquiry, being entailed in its very nature. And in this sense I hold that 'pure', value-free, anthropology is an illusion.

Philosophers might even go further and deny the possibility of value-free judgments in any pursuit of knowledge. Let me quote this passage: On closer analysis 'the opposition between value and fact breaks down. "Facts" are themselves values, values established in the endeavour to analyze out the factor of givenness contained in experience, and presupposing purposive manipulations of apparent "facts". . . . [Thus] the notion of value as something gratuitously superadded upon fact must be modified. . . . Reality in its fullness contains and exhibits values, and they are ejected from it only by an effort of abstraction, which is relative to certain restricted purposes, and is never quite successful'.[1] Certainly, in all human sciences a great many statements and categories which might appear to be free from valuation are in fact based upon the assumption at least of ultimate values. 'We are . . . constantly passing value judgments . . . when we speak of things as normal or abnormal, the average man, and especially when we use the term "pathological".'[2] My point is that in the study of society we can 'eject' values least of all.

Since the whole realm of social action is pervaded by purpose, we must at every step make judgments on the adequacy or otherwise of means to ends and of actual behaviour to the aim behind it. In a 'value-free' enquiry we should be judging this adequacy entirely by relative standards, measuring the end-results achieved against those aimed at by the actors. But as we shall see, in at least three instances we must apply absolute standards of adequacy, that is, evaluate the end-results of behaviour in terms of purposes *we* believe in or postulate. This occurs, first, when we speak of the

[1] F. C. S. Schiller (1921), in Hastings's *Encyclopædia*, vol. xii, p. 589.
[2] M. Cohen (1946), p. 171.

satisfaction of psycho-physical 'needs' offered by any culture; secondly, when we assess the bearing of social facts upon survival; and thirdly, when we pronounce upon social integration and stability. In each case our statements imply judgments as to the worthwhileness of actions, as to 'good' or 'bad' cultural solutions of the problems of human life, and as to 'normal' and 'abnormal' states of affairs. These are basic judgments which we cannot do without in social enquiry and which clearly do not express a purely personal philosophy of the enquirer or values arbitrarily assumed. Rather do they grow out of the history of human thought, from which the anthropologist can seclude himself as little as can anyone else. Yet as the history of human thought has led not to one philosophy but to several, so the value attitudes implicit in our ways of thinking will differ and sometimes conflict. Even if such conflicts seem absent when we treat of psycho-physical needs, survival, or social stability, this is so only because on this level many implications remain tacit and unexpressed. But from these basic evaluations a great many others follow, which lead us to view specific modes of social action under the aspect of their ultimate worth-whileness, and here the divergence in our philosophies must become apparent. We might again leave these evaluations unexpressed and so lull ourselves in a false sense of 'objectivity'; alternatively, we can make them explicit and thus, admitting our 'subjectivity', lay it open to scrutiny and criticism. There can be no doubt as to the right course.[1]

It is only a short and logical step from admitting the presence of these value judgments to admitting that we are indeed stirred by the social and ethical issues of our time and influenced by them in every phase of our work. It is a short step again to accepting also the right and duty of anthropologists to judge, criticize, and add constructively to social developments and political planning of all kinds. I said 'of all kinds'; for the application of anthropology to problems of colonial policy is only one special aspect of a wider issue. To say it again, there are a good many practical reasons why anthropologists might not wish to be drawn into political controversies (colonial or otherwise). But there is nothing in the nature of a principle to preclude or discourage such a step; rather on the

[1] To quote again from a philosopher: 'The fact is that all people who pretend to be indifferent to considerations of right and wrong actually make judgments of right and wrong, implicitly if not avowedly, and these judgments are not better by reason of their failure to receive explicit critical examination.' M. Cohen (1946), p. 169.

contrary. It may be necessary to make out a special case why to-day the natural scientist should cease to be the 'disinterested' enquirer and should concern himself also with the 'application' of his science for the benefit of society (or whatever you like to call it).[1] But the case of anthropology is not analogous. If, for example, a physicist also pronounces upon the use (or abuse) to which the theoretical advances of his science are put by his society, he argues no longer as a scientist but as a citizen or social being, and from the conscience he possesses as such. But the anthropologist in a similar position would criticize the very thing he also studies, society. As a scientist he is bound to make judgments on the nature of society and on the purpose of human behaviour; as a critic or perhaps planner of policy he merely applies the same kind of judgment to problems of which he happens to have cognizance as a citizen or social being. The anthropologist, then, being an anthropologist, already takes a stand in the controversy about the 'right' kind of society, or the right kind under given conditions, though he does so in a sphere in which he has no axes to grind. When it comes to the grinding of axes his decision to keep aloof is merely a refusal to draw conclusions from such knowledge as he possesses and such criteria as he always (even if tacitly) applies. No doubt, he can leave the drawing of conclusions to others. Yet it seems to me that he is the one best qualified to do this. I do not mean merely that the anthropologist should 'diagnose and predict' (Firth), that is, demonstrate from his findings the probable effects which this or that policy will have or the probable direction in which a society under given conditions will develop. Since the anthropologist investigates social regularities he will do this in any case, though he can clearly refer more or less openly and specifically to the social issues of the day. If he chooses the open and specific reference, he is bound to criticize, and if he is to criticize constructively, he is bound to suggest and recommend, and, perhaps, to draw up blueprints. Nor am I so rash as to prophesy immediate success: often, we shall have to plead ignorance as to the 'right' answer; as often we shall err and blunder. But blunders are always being committed—often by men insensible of the premises from which they argue and ignorant about the nature of the processes they attempt to influence or better. The blunders of the anthropologist will be 'better' blunders.

[1] See L. Hogben (1940), pp. 12, 736–7; and J. D. Bernal (1939), esp. pp. xiv, 41, 186.

CHAPTER IV

Psychology in Observation

---

1. THE PROBLEM

N eedless to say, anthropological literature is full of observations of a psychological nature. Actions are liberally
described as expressing motives, emotions, thoughts, interests, states of consciousness or, for that matter, the impact of
the unconscious. We read that members of a group are conscious
of their unity or proud of their status; that there are bonds of sentiment between parents and children or between kinsmen; that
people are afraid of witchcraft; or that a group encourages or re-
presses violent emotions.

Here I should find nothing to criticize, though I might wish to
know more about the method of observation on which statements
such as these are based. But other scholars might point to two
grave offences: first, the offence of admitting psychology at all, and
second, of admitting, not the innocuous 'objective' behaviourism,
but the highly suspect introspective psychology. Now, in a rigidly
non-psychological or fully behaviouristic approach the statements
just quoted would indeed be out of order; more precisely, they
would be out of order unless the psychological terms were used
merely as labels conveniently summarizing a chain of 'objective'
observations. 'Fear', then, would only mean a visible behaviour
response to certain events or objects, characterized by self-removal
and avoidance; 'pride'—another form of visible response in particular contexts; 'bonds of sentiment'—the fact that persons have
been 'conditioned' to seek each other out and do each other favours;
'emotion'—a muscular and vasomotoric reflex caused by or accompanying certain physical actions; 'thought'—perhaps 'sub-
vocal speech' (as some behaviourists would put it), though I do not
really know how to render 'thought' in such an 'objective' language.
However, in the statements of anthropologists obviously more is
meant: what is meant is these visible reactions *and* consciousness,

the latter providing in some fashion the motivations and concomitants of the former. In other words, these statements presume a psychological unity behind regulated behaviour, which is ultimately accessible only through introspection.

Although, logically, we ought to examine first the case of 'pure' sociology (to borrow a term from Rivers), which would banish psychology altogether from anthropological enquiry, we may leave this argument until later; for sociologists of this persuasion object primarily to the employment of psychological concepts in the *explanation*, and not in the *description* of social facts. Our problem, then, is behaviourism, which would permit not even description in 'subjective' terms. A few sociologists and anthropologists have fully accepted the tenets of behaviourism; many more make concessions to it. If the use of the term 'conditioning' is any evidence, almost the whole of modern anthropology has gone behaviourist. But mostly this and similar verbal concessions are only just that—whether they result from lip service or eclecticism. In either case the essence of behaviourism has been misunderstood: it offers a challenge, not an expedient.

2. BEHAVIOURISM

Behaviourism has its roots in the animal experiments of Pavlov and Bechterew. Its crucial concept is the 'conditioned reflex'; its *leitmotif*, revolt—against allegedly metaphysical, subjective, introspective classical psychology.[1] Behaviourism offers a psychology without the mind; it opens an approach to mental phenomena without the assumption of consciousness.[2] The 'introspective' reports of experimental subjects used in classical psychology, and the more dubious introspections of the psychologists themselves, are replaced by the experimental observation of behaviour. Under such conditions of rigidly 'objective' enquiry the mind, or what is normally and misleadingly called the mind, turns out to be merely a mechanism for the acquisition or 'learning' of responses. The acquisition follows a simple formula; it rests, in essence, on the

---

[1] This 'leitmotif' certainly pervaded early behaviourist literature, but is not absent even in more recent writings. Thus Professor Hull still finds it necessary to stigmatize the 'medieval' and 'theological' outlook of classical psychology in an article written in 1937 (Clark L. Hull, 1937, pp. 12–13).

[2] See John B. Watson (1930), Chap. X, which is intended to do away with the 'fiction that there is such a thing as "mental" life' (p. 224).

repeated association of stimuli, whereby an already established response to one stimulus is extended and transferred to the other.

In the simplest case the established response is an automatic, 'unlearned' reflex—the result of innate mechanisms such as hunger or physical pain: a hungry dog salivates at the sight of food; a child touching a hot radiator at once withdraws the hand. If a secondary stimulus—the sound of a bell, a flash of light, or the sight of the pain-causing object—is repeatedly associated with the original stimulus, the former will after a time by itself produce the same response (salivation, the retraction of the hand): the response becomes 'conditioned' or 'learned'. To remain effective, however, the conditioning must be 'reinforced'; left to itself, the conditioned reflex will in due course be 'extinguished'.

With the help of a few additional principles this simple model is made to account for the most complex learning processes. One such principle is the substitution of similar stimuli for each other, which leads to a 'generalization' of the response; a second, the equivalence of unlearned and conditioned reflexes as starting points for new conditioning; a third, of utmost importance, the equivalence of physical stimuli and symbolic-verbal ones. The artificial association of stimuli practised in the laboratory reappears in human life once more in the form of learning—planned or fortuitous. But it is also replaced by self-instruction, and thus by something like self-conditioning.[1] The random responses of the organism to the various stimuli offered by the environment are sifted by trial and error; certain responses are learnt to be rewarding and to lead to satisfaction, while others prove to lead to fatigue, discomfort, or pain, that is, to 'punishment'. Successful, rewarding responses tend to become fixed and habitual, unsuccessful ones drop out; responses originally rewarding but subsequently unsuccessful, are 'extinguished'.[2] Everything in human behaviour, then, is 'learning'; and all learning can be reduced to such simple stimulus-response sequences. The interlocked chains of sequences built up in the course of individual life embrace the totality of regulated behaviour. Or so it is claimed.

No one will wish to deny that the behaviourist analysis of lower mental processes is brilliant and effective; or that behaviourists

---

[1] The concept of 'self-instruction' is used by Hilgard and Marquis (1940) pp. 273–4, 276.

[2] This is, in essence, Thorndike's famous Law of Effect (1911).

have greatly served the cause of psychology as well as social enquiry in focusing attention upon behaviour, learning, and habit,
and in thus checking the preoccupation with the subjective aspects
of mental life. But perhaps this danger is not as great as behaviourists imagine and the rescue offered not as rewarding. Certainly,
behaviouristic psychology in its early and extreme form was as
naïve as it was ambitious. Its attack upon the higher mental processes was so crude as to be almost disarming.[1] There is no need
here to repeat the various criticisms it received, for example, at the
hands of such psychologists as Köhler or Koffka.[2] Moreover, most
behaviourists would claim that they have outgrown the crudeness
and assurance of this early approach.[3] To-day reflexes are no
longer self-evidently the 'basic units' of psychology, which,
'organized into chain sequences through conditioning', account
for the higher and highest mental processes; indeed it seems more
probable that conditioned reflexes represent merely a 'simple type
of learning' through whose study 'basic mechanisms can be laid
bare with relative ease'.[4] Yet the earlier claims of behaviourism to
be all-embracing are only slightly toned down; for these basic
mechanisms, it is held, will prove applicable to the fields of social
psychology, moral behaviour, psychoanalysis, the theory of
empirical knowledge, also to insight, thought and reasoning—'in
short, wherever in human or animal behaviour habits play a
significant role.'[5]

I am not certain how real is the distinction between studying
conditioned reflexes as 'basic units' and studying them as something that 'lays bare basic mechanisms'. However, the crucial
feature of the new behaviourism appears to lie elsewhere. For if

[1] Consider, for example, Watson's instance of choice and motivation: 'Under
the action of a group of stimuli coming from the sex organs [the individual] may
start to seek a mate, but the flabby condition of his purse may hold in abeyance
conventional courtship and marriage, and verbal precepts instilled in his youth
(laryngeal verbal stimuli) may check association with a temporary mate' (1930,
p. 198). Or take Watson's interpretation of creative thought: 'One natural
question often raised is: How do we ever get a new verbal creation such as a poem
or a brilliant essay? The answer is that we get them by manipulating words,
shifting them about until a new pattern is hit upon' (Ibid., p. 247).

[2] See W. Köhler (1947), Chap. I, and K. Koffka (1935), pp. 26 ff.

[3] Some anthropologists, however, still subscribe to it. The textbook on
Anthropology by Chapple and Coon (1942) is an example. G. P. Murdock's
article on 'The Common Denominator of Culture' (in Linton, 1947) at least
savours of 'primitive' behaviourism.

[4] Clark L. Hull (1934), pp. 448–9.   [5] Ibid., p. 450.

behaviourists now admit thought, reasoning, insight, and so forth, as phenomena for study, it would seem to follow that they must admit also the sphere in which these phenomena can alone be observed—the sphere of mind and consciousness. If behaviourists are to attack the field of psychoanalysis, the discipline of the unconscious, they must by implication accept the mind conscious of itself. A glance at modern behaviourist literature (of the more ambitious kind) might seem to bear out this new trend; for there we meet with studies of such things as generalization and abstraction, insight or reasoning, voluntary and purposive behaviour, and with explanatory concepts such as anticipation, expectation, disappointment, hypothesis, demand, intent, and many more.[1] This new orientation is apparent rather than real. For these concepts are used without the connotation we usually give to them, namely, the implicit reference to contents of consciousness and to the fact that these are open to inspection (or 'introspection'). The mention of states or contents of consciousness is still inadmissible. The behaviourist admits these 'subjective' phenomena only, as it were, pre-scientifically—as something that exists before it is 'objectively' examined; their examination shows them to be, after all, only more instances of stimulus and response. Actually, the reduction of these phenomena to stimulus-and-response mechanisms fails in its purpose; it is incomplete and leaves residues, though these are unacknowledged. And, what is more important, the explanatory weight of these new concepts, as they are used by the behaviourist, lies precisely in that unacknowledged and unexplained residue. It simply *sounds* convincing if one speaks of expectation or anticipation, purpose and interest, and what not, and it does so to behaviourists because they leave these concepts ultimately unanalyzed. In other words, in introducing some such explanatory concept, the behaviourist only uses the magic that is in names.

Admittedly, he will hasten to qualify any term that savours of consciousness or introspection by adding that it is 'only meant behaviouristically'; but put into words, this 'behaviouristic meaning' turns out to be little better than a circumlocution. Not infrequently the subjective residue creeps in unawares;[2] or it is

[1] For an instructive critical summary of these new trends in behaviourism see Hilgard and Marquis (1940).

[2] See, for example, Miller and Dollard (1941), where the authors go to great length in trying to avoid 'subjective terms' in describing hunger and thirst (p. 18,

pushed back from one phrase to another, until it is hidden away under some less suspicious name.[1] I have come across one open admission of this nominalist trend in modern behaviourism, which makes rather curious reading. Professor Tolman says this about his rat experiments:—In planning and analyzing them 'I am openly and consciously (*sic!*) just as anthropomorphic about it as I please ... casting (my) concepts into a mould such that one can derive from one's own human, everyday experience. These hunches may then, later, be translated into objective terms. ... In my future work [I] intend to go ahead imagining (*sic!*) how, *if I were a rat*, I would behave. ... And then eventually I shall try to state [the rules so derived] in some kind of objective and respectable sounding terms such as vectors, valences, barriers, and the like.'[2]

I will add no comment. But the passages just quoted are themselves a comment on such sweeping statements as Professor Hull's: 'We have been quite unable to find any other scientific system of behaviour which ... has found consciousness a necessary presupposition. ... Considering the practically complete failure of all this effort to yield even a small scientific system of adaptive or moral behaviour in which consciousness finds a position of logical priority as a postulate, one may, perhaps, be pardoned for entertaining a certain amount of pessimism regarding such eventuality.'[3] My answer is that at least one fact provides the evidence which Professor Hull denies. The very fact that he and others write books, develop systems, plan and describe their experiments so as to convince others, and suggest hypotheses for others to understand, proves, as strongly as it can be proved, the 'logical priority' of con-

N.). But elsewhere the fear-responses of a child are described thus: The child 'feels' the tenseness of muscles; it has 'a stirred-up, taut feeling in the pit of the stomach' (p. 58).

[1] Professor Hull's 'miniature scientific systems' seem to me to be a clear example. In one of these systems he rigorously applies a set of definitions meant to reduce all the operative concepts occurring in the system to behaviourist terms. Thus 'goal', 'disappointment', 'frustration', 'striving', etc., are treated in this way; but 'striving' is defined (Definition No. 12) as 'that behaviour of organisms which, upon frustration, displays varied alternative action sequences, all *directed* by an *intent* to the attainment of the same ... state of affairs' (italics mine); and 'intent' is nowhere defined (Clark L. Hull, 1937, p. 16). Hull's approach has, in fact, been criticized on the ground that he operates with 'concealed undefined notions that have not been exhibited (e.g. mind, psychological space, etc.) and of the assumption of which the definer is not aware, some of which he might scornfully repudiate' (D. K. Adams, 1937, p. 214).

[2] E. C. Tolman (1938 a), p. 24. [3] C. L. Hull (1937), pp. 30–31.

E

sciousness; unless, of course, we are to assume that these books, arguments, experiments, and hypotheses are merely themselves responses to some form of conditioning and nothing better than the Watsonian 'manipulation of words' (see p. 59 above, N.).[1] In which case further discussion of anything seems futile.

One of the essential things about recognizing consciousness is that we recognize the active part of the mind, even if by 'mind' we merely mean the sphere where conditioning takes place. For old-fashioned behaviourism the problem of consciousness does not arise merely because this sphere is thought of as a passive medium; conditioning is, as it were, done to it: a stimulus is impressed, and the response follows. There may be some competition between conflicting stimuli, but one would eventually win through by some mechanical, self-selecting device. From this point of view all sorts of 'higher' mental processes can be broken down to the crude mechanism of conditioning. You can argue that the national flag, by careful conditioning, becomes associated with patriotic behaviour, so that the sight of that symbol activates the conditioned response and makes you behave patriotically.[2] A word conditions you so that you behave in a certain way whenever you hear a person called by that word: you behave aggressively towards those whom you or others call 'enemy', and in an opposite manner to those whom you call 'friend'.[3] In modern behaviourism, or behaviourism at its best, the sphere where conditioning takes place has mysteriously become active, and itself contributes to the chains of stimuli. It is credited with 'self-instruction', anticipation, intent, and the making of 'hypotheses' (Tolman). The same conditioning stimulus is seen to provoke different responses in different contexts, since there exists a 'hierarchy of responses' implying the selection and rejection of presented stimuli according to their relevance.[4] In other words, I do not wax patriotic every time I see the national flag; and I do not exhibit aggressive behaviour when the word 'enemy' is mentioned in conversation. Finally, different stimuli provoke the same response, the mind (what else?) possessing the faculty of abstracting 'obscure cues' common to different stimulus

[1] Or unless, with Pavlov, we divide the world of our experience in two: 'It is one thing to live according to subjective states and quite another thing to analyze purely scientifically their mechanism' (1941, p. 26).

[2] Chapple and Coon (1942), pp. 30, 470.

[3] Miller and Dollard (1941), p. 75.

[4] Ibid. pp. 27, 72.

situations, and even of laying into them a 'degree of acquired similarity'.[1] Thus a political speech or the account of some national exploit will fan my patriotism as effectively as the flag since they both share an 'obscure cue'; and seeing obnoxious behaviour will stimulate me into the sort of aggressiveness I have learned to produce against enemies if I discover a relevant 'similarity' between the observed behaviour and the 'generalised' application of the word 'enemy'. All this is still tortuous circumlocution. But it means—if it means anything—that the sphere where conditioning is formed is an agency, not merely a medium, and that its manner of acting lies in examining, selecting, and integrating the stimuli which it absorbs. The concepts 'mind', 'consciousness', say nothing else save that they also imply the possibility of self-inspection. In animal experiments this possibility is ruled out. But with humans it is demonstrated, simply and conclusively, by the intelligible verbal reports which people can make about their 'subjective' experiences. But of this more later.

Behaviourists to-day, then, are as near accepting consciousness as they can be without ceasing to be behaviourists. That they have not taken the final step involves them in inadequacies which no refinement of terminology can conceal. There remains, in human conduct, a field which behaviourism cannot reach; 'the . . . behaviourist simply did all he could to minimise the difference.'[2] Yet he has not proved that consciousness and mind are propositions to be avoided, since he himself cannot avoid them. All that he proves is that mind and consciousness come to pieces in his hands. He will no doubt say that this is as it should be—the price paid for 'verification'. With other psychologists I would call it the cost of inadequate methods. For this 'verification' requires that 'subjective' phenomena must be reduced to behaviour observable under very special experimental conditions. This can be expressed more unkindly: 'The mistake of behaviourism is not so much refusing to take account of consciousness as refusing to take account of any facts except those revealed by a special kind of laboratory technique. The evidence attained by their methods is biased and incomplete and resembles too much confession of crime obtained by torture.'[3] Indeed, one cannot help feeling sometimes that to the behaviourist, old or new, nothing is evidence that cannot be verified on rats and

[1] Miller and Dollard (1941), p. 77.
[2] George H. Mead (1934), pp. 8–9.   [3] A. D. Ritchie (1936), p. 277.

dogs. Let me, in conclusion, quote this 'confession of faith' of an outstanding psychologist: 'I believe that everything important in psychology (except perhaps such matters as the building up of a super-ego, that is, everything save such matters as involve society and words) can be investigated in essence through the continued experimental and theoretical analysis of the determiners of rat behaviour at a choice point in a maze.'[1] As an anthropologist, who treats of society and words, I rest content.

3. THE ALTER EGO

Accepting consciousness behind behaviour is one thing, identifying its operations, another. Here the anthropologist's position seems more precarious than that of other students of humanity. He is not of the group which he studies; he observes individuals whose motivations, thoughts, and feelings may differ widely from those which are to him habitual and self-evident. Now the question—what is it that makes us certain about the mental processes behind another person's behaviour?—is a difficult one without the barriers of culture. Indeed, it is often treated as a fundamental problem of epistemology.[2] Within the sphere of our own civilization, however, psychologists, especially psychologists of the Gestalt school, have shown how it can be solved, and there is no need to go into the theoretical issues involved.[3] For all practical purposes sufficient corroboration exists to confirm the intelligibility of mental states and processes in others. That is, we can judge, if only roughly and on occasion, that the expressive gestures of others exhibit feelings or thoughts which we also have; and we can understand what other persons report on their mental states since these duplicate, at least so far as it is relevant, our own under similar conditions; so that our 'private' experiences, although we share them with no other, yet give us what Driesch calls the You-certainty. Yet where there are the barriers of different upbringing, of widely different conditions of experiencing, and of alien ideas and values, this kind of judgment might seem easily at fault. Thus, when anthropologists speak of emotions and sentiments, and diagnose motivations or mental states, are they merely guessing?

[1] E. C. Tolman (1938 a), p. 34.
[2] See Hans Driesch (1925), pp. 105–112, or C. D. Broad (1937), pp. 318–49.
[3] See W. Köhler (1947), pp. 216 ff.; K. Koffka (1935), pp. 655 ff.

This problem has a preliminary aspect, with which we may briefly deal. It concerns the spontaneous expression of mental states, above all affective states, in motor behaviour. This is not, of course, social behaviour in the sense previously defined—it does not, by itself, satisfy the conditions of aim-control and standardization. But it may enter into standardized action patterns; and it may amount to *signs* indicating the mental states behind such behaviour.

These spontaneous expressions are basically reflexes, innate in the human organism, and so universal. They present no problems of identification, weeping, crying, shouting, laughing, gesticulations, are the same 'signs' the world over. These reflexes are not unambiguous 'signs'—we may cry for joy or laugh from embarrassment; but the context in which these expressions occur will enable us to correct their ambiguity, which, moreover, is again the same the world over. That people of different races and cultures do not always laugh or weep at the same things or show the same excitement in danger or joy, is obvious. Custom and convention decree what is ridiculous or tragic, dangerous or joyful. But this is no problem either; the signs remain signs. They may be conventionalized in the sense that a particular reflex action is given a habitual form and occasion. The Chinese open their eyes wide in anger;[1] the Ethiopians show horror by placing their hand over the mouth. Examples of this kind can easily be multiplied.[2] They would, however, show another feature also, namely, habitual differences in the frequency and intensity of the expressive motor behaviour. Different races (using the term in a very loose sense) show different levels of this kind. Compared with ourselves, for example, certain orientals or the Latins in our own civilization seem to gesticulate more readily and vehemently, and to speak habitually in a louder voice. These are, once more, 'signs' for mental states, and we shall conclude that these people are more 'excitable', that is, that in their case affective stimuli are more readily effective. We may add that it is only the nexus between mental states and expressive behaviour which is innate; the appearance of the latter tells us nothing about the innateness or otherwise of the mental states it indicates.

[1] O. Klineberg, 'Emotional Expressions in China': quoted from Kimball Young (1946), p. 89.

[2] For an exhaustive discussion see O. Klineberg (1935), Chap. XV, and Kimball Young (1946), pp. 88–91.

Now the fact that the various forms of expressive behaviour can become habitual and conventionalized is not in itself a source of error (for the convention can easily be elicited through verbal information). The source of error lies in the fact that, through cultural training (or 'conditioning'), the 'signs' may be separated from the spontaneous response. Thus reflex-like expressions are often decreed in specific situations irrespective of the true subjective state or may be rigidly inhibited in spite of it. Ceremonial weeping, for instance, seems widespread—it has been recorded of the Andaman Islanders,[1] and I have witnessed it in the Nuba Mountains; the Chinese and Japanese smile as a matter of etiquette; the American Indian, proverbially impassive, is another example. What we may find, then, is simulation. Let us be clear where the source of error would lie. Even if simulated—or rather, because it is simulated—the behaviour in question still signifies the affective state: at funerals there is meant to be a show of grief, expressed in weeping; at a cruel test of manhood there is meant to be a show of equanimity, and so an impassive face. What remains in doubt is whether the mental states so shown are genuine.

Usually, this question can be answered from our general knowledge of the working of the emotions which lead to such expressive motor behaviour. If they are genuine, they cannot, for example, be switched on and off *ad lib*. Radcliffe-Brown reports that the Andamanese readily wept 'real tears' at his request—which settles the question conclusively.[2] At a Nuba funeral I saw women weep and cry, in utmost frenzy—for about half an hour; after which time they retired to a hut where they immediately dropped their emotional exuberance, being replaced by other women who equally readily switched on the same violent expressions. Nor was this all; for I was given the rules laying down, for each kinship degree, male and female, the precise number of days during which each must mourn. Here again, genuine emotion cannot be assumed (at least, to the extent to which its expression is prescribed by the rules). In the Fulani *tsoro*, a most cruel initiation rite which adolescents must undergo, the initiates keep a straight face, moving not a muscle when leather thongs lash their chest and back, and even smile and joke under the ordeal. That it must be an ordeal, we can judge by the weals which the lashes leave; and we know (or can guess) that

[1] A. R. Radcliffe-Brown (1933 a), pp. 116–17, 239 ff.
[2] Ibid., p. 117.

under these conditions the impassivity is only 'put on'. Indeed, now and again, an involuntary contortion of the face and rapid winking when new lashes are threatening will betray the pain and fear. Simulation implies training, and not all individuals will be equally well trained; younger people may laugh or cry when the older remain impassive. Sometimes, too, we discover artificial aids, such as drugs to produce insensitiveness to pain or to evoke frenzy. Perhaps there are cases where the simulation is without flaw. Here indeed we may be misled, though I do not myself think that the danger is very great.

If in the preceding examples reflex-like behaviour appears detached from the mental states it normally expresses, behaviour of no reflex character may serve as an expression of mental states. Here we are dealing with *symbols*, often physically detachable, for feelings, thoughts, interests, or pervasive attitudes, forms of dress to indicate grief, conventional gestures of obeisance or endearment, emblems of loyalty or sentimental attachment.[1] Their meaning is decided by the existing cultural norms, and varies with them. Why this and not that symbol is chosen by a culture is a problem which goes beyond the present context. The main fact, for us, is that these symbols are employed by the individuals in accordance with the cultural canon; they are intentional acts—social behaviour in the full sense of the word. Yet being symbols, they also stand apart from other forms of social behaviour. They belong to what I shall call the *diacritical* elements in culture.[2] These are, briefly, means of demonstrating the differential position of individuals in the group, and so the range of social tasks consequent upon that position. Whenever these means are employed, they indicate that behaviour conforming to the social tasks in question is taking place or may be expected to take place. The wearing of mourning dress, the conventional gestures of obeisance, and other symbols of this kind, are such indicators. They are indicators of a special kind in that they indicate, not only that such-and-such actions may be expected on the part of the individuals, but also that these actions are con-

[1] The criterion for my use of 'sign' and 'symbol' respectively is briefly this: *Signs* derive their representative capacity from their commonly experienced, 'intrinsic' or 'natural', connection with the things they signify; while the representative capacity of *symbols* is artificial, valid only under prescribed conditions, and determined by rules of usage. Here I am closely following Dewey's distinction (see 1938, pp. 51–2).

[2] See below, p. 157.

sequences of a particular mental state—grief, humility, and so forth. Like the conventionalized 'sign' of ceremonial weeping, the conventional symbol of a mourning dress might merely simulate the feeling of grief: whether it does more than this, can be seen only from the manner in which this as all the other 'indicated' social tasks are fulfilled.

In this 'fulfilment of social tasks' lies our main problem. It concerns the method of identifying behaviour, not only as an expression, but as a consequence of mental processes and states of consciousness, that is, as the result of motivations.

4. MOTIVES BEHIND BEHAVIOUR

The answer lies in these facts. The people we observe act with choice, that is, they act in a certain way while other ways of acting are in principle equally possible; furthermore, the people can report on how and why they have made the choice and comment on the mental state which is its antecedent or concomitant; finally, people formulate certain states of consciousness as specific socially sanctioned aims. On this threefold evidence, of choice, of verbal reports, and of aimed-at mental states (again verbally reported), all identification of consciousness behind behaviour must rest. Let us examine a few examples.

An anthropologist would state that the father, say in the Trobriands, loves his children; that tribesmen feel respect towards their chiefs or priests; that in some tribes incest is regarded with horror; or that clans exhibit strong sentiments of group-loyalty. Each of these statements means the summing-up of numerous observations—a shorthand for a whole range of behaviour. Some of these observations refer to spontaneous or conventionalized expressions of emotional states—a father fondling his child, smiling at his pranks or grieving at his illness; people looking aghast at the mention of incest, or exhibiting anger when witnessing disrespectful or disloyal conduct. Other observations refer to conventionalized conduct and gestures whose meaning I understand through comparing them with conduct and gestures in different contexts; thus I may observe that tribesmen bow low in the presence of a chief but not when meeting fellow tribesmen, or that they bare their heads only in sacred places.

In yet other situations I observe more than merely reflexive motions or conventional expressions; and here I also do more than merely 'sum up', namely, point to and name a common denominator in diverse modes and contexts of behaviour. Essentially, this common denominator refers to a definite directedness of consciousness in one way or other, rendered visible in action from choice. The father to whom I ascribe love for his child will be seen picking up the infant when it stumbles, going out of his way to help and protect his child, doing things for it which the child (visibly) enjoys, and trying to be with the child whenever he can. In theory, as I know from general experience, the father might be annoyed with the child's pranks, indifferent to its illness, and unwilling to spend property for the sake of a son's brideprice or a daughter's dowry; yet he is not. The tribesmen will obey orders given by chief or priest; they will meticulously observe the often cumbrous rules of etiquette. Again, they might resent the former and find the latter inconvenient—yet they observe the rules nonetheless, without having to be forced. Clansmen will forgo benefits for the sake of their fellow-members; run dangers to aid, protect or avenge them; and (in some groups) refrain from flirting with the wives of clansfellows. They might decline to sacrifice their comfort and pleasures or to risk their safety for the sake of clan morality; yet they do not do so. It is this consistent choice amidst competing motivations which I identify as the 'common denominator' and as evidence of a consciousness 'directed' in a definite way. The consistency of behaviour demands, and permits, expression in terms, let us say, of some mental energy which supplies the overriding impulse in a variety of contexts. I can name this mental energy; in the present examples I call it 'sentiment'—of paternal love, or respect, or loyalty.

Let me emphasize that we are not merely assuming, as a theoretical possibility, the existence of competing motivations or the actors' awareness of them. Their existence is observable and is assumed by the society we study. For there is variability of conduct; there are good and bad fathers; respectful and disrespectful followers of a chief or priest; there are loyal and not-so-loyal members of the clan. Even in strongly standardized behaviour there is deviation from the norm—as in offences against exogamy or even, sometimes, against incest prohibitions. These deviations are known or remembered; they are also anticipated, since one conceives of sanctions or other forms of disapproval consequent upon 'abnormal' or 'improper' conduct. Yet though society limits the variability of behaviour through approval and disapproval and hence in a sense chooses for the individual, he must choose all over again. The possibility of alternative courses of action is given; if it is disregarded, it is disregarded although it is known; it is over-ruled by a conscious aim direction.

We must clearly not overstate the case for consciousness behind regulated action. In many respects social conduct runs a smooth, given course, and its phases need not be carried by fully conscious aims. At any moment of acting the individual may well have no real choice, in the sense that he is simply carried forward by a habitual and unanalysed impulse without asking himself what satisfaction this will gain him, or whether this is the 'normal' and 'proper' way to act. Nor will he argue at every step—since I love my child I must act so and so, or since I wish to be loyal to my clan, this is the correct course to follow. But though these motives may have no emphasis or may not be present at all in his awareness, they can at any moment be lifted into awareness and made available for in-spection. For people comment on their own actions as well as those of others; they justify, in words, their attitudes and motives, or criticize those of others. This happens, above all, when new situa-tions have to be faced; when conflicts arise and competing motiva-tions cannot simply be disregarded; or when motives are queried, by an enquirer or by the society itself. We meet everywhere with institutionalized occasions of this nature. Think of legal disputes, where actions and motives are explained and called in question, or weighed and judged by the standards of right and wrong.

Full consciousness of action, then, is mostly absent in 'routine' behaviour. It is revealed where the routine is broken or threatened. It is revealed also *when routine starts*—when aims, sentiments, or thoughts are in some manner implanted, perhaps once more on institutionalized occasions. These are the occasions when cultural norms are demonstrated and transmitted—in initiation rites, in the course of religious ceremonials, or through teaching of all kinds. Behaviourists may still speak of 'learning' and 'conditioning'. But this 'conditioning' starts somewhere; and it starts because someone wants it to start, that is, in consequence of consciously held aims. Equally, it operates through consciousness; for though this learning of the cultural norms may involve the immediate concrete stimuli of 'reward' and 'punishment', it also involves, in at least equal measure, those abstract 'anticipations' and remote 'goals' for which the crude concept of conditioning fails to account. Once implanted, the cultural norms may well become 'routine', but a routine made possible by that 'directedness' of consciousness which sustains the consistency of behaviour in the presence of choice.

But, if I am right, the sentiments, thoughts, and other motives behind behaviour are accessible only within set limits. Where no alternative courses of action are observable, where there is no evidence of competing desires, where actors do not comment on reasons or motives and do not verbally weigh right against wrong, we cannot logically presume the working of consciousness. Other factors may here be at work—true conditioned reflexes or responses, rigid instincts, automatic habits, or perhaps the subterranean forces of the unconscious. This last aspect we may, in this chapter on Description, disregard. Doubtless, many forms of regulated behaviour are of this automatic type—dress habits, table manners, habitual postures, and the like. But these are patterns of behaviour of relatively minor social significance, or, more precisely, they are automatic only when they have such minor significance. I doubt whether there are behaviour patterns of greater social weight which would force us to abandon our search for mental processes even behind 'routine'.

But we must not restrict our search too rigidly. This is, I think, a telling example. In primitive communities incest prohibitions are frequently observed with absolute regularity. There are no sanctions, and no conceptions that the rule may ever be broken. No choice or possible conflict is ever visible—the people 'just behave like that', and the comments they make state precisely this. Here the approach to consciousness as I envisage it may indeed seem barred. Westermarck, who saw in the incest prohibitions the result of a gradual weakening of sexual attraction between individuals living in close proximity, presumed some such situation. His theory is insufficiently documented, anthropologically as well as psychologically, but let that pass. Now I did find, in the Nuba Mountains, tribes where the incest rules appeared to operate with such absolute regularity, so far as this could be deduced from observable and remembered conduct. Yet assuming the accuracy of this deduction, there was one indication of an interplay of motivations and a conflict of impulses: the people had incest dreams, and talked about them. The possibility of incest was conceived of, if only in dreams and phantasies. The alternative course of action was present—we may now say—in consciousness.

5. NOMENCLATURE

We conclude, then, that we can point to some 'mental energy' as the concomitant of regulated conduct. The question remains how we know whether to call this energy thought, desire, emotion, or sentiment. It may be that, say, death and danger evoke only thoughts, and not emotions; that the clansfellows pursuing a blood-feud act from a notion of equity rather than from sentiments of loyalty or emotions of revenge; that a father would aid and protect his child not from love but from a sense of duty, or perhaps the desire to conform to the customary model of a 'good father'.

Here we cannot but let ourselves be guided by language—both the language which developed in the culture to which we belong, and the technical language of psychologists. We observe actions and responses for which language—general or psychological—has devised fitting terms. For the spontaneous, consistent, and occasionally excited behaviour of the father or tribesman which we have sketched there is no other word save 'love', 'respect', or 'loyalty'. When a person disdains to do certain work considered unfitting for his elevated social status, we have no word other than 'pride'—which traditional psychology calls a 'sentiment'. Blood feud is an action requiring a high degree of determination and some spur of violent nature; psychology classes this kind of impulse as emotional. And when the people we observe act with deliberation and without signs of passion, perhaps hesitatingly and with ample comments on their course of action, we shall call this acting from a 'sense of duty' or from thought; while unexcited, 'unthinking', routine behaviour must be identified as 'customary' or 'habitual'.

Thus the final choice rests on our appreciation of the whole range of connected situations, our ability to identify expressive behaviour, and, above all, on the adequacy of our linguistic 'summaries'. An ultimate inaccuracy must perhaps remain, since the linguistic categories we must employ are far from precise or unequivocal. Furthermore, they are introspective in nature; for whatever we discover (or think we discover) of mental states and events in others is only intelligible in so far as it duplicates our own experiencing, and can only be expressed in terms verified through that.

Here, then, we are fully committed to introspection, with all its dangers and pitfalls of subjectivity. The only alternative is to define, say, the common denominator in the father-child relationship, by some non-committal term. I might enumerate all the typical aspects of the relationship and say that they reflect a mental 'energy' (or 'directedness', or 'vector') X. I should find the same energy at work in husband-wife relationship, or between friends. Between enemies, on the other hand, the opposite relationship would imply an opposite mental 'energy', which I might call $\frac{\text{I}}{\text{x}}$.

Certain psychologists have indeed been experimenting on some such lines.[1] Here I cannot refrain from quoting this little poem which I found in Eddington's *Philosophy of Physical Science*, and which I consider an admirable (if somewhat frivolous) comment on 'mathematical psychology'.[2]

> Let x denote beauty, y manners well-bred,
> z fortune (this last is essential),
> Let L stand for love—one philosopher said—
> Then L is a function of x, y and z,
>   Of the kind that is known as potential.
>
> Now integrate L with respect to dt
>   (t standing for time and persuasion),
> Then, between proper limits, 'tis easy to see
> The definite integral Marriage must be
>   (A very concise demonstration).

But to return to more serious matters. The replacement of the 'subjective' psychological phraseology by a quasi-mathematical symbolism seems to me to be excessive caution. Nor is it warranted, since the crucial, compromising step lies in the admission of consciousness and in the diagnosis of its forms or states. Once I diagnose these, I must give them a name which reflects the phenomenal characteristics by which I judged. To do otherwise is mere circumlocution if not dishonesty. To say it again, this name is the result of introspection. More precisely, it implies a projection of what is observable on the surface of behaviour, below this surface. We interpret what we see in terms of factors which, in the last resort,

---

[1] See K. Lewin (1938). In animal experiments such 'noncommittal' symbolism clearly represents the most adequate method (see, e.g. E. C. Tolman, 1938 a).

[2] The poem is by W. J. M. Rankine, *Songs and Fables*, 1874.

we can grasp only through self-analysis. This self-analysis psychologists obligingly carry out for us through 'introspection'. But the same self-analysis is also at the root of our language as mankind created it. If we are loth to accept the results of professional introspection, we can with better grace accept the results of human evolution.

Nor is 'introspection' so formidable and dubious as it is sometimes made out to be. The word is inaccurate and misleading. We might, with Köhler, speak of 'direct experience', since all we do when we 'introspect' is to observe what is most directly and immediately given in *any* form of experiencing—including that which underlies physical observation or measurement.[1] Other scholars have suggested 'inspection', a term reducing the process to what it really is—the scrutiny of data in our awareness, which proceeds in precisely the same manner and with the same validity as the empirical scrutiny of the so-called 'objective' data of the physical world or indeed of behaviourist experiments.[2] Do not ask me to define 'awareness', or 'immediate experience', or for that matter 'consciousness' (which is only another word for the same thing). These are primary concepts, which we must accept before we can start talking intelligently about anything. No one can honestly say that he does not know what they mean. And even physicists who insist most rigorously on the 'operational' definition of all terms admit these undefinables.[3]

[1] W. Köhler (1947), p. 26.

[2] C. D. Broad (1937), pp. 259 et seq.; A. D. Ritchie (1936), pp. 94–5, 148. Confirmation comes from an unexpected quarter: 'Psychology in so far as it concerns the subjective state of man has a natural right to existence; for our subjective world is the first reality with which we are confronted' (J. P. Pavlov, 1928, p. 329).

[3] 'The concept of consciousness is perhaps the ultimate unanalyzable, and when we attempt to express the possibility of getting away from it we attempt the impossible' (P. W. Bridgman, 1938, p. 142).

CHAPTER V

The Material of Observation

1. THE NEXUS OF BEHAVIOUR

We have stated that anthropological observation and description deal with standardized, task-like patterns of behaviour. Wherever we touch upon the realm of things we call 'social', we touch upon material of that nature. Its definition must also be the definition of the basic units that can be isolated in that totality of human behaviour which is culture or society.

Let me explain the 'must' in this sentence. If scientific insight is insight into an order of things, observation must be directed towards breaking up the continuum of data into units—units which can be manipulated and ordered in a fashion more systematic than the ambiguous and fortuitous ordering inherent in naïve observation. Here lies the danger of 'atomism'; for it is, to-day, an accepted postulate that culture and society represent wholes, complexes of a quasi-organic nature, which do not break up into atomic units as do complexes which are merely sum-totals of component parts. The difficulty is resolved if the units we seek to isolate satisfy the conditions of the whole, that is, if each bears the characteristics pertaining to that total entity, culture or society. We are not, then, operating with indeterminate 'atoms', but with elements whose nature is also that of the universe they build up. The whole is not the sum-total of its parts, but their integration or nexus. Society and culture are broken down, not to, say, individuals, nor to the 'works of man' (Kroeber), but to 'man-acting'. In this sense no legitimate isolate can be discovered more basic than that of a standardized pattern of behaviour rendered unitary and relatively self-contained by its task-like nature and its direction upon a single aim.

On this basic level the behaviour pattern runs its course in time; it consists of a sequence of part-actions which has a beginning and an end—the assumption of a particular task, its execution, and completion. The essential aspect is biographical, and the unit of action so

75

viewed is best termed a *behaviour cycle*. A mother tending her child, farmers working on the land, the performances of a sacrifice, a dance or court session—all these are instances of such basic 'isolates'.

I have called this basic isolate 'relatively self-contained'; for it represents, internally, a fully unitary pattern, while its external relations in time and space are irrelevant and shadowy, somewhat like the background of any visual pattern on which attention is concentrated. As soon as observation goes beyond any one isolate, the background turns into a 'foreground'; we face a continuum of features extending in time and space which may, once more, be grasped through acts of breaking-up and re-ordering, that is, through the collection of what is given into categories of 'belonging'. In this new ordering the self-containedness of the basic isolate is absorbed in wider patterns; here, too, its unitary identity disappears. For a dualism inherent in the basic pattern but unimportant in this narrow range becomes a relevant criterion for the wide-range alignment. The dualism is that of 'man-acting', of people behaving, that is, of the human beings and their tasks. Beyond the single behaviour cycle, this dualism entails a divergent alignment, in the sense of relations between the human beings, and in the sense of relations between their tasks or actions. Each, then, becomes the starting point for the ordered collection of data.

When starting from 'action' we can operate with two criteria— the criterion of means-to-end relations between behaviour patterns and the criterion of similarity or difference in their aim contents. It is clear that every social task exists within a nexus of other social tasks. Its performance requires other instrumental or prerequisite actions, and is in turn a prerequisite or starting point for further actions. Take the simple action pattern of a mother nursing her child. It implies numerous such means-to-end connections—there are, perhaps, dietetic rules to ensure the mother's milk; there must be cooking arrangements to heat the water for the infant's bath, and special productive activities to procure oil for rubbing on the babe's body. Always, there must be some arrangement whereby the young mother learns how to treat the infant in conformity with accepted standards, and some arrangement, too, which ensures the time and safety needed for the performance of the maternal duties. On the other hand, the activity 'nursing a child' is by its aim contents linked with all activities similarly implying care for infants—educating them, playing with them, or observing some religious rule to safeguard their health or spiritual welfare; while 'feeding the child' leads in the same way to all other tasks concerned with food production and consumption. Thus we arrive at a two-fold nexus, one establishing complexes of behaviour of an *instrumental* or *pragmatic* nature, the other, *logical classes* of behaviour.

When starting from the individuals involved in any action pattern we are again led towards a two-fold nexus, of a somewhat different kind. One nexus concerns the identical individuals who appear in different action patterns; the other, the sets of action patterns which regularly occur between particular individuals. Such a set of regular action patterns between given individuals defines their position towards each other in a wide range of contexts, and we summarize it, by a sort of shorthand, as their *relationship*. But now these two criteria refer to successive steps of observation. In the first step we search for all the contexts of activity involving the same individuals, say, A and B, which is bound to lead us also to contexts linking A with, say, C and D, or B with E and F. In the second step, we summarize the set of behaviour patterns between A and B (or A and C and D, or B and E and F), and search for identical or similar sets, that is, for identical or similar relationships, throughout the individuals of the society.

The mother and child in our example are linked with one another by more than one action pattern; equally, the same set of action patterns will be visible between many, perhaps all, mothers and children in the society. Each set defines an individual or personal relationship, while for their totality we devise the further shorthand of a *social relationship*; in this case, of the mother-child relationship in such-and-such a society. Again, both mother and child are also linked, by other action patterns, with other individuals. The mother-child relationship operates within the family, the household, the local community, ultimately the political group, each of which names refers to a human aggregate where both mother and child have their appointed 'position'. The mother-child relationship, finally, which may be summarily described as one of care, protection, and authority, fits in with other relationships similarly resting on the dependence of one individual upon another, and can accordingly be classed with them. Each individual relationship, then, falls into wider and wider categories both as regards the physical *locus* (the human aggregate) in which it operates, and the logical classification to which it yields.

F

To sum up. When extending our observation beyond the single behaviour cycle we can use both the aim contents of actions and the actors themselves as our starting points. In the former case we are led towards a pragmatic network and a logical order of social tasks; in the latter, towards a human-physical network and a logical order of inter-personal relatedness.

2. SOCIAL DIMENSIONS

Social reality, then, is perceived under two aspects and collected into two orders of things social. One rests on the criterion of the aim content or the purposive character of action patterns; the other, on the criterion of the relationships between individuals and of their position towards or in regard to each other. The order of standardized purposive action patterns contains the social entities we know as *institutions*; the order of relationships, the social entities we know as *groups* or *groupings*. Institutions and groupings will be fully analyzed in the subsequent chapters. Here we propose to examine the interrelation and interdependence of these two orders of things social. It follows from what we have said that every social fact belongs to both orders at once, having in each some determinate place or range of places; furthermore, its places in the two orders are in some measure independently variable. In other words, there can be no grouping which does not imply some definite action pattern or patterns, through which it is mobilized or 'activated', and alone visible; and there can be no action pattern which does not imply some form of grouping, through which alone it operates. We can make no statements about one without referring at least implicitly to the other, although there are certain exceptions and borderline cases, which ,we may for the moment disregard. The same kind of grouping, however, built out of particular relationships (say, the family), will be visible in a series of action patterns—care for children, productive cooperation, religious observances, and so forth; while conversely a particular action pattern, having such-and-such aim contents (say, protection of infants), may activate a series of relationships and groupings— the family, the local community, the State.[1]

---

[1] This holds good for any given society or culture. If we go beyond one society or culture, the two 'orders' appear as independent variables in a much fuller sense of the word. Here the same kind of grouping will be visible, not only in a series of different action patterns, but in different series of this kind, and the

For this dual nature of social facts we may seek an analogy in the physical world, namely, in the concept of spatial dimensions. This concept allows us to visualize the pervasive twofold order to which all social facts belong and in which they can alone be conceived to exist. But this is no more than an analogy, and hence not a faithful picture. The analogy fails to account more particularly for two facts. First, the social 'dimensions' are independently variable only within set limits; that is to say, any social fact occupying a certain place in one dimension can at the same time occupy only a certain number of places (but not all possible places) in the other. The care for infants, a productive task, some religious observance—each of these instances of standardized action patterns mobilizes only certain relationships and groupings out of the totality of relationships and groupings occurring in the society; conversely, the institutionalized group, such as the family, the clan, a religious congregation, or the State, materialize only through a certain range of action patterns within the given 'dimension' of action. Secondly, the physical analogy refers to an order of existence which is entirely reducible to quantitative data and to measurements on a uniform scale. In the social 'dimensions' the data are essentially qualitative, being given in the diversity of aim contents and action patterns, and in the diversity of relationships. In one respect, however, our analogy is precise. As in any concrete physical situation only certain of the possible spatial positions appear occupied or filled out, so any social or cultural state of affairs only 'fills out' certain positions in the social dimensions out of the total of theoretically possible ones. Even in human culture and society at large there are apparently many 'empty' places within the space embraced by the two dimensions.

In this sense, then, social facts are two-dimensional. Like any two-dimensional entity, they can be projected on to one or the other co-ordinate, and so viewed under one or the other aspect. If we wish to find names also for the dimensions themselves, they seem suggested by the familiar words *Society* and *Culture*. Society,

same institution will be found to mobilize different kinds of relationships and groupings. Thus the family may in one society operate in the contexts of infant care, education, religious observances, and economic production, and in another in the contexts of infant care, political activities, and legal responsibilities; similarly the institutionalized tasks of education may in one society be entrusted to the family and to kinsmen, and in another to age grade associations, secret societies, or the State.

as I see it, means the totality of social facts projected on to the dimension of relationships and groupings; culture, the same totality in the dimension of action. This is not merely playing with words. In recent anthropological literature, in fact, the terms 'society' and 'culture' are accepted as referring to somewhat different things or, more precisely, to different ways of looking at the same thing.[1] And indeed, the very existence of these two words would seem to support our two-dimensional schema: categorizing thought, as expressed in language, has been led towards the same twoness-in-oneness.

The consistent distinction between these two concepts entails considerable linguistic difficulties. Mostly, when we speak of 'culture' and 'society' we mean a totality of facts viewed in both dimensions; the adjective 'social' especially, for example, in the familiar phrase 'social facts'; or in the less familiar one, 'things social' (which is my translation of Durkheim's *choses sociales*), has always this double connotation. Nor do we possess a convenient term summarizing this twofold reality as such save the clumsy word socio-cultural. I can, therefore, only hope that the sense in which the terms social and cultural, society and culture, will subsequently be used will become clear from their context.

Now, anthropologists sometimes assign to the two 'dimensions' a different degree of concreteness and reality. Radcliffe-Brown, for example, regards only social relations as real and concrete, and culture as a mere abstraction;[2] while Malinowski's whole work seems to imply that culture is the only reality and the only realm of concrete facts. Understood in so absolute a sense, both views are misconceptions. Social relations and the groupings into which they merge are as much of an abstraction as is culture. Both, too, are abstractions evolved from the same observational data—individuals in co-activity; but they are not, I think, abstractions of the same level.

To abstract is 'to transcend particular concrete occasions of actual happenings'.[3] In creating our two orders of things social we

[1] Radcliffe-Brown contrasts 'culture' with 'social structure' in much the same sense, though he leaves 'society', apparently on purpose, unexplained (1940 a, pp. 2, 4, 5, 12.) See also R. Linton (1946), p. 206; R. Linton, in A. Kardiner (1939), p. 7; C. Kluckhohn in R. Linton (1946), pp. 79–80; M. J. Herskovits (1948), pp. 29–30. The formulations put forth by these scholars, incidentally, differ from mine, as they also differ from each other.

[2] (1940), p. 2.   [3] A. N. Whitehead (1937), p. 196.

'transcend actual happenings' to a different degree. In either case we go beyond the concrete, particular individuals between whom we observe the social happenings (co-activities, or forms of behaviour), since in linking actions with actions we are concerned only with their aim contents, and in formulating social relationships, with instances of mutual behaviour occurring throughout the society, that is, between anonymous persons ('the' mother, or 'the' child). In other words, we operate with *classes* or *types* of action, and *classes* or *types* of actors. Equally, we 'transcend' the concrete time and place in which things happen, since we are dealing with standardized and repetitive patterns of behaviour. Yet in constructing the order of action we still base ourselves on the qualitative character, the particular aim contents, of the behaviour patterns, which is not further reducible and remains a feature immediately apprehended by observation; while in constructing the order of relationships, we go beyond these features also. They are, as it were, 'bracketed away' in a new formula, which aims at expressing the relative position of the actors and some general coordination between them. Thus, in formulating the relationship between mother and child, we leave behind the nursing of the child, the care for its health, and any other particular activity observable between these two classes of persons. The mother-child relationship is *all* these activities, in the sense in which a shorthand symbol is all the particular items or operations for which it is made to stand, and can be so analyzed. But this analysis is all 'in brackets', and the shorthand itself, unanalyzed, represents an essentially positional formula.

There are, of course, degrees of abstraction, that is, of such 'shorthanding'. In the present example the positional formula still bears a fairly explicit reference to 'actual happenings'—the particular co-activities and their aim contents. For 'mother' and 'child' describe moderately narrow classes of persons, that is, individuals observable in relatively few and specific contexts of behaviour; it is only these which are put 'in brackets'. But any social relationship can be subjected to further abstraction, through a more far-reaching 'bracketing-away' of actual happenings; and the relationships so constructed apply, not only to narrow classes of persons such as mother and child, or priest and layman, or trader and customer, and so forth, but to the widest class of person, encountered in any conceivable context of behaviour, namely, to the 'member of the society', or perhaps to 'human being'. We operate with such abstractions when we speak of the relationship of dominance and submission (between any kind of person), or reciprocity, equal and unequal status, or of symmetrical and asymmetrical relationships. Here we have a shorthand for behaviour patterns between individuals which may be of greatly varying kind or aim contents, and are alike only in the general positional picture they present. A long and varied series of human behaviour being thus put 'in brackets', the social relationships are emptied of all explicit reference to particular 'actual happenings' and stand fully for positional formulae—so fully that they can be expressed in mathematical symbols, pluses and minuses, equal-signs, and the like. Whether these highest abstractions are useful or not I will not for the moment discuss. Yet it has been shown, I think, that any class of relationships is more completely removed from 'actual happenings' than is any class of action, so that the order of phenomena to which relationships belong—the order of grouping or Society—represents an abstraction of a higher order than the order of action or Culture.

Paradoxically, though relationships are so highly abstract, groups and societies, which are built of them, appear to be fully concrete and to have a certain crude solidity; for we are surely able at any moment to point to a collection of human beings and say: They form such-and-such a group or society. The paradox is easily resolved. For here we consider only the population, the human aggregate, which, at that moment, embodies a society; and this human aggregate is indeed concrete enough to be enumerated in censuses or listed in directories. But the society itself is clearly not found in censuses or directories. Nor is it, simply, the collection of concrete living individuals who have a certain culture in common and 'live together by its institutions'.[1] This naïve formula fails as soon as we go beyond a given time-phase; for the thing we call a society persists while its individuals die and are replaced by others, and also when changes remodel its institutions or even the physical foundations of this 'living-together', that is, the association of the society with a particular territory. Even so, societies seem to retain something of their crude solidity. But this, it seems to me, comes essentially from the fact that they have names, and that the

---

[1] R. Linton, in A. Kardiner (1939), p. 7. Linton has later modified his views, accepting the perpetuation of societies as 'distinct entities', independent of their ever-changing populations (see 1947, p. 12).

names which people invent for themselves continue to be borne by successive populations.

Our conclusion, that relationships and groupings are more abstract than action patterns and their nexus, upsets somewhat the analogy with spatial dimensions, and one might perhaps suggest another, more convincing, parallel. Since relationships rest on positional qualities, the 'order' of relationships might be identified with *structure*, while the nexus of action patterns, resting as it does on aim contents, would fall in the category of *content* (or perhaps *function*, in the sense of purpose).[1] I hesitate to adopt this familiar antithesis in spite of the inaccuracy of my own analogy. For one thing it is doubtful if we can generally regard the apprehension of 'structure' to be less immediate or concrete than that of 'content'; in one field of observation at least, in perception, this is certainly not so: so that this analogy, too, has its weak spot. And for another, 'structure' (or the kindred concept 'form') is a category of such wide validity that it can be applied throughout the field of social phenomena; culture, too, has a 'pattern' or 'form', as institutions or action patterns also exhibit 'structural' features. It seems preferable, therefore, not to re-name our two orders of things social; all we need add is that in the dimension of Society, whose elements are relationships, the aspect of structure is more pervasive, since these elements are themselves positional abstractions and so structural concepts.

Our two-dimensional scheme, however, is incomplete in another sense. For there are two further orders of facts which are so pervasive that every social event may be said to belong to them also and to have a determinate place within them. I am thinking of *language*, and of the cognitive constructions, the ideas current among people, in short, of the *idea systems* of societies. As regards language, there is no need to emphasize again that all social behaviour happens in a world of language, amidst and through verbal communication. We may, however, point out these two aspects in the pervasiveness of language. Generally speaking, language operates in two ways. First, it *names* (and so orders and classifies) the features of the universe in which we move and with regard to which we act, so that these can be indicated in 'ordered discourse and reasoning' (Dewey). Secondly, language operates pragmatically, in the manner of

[1] In defining *structure* as resting on 'positional qualities' I follow C. D. Broad (1937), p. 595.

signals, initiating and controlling behaviour, so that this may follow a required course. These are aspects or phases of the *modus operandi* of language, and hence not sharply separable; for the signal function of language essentially rests on its capacity to name that with which behaviour is concerned; and even the purely indicative use of language may at any moment provide a 'signal' for further behaviour. Now it is clear that both aspects of language relate to both dimensions of social facts. All regulated action involves language-as-signals, since it is always action initiated and controlled by language, and actions as well as relationships or groupings are among the things named by language. That these names will again operate as intellectual aids in regulating behaviour need not be specially mentioned. But these acts of naming do more. In the case of actions, they group together instances of behaving in diverse classes and complexes, so that any manner of behaving is shown as belonging to a defined area in the dimension of action. While in indicating relationships and groupings the names also demonstrate their existence; for since any such act of naming consists in furnishing a 'shorthand' for a series of behaviour patterns, it exhibits the very fact that this series makes up—*is*— that novel entity, a particular relationship or grouping. In other words, language indicates the units of action, and renders relationships and groupings visible, incidentally lending them that 'solidity' of which we spoke before.[1]

The position of idea systems in our schema of social dimensions is less easy to define. To begin with, these cognitive constructions are not only, tacitly, in the minds of people before and while they act, but are also specifically expressed, explained, taught, that is, enacted in task-like fashion. Thus they both result in action (in the manner of motives) and are exhibited by means of actions. In certain respects, however, idea systems seem to command their own peculiar class of actions; for unlike language, idea systems also form the aim contents of specific behaviour patterns in which individuals—the philosophers, scholars, and moralists of any society—do nothing but produce and fashion ideas (while there are clearly no specific action patterns in which language is similarly

---

[1] The last remark applies only to the *proper names* borne by individual groups, while the preceding remarks apply both to them and to *terms* devised for types of groups. This distinction, however, is not further relevant (see below, pp. 147–8).

'made').[1] Yet ideas thus given currency, and other ideas not as specifically fashioned, are also implicit in all other forms of action, whatever their aim contents, and in all relationships and forms of grouping. Thus technical processes are based upon given theoretical assumptions; political activities have their ideology and ethics; religious observances their dogma, and so forth. Similarly, all relationships and groupings have their code of ethics, that is, a body of ideas about the rights and obligations valid for the individuals concerned. In this sense, then, social behaviour happens amidst and through idea systems, as it happens amidst and through language.

Language and idea systems are clearly closely linked, since the latter become effective only through being communicated; and both represent special cases of the dimension of action. If all actions 'are intended to have consequences' (see above, p. 30), the consequences of language lie in communicating ideas or intentions so that further action may follow; the consequences of idea systems, in producing precepts for action; while all other forms of action achieve their consequences ('changes in the environment or in the relations between actor and environment') by more direct and physical means. In thus splitting up the dimension of action we remain close to our physical analogy, though we must think, not of the spatial dimensions of Euclidian geometry, but of the time-space continuum of modern physics. Culture (or Action in the wider sense), with its three coordinates Language, Idea Systems, and 'Physical Action', corresponds in this simile to three-dimensional space; Society, to the dimension of time. Again, we can project the total reality of things social upon these new dimensions, that is, we can study language for its social or cultural implications, and idea systems for their bearing on groupings or social tasks.

Let me conclude with a graphic representation of 'social reality' as I conceive it. Though my diagram is hazardous and over-simplified it offers, I suggest, a useful visual aid. A few comments are necessary. The curved lines represent the four dimensions, and the points or stretches marked on them the social facts projected upon a particular dimension, that is, viewed under that one aspect only. The complete social fact as it occurs 'in reality' appears in the space between the coordinates. I chose for

[1] The activities of linguists or of such bodies as the French Academy, which watch over the correct use of language, are perhaps borderline cases.

my paradigm a well-defined social task—blood revenge—which we will take to be entrusted to a body of persons acknowledging common descent and, on these grounds, the obligations of mutual aid and collective responsibility. The social task thus has its place, in the order of Action, among the logically related aim contents, that is, among 'legal' activities; and it has its place also in the order

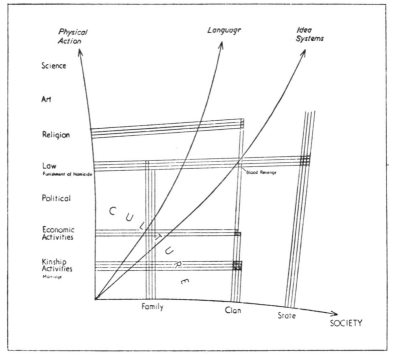

of Grouping, in the *locus* 'clan'. In the diagram, then, blood revenge will be placed at the intersection of the respective coordinates and abscissae, thus indicating relationships activated and aim contents operating through relationships. Blood revenge further involves language and a particular ideology, which could be indicated by similar intersections, though these have been omitted for the sake of simplicity. We can in the same manner symbolize the whole grouping 'clan' by showing it to be activated in the sphere of economic and religious activities, and in marriage (a specific kinship activity), but not, for example, in political or aesthetic activities or in legal actions other than punishment of homicide;

conversely, we are symbolizing the fact that such-and-such aim contents operate through the clan, while others do so through the groupings 'family' or 'State'. Let me add that the bundles of abscissae stretching upwards from each grouping must be thought of as indicating a whole range of relationships, which I could not represent more adequately. Finally, in drawing the dimensions as curved lines I meant to indicate certain exceptions which will occupy us presently. Where the dimensions curve away, the corresponding coordinates and abscissae can no longer intersect, so that the social facts occurring in that range of actions or groupings would no longer belong to all dimensions at once; which is precisely what I attempted to symbolize.

3. Action Autonomous

For the sake of simplicity I shall in the following refer only to two social dimensions, ignoring the subdivision of the dimension of Culture. The question I now wish to consider is whether we do not also meet with social and cultural facts which contradict our two-dimensional schema. Ethnologists describe the distribution of technological objects and processes, or of cultural data such as myths and religious beliefs, without reference to social relationships or groupings. Works of art can be studied and understood in a like manner; so can, of course, languages and scientific systems. Are these, then, items of culture which exist only in one dimension, and which can be fully embraced by an approach under the aspect of 'action' only?

Whether the ethnologist who traces the diffusion of elements of material culture or considers only the contents and form of myths or religious beliefs is right or wrong, scientific or unscientific, is not a valid question. His methods are adequate for his aims; and his aims are not those of social anthropology as here understood. From our point of view these efforts have little informative value since they approach a two-dimensional entity under one aspect only. Expressed in convenient though somewhat loose phraseology, such an ethnological collection and comparison of cultural data ignores their function in society.

But let us not judge too sweepingly. In certain sectors of culture this 'function in society' seems indeed to disappear; certain orders of cultural facts are without even a tacit implication of determinate social relationships and groupings. They seem indeed open to 'one-dimensional' study only. This, as I shall attempt to show, is true of language, of art (in the widest sense), and of technology and science. All that these social phenomena imply is human beings, through whose actions these cultural forms materialize and for whose needs, aims, desires they exist. They are linked with social groupings only in that they must be intelligible to and manageable by them.

Language, as speech, is bound up with social groups and relationships. Social classes are differentiated by dialect as much as by other characteristics of behaviour; social relationships entail the use of special language, not only in nomenclature but in habitual communication—as in the 'baby talk' a mother uses towards her child, in the slang of occupational groups, in the ceremonial language laid down by etiquette, secular or religious, or in the private language of secret societies. All these examples, however, refer only to the operational aspect of language. Its phonology, grammar, and partly its semantic system, in one word, its *structure*, is in no way bound to group arrangements; it neither mobilizes determinate social relationships nor bears within itself a reference to them.[1]

The position of art is closely similar. What art depicts, poems and stories describe, dramas represent, is society in all its aspects; relationships and group arrangements enter into these themes as do all features of cultural and social life. The execution of works of art remains tied to forms of group organization; painters and sculptors form occupational groups, which presuppose another group—the public for which they work; large-scale architecture (a Gothic cathedral, an Egyptian or Aztec pyramid) implies large-scale labour units and a stratification of social groups; drama, dance, part-singing or orchestral music mobilize at least temporary groupings. But there is no link between group organization and, say, painting in oils, perspective in drawing, ornamental designs in sculpture rather than naturalistic ones, blank verse rather than rhyme, polyphony rather than homophony in music, or realistic drama rather than classical tragedy. The *style* in art, then, exists in its own right, entailing and presupposing no determinate social relationships.

[1] A similar view has been expressed by Professor Radcliffe-Brown (1940 a), pp. 6–7.

This autonomous nature of cultural activities is somewhat weaker in the field of technology and science; for the execution of technological processes or scientific pursuits is bound up with group organization, and the latter also determines a wide range among the problems which technology and science set themselves. But here, too, we meet with the formal manner, the 'style', in which the problems are solved; and problems and solutions follow from one another by the autonomous, structural laws of logic.

Language, art, and science, therefore, entail determinate social relationships only with that side of their nature which we may term their content or their operational aspect; their 'style' and 'structure' have no bearing on the dimension of grouping. For these phenomena we can establish only one kind of nexus, of purely intrinsic nature, which gives us simply behaviour patterns following from behaviour patterns, without any implication of relationships or forms of grouping. Such a nexus is represented, for language, in Grimm's Law; for art, in the often cyclical evolution of styles; for science, in the logic and history of problem-solving. The dimension of action is here autonomous; in describing these sectors of culture we describe 'all-culture'.

It might seem that the same could be said of certain other cultural forms—of cosmological speculations embodied in religious systems, and of artistic or quasi-scientific motifs in religion or myth. Admittedly, not everywhere can a sharp line be drawn. But though there may be overlapping, the criterion for dividing the zone of 'all-culture' from the two-dimensional entity which is culture *and* society is unambiguous. The criterion hinges, as has been said, on the determinacy or indeterminacy of the social relationships involved. Guided by it, we discover that cosmology or myths operate with anthropomorphous beings seen in determinate relationships, and so bear by clear implication upon the dimension of grouping; and that, in religion, even the aesthetic or quasi-scientific features cannot be conceived of without the implication that they exist for officiants and a congregation, that is, for determined groupings.

Perhaps one further point needs to be clarified. The definition of a realm of 'all-culture' does not rest merely on the fact that the same language, styles of art, and forms of technology or science are found distributed over different societies and societies differently organized. This might be equally true of any institution. The essential fact is that, whether or not they are so distributed, they do not require specific group organizations for their realization. If the ethnologist, linguist or historian of culture traces the same institution through different societies or ages regardless of their implications as to relationships and group organization, he chooses to view, as I have put it, a two-dimensional whole under one aspect only. If he describes and studies language (not speech), the styles of art, and certain problems of technology and science in this manner, he follows an inevitable course.

4. GROUPING AUTONOMÓUS

In the order of groupings we find no exactly equivalent instances of 'one-dimensionality'. I believe, however, that we meet with approximations, with social phenomena which are almost 'all-grouping' or almost 'only-relationship'. They are not, of course, independent of action, nor can they be, since relationships and forms of grouping are abstractions from patterns of co-activity and imply, at least 'in brackets', some reference to them. But in the case of certain groupings this reference is almost random and indeterminate. I can think of two instances—the crowd, and the community (as understood by MacIver).[1]

In either case the aggregate of individuals (fortuitous and fleeting in the crowd, and enduring in the community) exhibits a general coordination of behaviour whose precise aim contents is indeterminate. We have simply a multitude of individuals in physical proximity in which any kind of happening or activity will serve as an occasion for this coordination of behaviour.[2] A crowd behaves as a crowd in situations of common fear or joy, under the stimulus of curiosity or aggressiveness, in response to a collectively felt wrong or admiration or awe, and in many other situations. In a community individuals adjust their behaviour to each other on any of the multifarious and random occasions which an 'area of common life' (MacIver) offers. In either case, too, the coordination of behaviour takes the form of a spontaneous conformity or submission to leadership; it springs essentially from psychological responses entailed in proximity, and is therefore in large measure independent of the aim contents of the actual behaviour. Crowd

[1] R. M. MacIver (1924) especially pp. 23, 98 et seq.; (1931), pp. 9–11.

[2] The crowd and community, in other words, consist entirely of relationships of a purely 'positional' nature, here carried to the extreme (see above, p. 82).

and community are, as I have said, only approximations to 'all-groupings'; for the behaviour patterns through which they operate are not entirely random and indeterminate. The crowd, to behave as a crowd, requires some occasion or aim which is intensely stimulating; and the community presupposes one (though elementary) form of co-activity, namely, common residence.

I am inclined to add here, as a third approximation, friendship. Here again we have a general coordination of behaviour whose precise aim contents is mostly indeterminate. In other words, friends will act as such, assisting and showing their regard for one another, on almost any occasion, no activity being excluded or specifically referred to ('bracketed') in the relationship formula. Again, the relationship rests essentially on emotional responses spontaneously emerged from physical contact. All this is strictly true, however, only when we speak of friendship in general terms. In given societies, friendship usually entails some more closely defined action patterns, and only certain forms of behaviour are 'bracketed' in the relationship while others—by convention if not by definition—remain outside it.

5. THE INDIVIDUAL

The two coordinates of culture and society meet at the same zero point—the individual. The place occupied by the individual in the sort of world anthropologists describe is clearly of fundamental theoretical importance. In older literature this question is usually settled by a tacit compromise between the respective claims upon our attention of the 'individual' and 'society', rather than subjected to explicit analysis. Sometimes there is explicit disagreement. Various students of primitive society have voiced the warning that the individual must not be forgotten or his role minimized;[1] while a few had the courage (or onesidedness) to express the conviction that the individual counts for nought.[2] The controversy, such as it is, seems to miss the point and to rest on arguments which miss each other; the defenders and assailants of the individual simply mean different things. Though this particular controversy has almost disappeared from recent anthropology, and few would now

[1] E.g. Lowie (1938), pp. 268 ff.; A. Goldenweiser (1937), p. 413; B. Malinowski (1934), p. xxxviii.

[2] A. L. Kroeber (1915); (1944), p. 5. Leslie A. White (1947 b), pp. 191, 197. Nor, of course, has the individual any part in the society as Durkheim sees it, dominated by 'collective representations' and 'group consciousness'.

dispute that it is relevant to study the individual as well as the society, the two are still being held apart as though they were disparate and essentially opposed entities, which must be approached by different routes and perhaps even by different techniques. Again, the question is often wrongly put; indeed, the whole familiar antithesis individual-society is in certain respects a false one.

Action patterns are realized by individuals; groupings and relationships exist through individuals. Yet if the action pattern is conceived of as standardized, regular, and recurrent, it is also independent of the concrete living individual. Clearly, institutionalized action patterns exist in a relatively timeless and ubiquitous sense, being available for all or for numerous individuals in the society and recurring irrespective of the life span of concrete individuals. Similarly the set of action patterns which makes up any social relationship or grouping exists for numerous varying individuals and successive generations. The relationships between fellow citizens, mother and child, chief and subject, and the rest, are repetitive throughout the group, and groups exist and persist while their human material changes with age and death and is renewed with every birth. At every step of our enquiry, then, we observe individuals; yet step by step our analysis also leads us away from the individual to something else.

We need a word for this 'something else', that is, for the human being who is the pivot of all things social yet is not a concrete, uniquely existing human being. More precisely, we need a *type* concept which we must superimpose upon this changing, fluid reality before we can attempt its analysis.[1] This concept, as Radcliffe-Brown has shown, is given in our language, in the word *person*.[2] Its legal sense, in particular, bears on our problem. Jurists mean by a 'person' (to quote from the *Oxford Dictionary*) a 'human being with recognized rights and duties'. Yet any human being has numerous such rights and duties, of various kinds and effective in different contexts; and among them we can distinguish sets or series of rights and duties, each set or series being composed of a number of modes of action which hang together

---

[1] Cf. Max Weber: 'It is necessary to know what a "king", an "official" . . . or a "magician" does; that is, what kind of *typical* action, which justifies classifying an individual in one of these categories, is important and relevant for an analysis, before it is possible to undertake the analysis itself' (1947, p. 97).

[2] A. R. Radcliffe-Brown (1940), p. 5.

pragmatically or logically. In any legal situation only one such set will normally be put in question—say, an individual's rights and duties as an employer (but not as a married man), or as a husband (but not as an employer). We might here speak of different 'aspects' of a person, or of different 'roles' assumed by it, or simply of different 'persons'. Though this is a question of words, the last-named usage seems to me to be the most consistent as well as convenient one. Understood in this sense, the person is more than the individual; it is the individual with certain recognized, or institutionalized, tasks and relationships, and is *all* the individuals who act in that way. The person is also less than the individual; for an individual may be several persons, and out of his physical and mental qualities only some will enter into the ways of acting which define the person. The 'chief', or 'priest', or 'soldier', or 'father', or 'brother', are persons, who at any given moment are represented in numerous individuals; yet the same man may be chief, soldier, father and brother, all at once and with different parts of his being, acting as one or the other in different contexts and in respect of different other individuals (seen as persons).[1]

On any given occasion of observation person and individual coincide; in any extension of observation beyond one occasion, they diverge. The position is much the same as in any play we watch. The actors are individuals appearing in this or that role, as this or that person, and all the actions they perform 'hang together' in a set or series. The same actor, if I see him in more than one play, will play different parts; and the same part, if I see more than one performance of the play, may be taken by different actors. And there is this, too. The actor's individuality will be visible in all the parts he acts, yet the same part must also require some uniformity of appearance and behaviour in all the individuals who act it, whether natural or simulated.[2]

---

[1] The legal concept of the 'person' goes together with the legal concept of 'status', which denotes the recognized 'conditions of persons' and their legal relations with one another, which means, again, individuals *cum* their rights and duties. Linton uses 'status' in this sense, to describe what I have called the 'person' (1936, pp. 113–14). This is once more a question of words. But I would hold that 'person' is the more logical and useful concept at this stage, since 'status' also connotes a more advanced stage of analysis, where the additional word is in fact required (see below, p. 171).

[2] It may here be noted that, etymologically, 'person' comes from the character assumed by actors in a play, more precisely, from the masks (*personae*) worn in Rome by the players.

The analogy must not be driven too far. The 'play' which we watch on the anthropological scene has no script; we cannot from it construct the part as 'it really is', uninfluenced by the varying individualities of the actors. The social play, moreover, is enacted in a multitude of simultaneous performances. The role, the person, thus amounts to something like a common pattern or norm that emerges for us from the varying performances. Certain features will be common in every acting of a given social part; others will vary with the actor—when the script which exists only in the actor's brains leaves that latitude. The anthropologist, then, intent upon discovering the standardized pattern in social acting, must abstract the norm from the varying performances. Yet he cannot fail to observe the latitude left to individuality. One is the background for the other; and the relations between 'norm' and actual 'performance' yield the strength of the standardization. The individuality of an actor may turn a part upside down; but we have no script to consult, nor has the producer who permits such latitude taken us into his confidence. Whether we see a norm broken, or merely a role variously conceived, we can assess only with the help of those simultaneous performances which we have come to watch. In the terminology of anthropological technique, we observe a wide range of activities, we compile biographies, and collect case studies.

The discussion of the place of individuals in their society nearly always turns upon the dichotomy between the two and upon some kind of special relationship supposed to exist 'between the individual and the group'. This is a loose way of describing a variety of things. In juxtaposing the individual and the group (or society) we may mean to contrast the individual and the multitude; referring to the density of contacts in which he happens to be enveloped, to his solitude or sociability, and to the degree to which he participates in the life around him. Or we may mean the 'individual *versus* the rest', that is, the reformer, genius, rebel, or criminal, who goes counter to the norms and values accepted by the majority; let us be clear, however, that here the individual may still be *of* his group; even as one who defies the norm, he may still fit an accepted role or 'person'. Again, holding the individual apart from the society may be a descriptive device to exhibit the gradual adjustment of behaviour through which he is shaped into conformity with the rest. Or the juxtaposition may have a legal or statutory meaning, bearing on the rights and obligations of individuals within the corporate group of which they are members (that is, in which they are particular 'persons'). Finally, the juxtaposition may describe individuals completely severed from the rest of the group, both in their human contacts and their statutory position; here the social norm will be understood to offer no niche for the behaviour or ambitions of a particular individual: he is an outcast, a misfit, Margaret Mead's 'deviant', or Durkheim's *individu désagrégé*.[1]

There may be more situations of this kind. All, however, belong to one of two types, though there is some overlapping. They involve either relations between one *person* and all other persons in the group, or relations between one *individual* and all others. The first type is most clearly exemplified in legal contexts, when we consider the rights and obligations pertaining to persons. Here we may conveniently summarize 'all other persons' in the collective noun 'society'. But the relationship is essentially one between a part and the whole; for the single person is such, and has his 'statutory' rights and obligations (or his 'niche'), only inasmuch as he belongs to that sum-total of persons we call a Society. In other words Society here means the 'summation' of persons. The second type is exemplified most clearly in the case of solitude or sociability. Here we consider the fortuitous position of a concrete individual amidst others, which will be determined by his, or their, temperament, interests, moods, and the like. Again, we may summarize 'all other individuals' in the collectives 'group' or 'society'; but we must be clear that this is only a convenient and inaccurate way of speaking. Now I hold that only these two kinds of statement can legitimately be made about the relations between individual and group. If more is meant, if the juxtaposition is taken to mean some fundamental dichotomy between the norms and values obtaining in the group on one side, and the independent leanings or desires of individuals on the other, then it is based on a fallacy. The group is an abstraction; the individual is a concrete, unique reality; there cannot logically be actual relations (that is, interactions) between them. To say that there are, would be like saying that it is Mr. Gielgud and not Hamlet who has a quarrel with the State of Denmark.

The theoretical position has been admirably summed up by Bentley (though his omission to introduce some such concept as the 'person' somewhat weakens his argument). Society consists of

[1] E. Durkheim (1897), p. 229.

individuals; and the 'summation of individuals' (I would say, 'persons') is the society. 'Such being the case a discussion of the relation of the individuals as such to society can have no exact meaning. We must change our statement to that of the relation of the individual to other individuals.' The field of social enquiry lies in 'Man-Society'.[1]

Yet a dichotomy there is. It exists, for the observer, on the logical plane, between the norm he abstracts from a fluid variety of happenings and the happenings themselves; where the dichotomy is projected into the human material we observe, it lies within each human being—between his wishes to behave in such-and-such a fashion and his knowledge of 'normal' behaviour, that is, between that part of his being which is his psycho-physical individuality, and the other part, which is his conception of the person he is or is meant to be.

The dichotomy poses important problems, though their exploration goes beyond our theme. But this much may be said here. All these problems revolve upon the conception of a 'fit', of some adaptation between individuality and person. Now the smaller and simpler a society, the fewer and more sharply defined are the 'persons' available for individuals. Each individual may be almost every person that exists. It may seem, therefore, that there is more chance in primitive societies of individualities not 'fitting' the given selection of 'persons' and so being left without an appropriate social niche. Yet it is equally true that in simpler societies individualities are more firmly modelled into persons. For here individuals in their various roles constantly confront each other and are aware of all 'persons' existing in the society; thus the person is fashioned and modelled by direct observation and assimilation, and by constant mutual correction and criticism. Each person contributes to shaping all other persons.

In large and complex societies the persons are much more numerous, more diffuse and ill-defined. They are also less well and less directly known. An individual may only have a theoretical knowledge, from reading or hearsay, of many 'persons' existing in the group, and if he attempted to model himself on them, he would do so with such uncertain knowledge; the proverbial *nouveau riche* or the philistine masquerading as artist are familiar examples. To the individual as well as to the observer, the precise connotation

[1] A. F. Bentley (1926), pp. 88–9, 90.

of a 'person' may here seem elusive, so that all save a small core of behaviour patterns have to be ascribed, instead, to the 'individuality'. Social change would further blur the picture of existing persons, since it may create new ones, as yet of vague outline. During my stay in Nupe a rich merchant bought a title of nobility and so entry into the upper classes; this was a new departure, and at the time no 'person' fitted this individual, though there were already signs that this new 'person', the 'merchant prince', would in due course be accepted. In our own society we should find it difficult to define unequivocally the 'person' of a doctor, parson or politician, apart from their occupational activities and legal status. Convention and popular opinion no doubt paint a fuller (and onesided) picture of their appropriate conduct and relationships; and moralists will readily decide whether the 'father' and 'husband' are identical with the person 'breadwinner'; the student of society might find little more to describe than individualities.

We note, however, that there are two sides to this problem. The first concerns the latitude which a social role or 'person' leaves to the individual actor; the second, the series of different 'persons' which any individual may assume and combine. To some extent the two aspects must coincide; for it will often depend, fortuitously, on the individual whether he desires or is able to be different persons at the same time, say a scholar as well as a soldier, a family man as well as a political leader. But equally, this combination of persons in the same individual will in some measure be laid down by the obtaining social norms. We know that certain roles are mutually exclusive as when a society expects its priests to be celibate or its military caste to keep aloof from business; others are complementary—as when the leaders of the community are expected to be husbands and fathers, and perhaps landowners or successful businessmen. In either case we have something like an extension of the concept of 'social persons', which might seem to warrant a special name—'social personality'. Let me stress that, as the term is here used, it is purely descriptive; it merely denotes the more or less fixed sum-total of roles which societies, as it were, load upon their individuals. Also, the emphasis is on 'more or less fixed'; for the fluidity of the social personality is of necessity even greater than that of the social person. In simple societies the former like the latter can be circumscribed relatively easily and accurately. Where, as I put it before, each individual is very nearly every person that exists in the society, we might indeed be able to speak of *one* typical social personality. But here, too, there will be some latitude in the choice of roles and only a potential coincidence of all roles; clearly, not every peasant will also be a priest or chief, though he might be eligible for either position; above all, there will be the unalterable differences of age and sex. In complex and internally differentiated societies, however, the concept of a social personality would seem to lose all value. Certainly, we can no longer intelligently speak of a single or pervasive social personality; if we did, we should be referring to a synthetic personality to which nothing corresponds in practice, and to a hypothetical individual whom we made into a summary of all the social persons existing in the society. Nor is it possible to define with any precision even the series of social personalities existing in the society. The examples quoted above, just as they illustrate the latitude in the choice of persons open to the individual in complex societies, so they demonstrate the fluid boundaries of the social personalities. In defining the latter we should in fact be describing the whole working of a culture or society—its rules governing the assumption of social roles, the entry into groups and relationships, their 'openness' or 'closure', and the mobility permitted between them. All these facts will occupy us later. Here I would only suggest that, necessary though we must consider the concept of a 'social person', that of a 'social personality' has only restricted heuristic value; indeed, on occasion its value is deceptive, since it affords a picture of neatness and simplicity which is altogether illusory.[1]

6. POINTER RELATIONS

One final logical difficulty needs examination. We regard a social relationship as an abstraction standing for a set of regular behaviour patterns between individuals. Yet we have also stated that the individuals so considered are 'anonymous' or, as we may now say, 'persons' (another abstraction), since the behaviour patterns hold good irrespective of concrete, living individuals. Thus we seem to hold that relationships attach to beings (persons) who are such beings only in virtue of the social part they play, that

[1] Here I seem to be questioning the usefulness of a concept which figures prominently in recent literature. The 'social personality' of Linton, Kardiner, and others, however, is essentially an explanatory, not a descriptive concept, and will be discussed in Chapter XIII.

is, to individuals-*cum*-their-relationships, which is an obvious circle.

The circle disappears, however, when we trace this process step by step. For in constructing the relationship out of observed behaviour patterns we fasten upon one relation or event as a 'pointer'. This crucial relation or event need not itself be a behaviour pattern; it may represent an extraneous physical feature, such as the biological fact of procreation, on which we base ourselves when speaking of the mother-child relationship, or the physiological criterion of age which we use when speaking of the relationship between adults and youths. Where the 'pointer' consists itself in behaviour, this is of a basic and preliminary kind, corresponding to a prerequisite condition or formality rather than to a behaviour pattern in its own right. Thus, in defining the relationship between fellow citizens we usually take residence in the same territory as our 'pointer relation'; in defining the relationship between chief and subject we base ourselves on some formal act of allegiance or on the formalities of chiefly accession; while in the relationship husband-wife the formality of marriage furnishes the necessary 'pointer'. Starting from the pointer relation, we trace the cluster of other behaviour patterns occurring with it or in consequence of it. It is this cluster that gives us the full social relationship and also completes our picture of the 'persons' involved in the relationship. The person, then, is not merely an anonymous individual somehow appearing in given relationships; at least, the person only becomes that when our analysis of the society is complete (and our description of it all on paper). To begin with, the person is any concrete individual who is marked off, *qua* individual and at some period of his life, by a particular pointer relation; and from this fact all others follow—the roles which individuals are seen to play, their 'persons', and the variety of relationships which we abstract from their behaviour.

It is clear that we can proceed in this fashion only if we know what pointer relations are in use in a society and precisely what relevance they possess; and this knowledge will once more only emerge in the course of our analysis. But we can always start experimentally with some situation or forms of behaviour which seem likely to have this significance, such as the biological facts of descent, the physiological facts of age, any kind of behaviour looking like a test or qualifying event, and so forth. Often we shall have to change our approach; we might, for example, discover that the parent-child relationship rests as much on adoption as on biological parenthood, or that the duties towards each other of fellow citizens do not follow from common residence but from common descent or extraction. However this may be, the true 'pointer relation' is always more basic than all the other relationships in which persons may stand. I spoke of it as a prerequisite condition. But its nature can be expressed more precisely in this fashion: The pointer relation or event represents a principle of *recruitment* for relationships and groupings; it makes these possible, but is not yet part of them. In this sense the term will be used in the discussion that follows.

7. NOTE ON CHANGE AND EVOLUTION

In conclusion, it might be asked whether our schema of social dimensions has not omitted perhaps the most important one, namely, time, that is, the dimension which would contain the social *processes* and the phenomena of cultural or social change. Now in a sense I have taken the time dimension for granted. Indeed, our previous statements, that behaviour cycles happen in time and that our subject matter consists in regular, repetitive behaviour, would make no sense otherwise. Yet in taking the time dimension for granted we seem to ignore the well established distinction between two types of social enquiry, one concerned with the static, simultaneous array of social facts in cultures and societies (a 'synchronic' enquiry), and the other with situations or phases separated in time (a 'diachronic' enquiry). If the two terms 'synchronic' and 'diachronic' are understood very rigidly, the distinction clearly makes no sense; for nothing in the sphere of social facts is literally static, and 'regularity' in behaviour is only visible over a period of time. But the two concepts can of course be understood both more loosely and with a certain shift of emphasis. The 'synchronic' approach would then be concerned with a (roughly) simultaneous as well as continuous state of affairs in any one society, that is, with a state of affairs assumed to be uniformly repetitive within an (undefined) time span; while the diachronic approach would be concerned with broadly separated time phases and with broken uniformities. In other words, in one case we view social situations *as though* they were static (or endlessly repetitive), while in the other we seek out situations furnishing evidence of developments or other forms of change.

Most anthropologists seem to regard the latter phenomena as being of a specific kind, forming a separate field of enquiry, and yielding specific information—on 'laws of change' and the like. Now I cannot share this view; I cannot agree that cultural and social change form a special chapter and their study a special method of social enquiry. It seems to me that social change merely constitutes that aspect of our field of enquiry which makes social analysis at all possible; and that the method employed in studying the former is the general method of social analysis. Nor yet are there any 'laws of change' (with few exceptions to be stated presently) which are not simply the sort of laws we can hope to arrive at by any kind of social enquiry.

Let me explain this—though in doing so I must anticipate the terms and results of a later discussion. In *describing* social phenomena we can choose whether to consider some roughly contemporaneous phase or several such phases stretching back in time; in the latter case, we might well be describing also processes, developments, that is, phenomena of change. But in *explaining* social phenomena we have only one method at our disposal, namely, that of examining their interdependence (or the *co-variations* between them, as we shall later say); and this, in turn, is visible most clearly when change sets in, that is, when some variation in one phenomenon can be seen to provoke concomitant variations in others. It makes no difference in principle whether the initial change appears to arise within an apparently undisturbed culture and society or is imposed by happenings outside, in situations commonly referred to as 'culture contact', though in the latter case certain additional variables will have to be considered, such as the compulsion, physical or otherwise, sustaining the initial change. Nor do the modern forms of culture change or contact in primitive communities add any novel feature apart from the magnitude of the changes so produced and, again, the element of compulsion usually behind them. Even so, they are only more instances of the kind we require for our analysis, and more evidence for the interdependence of social phenomena. Indeed, they are most valuable evidence, for the often unprecedented scale of these changes demonstrates extremes in the scale of variations such as are not easily found in the study of self-contained societies.

The processes and connections so elucidated give us no 'laws of change'; at least, they give us only laws governing changes in determinate social phenomena. That is, they define the 'invariant relations' between such-and-such institutions, groupings, and so forth; and this is what any 'social law' does. If there exist any 'laws of change' pure and proper, namely, statements on the invariant course of social change in the abstract, regardless of the particular social facts involved, I do not know what they can be like. I can only visualize useless truisms, to wit: 'The impulse to change may come either from without or from within the society.' Or: 'The primary changes introduced into societies by changes in the external environment may involve either an increase or a decrease of scale' ('scale' meaning the 'number of people in relation and the intensity of those relations'); since constancy of scale would presumably mean 'no change', this statement merely affirms that societies can change in any way possible. Or again: 'When primary changes involve an increase of scale, the resulting disequilibrium "is resolved" either by the increase in the range of narrower scale elements to match the wider, or by a decrease in the range of the wider-scale elements to match the narrower, or by both at once.' Since disequilibrium is here defined as 'unevenness of scale', we are merely being told that an uneven scale can only be remedied by being made even.[1] Concern with the oft-quoted 'cultural lag' seems to me to reflect a similar misdirected interest in 'pure' laws of change. The 'culture lag' of course exists; but it indicates merely the 'lack of synchronization between variables',[2] that is, between the concomitant changes in related social facts. Now a precise synchronization is as unthinkable as a rigidly 'synchronic' view. And though the magnitude of the lag does indicate the varying capacity of social facts, when changed, to provoke a more or less rapid adjustment in others, this indication only adds to our general knowledge of these facts and their interdependence. If we attempted to speak of 'cultural lag' in the abstract, we should be able to say no more than 'it is bigger or smaller', and often 'bigger'.

As I anticipated, however, there are exceptions. I believe that there are these three instances in which we can speak of laws of change in their own right, and can conversely no longer take the time dimension for granted.

[1] The passages quoted are from G. and M. Wilson (1945), pp. 131-5.
[2] G. A. Lundberg (1939), p. 523.

(1) It is likely that change as such, if it is of sufficient magnitude, has a peculiar shock-like effect, disturbing or stimulating, upon the group experiencing it, so that the manner and speed with which the change in any one cultural fact produces concomitant changes elsewhere would reflect not only the group's ability to adjust itself eventually and rationally to the new conditions, but also its spontaneous reaction to the novelty *per se*. Thus we often visualize societies being stunned by a sudden change, or conversely stimulated into new activities. And we also visualize the appearance of some new social phenomenon, say, a religious or aesthetic movement, which would reflect, not the response to a particular change that has taken place, but a response to the fact that there has been radical change. These two processes (if there be two processes) are clearly difficult to isolate. Also, this is essentially a psychological problem, the discussion of which belongs to a later context. But this much may here be said. Inasmuch as the shock-like effect of change is psychological, we may assume that it will vary with the habituation of the group to change and rates of change. It should therefore be possible to isolate it in two ways. First, we could compare different societies which are exposed to the same kind of change but in which this is preceded by unequal periods of relative stability. Secondly, we could investigate whether certain social phenomena which seem to follow upon changes in some cultural fact persist or disappear when this change has become permanent and lost its novelty. Either method might well enable us to formulate specific 'laws' of change, that is, laws bearing on some invariant relation between the relative stability of cultural situations and their sensitiveness to change.

(2) Again, the search for specific laws of change would be legitimate if it could be shown that something in the nature of an autonomous force operated in cultures and societies and drove them on to successive metamorphoses. This force could be visualized as moving in cycles or curves of periodicity, such as various historians and philosophers claim to have discovered in the development of art, in systems of thought, in the appearance of genius, or even, on the widest plane, in the growth, maturity, and decline of societies and civilizations. The verification of such cyclical processes rests on criteria so delicate and so easily misread that it will probably convince only the converted. However this may be, all such hypotheses ultimately involve a psychological

assumption, namely, the assumption of some condition in the human organism which causes action and thought to oscillate in a determinate rhythm between given goals and potentialities of satisfaction. Which assumption of a 'pendulum swing' will occupy us later.

(3) The autonomous force can also be understood to move, arrow-like, in one direction; the concept of social or cultural evolution means precisely this. Now this concept is only a little less difficult to handle than that of the cyclical laws, in spite of its apparent persuasiveness and the deceptively close parallel with biology. At least, it seemed at one time to be so directly and simply convincing. It was essentially this over-simplification of the methodological issues involved which reduced early evolutionary anthropology to futility. But when anthropologists later criticized the evolutionary viewpoint out of existence, they demonstrated only the inadequacy of the method, not the wrongness of the evolutionary concept itself. Indeed, the import of that concept goes far beyond the conventional province of anthropology; the ultimate issue of evolution in societies and cultures concerns anthropology no more closely than it does any enquiry into the achievements and fate of humanity. If anthropology had not produced its evidence on 'primitive' societies, the idea of evolution would presumably still have been conceived, by historians or philosophers. And however anthropologists may read that evidence, the more general concern with evolution will remain unaffected.

In fact, however, the concept of evolution has never disappeared even from anthropological enquiries, though it may be disguised in the more non-committal word 'development' or relegated to incidental mention and inconspicuous places. Nor is it conceivable that the evolutionary viewpoint should disappear altogether from social enquiry. The fact remains that the vast variety of societies and cultures which have arisen in the history of mankind exhibit an increasingly powerful and efficient command over the physical conditions of existence, an increasing measure of independence of fortuitously given environments, and hence an increasing capacity for survival.[1] Or, expressed in narrower terms, we have the evidence of an increasing capacity for 'harnessing

---

[1] 'The criteria for [evolutionary] advance have been variously defined ... but perhaps the most satisfactory criterion is the degree of independence of a particular environment' (M. Ginsberg, 1947, p. 29).

energy', which is at the root of that wider advance and progress.[1]
'Advance' and 'progress' there is, and it is futile to jib at the words.
If it is said that, in speaking of 'advance' we are being hopelessly
'ethnocentric',[2] my answer is that our modern civilization is as much
a fact as are the more 'primitive' civilizations, and that the inevitable comparison of the two as inevitably demonstrates that
difference in the 'command' over the material conditions of
existence which causes us to call one 'primitive' and the other
'advanced'. And if it is said that this difference does not necessarily imply a 'progress' to better things, or that our technical advances may well lead to the self-destruction of our civilization, this
is neither here nor there. What is 'better' or 'worse' depends on
your own philosophy, which you bring to the empirical enquiry
but do not derive from it; the empirical enquiry merely shows a
cumulative process moving (or *progressing*) in one direction. Nor is
this in any way denied by the possibility of a sinister end to all
human efforts, though this might make us more cautious when
equating command over the environment with survival. But then
this is a question of ultimate limits. Perhaps the cumulative process
of technical advance will finally recoil upon itself; but we are only
in the middle of that process and cannot yet sight the final goal.
At the point at which we find ourselves the cumulative process is
simply there, and thousands of things would make no sense if we
denied it.

It is, however, a valid question whether the concept of evolution
is applicable only to the material and utilitarian command over the
conditions of existence, or also to the 'spiritual' achievements of
mankind. Both views have been defended. We might hold that all
intellectual achievements are merely consequences of the 'technological' mastery over material conditions.[3] Or we might argue that
only the utilitarian realm is susceptible of evolutionary interpretation, while the 'spiritual' realm moves by an impetus of its own—
which might be of the cyclical nature referred to before; or visible
only in irregular and sporadic happenings;[4] or perhaps reflect a

[1] See Leslie A. White (1943), p. 338.   [2] J. M. Herskovits (1948), p. 474.

[3] This is essentially the materialist view of history; among anthropologists,
Leslie A. White has recently defended it (1943, pp. 353–4).

[4] I gather that a radical seperation of this kind into 'civilization', which exhibits the unilinear and cumulative movement of evolution, and 'culture', which
reveals no definite order of growth but happens sporadically and in bursts, has
been upheld by Alfred Weber (see M. Ginsberg, 1947, pp. 114–15).

groping approach to ideals, glimpsed here and there in the history of mankind, and born of the power of thought and imagination that is man's everywhere and at all times. If such a moving force be true, it would play within the realm of events which Whitehead has called the Adventures of Ideas, and the paths taken by this force capable of 'energizing two or three main ideas, whose effective entertainment constitutes civilization', would be visible only to the philosopher's eye.[1]

I will not venture an answer. But it seems clear that we all—anthropologists, historians of civilization, philosophers—require the concept of evolution. So far as social enquiry is concerned, the concept we inherited from Spencer, Tylor, or Morgan, needs careful revision.[2] But by the same token it is also true that even the most careful restatement will never return to the concept the explanatory value it once possessed. The truth of the matter is that evolution belongs to those all-embracing concepts which, though inescapable, are too remote from the concrete problems of empirical enquiry to be much use in solving them. We need the concept of evolution, as it were, to satisfy our philosophical conscience; but the 'laws' of evolution are of too huge a scale to help us in understanding the behaviour of the Toms, Dicks and Harrys among societies and cultures, which after all is our main concern. Perhaps, indeed, there are no particular 'laws' of evolution but only one 'law'—or postulate, if you like—that there *is* evolution.

[1] A. N. Whitehead (1933), p. 9.
[2] For sociology, this has been attempted by MacIver (1937, pp. 407–12), for anthropology by Leslie A. White (op. cit.).

CHAPTER VI

Institutions

1. Problems of Definition

We have held that the order of things to which social institutions belong is built up through collecting together standardized action patterns on the grounds of their aim contents—more specifically, on the grounds of some relation, pragmatic or logical, between the aim contents. Institutions are thus units within that order; we can say at once that they are 'functional' units, that is, that they are made up of action patterns which operate in conjunction and whose aims require each other in a practical sense. Here, then, we collect together a series of action patterns on the grounds of their pragmatic relatedness; we also summarize this collection by giving it a name—the name we have for an institution. The institution would thus appear to be once more an action pattern, though magnified and more abstract than any elementary action pattern, embodying a class of aims and a series of ways of behaving rather than a single aim and behaviour cycle. It might also seem that the institution exists or is valid only for the observer, that is, the person carrying out this collection and summary. That this is not so is of course shown by the fact that the people we observe themselves have names for these 'summaries' of related action patterns—'marriage', 'family', 'chieftainship,' 'property', and the like. All such names, as we shall see, stand for normative concepts; the institution represents, for the actor, a rule or norm, and has that kind of reality, that is, the non-spatial and in a sense timeless validity of concepts. At least, this will always be true for some of the actors; others will at any given moment be concerned with translating the norm into concrete reality or, as I shall put it, with 'activating' the institution. Whenever we say that such-and-such institution exists we therefore indicate two things: first, that we can collect together and summarize ('conceptualize') certain regularly performed action patterns bearing on a class of aims; and second, that for a certain class of aims a mode of behaviour is *laid down*. The two viewpoints must converge in our formulation of the regularity or standardization of the behaviour we describe, in the sense that our summary must in some fashion match the conception of a norm which guides the actors.

The concept 'social institution' has become an almost indispensable tool in modern social enquiry, though unhappily its usage and definition are far from uniform.[1] The definition, however, towards which these introductory remarks have led us seems to me to lie at the root also of a great many other formulations. By institution, then, we shall mean a standardized mode of social behaviour or, since social behaviour means co-activity, a *standardized mode of co-activity*.

Let me quote some other definitions. Hobhouse (1924, p. 48) records these two main meanings of 'social institution'—the 'recognized and established usages governing certain relations of men (e.g. the institution of Law)'; and the 'organization [of men] supporting a complex of usages (e.g. the institution of the Church)'. Sumner (1907, pp. 53–4) notes the twofold aspect of all institutions, which always consist, first, of a 'concept' (of purposive nature, e.g. an interest), and second, of a 'structure' (i.e. the machinery, human or material, through which the concept is realized). Becker-Wiese (1932, p. 402) phrase the same distinction more carefully: The 'concept' of institutions lies in the function or purpose 'which the investigator ascribes to the institution as a result of careful analysis of the behaviour of its members'; and it is also he who 'discovers' the means whereby the 'concept' is realized. The authors point out the further, 'normative', aspect of institutions, which always act also as the 'moulds or channels within which the behaviour of individuals should be confined' (p. 404). MacIver (1924, pp. 8, 154–5) defines institutions as 'determined forms in accordance with which men enter into social relations', and Ginsberg (1934, p. 42) similarly sees in institutions 'recognized and established usages governing the relations between individuals and groups'. Allport (1933, p. 21) once more emphasizes the conceptual nature of institutions, which 'take on a reality' for the observer when he regards human beings as 'cooperating, in a

---

[1] Cf. L. T. Hobhouse (1924): 'The term (institution), in fact, is so variously used that it is doubtful if it has a single meaning common to all its applications' (p. 48). But this, I would suggest, is too pessimistic a view.

regular and habitual fashion' and on a 'multi-individual scale' towards the fulfilment of some purpose. In Durkheim's sociological system institutions play the part of normative rules defining 'modes and conditions under which actions in the pursuit of immediate ends should or may be performed' (quoted from Parsons, 1937, p. 400). Among anthropologists Radcliffe-Brown's definition is closest to ours (1940, p. 9); he sees in institutions 'standardized modes of behaviour' and so the machinery by which the network of social relations 'maintains its existence and continuity'. In Malinowski's more discursive interpretation (1946, pp. 39, 52) institutions appear as 'units' of organized human activity, which have purpose in that they are directed towards the satisfaction of needs; which rest on a 'charter', that is, on some agreement on the set of values underlying the organization; and which imply a 'personnel' (the group so organized) and 'norms' (acquired skills, habits, legal and ethical norms). Finally, Kardiner calls the institution 'a fixed mode of thought and behaviour which can be communicated, which enjoys common acceptance and the infringement of or deviation from which creates some disturbance in the individual or group' (1945, p. 24).

I quote these different formulations without comment since their correspondence with each other and with our definition is clear enough, in spite of the varying phraseology. Two comments of a different kind, however, are necessary.

The first concerns the purposive nature of institutions, which is emphasized, in one way or another, in the majority of definitions just quoted. The purposiveness of institutions is, of course, implied in the words 'social behaviour' in our definition, which we understood to mean intentional and purposive behaviour. But it may not be unnecessary to point out once more that this purposive aspect refers only to the task-like nature of organized behaviour, to the aim-contents implicit in the action patterns themselves, and not to any ulterior or ultimate purpose which the investigator might claim to have discovered in them. Allport has warned against the danger of dealing with institutions as though they were 'substantive things', capable of 'explicit denotation' and having 'ulterior ends', instead of merely describing the 'work' they are supposed to do.[1] We must treat institutions as 'conceptual fields', 'capable only of implicit denotation'; and we must realize, too, that

[1] (1933) p. 46.

H

the teleological approach is only preliminary: it helps us to 'locate' institutions on a 'teleological map'; once having done this, 'we can lay the map aside . . . and shift our attitude from the . . . purposive approach to the observation of what the individuals are actually doing.'[1] I fully agree with the first part of the argument. But it seems to me inaccurate to say that the purposive approach is only preliminary and must be ignored once the institution has been 'mapped'; purposiveness is a constituent of institutions, and cannot be 'laid aside' lest the institution itself disappear under our eyes. It is also inaccurate to see in institutions conceptual constructions with which the observer alone operates. Institutions, as I have stressed, have validity for the people acting in or through them; thus they have some 'substantiveness', if only that of rules and models for behaviour, of 'social things' which people can see and manipulate. Nor, finally, can the 'explicit denotations' in terms of ulterior ends be ultimately excluded; but it is true that this purposive aspect belongs to the order of *explanatory* concepts and has no place on our present, descriptive, level of enquiry.

The second comment concerns the perseverance which we must ascribe to institutions; for here it might seem necessary to specify the mechanisms ensuring this perseverance. Thus Professor Ginsberg would add that institutions entail sanctions, and are in this manner specifically sustained and safeguarded.[2] Malinowski's reference to 'legal norms' expresses a similar viewpoint. Obviously, being standardized and hence persevering modes of action, institutions are somehow safeguarded from infringements and deviations, and entail definite consequences in such events. Yet if these safeguards and consequences are said to lie in sanctions, these must be given a very wide and fluid meaning since otherwise the institution in a general sense would come to be identical with legal or legally protected institutions. This view is carried to the extreme by Kardiner when he speaks of some 'disturbance in the individual or group' which would follow upon deviations from the institutionalized 'mode of thought and behaviour'. So vaguely defined a consequence is almost meaningless. The solution, then, would seem to lie somewhere between the two extremes. We might say that institutions are safeguarded by at least one kind of 'sanction', namely, disapproval of departures from the given mode of action

[1] Ibid., pp. 24, 27.
[2] In his lectures and in verbal statements.

and approval for adherence to it; and we should admit also disapproval and approval of an informal or even tacit kind, perhaps
capable of being elicited only through interrogation. In a sense,
however, these remarks are redundant; for as we shall see, they
merely affirm that institutions are norms—the kind of norms
found in social behaviour.

Now, it is not the aim of this discussion to describe and analyze
concrete institutions, but rather to show how this is best done. We
shall also, to borrow Allport's simile, draw up the map on which
all institutions will be found, but we shall disregard its detailed
design. The points upon which we shall fasten in this twofold task
follow from our definition of institutions. They are: (1) the degree
and nature of the standardization visible in the co-activity; (2) the
group of individuals or the 'personnel' who are its carriers; and (3)
the purposive orientation, the aim-contents, of the activity. In
addition, we should also include data which, though they do not
add to the knowledge of particular institutions, represent prerequisite conditions, namely, the physical environment in which,
and the material tools with which, any institution is realized. But
since little can be said in general terms about these, they will be
disregarded.

2. STANDARDIZATION

We have said that institutions represent both summaries of
behaviour and rules for behaviour. These two aspects appear combined in the usual way of describing institutions, which is by
means of *if-situations*. In other words, to indicate that a certain
institution exists, we state that, in such-and-such observable
situations, people of a certain description act regularly in a particular fashion. Any anthropological description of an institution
will therefore read somewhat like this statement on bloodfeud:
If a Nuba (or whatever the tribe may be) is killed by another
Nuba, the kinsmen of the victim will exact revenge of the kind
known as talion or *lex talionis*, that is, they will kill one of
the assailant's kin who must be of the same age, sex, and status
as the victim.

Statements such as this can of course be made in much fuller
form. Even so, certain variable features in the situations considered
will always be neglected or at least mentioned only as irrelevant
details which do not affect the if-rule we extract. For clearly each

individual differs from the next, no two behave exactly alike, nor are situations ever exactly alike. Yet we shall judge the if-situation to hold good and the particular ways of acting to be in fact standardized, or institutionalized, in spite of these variations. On what grounds do we make this judgment? In the simplest case the variations will only concern the event which sets the action in motion. Thus in our example the victim may be clever or stupid, a fellow villager of the assailant or not, and the homicide might take place in the village or outside. If I consider these variations to be irrelevant and still to represent the same class of events, I do so because they do not affect the course of action that follows. At some point, however, the variations may become relevant in this sense, and must be embodied in the if-rule or added to it as provisos or qualifications. Thus it is relevant (in our example) whether the assailant is a clansfellow of the victim, and whether the homicide took place on cultivated soil; for in the former case there will be no revenge; and in the latter there will be a ritual expiation as well.

The position is more complicated where the variations concern the course of action itself. For example, we might find that the revenge can take place by day or night, and at different times of the year; in a formal battle or on some chance occasion; in the village or in no-man's-land. The number and kinship position of the individuals involved may also vary, so may the period within which the revenge is exacted; even the exact balance of the revenge may sometimes be missed or may be exceeded in the heat of the fight. Here our only objective criterion as to the standardized way of acting lies in the frequency with which the different ways of acting occur; we shall speak of a course of action 'mostly' or 'usually' followed, and phrase the 'if-situation' accordingly. Finally, there might also be instances in which the revenge does not take place at all; but provided it takes place in the majority of cases of which we have knowledge, we shall take it that these instances are exceptions and do not invalidate the rule. In other words, we call a mode of action standardized or institutionalized if it represents the *typical* or *normal* conduct in response to a given event or class of events. To be sure, frequency of incidence is not the only 'objective' criterion; the occurrence or non-occurrence of sanctions is another. If a certain variation in the response is followed by some action on the part of others which more or less clearly penalizes the original actors, we shall know that their varied conduct is not part of our 'if-situation'. Yet as I have stressed, sanctions are often tenuous, so that they might be discoverable only if we already suspect a certain way of acting to be a-typical or abnormal.

All these facts we can discover through observation and from informants. By both means we can establish the proportion of the numerically *predominant* responses (which we call typical) to all *recorded* responses, past and present. Informants, however, may state this regularity in a more absolute form, namely, as the proportion of the *typical* responses to all *possible* responses, in the future as well as in the present or past. But even if the pronouncements of informants are less positive, it is clear that institutions, if they are valid at all, are valid in this relatively absolute and timeless sense. So that they imply, not merely a regularity of conduct that exists and has existed, but one that is predictable.

Such predictable regularities emerging from individual variability are represented statistically in the familiar 'normal curve of error'. It demonstrates that among the quantitative variations in which a given event or property occurs, a mean value will occur with the highest frequency, while extreme values will occur with correspondingly lesser frequency. Once the curve is established, the probability with which any variation will appear can then be calculated. If we read any institution correctly, the responses in conduct which we define as 'typical' must correspond to such a mean, and the a-typical responses to values deviating from the mean. The institution itself is, ideally, nothing but a curve of error operating for social data, and its standardization the predictability, or what Max Weber calls the 'objective probability', of actions.[1]

I can thus represent an institution such as the Nuba bloodfeud on the curve given below, the cases I observe or record enabling me to draw the curve. For example, the typical response of talion revenge appears as the mean, and so figures as the peak of the curve; responses to the event of homicide which fall short of or exceed the precise balance are placed on the ascending and descending arcs respectively. If my observation is adequate, all future cases—while the institution remains valid—will fit the

[1] (1914, p. 420). Max Weber's concept of 'objective probability' (*objektive Chancen*) has a second meaning also, to which we shall turn presently, namely, that of 'chances of expectation' existing for the people acting in institutions and capable of being assessed by the observer.

curve also. The more ample my evidence, the more accurate my calculation of typical and a-typical responses, and so my understanding of the institution.

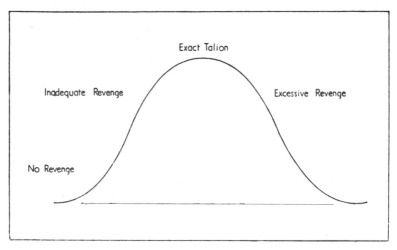

Exact Talion

Inadequate Revenge

Excessive Revenge

No Revenge

I have said that, 'ideally', social institutions are curves of error operating for social data. Let me underline this qualification, which holds good in several respects. To begin with, it is hardly ever possible to record instances sufficiently numerous to have statistical validity.[1] Yet whenever we pronounce upon typical and standardized behaviour, we imply such a validity and operate with approximations, however rough, to the 'ideal'. Furthermore, for each case we should need numerous curves, referring to the variety of features that must be considered—the character of the revenge, the time taken over it, the number and kinship position of the participants, differences in the 'if-situations', and so forth. Finally, the curve of error is legitimately applicable only to quantitative variations in events or properties, while in the social field we are predominantly dealing with qualitative variations, such as the nature of the revenge in our example, or differences in religious beliefs, in kinship practices, legal usage, and the like. The field of economics would appear to be the only one where quantitative variability rules relatively absolute. But let us note that even in the case of our qualitative variations the very aspect of standardization introduces a quantitative principle, so that the degree to which a

[1] This question will be discussed more fully at a later stage (see pp. 248–51).

given practice or belief is maintained or deviated from requires projection on some scale of measurement. Withal, then, our reference to the normal curve of error is more than an analogy or illustrative device. It serves to define an essential characteristic of institutionalized behaviour. It serves to emphasize, above all, that institutions are not (to borrow a phrase from physiology) 'all-or-nothing-reactions', that is, refer to modes of action which either occur or do not occur; rather, the modes of action occur with varying accuracy and completeness, and so admit of the chances of 'normal error'.[1]

In one respect, however, the statistical ideal, even if it can be achieved, offers to the anthropologist only inconclusive data; for it produces only half the knowledge at which he must aim. Since we are concerned with intended and task-like behaviour, we must require its standardization in a statisticial sense to have also a 'subjective' significance. This lies in the *expectations* by which the actors are guided when behaving in the standardized fashion. Unless these, too, are given, the statistically regular and probable modes of acting remain for us meaningless.[2] In other words, we understand institutions when we understand that what is for us, the observers, a statistical probability, is for the actors a 'chance of expectation';[3] and that what is for us an objectively ascertainable range of variability, is for the actors a permitted and expected latitude of acting. By 'actors' we must mean, further, not only the individuals actually executing the standardized mode of action, but all the potential actors, that is, the whole group for which the institution is valid. Any single actor knows, and trusts, that when he does a certain thing others will respond in a predictable fashion. Equally, he knows what is expected of him. He knows that, if a

[1] The 'curve of error', incidentally, would reflect, not only the rigidity of standardization, but also the existence of alternative standardizations; e.g. homicide in the tribe might entail *either* bloodfeud *or* the payment of compensation. If the two practices are equally relevant, that is, occur with approximately the same frequency in the same if-situation, this will be visible in a two-peaked ('bi-modal') curve.

[2] Max Weber speaks of 'adequacy on the level of meaning'. 'If adequacy in respect of meaning is lacking, then no matter how high the degree of uniformity (in acting) and how precisely its probability can be numerically determined, it is still an incomprehensible statistical probability. . . . Statistical uniformities constitute understandable types of action . . . only when they can be regarded as manifestations of the subjective meaning of a course of social action' (1947, pp. 90-1).

[3] Max Weber (1914), p. 420.

certain event occurs, he will be expected to do certain things and to have the purpose or desire of doing them (for example, to avenge the killing); as in turn he knows that, if he happens to have certain desires or aims, he will be expected to follow the procedure laid down for their realization (for example, to go to court if he wishes to obtain redress for a wrong). For the actor, then, the institution imposes both aims of acting, and the procedure or means for attaining them. And any individual does not only act in if-situations (of both kinds) whose outcome the observer can predict, but has knowledge of them, acts upon this knowledge and can also make statements about it.

This knowledge belongs to the dimension of idea systems, whichever way we call it—the concept or theory of institutions, or perhaps, with Malinowski, their 'charter'. It gives us the believed-in (as against the statistical) norm of acting, and is communicable through verbal information. Yet the believed-in norm requires as its corollary the statistical norm and may have to be corrected against it. Informants formulating their knowledge of institutions for our benefit will often exaggerate their rigidity, framing their knowledge in absolute terms, as a dogmatic certainty rather than a 'chance of expectation'. But even if the informants speak only of 'normal' or 'typical' behaviour, their statements might not be borne out by actual observation. Subjective expectation and objective probability will thus be at variance, each defining a different 'normality'. Any marked conflict of this kind is probably always a symptom of change, indicating a decline in the validity of institutions and foreshadowing some readjustment. The sphere of law offers perhaps the best illustrations since here the codification and enforcement of 'normal' behaviour render the conflict most acute. Thus a law may still be presented as the believed-in norm of conduct (and may still be enforced), while its infringements have become so frequent that they cease to be mere deviations and become themselves, in an objective sense, 'typical' and 'normal' behaviour. It might then be expected that the law, the formalized norm, will eventually itself change, as is amply shown in the history of Western legal systems. In the study of primitive societies we mostly observe only a phase in this process and must guess at its further course. We might, for example, find the old men maintaining that a certain course of action is 'normal' and in conformity with accepted practice (say, observance of exogamy), while our case studies would show that this kind of behaviour does not, or does no longer, figure on the peak of the curve of error. Perhaps the old men are merely idly harking back to a spurious golden age when everything was 'better than it is now'. Yet as old men, they may also be the active guardians of custom, and in a position to obstruct the new kind of conduct or at least to withhold their blessing. How long an ambiguous situation of this kind can persist, it is impossible to say in general terms since too many different factors are involved. However this may be, we have here a true clash between the 'theory' and 'practice' of institutions, which only the twofold orientation of our study can reveal.

Equally, we have a clash of values. For any believed-in norm of conduct implicitly refers to approved and desirable conduct; the modes of acting indicated by the 'theory' of institutions are always 'good' modes of acting. To the normative aspect of institutions we must therefore add their value aspect. This step, which seems to me inevitable, has important consequences; for it requires us to exclude from any list of institutions certain regular modes of action which in all other respects might seem to belong to it. This applies to all modes of action which a society would enter in its debit ledger, among its failures and blunders, and of which sociologists sometimes speak as symptoms of 'social pathology'. The recurrence of suicide, or of crimes, perhaps war, and the creation of unemployment are instances. All these facts are social facts, since they consist in intentional co-activity or result from it; they may also be statistically predictable, and may even be expected by the actors in the sense in which inevitable consequences are expected. Yet we shall not normally call them institutions.[1] For though suicides, crimes, war, and unemployment represent task-like behaviour or consequences of such behaviour, the aims of these tasks are not *approved*, and the consequences not thought of as 'good' consequences; nor, of course, is their non-occurrence sanctioned. On the contrary, the people (or at least the majority of people) trust that these events will not or need not occur and will certainly do their best to prevent them from occurring. Certain regular and expected modes of acting, then, are without a 'theory' or 'charter'; the theory is, rather, that they are 'abnormal' and the aims behind them illegitimate. We know that the dividing line

[1] On this, I think, there will be wide agreement. On the other hand, Herskovits calls 'technological unemployment' an institution (1940), p. 10.

between 'normal' and 'abnormal' modes of action is far from rigid; for war and suicide are sometimes fully institutionalized in the sense here understood, and 'crimes' in one society will be 'approved' behaviour in others. Equally, the dividing line may not be easy to draw even in the same society if different sections uphold different norms. Yet it must be drawn unless we abandon the concept of institutions altogether. The dividing line will always follow from the 'if-situation' we can formulate; it must now read: 'if so-and-so happens, people will be *trusted* to act in a given manner.' If we cannot say 'trusted', but only 'will probably act' or 'will be expected to act', then we are not dealing with true institutions.[1]

3. INSTITUTION AND ·GROUP

Though any institution is valid for a group and activated by it, the relations between the two are complicated and of great variety. In fact, we over-simplify the position when we speak of 'a group' or simply of the 'personnel' of institutions. For at least two different human aggregates are involved in every institutionalized activity. There is, first, the co-acting group (the 'actors') which on a given occasion translates the norm of the institution into action; and there is, secondly, the group from which the actors are drawn, that is, the group for which the norm is 'valid'. As we shall see, it is sometimes also necessary to distinguish 'actors' from 'co-actors', and to add a further group, namely, the group recognizing the validity of the norm without being implicated in its actuation. The main issues here involved seem to be three: (1) the time perspective of institutions; (2) their group scale; and (3) the relations between the 'validity' and 'actuation' of institutions.

One point must be clarified in advance. When we say that an institution is 'valid for a group' we mean that, objectively, the regular mode of behaviour is observed only in the case of individuals of such-and-such a description, the latter being derived from contexts other than the mode of action considered. Similarly, the formulated norm of the institution will itself state who the actors shall be. In the simplest case the norm as well as our description will refer to some non-social trait, say, biological descent, or age and sex. Often, however, the reference is to some social

---

[1] I owe this distinction between the 'expected' and the 'fiduciary' character of social actions to Professor Radcliffe-Brown.

qualification, that is, to participation past, present or future, in some other institution. Thus carrying on a bloodfeud might be expected only of men who are already married; some religious observance, only of men already circumcised; military service, only of those who have as yet no family, and so forth. In addition to this general rule of the institution there may of course be other more specific ones, allocating particular roles or functions to the various co-actors, once more in accordance with required qualifications. We note that, while the liability to act in a particular institutional capacity adds to the social tasks which make up a 'person', the rule that certain individuals (and not others) shall be so liable also presupposes that they are already in some other respects particular 'persons'. Or, expressed differently, the actor in an institution must have been 'recruited' into the group for which the institution is valid.[1]

(1) Certain institutions are activated periodically, on regular occasions, and may involve on each occasion the same 'personnel' of actors. A seasonal religious ritual, always performed with the same congregation, is perhaps the best example. Let us call such institutions *repetitive*, and add that their validity is measurable in terms of the frequency with which they are activated in a given space of time. Other institutions have a validity which, though equally measurable, is of a *contingent* nature. This is to say, the institution is activated irregularly and perhaps by varying individuals, as the occasion (the 'if-situation') demands. The institution is, as it were, always available though periodically latent for some or all actors, being translated into action only when the need arises; think of marriage, of primitive courts of law, or of magic rites invoked in the case of illness, misfortune, and the like. Yet other institutions have a *continuous* validity, in the sense that they operate without periods of latency, every member of the group being at all times an actor—for example, the family, sovereignty, or the institution of property. Sometimes such institutions are strictly continuous only for certain selected individuals who operate or 'administer' the institution, while others are only on occasion drawn into it; this is true, especially, of political institutions with their administrative staff and their intermittent importance for the average individual.

These divisions are obviously not rigid. The difference between

---

[1] See below, p. 151.

contingent and continuous institutions, for example, will often depend on the viewpoint. Thus the modern court of law may be said to operate continuously for the society at large, being kept in operation by the permanent judiciary; but for the parties which invoke the court in the event of legal disputes the institution has only contingent validity. The same institution (if it is sufficiently complex) may also show all those aspects. Thus the Church, considered as an organization upholding a body of moral and spiritual doctrine, has continuous validity; many of its observances take care of contingent needs or events (baptism, confession, prayer); while others are repetitive as well (Sunday service, feast days).

Institutions may be 'contingent' also in another sense, namely, in that they are simply available, individuals being free to make use of them or not as they wish; our own society is full of institutions of this kind. We may call them 'alternative' or 'free' institutions, as against others which are 'exclusive' or 'compulsory', that is, which must be activated by all individuals in given if-situations. Needless to say, the same kind of institution may be compulsory in one society and free in another, or may occupy any place between these extremes. Let me add that the degree of compulsion peculiar to an institution will be visible not only in the 'chances of expectation' but also, often, in the existence of formal sanctions which enforce the expected mode of behaviour. Of these enforcing mechanisms we shall speak later.

(2) As regards the scale on which institutions are activated, I would distinguish between *associative* and *parallel* institutions. In the former the institutionalized mode of action is executed more or less collectively by the whole group for which the institution is valid, and which thus coincides with the group of actors—as in hunting expeditions or communal ceremonials. In the latter kind of institution varying bodies of persons within the wider group (the 'co-actors') would act severally and on different occasions in the same standardized manner: the family operates in this 'parallel' fashion, so do marriage, hospitality, most laws, property. Probably many institutions can take either form, and it may well be a relevant characteristic of societies whether they tend to choose one or the other, for example, associative religious observances (i.e. communal rituals) rather than parallel ones (individual or family worship).

Now, in associative institutions all actors are obviously also co-actors in the same actuation (though possibly with different roles or functions). But in parallel institutions, where this does not apply, there must be some rule as to who shall be the actors in any actuation. Mostly this rule is stated in positive terms, as part of the institutional norm, and needs no separate mention. Sometimes, however, the rule is stated negatively, as is the case in exogamy, which defines the main co-actors in marriage by exclusion (in terms of non-common descent or non-common residence). Admittedly, exogamy is sometimes regarded as an institution in its own right. This is, I think, incorrect; exogamy only expresses a particular validity of the 'parallel' institution, Marriage.

The distinction between associative and parallel institutions depends once more, to some extent, on the viewpoint of the observer and the scope of his enquiry. If we study, for example, a single village community of a large tribe we may find that funeral ceremonies or age grade activities operate as associative institutions; while if we study the whole tribe, whose several communities might all share the same institutions, these would appear to operate in parallel fashion.

(3) In more complex societies we often meet with institutions which are valid only for certain sections, and do not embrace the whole of the society. In so far as the other sections are not implicated in the actuation of the institution in question, the situation presents no problem; we are here dealing merely with an internal cultural differentiation familiar from stratified or ethnically heterogeneous societies. Again the distinction may be largely a matter of viewpoint. Considering the society at large, we should say that a certain institution found in it 'belongs' to one of its sections; considering this, we should call the validity of the institution 'embracing'. Yet sometimes this simple rule does not apply. Thus military service will normally concern only the able-bodied male population of a given society; age grade activities concern directly only a certain age set, male or female or both; certain institutionalized activities might be restricted to the women; others to persons possessing certain economic qualifications, and so forth. Yet though these modes of behaviour are directly valid only for this or that section of the society (defined by age, sex, physical fitness, etc.), in an indirect and more theoretical sense they are also valid for, or 'belong' to, the society at large. In other words, the society knows

of the existence of these varying modes of behaviour and expects them to be activated by the individuals possessing the required qualifications; the modes of behaviour are viewed as cultural possessions of the group at large, not only by the observer, but by that group itself, though their execution is *apportioned* and *delegated* to the particular section. Here, then, the validity and the actuation of institutions cease to coincide; the former is 'embracing', and the latter 'sectional', whichever viewpoint we apply; for the society at large will regard the particular institution as a task falling to one of its sections, and the section will execute the cultural task as a right or obligation vested in it *qua* section.[1]

Where the sectional institutions are based on differences of wealth, age, physical fitness, or on some other 'open' principle of 'recruitment' which everyone might satisfy, they would seem to amount merely to a sub-species of 'contingent' institutions, and the discrepancy between validity and actuation would be fully accounted for by the existence of the 'periods of latency' of which we spoke before. But this is no longer true where the institutions are apportioned to the respective sections in a rigid and 'closed' fashion, on the grounds of qualifications which are beyond individual control or hope of attainment.[2] Such qualifications are sex, descent, ethnic extraction, or some particular ability or form of wealth which not everyone can hope to acquire. Here, I think, it is relevant to distinguish 'sectional' institutions from 'embracing' ones; as it is also relevant to distinguish sectional institutions in the sense here defined from other, similarly differential, institutions which are not truly sectional. For there is a fundamental sociological difference between, say, a village ritual which is unknown to the rest of the tribe or of no consequence for it, and a ritual performed by one community with the knowledge of the whole tribe, in conformity with the tribe's expectation, and as an 'apportioned' task. Or again, we meet with the different modes of behaviour in different social classes or castes, or even clans and kinship groups, which the observer will record but in which the people themselves take no interest, being only vaguely aware of 'how the other half live'; yet a similar differentiation of behaviour may also be generally known and expected, and

---

[1] Linton refers to this aspect of institutionalized behaviour when he speaks, somewhat less sharply, of the varying 'participation in culture' exhibited by the individuals and sections of any society (1936), pp. 271–2.

[2] As regards the terms 'open' and 'closed' recruitment, see below, p. 152.

conceived of as a valid 'embracing' norm—as an as-it-should-be rather than an as-it-is situation. In one case, to say it again, the situation reflects merely a cultural diversity of no intrinsic sociological significance, interesting though it may be to the ethnographer. In the other, the cultural diversity is complementary within the wider system; it has the relevance of an internal social rule in that system and bears on some required coexistence—some 'co-adaptation'—of diverse modes of action. As we shall see, this kind of situation is typical of societies which are segmentary in structure.

Let me add this. We were here regarding a particular standardized mode of behaviour, for example, a specific form of marriage or taboo, as an institution. But one can obviously also apply the term 'institution' to marriage or taboo in general, and call their various forms instances of such institutions. These are two ways of speaking, based on different levels of abstraction and on classifications of varying inclusiveness: to which point we shall presently return.

4. AIM CONTENTS

The aim contents of institutions constitute their qualitative character. Here one often speaks of 'interests', 'wants', or 'needs' realized in an institution. What is legitimately meant by these terms is always a *task*, or series of tasks, set as well as fulfilled by the institution and present as such in the minds of the actors. This consciousness is expressed in statements bearing on the achievement of the tasks—in requests, orders, instructions, or verbalized anticipations.

In our introductory remarks we spoke of institutions as embodying a class of aims rather than single aims. This plurality of purposes in institutions will, I think, be readily accepted. Malinowski, for example, speaks of their 'amalgamation of functions'; Allport of an 'institutionalized field of action'.[1] Statements such as these, however, are easily misleading; for they may be taken to refer both to the professed aims of institutions, as laid down in their norms, and to the tacit and, as it were, incidental purposes which we, the observers, discern in the results of the modes of acting. In the latter sense probably no institution can be said to exhibit a single aim only. As we shall see, any institutionalized mode of

[1] B. Malinowski (1931), p. 626.—F. H. Allport (1933), p. 21.

action, merely through being activated, aimfully bears on the functioning of other institutions (as well as of groupings). But considering only the professed aims of institutions, there are doubtless a few which revolve upon single aim contents, or which include several aims merely as consecutive phases in the achievement of the one professed aim. This phase character is in fact the outstanding feature of these single-contents institutions. Their actuation represents a single-minded task, which has a beginning and an end and describes an easily measured time span. The action pattern is essentially *biographical*, corresponding to a sharply defined section in the biography of any actor. The type of blood-feud we described; the institution of tribal hospitality; or a sacrifice performed with a particular end in view, without dancing, feasting or any other distraction from its quasi-utilitarian aim, are examples.

The large majority of institutions, however, are of composite nature, comprising several aim contents and a series of more or less separate tasks. Such institutions can be analyzed into their part tasks or *elements*, each of which corresponds in design to a single-contents institution. Thus we can analyze, say, marriage in a certain primitive society into these elements—courtship, bride-price, solemnization, sex relations, cohabitation (in the literal sense), division of labour and property, rules of etiquette (between the spouses and towards third persons), parentage, widowhood, divorce. It is not important whether or not this is an exhaustive list; what is important is that it seems to be put together almost at random. Indeed I doubt whether the elements composing any complex institution can be put together in any other way. In fact, the systematic and ordered description of any such institution presents great and partly insoluble difficulties. They lie, I think, not so much in the varied purposive character of the elements as in the intractability of these composite institutions in terms of a biographical schema, which always represents the most convincing order in which to place facts of behaviour. Now, marriage does contain several elements which can easily be treated in this way, as successive phases in a total time span—courtship, brideprice, solemnization, widowhood. But it is clear that such a definite time span, whose beginning and end are in fact signified by specific elements (solemnization, widowhood, divorce), is not true of other institutions, especially continuous ones, such as the family, sovereignty, or property. Even in marriage many elements do not fall into a clear and simple biographical pattern. Some are contingent and thus represent irregular happenings—care for offspring, or divorce; others are repetitive—say, periodical visits to relations required of the spouses on festive occasions; yet other elements are, within that contingent institution, continuous—sex relations, division of labour and property, cohabitation, etiquette. Again, the last three elements have the same time span as marriage itself; but in most forms of marriage sex relations will come to an end while the other elements (and marriage as such) continue functioning. Finally, certain elements represent alternative modes of behaviour—if the marriage is dissolved by divorce, the element 'widowhood' will not be activated at all; and if the wife does not give birth to children, etiquette might take a different form, the brideprice might have to be refunded, or the obligations of widowhood might be of a special kind.

We might summarize the whole issue by saying that the elements of any institution represent relatively self-contained modes of action, realizing relatively self-contained aims. In as much as they are self-contained, they can be described *seriatim*, in any order; yet in as much as they also hang together they imply constant cross references and re-grouping. Now, the elements in an institution hang together in two ways: they require each other ('pragmatically') for the realization of their several aims, and so fall into a 'functional' unit; and they also fit or subserve, as part-purposes and part-actions, some over-all purposive orientation which seems to attach to the institution as such.

The pragmatic unity of the institution is obvious enough. Each element has its own 'if-situation', being the appropriate, standardized response to it. Yet each if-situation entails all others, if the institution is at all valid and observed. Thus a man cannot enter into sexual intimacy with a woman in accordance with the norm of marriage, without being required (and requiring others) to act in a definite prescribed manner as regards the children, residence, economic activities, and the rest. If no such requirements exist, then the respective modes of action are simply not elements of the institution. Again, each element has its own 'expected' variability and curve of error; but each fits into the way the institution as a whole is intended to operate. That is to say, the institution, if it is to operate adequately, depends on the presence of all elements with their normal range of variability, and there is no 'chance of expec-

I

tation' that any element can be absent or variable beyond a certain latitude. Thus the temporary living-apart of husband and wife will fall within the permitted latitude of the element 'co-habitation'; while their permanent separation would represent an 'unexpected' variation, an abnormal form of conduct, disturbing the adequate functioning of marriage. We cannot of course speak of the 'expected' absence of an element; for in this case the institution would no longer be the same, and if I called the absent mode of behaviour an element I should have misread the institution. Thus in certain types of marriage the separate residence of the spouses is 'expected' and has no disturbing effects; here, then, 'co-habitation' is not an element of marriage, but is replaced or replaceable by some other mode of action enabling the rest of the elements to continue functioning, for example, regular visits between the spouses.

Yet it is possible to define a certain mode of action as the element of an institution while pointing out that it varies so widely that in numerous instances it altogether disappears. Here the following possibilities might occur. In the absence of the element in question the institution in fact fails to work; thus a form of marriage normally implying a division of labour and property in which the man is the bread-winner and the wife works in the house might be seriously disturbed when the wife has an independent profession and income. Or again, the instances showing the absence of the element include some new arrangement whereby the institution as a whole can operate adequately, though this new arrangement is still regarded as not 'quite the right thing' and not 'what one expects'. The Nupe peasants take this attitude towards wives who have children but follow an independent profession or trade. Here we are merely restating the familiar conflict of the theory and practice of institutions. Or finally, the two kinds of practice, one including the element and the other omitting it, both work adequately and are accepted as 'normal', though under different conditions. Thus the Nupe expect their wives to have an independent profession if they are childless, but not otherwise. In this case we have no longer an 'unexpected' variability of aims or elements, but alternative aims or elements in the same institution, or perhaps variants of the same institution.

The 'over-all' purposiveness of institutions presents a more difficult problem. I suggested that this character attaches to the institution as such, that is, that it is not visible in the elements considered separately. Yet clearly, it must also in some way be built out of the elements and their aim contents; it must at least partly be visible in them, in the sense that each element contributes something towards this total purpose and exhibits one or the other aspect of it. The analysis of any institution will show this to be true. In primitive marriage, for example, the payment of bride-price often bears conspicuously on the attractiveness of the bride (being assessed in accordance with it), or on the sexual prerogatives of the husband (which start after the payment). But marriage obviously does more than enable people to achieve these aims. Marriage also achieves an enduring union of man and woman and safe-guards care for offspring, which aspects might not be expressed in the part purposes discernible in the element 'brideprice'. These aspects will, however, be embodied in other elements of marriage, such as the division of labour and property and the specific task of 'parentage': and these are in turn independent of the sexual aims which the brideprice may express so conspicuously. Indeed, the different part purposes may conflict with one another, as when sexual rela-tions are interrupted during pregnancy or before weaning. Or take a different example, the institution of chieftainship. It mostly in-cludes among its elements the apportionment of land to the chief's subjects. Now this rule appears, from the point of view of the people, as an aimed-at benefit. But other elements equally implied in chieftainship point in a different direction and may represent disadvantages, tasks felt to be cumbersome by the people, such as services or payments exacted by the chief. These diverse and even conflicting part purposes together build up the purposiveness of the institution as a whole, which we may summarize as the control of internal security and external solidarity. The 'over-all' purposiveness of an institution, then, lies in what all the elements together achieve. The aims visible in the elements do not simply add up to the aim of the institution as a whole; the latter is the product or *resultant* of the former rather than their sum total. More precisely, the resultant purpose of the institution rests upon the part purposes of the elements as on steps or means towards its realization.

Here one might ask whether this resultant purpose can be assumed to be present in the minds of the actors. The answer is—yes, though there will be degrees of this. Some individuals will have a fuller insight into the situation than others; a judge will know more about all the implications of marriage than perhaps the bridegroom and bride; a chief more about how chieftainship is intended to work than the average villager. Perhaps, too, at any moment of acting individuals will not consciously anticipate the whole norm of behaviour in which they become involved, as when one marries to be with the beloved or because one is fond of children or for reasons of economic security, without working out beforehand all the consequences of marriage. More generally speaking, individuals act in the institutionalized manner when they are faced with particular if-situations, which provoke immediately only the appropriate element of the institution, while all the other if-situations implicit in it remain in the background. Yet these will follow in due course, and can also at any moment be observed in the case of others. Thus the institution is present as a whole to the actors, though an individual picked at random might have to piece it together in time and through learning. The institution as a whole exists for the actors as any concept exists for those who use it—as a summary of many items of which one keeps only a few in the mind at any moment, though one can make oneself aware of all. This analogy is not, I think, too far-fetched. For having a common concept and word for a number of situations indicates that these are seen to be related and to have some unity. And, as I have said, people have words for marriage or chieftainship, and not only for courtship, brideprice, sex relations, land titles, tribute, and so forth. People do conceive of total institutions and all they entail, and not only of single if-situations and the diverse part-purposes concerned with them. When our reading of a total institution is not supported by such linguistic evidence, we might have to choose between our idea of grouping together a class of aims and the actors' idea of breaking it up. Let me for the moment disregard this point.

The foregoing discussion seems to indicate that all there is of purpose in an institution is contained or grows out of the specific qualitatively defined modes of action we have called elements. This is not quite correct, however. As we have seen, the make-up of institutions exhibits certain measurable factors—degree of standardization, contingency, rate of recurrence, time span. Note that these are quantitative data only if stated statistically in terms of objective frequency or duration. Considered as chances of expectation they belong to the qualitative, or purposive, side of actions.

Thus the enduring character of marriage, although it can only be expressed in measurements of time, represents a purpose among others in that institution. Nor can this purpose be assigned to any specific mode of action; paradoxically, it is the absence of a particular element, divorce, which determines the duration of marriage. In other institutions we cannot even isolate such a negatively controlling element—controlling, for example, the length and repetitiveness of hospitality, the duration of services a chief will expect, or the recurrence of religious ceremonies. We must therefore admit the presence in the institution of aim contents which are not realized by any one of its 'elements', but operate, as it were, through its total curve and lie in the quantitative features themselves.

5. ON CLASSIFICATION

Our next task is to construct the whole order to which institutions belong, that is, to relate institutions to one another and to classify them. We relate and classify of course at every step of our enquiry. We classify when we say that certain ways of acting belong together to one institution; we classify when we say that certain procedures are instances or variants of the same type of institution. In neither case can we claim that ours is the only possible classification. There cannot be such a thing. For any classification implies some criterion of relevance which the classifier brings to the situation. In grouping together a number of items of any kind— objects, concepts, or forms of behaviour—as belonging to the same class or category, we do not simply go by the identical or otherwise comparable properties they exhibit, but also judge what sort of identity shall count, and what sort of difference shall not count. Any *fundamentum divisionis* implies such a judgment, and there may be differences of opinion. I have, for example, classed courtship as an element of marriage; but it might be argued that the difference between this and other elements is more relevant than their unity, so that courtship should count as an institution in its own right. Again, we mostly call 'marriage' any enduring union of man and woman which implies sex relations and duties of parentage, whether the spouses are required to reside together or not, and whether the union is required to be solemnized or not; these differences are considered to have secondary relevance only and to establish only variants of the practice 'marriage'. Yet we might also separate these different modes of action and argue that only the institution implying solemnization should be called marriage, and the other practices something else. I do not mean to say that this particular argument has ever been put forward. But there have been endless controversies about similar issues—about what is or is not totemism, or animism, or magic. These are futile arguments; crudely speaking, marriage, or totemism, and the rest are what we say they are (though, as we shall see, we are not quite free in this matter).

In the present section, however, we are concerned with classification in a more specific sense, namely, with the ordering of institutions into categories in accordance with the similarity or diversity of their aim contents. Conventionally, we carry out such an ordering when we call certain institutions political, others economic or religious, and so forth. Now since most institutions embody several aim contents, different alignments may appear possible. Often, there will be little disagreement since we have a convincing criterion of relevance in the subordination of the part purposes in any institution to its 'resultant' purposiveness. Thus we shall not group marriage with prostitution or circumcision although all these bear upon sex, nor with markets or trade, although the element 'brideprice' bears on economic aims. Rather, we shall group marriage with other institutions which similarly bear upon procreation and parentage, such as inheritance, adoption, family. The elements of any given institution remain, however, part purposes, and may as such fall within different classes of institutions. We usually refer to this fact by saying that, say, marriage also has an economic or legal aspect, chieftainship a religious one, a religious ceremony a kinship aspect, and so forth. We should, more precisely, say that the purposive orientation of marriage, chieftainship, or of a religious ceremony implies, as steps or means towards its realization, modes of action which, considered as ends in themselves, would fall within a different class of institutions.

However, the criterion of relevance might prove an ambiguous guide and the 'resultant' purpose not fall squarely into any one of the conventional classes of institutions. Is property an economic or legal institution? It is probably both, though this is rather a special case since legal aims or interests, being as we shall see 'regulative', enter almost *ex definitione* into all institutionalized activities.[1]

----

[1] See below, p. 141.

But again, Malinowski felt that the *kula* exchange could be classed neither fully with economic nor fully with religious or ceremonial activities, but required a mixed classification, as a 'semi-economic, semi-ceremonial' activity.[1] Similarly, the *potlach* of North West America would seem to be as much economic (since it deals with the disposal of wealth) as political (since it is meant to validate rank and noble status). In cases of this kind much can apparently be done, in a simple manner, by hyphenating the conventional categories; or we might again speak of 'different' aspects of an institution, taking them here to be of equal weight and relevance.

All these questions revolve essentially upon the extent to which we are prepared to go when abstracting from the phenomena we study, and whose character we wish to describe, such traits as would form a basis for their classification. More precisely, these questions involve some adjustment between two points of view— on the one side our own *ad hoc* readiness to abstract, and on the other the degree or kind of abstraction required by the conventional categories in which the phenomena may be subsumed. Now, these conventional categories have evolved, often haphazard, in the history of our thought, and we inherited them such as they are; where they have been more rigidly defined, the definitions grew out of the experiences gathered in our own society and reflect our concern with its nature and history. Nor is there only one agreed definition for each category of institutions; rather, volumes have been written on the nature of economics, political systems, law, and so forth. Not unnaturally, therefore, the anthropologist will often find that the phenomena he studies fall into several of the conventional categories or into none. Or, differently expressed, he will find that the degree of abstraction required by these categories goes both further and less far than he is prepared to go. Modern economic theory, for example, defines as 'economic' any exchange of possessions or services in the command of a person for the sake of any other possessions or benefits:[2] if we accept this criterion, then the *kula* or *potlach* fall undoubtedly under the heading 'economic', but so would practically every form of human action. On the other hand, 'law' has been defined as resting on the enforcement of norms of conduct by means of formal 'statutes' and 'the systematic

---

[1] B. Malinowski (1932), pp. 510, 513, 514.
[2] P. H. Wickstead (1933), vol. I, p. 167.

application of the force of politically organized society';[1] in which case a wide range of primitive institutions concerned with the enforcement of norms of conduct would not be law.

Yet we cannot ask whether the game is worth the candle. Obviously, we must classify; obviously, too, it is not a matter of indifference whether we call a mode of behaviour 'economic', 'semi-economic', or something else. And in calling a mode of behaviour anything we are not free to disregard or replace the conventional categories and the terms denoting them. We can to some extent manipulate them, restricting or extending their meaning, or use circumlocutions in Latin or Greek. But we cannot move too far from the known, conventional concepts, inaccurate though they may be for our purpose. This is not, I think, merely a question of technical *versus* non-technical language. Rather does it bear on the very unity of our subject matter. For we study Society with a capital S, which means all forms of social existence, including our own. If we ceased to speak of law, economics, or religion because nothing quite like them (as the words are conventionally understood) is found in the primitive society we study, we should also cease to speak of phenomena identifiable wherever Society exists.

Perhaps there is this, too. We do not classify forms of organisms, or rocks, or machines, or any other series of items which is only progressively explorable and may well be infinite. We classify purposes, the relevantly different purposes in the human universe. We probably cannot conceive of them as infinite in number. But however this may be, in the history of our thought they have all been explored and mapped. The conventional categories of institutionalized action give us such a map of relevances which we have come to accept as exhaustive and faithful. Differently expressed, these categories give us *sectors* of that totality we call human culture, each defined in terms of a relevant purpose and each presupposing the other sectors with their purposes; none can be thought away, and all together embrace every possible form of social action. When I call an action, even in a rough sense, economic or legal I indicate its place on this map of relevances; we then understand that this action has a known part to play, which other kinds of action do not play, and that it fits in a definite manner into a universe of discourse. As students of primitive society we may have to redraw this map here and there, but we shall still speak of 'semi-

[1] A. R. Radcliffe-Brown (1933 b.), p. 202.

economic' actions, or perhaps of 'rudimentary' law.[1] If we ceased to speak of 'economics' or 'law' altogether, we should describe things hanging *in vacuo*. Indeed, the tacit assumption that there is such a map, and that on it all the forms of social action must be found, is behind many arguments about the conventional categories of action. When many anthropologists reject Radcliffe-Brown's narrow definition of law they do so, not because they deny that the kind of law he has in mind is a relevant category, but because, we might almost say, they feel that the thing we are used to call law cannot be absent in any form of social existence.[2]

The list of institutions I propose to give represents such a map of relevances, or of sectors of culture, and no more. To make its meaning quite clear I would state its items in this form—institutions concerned with aims of an economic, political, legal nature, and so forth. These broad categories leave room for finer and more precise subdivisions which refer to the particular means—procedures or machineries—employed in the achievement of these aims. Thus the 'legal' institutions would include constituted Law in Radcliffe-Brown's sense as well as institutions which, though still aiming at the enforcement of norms of conduct (which I take to be a 'legal' aim), do so by means of a different kind of machinery; and 'economic' aims would operate through price, profit, and market mechanisms, as well as through the machinery of 'personalized' transactions, which Firth has explored for primitive economics.[3] Beyond a few comments I shall not attempt to define the various

[1] See, for example, A. S. Diamond (1935), p. 280.

[2] See, for example, J. E. Lips on Radcliffe-Brown: 'If this method were generally applied we should have to deny also the existence of religion, art, and other fields of culture in primitive civilization. However, there is no people . . . without law' (1938), p. 489. Unless we understand this as an argument from the tacit assumption stated above, it ceases to be an argument at all. Much the same is true of the following passage from Malinowski (1934, p. xxv). In many primitive communities 'there is no "force of politically organized society" which acts to compel conformity to laws . . . yet the laws are kept.' Clearly, on the basis of the definition attacked by Malinowski it is not 'laws' that are kept: Malinowski only 'feels' (as I would say) that they must be called such.

[3] R. Firth (1939), p. 355. Modern economic theory tends to deny the existence of economic 'motives' and hence aims of action, admitting only economic relationships between actions or economic 'aspects' of any kind of action. (See Wickstead, 1933, vol. I, pp. 165, 167; L. Robbins, 1935, pp. 16–17; D. Goodfellow, 1939, p. 41.) But even economists will not deny that, say, a bank or a cooperative farming organization are qualitatively distinct, i.e. by their *aims*, from a religious system or friendship, the economic 'aspects' of the latter notwithstanding.

items on my list. No one can honestly say that he does not know what economic, political, or legal means. He may know it only roughly, for these inherited concepts have a broad and fluctuating meaning. Yet in order to draw that exhaustive map of purposes in the world precisely such broad meanings are required.

How to class particular institutions of dubious citizenship; and how to draw for each sector the subdivisions accounting for diverse procedures and machineries—these are questions which must at this stage be left to *ad hoc* enquiries. Only these general remarks may be made. Classifications, strictly speaking, cannot be right or wrong, only more or less adequate. This means, first, purely practically, that classifications will prove to be more or less economical. If my categories are too broad, I shall have to introduce subdivisions whose whys and wherefores have to be specially explained; and if my categories are too narrow, I shall have to account for the relations linking the phenomena I have separated. Secondly, classifications can make use of traits which will prove to be more or less 'significant in the sense that on the basis of the traits the subject matter can be organized into a system'.[1] In other words, the judgment of relevance underlying any form of classification will prove more or less fruitful when we attempt to expose the wider or widest interrelations between phenomena. Thus all classifications are in some measure arbitrary, tentative, and 'groping'. Here I am not referring to the discovery of new facts which may force us to revise our categories, but rather to the new way of looking at things which follows from any classification once it is adopted; for this new way of looking at things may be justified by further enquiries or not, and contribute more or less usefully towards that 'organizing of subject matter' which is science.

Nor are there any golden rules—save one: that we must not find more in our classification than we have put in. The concepts we employ must be used 'operationally' and not made to mean more than the observations and intellectual processes that have led us to adopt them.[2] In this sense economics, or political organization, or law are what we make them and no more. If we choose to regard (let me stress the 'choose') as economic also exchange transactions in equivalents like the *kula*, or as political also chiefless social

[1] Cohen and Nagel (1947), p. 133.
[2] The term 'operational' is borrowed from modern logic. See P. W. Bridgman (1927) and (1938), pp. 20–1, 56 *et passim*.

organizations, we cannot afterwards claim: We have now discovered that the profit motive is not essential to economic activities,
nor leadership to political ones. If, with Malinowski, we point out
that even societies without courts or police have law,[1] we have
decided beforehand what law is to be. All classifications are in this
sense pre-emptive. We do discover something new—namely, a
new way of looking at things; and this, as I have said, may be
important for the ordering (or 'understanding') of our subject
matter. But we do not discover—for there is no such thing—their
'real nature'.[2]

This, then, is my list of institutions. Having said enough about
the nature of classification I do not propose to compare my list
with, or defend it against, the different methods of classifying
institutions suggested by other scholars.[3] Most of the items are
self-explanatory, though these two remarks must be added.

Operative	*Regulative*
Somatic	
Economic	
Recreational—aesthetic	
Scientific	
Religious (incl. magical)	
Educational	
Political	
Legal	
Kinship	

The term 'somatic' is intended to account for all standardized
modes of action whose aims bear specifically on the phases and
facts of individual physical existence, such as sex, age, treatment of
disease, circumcision, and the like. The two terms 'operative' and
'regulative' will be explained in the following section; let me here
emphasize that they imply, not a sharp division between two categories of institutions, but a gradual transition from one to the

[1] See p. 133 above, Note, and B. Malinowski (1926).

[2] Perhaps this is not always fully realized. Linton makes this point forcibly
(though I do not quite follow his use of the word 'real'). He warns us against
considering classifications of social facts as though they were 'objectively real. . . .
Classifications of institutions are convenient tools for descriptive purposes . . .
but they can aid us very little in understanding the real significance of institutions' (1936, p. 259).

[3] See, e.g. Park and Burgess (1924), p. 51; Sumner and Keller (1927), vol. I,
p. 99; Malinowski (1944), pp. 62–5.

other, any class of institutions being only more or less operative or regulative.

6. Interaction of Institutions

The interrelation of institutions may now be considered from a different viewpoint, namely, with regard to the manner in which they, or classes of institutions, are linked 'pragmatically'. By this I mean that whole institutions (like their 'elements') may require each other, certain institutions being so designed as to aid or control the working of others. A distinction of this kind has been suggested by some sociologists. E. A. Ross seems to hint at this when he points out that institutions appear both as forms of 'social practice' and as 'means of control'.[1] Becker-Wiese speak of 'operative' institutions, which are 'expected to render a definite service' to the society 'in their institutional capacity', normative guidance being secondary, as against 'regulative' institutions, which emphasize the normative aspect, representing 'moulds or channels within which the behaviour of individuals should be confined'.[2] I propose to adopt this distinction, though slightly modified, in this sense. In the *operative* institution we see a professed purpose immediately fulfilled; the institution achieves its task within itself and so, in a relatively self-contained fashion, renders its specific 'service'. The *regulative* institution bears upon the operation of other institutions; it achieves its purpose or task in enabling the purpose and task of other institutions to be achieved; so that the regulative institution does not merely represent the 'moulds and channels' of behaviour (for this is a characteristic of all institutions), but safeguards them. Let me add at once that regulative institutions bear in the same sense also on groupings and their manner of operation. And let me repeat that the distinction is fluid, describing a difference in degree and aspect rather than in invariant properties. Institutions are rarely one or the other thing; and the same institution or class of institutions may appear, in different contexts, as (predominantly) operative or regulative respectively.

We can now attempt to answer a question which our analysis of institutions was bound to raise: How is their standardization maintained? There appear to be only two solutions. Either the aim contents of an institution, supported by the ubiquitous trend of

[1] (1901), pp. 247, 254.   [2] (1932), p. 404 ff.

habituation, satisfies requirements or 'needs' sufficiently cogent or undisputed to sustain the standardized mode of behaviour, so that the institution becomes self-regulating. Or the institution requires the additional support of some independent, regulative mechanism. There are, however, transitional forms. Where non-observance of an institutional mode of behaviour is accompanied only by diffuse expressions of disapproval, we should speak of it as self-regulating; but such forms of disapproval often shade over into formal and public sanctions, which we take to represent regulative mechanisms. Moreover, fully self-regulating institutions are rare. They are perhaps exemplified only in economic institutions,[1] in aesthetic, and, in a different manner, in kinship institutions (as will be seen presently).

The regulative effects of institutions upon each other appear to take these main forms (between which there is, once more, considerable overlapping)—threats of sanctions; positive inducements; instruction; and a more subtle kind of inculcation which I will call dramatization. We may disregard the nature of the sanctions— whether they inflict physical or social deprivations, or mental suffering or discomfort; the essential thing is that they represent regular modes of behaviour having some such aim, and being contingent upon the non-observance of some other regular mode of behaviour. Conversely, people are induced to behave in the institutional manner through the promise of rewards, prizes, or other benefits expressing public appreciation. The regulative effect of instruction, as exemplified in schools or other educational activities, is self-explanatory. We might only add that the so-called spiritual or supernatural sanctions and rewards fall properly in the category of 'instruction', through which alone this kind of expectation is fostered. The teaching and telling of myths and legends, in particular, often conspicuously serve this purpose.

As I have stressed, institutions need not be concerned *in toto* with these regulative tasks or involve a specifically constituted body of actors to carry them out (e.g. a legal executive, or professional teachers). The regulative aims and effects may attach only to one element of an institution 'operative' in all other respects or to one aspect of its actuation. Many instances can here be quoted. Marriage, through its element 'brideprice', has an inducement

---

[1] I presume this is implied in the following statement: 'What gives their immense social significance and importance to the economic forces is that they *always look after themselves*' (my italics; P. H. Wickstead, 1933, vol. I, p. 209).

effect upon thrift and economic enterprise; the institution of a tribal council or of priesthood, though concerned with specifically political and religious tasks, may also, by the method of appointment employed, penalize immoral or reward moral conduct. In the Nuba Mountains I saw a girls' dance in which the dancers selected their partners among the young men in accordance with their bravery and skill in raiding; and many myths, while formulating the quasi-scientific or quasi-historical knowledge current in the society, also contain ethical judgments or illustrate desirable modes of behaviour. This kind of indirect regulative effect is typical, above all, of the 'dramatizations'. By this term I mean the demonstration of desired modes of action in the context of ceremonials and aesthetic performances. Such a demonstration may be conspicuously a 'drama', ritual or secular, whose theme and pronouncements, heroes or villains, bear directly upon approved and disapproved conduct. Often the dramatization will be more subtle and circuitous, the desired modes of behaving being exemplified only in formal features of the performance, that is, in the manner in which persons or situations are employed (or not employed). Think of the distinction between performers and public in any ceremonial, which might reflect differences in status or importance; of the exclusion of women from esoteric activities; of the banishing of quarrels during festive events, and so forth.[1] In either case the emotional appeal of the ritual or aesthetic context is made to serve as a vehicle for moral ideas and as a means of reinforcing their hold over people.

The mechanisms here at work may be called mechanisms of transference; a purposive attitude evoked or cultivated in one institutional context is transferred to another so that the validity of that institution might be maintained. Since the continued validity of institutional behaviour clearly contributes to the 'well-being of the society' as it is constituted, we may also say, adopting Professor Radcliffe-Brown's phraseology, that regulative institutions establish or underline the 'social value' of modes of behaviour required in other, operative, institutions, much as the way in which an object is handled or a manner of behaving treated in some religious ceremony makes the congregation realize that the object or manner of behaving is good, desirable, valuable (or the opposite).[2]

---

[1] I have elaborated this point in (1937 d), pp. 120–2.

[2] (1933 a), pp. 264 et passim.

Equally, however, such a transference of purposive attitudes may have a socially disruptive effect; for what you learn in school, are taught in church, or see on the stage, may conflict with the tasks set by everyday life. Whether or not such conflicts occur will be an index of the total integration of social life, which problem belongs to a later context. But it will readily be agreed that societies rarely exhibit a close adjustment between the efficiencies or values cultivated in different institutions; rather, different efficiencies and values will tend to develop apart at the risk of conflicts arising within the embracing body of culture. Let me stress that such conflicts need not arise only through the 'transference' of purposes; often they amount to a clash of practical advantages. One institution may develop, as it were, by its own momentum in such a manner that it interferes with the efficient working of others, even though it may bear on them in some regulative sense. Thus a society making adventure or military exploits a supreme aim may deplete itself of the hewers of wood and the drawers of water; a group encouraging the periodical dissipation of wealth, though inducing by these means intensive production, may well have to face periodical threats to its subsistence, famines and the like; and when seeing certain religious rituals at work which undoubtedly sustain initiative in practical tasks but also draw heavily on the resources of time and labour, one often cannot help thinking that they defeat their own purpose. In the economic sphere we can calculate these vicious circles in terms of costs and diminishing returns. In all other spheres of culture we can only note the diversity of purposes that exist in any society, and the dubious adjustment between their several efficiencies.

The list of such one-sided 'social values' could be infinitely expanded. But let us consider more closely their efficacy in the spheres in which they unquestionably obtain. The question here is—For whom are they so 'unquestionably' effective? For the actors or for the observer?

Now Radcliffe-Brown, in defining 'social value', appears to go further than most anthropologists will probably be prepared to go. He holds that rites or ceremonies make the individuals realize 'the social value of the thing in question', the social value of a thing being 'the way in which that thing affects or is capable of affecting social life'.[1] I do not think that the people generally realize all this;

[1] (1933 a), p. 264.

all they realize is, mostly, only the 'value-having' as such. This realization makes them transfer the purposive attitude so acquired to other contexts, and it is through this transference that the aimed-at effect upon social life is achieved. And here we must ask further, how far this effect is really, that is, consciously, aimed at. Often the regulative effects of institutions will indeed be fully understood by the actors (or some actors) and form part of the professed aims of the institution. Take the case of legal procedures or of religious ceremonials which conspicuously pronounce upon the right and wrong of specific actions, or of initiation rituals which demonstrate the various social duties henceforth facing the neophytes. But as often this may not be so. A dance or a drama on the stage is meant to entertain, not to teach; a religious ritual may be consciously performed for the sake of some utilitarian aim, say, increase of fertility, and not to demonstrate social relationships or status differences meant to be effective in other spheres of life. This would appear to be true, above all, of the circuitous dramatizations mentioned above, in which the *form* of the institutionalized performance, and not any directly expressed *contents*, carries the regulative effect. Perhaps, too, the regulative effects tend to be unwitting where they bear on relationships and groupings rather than on the aim contents of 'operative' institutions. If, then, we point to regulative aims in such situations we go beyond what is in the minds of the actors. We discern these aims, not in the intentional modes of action, but in their consequences, which are fully incidental to the actuation of the professed aims and represent only for us, the observers, the achievement of some 'purpose'. In other words, we no longer describe an institution but explain its *raison d'être*.

Finally, in distinguishing special regulative institutions we seem to face a *regressus ad infinitum*; for if one kind of institution is said to be safeguarded by another, we might obviously ask what is safeguarding the latter, and so forth. No doubt, we often meet with such cumulative safeguards. A conspicuously regulative institution such as kingship will often also utilize the support of 'dramatizations', in the pomp and circumstance with which it is surrounded; and the ceremonial, with its regulative aims, will be backed by the 'charter' of some myth taught in the community, which in turn 'regulates' the ceremonial. In this respect societies seem indeed to be designed upon the formula, The-house-that-Jack-built.

The arrangement of our chart of institutions will now have become clear. But the grouping together of political, legal, and kinship institutions under the head 'regulative' still requires explanation. Now by 'kinship institutions' I mean, briefly, all institutions intended to control and maintain groups based on descent (e.g. marriage, family, inheritance, adoption, etc.). By 'political', all institutions intended to control and maintain, ultimately by means of force, the widest corporate group, that is, the society.[1] By 'legal', all institutions intended to control and maintain, ultimately by means of sanctions, the adequate operation of all other institutions and groupings within the society ('international law' is in this sense an exception, being, in fact, altogether 'pseudo-law'). All three classes of institutions, then, are essentially regulative; all three, moreover, refer to groupings, and can be fully defined only in terms of that other 'dimension'.

The position of kinship institutions, however, still remains in a sense anomalous. Here the coexistence of the operative and regulative aspects in the same institution takes a peculiar form. For the modes of kinship action—marriage, adoption, parentage, inheritance—bear upon the physical creation and perpetuation of the group by which they are activated. Kinship, as a range of operative activities, thus regulates itself as a grouping, so that its aims can only be defined tautologically, as creating and sustaining a group resting on these aims. Thus marriage fulfils itself in extending and perpetuating groups based on descent, that is, ultimately on marriage; parentage (and similarly adoption) serves to protect and guide the offspring who will expand and perpetuate the descent group, once more through parentage; while inheritance endows members of the kinship group with such rights and possessions as will enable the group to persist (family-land, property, or status and position). To say it again, the group does not realize aims extraneous to itself, its own existence and survival being its aims. We can, of course, still distinguish between group and institution, but only in the elementary sense of pointing now to the 'personnel' activating the institution (say, the 'family group'), and now to its activities ('family life'). But one exists only in virtue of the other, so that in an ultimate sense the two coincide. Expressed in the terms of our schema of dimensions, in the case of kinship they cease to be independent variables.

[1] The terms 'widest corporate group' and 'society' will be explained in a later context (see pp. 183 ff.).

K

7. RESIDUAL CATEGORIES

Though institutions have their *locus* in the dimension of action, they do not constitute that whole field, nor yet the whole field of recurrent and standardized action. We must, therefore, in conclusion, deal with such 'residual' categories. If our analysis of institutions be correct, forms of action which are not, or are not yet, institutions must be characterized by the absence of one or more of the attributes of institutions as we defined them. This is indeed the case.

A first residual category comprises modes of action standardized, but not orientated upon a conscious purpose. Here we meet with the diffuse field of the customs, conventions, and *mores* of society.[1] Food and dress habits; ways in which tools are handled or perhaps children treated; forms of greeting or showing respect—all these forms of behaviour are 'just there' (MacIver). They enter into institutions, as their fabric as well as raw material; but the conscious norm, which is the bridge between habitual and intentional standardization, is absent, and we have uniformity of conduct rather than coordination of action. The boundary line, however, is thin and easily blurred, and institutions constantly grow out of customs and *mores*.[2] Etiquette is perhaps the most important example of this kind; mere 'manners' between persons are here seized upon and consciously standardized so as to symbolize and demonstrate social relationships, status, or group membership.

Conversely, purposively orientated actions obviously also appear without standardization. This is the realm of unpredictable, spontaneous activities of individuals or groups. As such, they are outside sociological understanding—they are the 'unique events' capable only of 'historical' statement, or description. But they may assume sociological relevance when their relationship to standardized modes of action is explored. The spontaneous actions are then studied as variants or deviations of the latter, or as relative innovations turning the standardized mode of action in a new

---

[1] Thus Sumner and Keller call *mores* a 'lowest form' of institutions (1927), p. 88.

[2] MacIver calls customs the raw material for institutions, various institutions having been customs 'before' they became institutions (1924, pp. 154-5). Becker-Wiese express a similar view, considering 'institutionalization' to take place when a custom 'acquires permanence and comes to fulfil a definite function' (1932, p. 402).

direction. Moreover, spontaneous action may become recurrent and permanent—'institutionalized'—like the Ghost Dance of the Plains Indians, or any other instance of effective cultural change.

We have already referred to the third residual category. It concerns the purposive modes of action which, for the observer, are recurrent and standardized in a statistical sense, but which the actors do not accept as 'normal' or 'typical' (see above, p. 117). We have also stressed that the 'abnormal' action in one society may be 'normal' and 'expected' in another; we may now add that one may also turn into the other in the same society. Some primitive societies like the Ngoni or Nuba in East Africa enjoin and commend theft or cattle raids in certain contexts (e.g. in the case of young bloods), while in others the same form of conduct is considered criminal. Suicide, generally 'abnormal', may be the 'expected' behaviour of offenders (as among the Ibo or Ashanti in West Africa) or the Trobrianders and Tikopia in the Pacific. Among fighting races all men live and plan for the contingency of war, which is both objectively recurrent and subjectively expected. The Holy War of Islam or the Crusades of the Middle Ages come close to institutions, if indeed they do not deserve that name. But let us note that even where actions such as these are not themselves embodied in institutions, institutions exist to cope with their regular though 'abnormal' occurrence—such as police forces, armies, or a body of laws.

Finally, there are the ideologies of peoples, their beliefs, their philosophies, and their styles of art. They may express themselves in and through institutional activities, but they also remain outside them, as idea systems which are perpetuated and developed autonomously.[1] There is, too, language (or communication in general). It does not constitute an institution; rather does it pervade all institutional activities and makes them possible; equally, it has its own autonomous structure.[2] All these phenomena belong to the

---

[1] L. v. Wiese speaks here of 'abstract collectives', which embrace ideologies and the 'image complexes' of art, music, and philosophy (1929, p. 202).

[2] See p. 88 above. J. Dewey calls language 'a cultural institution, and, from one point of view . . . but one among many such institutions.' He adds this, however: Language is also '(1) the agency by which other institutions and acquired habits are transmitted, and (2) it permeates both the form and the contents of all other cultural activities. Moreover, (3) it has its own distinctive structure which is capable of abstraction as a *form*' (1938, p. 45).

realm of intentional action; they are standardized; yet they lack, wholly or partly, one attribute of institutions—the implication of specific groupings. As I have put it, they belong or approximate to the field of 'all-culture'.

CHAPTER VII

Groupings

I. DEFINITIONS

Sociological literature is full of descriptions and classifications of social groups. Anthropologists, on the other hand, preoccupied rather with the field of culture and its typical isolate, the social institution, have used the group concept somewhat erratically. The usual sociological classification of groups is mostly based on the nature of the human contacts and relationships involved in the formation of groups; here such distinctions as that between 'primary' and 'secondary' contact groups (Cooley) are too familiar to need explanation. The classification suggested by Park and Burgess, into family, language or racial group, territorial communities, conflict groups and accommodation groups, operates with mixed criteria and is, in the author's own words, neither 'adequate nor wholly logical'.[1] The manner in which groups emerge and develop offers another criterion; it led to Toennies' familiar dichotomy which, somewhat shorn of its metaphysical fringes, reappears in MacIver's distinction of Communities and Associations. While the former are said to emerge spontaneously among people living in proximity and sharing a wide range of common interests, the latter evolve where an aggregate of individuals act in voluntary coordination for a specific common purpose.[2] L. v. Wiese distinguishes aggregates (*Massen*), A-groups (the pair, or group of three), and B-groups (plural groups), and subdivides the last in accordance with the interests and 'wishes' by which they are dominated.[3] These various definitions seem to me deficient at least in one respect; they all fail to account for the precise relationship between the group formation as such and the purposive action

[1] (1924), p. 50.

[2] R. M. MacIver (1931), pp. 9–10; (1924) pp. 23, 110; F. Toennies (1926), pp. 218–26.

[3] (1929), pp. 114, 180, 185.

145

patterns, that is, the institutions, through which groups operate and are alone visible. These definitions all imply institutions, for example, as 'the determinate forms in accordance with which men enter into social relations', and so produce groups.[1] But the mutual determination of the two 'dimensions' of social existence is left unexplored.

The institutional contexts in which groups appear offer another, and conveniently simple, basis for classification and description. Thus we often speak of political groups, kinship groups, religious communities, economic or technological associations, and so forth. These are useful working definitions, provided they are used for approximate and preliminary descriptions. If groups were described solely in terms of the institutions through which they operate, we should not know where they begin or end. A group appearing in the context of one institution need clearly not be defined by it alone; the people forming a 'political group' may also represent a kinship group; a military group may also be an age set, and the congregation of a fertility cult a cooperative labour unit. The group, even understood in a purely physical sense, is something that exists apart from and over and above such specified contexts of action. Any definition or description of groups must therefore account for these two facts—first, that groups operate through institutions, and second, that groups are also forms of social existence *per se*.[2]

A group, then, may be defined as a collection of individuals who stand in regular and relatively permanent relationships, that is, who act towards and in respect of each other, or towards and in respect of individuals outside the group, regularly in a specific, predictable, and expected fashion. The relationships making up the group are therefore visible only in the institutionalized modes of co-activity. The latter appear as the *rights and obligations* vested in or incumbent upon the individuals in virtue of their group membership, either as modes of action reserved for (or forbidden

---

[1] R. M. MacIver (1924), p. 155.

[2] The terms 'grouping' or 'group' may be taken to have a wider meaning than that of groups operating through institutions and firmly constituted like the latter. In other words, there may be 'groups' which are not 'institutionalized'. But again, there is no general agreement on the use of these terms. The following discussion will be mainly concerned with 'institutionalized groups'. But this is a clumsy phrase, and I shall instead speak simply of 'groups', unless there is the risk of confusion.

to) the members of the group, or as modes of action generally valid but typically modified when occurring between group members.

We shall make this definition more precise as we go along. But we can already see that a number of things follow from it. In our phraseology, the individual *cum* a series of rights and obligations is a 'person'.[1] A group is therefore composed of persons, and the person, always defined in terms of modes of action in respect of others, has its *locus* in the group. It is clear that an individual, as he may belong to different groups, will also be different persons; but some groups, as we shall see, operate through diverse contexts of activity, each implying a different series of rights and obligations, so that the individual may also be different persons in virtue of his membership of one group. Furthermore, since institutionalized rights and obligations, and the persons defined by them, are valid in a relatively timeless sense, the group has the same kind of validity, being independent of the concrete individuals who, at any given moment, are its members. Thus groups renew their human material in some manner, which poses the problem of their 'recruitment'.

When calling certain forms of observed behaviour 'rights and obligations' we assume of course that they have that meaning for the actors and that the behaviour follows from a definite contents of consciousness—some awareness of reasons and some expectation of demands. A group may therefore be said to be conscious of itself in that each actor is aware that he 'belongs' and that, in virtue of his belonging, he is entitled or required to act in a given way. The proverbial *esprit de corps* is only one, intensive and narrow, application of this awareness. There is nothing mystic or intangible about it; it is communicable in language; it is expressed in some formulated code or statutes governing group life; even the awareness of 'belonging' in the abstract takes tangible form in the terms and names which people have for their groups.

We already know about this importance of names. When we said before that they make groups visible, and now that they express the awareness of 'belonging', we were stating the same facts from different view points. The connecting link lies in the possessive use of group terms (*my* family, *my* people), and in the subjective use of group names (' I am an Englishman'). Let me add that I shall not otherwise distinguish between *terms* for types of groups and the

[1] See above pp. 92 ff.

proper *names* given to individual groups; in this context it is unnecessary to keep the two apart since in actual usage they prove interchangeable. It amounts to the same whether a person speaks of his people, his tribe, his clan, or says 'I am an Englishman', or Nupe, or Eaglehawk. In either case he indicates that a series of ways of behaving (the series implied in the 'shorthand' of the name or term) applies to him, and that, obviously, he is aware of it.[1]

But the names which people devise for their groups are not the only things that make them visible, and these other attributes of group existence may not tally with the evidence of names. The question arises whether there must be a name to make the group complete, that is, to entitle us to impute to the human aggregate in question the requisite consciousness of unity. This is clearly not so. It may simply not be important for the people to demonstrate their unity by the special pointer of a name if that unity is sufficiently visible in their co-activities or in their formulated codes and statutes; while, from the observer's point of view, these may offer sufficient evidence of the awareness of 'belonging'. There is one exception, however. In very large human aggregates, especially in those which we suspect to represent the widest kind of group (a people, nation, tribe), the name seems to be all-important. All-important for the people, since the unity of such wide aggregates is probably too tenuous to remain visible without a name; and certainly all-important for the observer, since across such wide units (if units they be) the co-activities are too diffuse and the statutes work too intermittently to evidence, by themselves, that awareness of belonging.

Let me leave this point for the present and turn to another aspect of the nexus between group existence and group name. If, for the observer, the names are pointers to a conscious group unity, they are also, for the people, a means of indicating and maintaining that unity *as they desire it to obtain*. In other words, the group name stands for the 'theory' and the 'believed-in norms' of acting, which pertain to groups no less than to institutions; and again, theory and

[1] The only difference lies in the knowledge required of the listeners. In the first case they must know the species of people, tribe, or clan which is being talked about; in the latter, that Englishman, Nupe, or Eaglehawk are names for a nation, tribe, and clan. Names and terms so used are therefore interdependent as well as interchangeable.

practice may conflict. We might, for example, be authoritatively told that everyone belonging to 'our group X' (a lineage, clan, or tribe) is of common descent; this would prove incorrect in fact, since individuals not fulfilling this requirement would yet be treated (and referred to) as members of group X. Thus the name would have one meaning when it is explained, and another when it is applied to the actually obtaining conditions. In cases such as this the theory is often saved, and the ambiguity cancelled, through accepting putative descent and spurious pedigrees. More importantly, there may be no theory to save. The ambiguity in the use of names may reflect an ambiguity in the 'obtaining conditions'; and the conflict will be, not only over the true meaning of a name, but over the privilege to bear it, and hence over the rights and obligations that shall go with the name. In Nupe country I found that the people of a certain district which had comparatively recently been conquered and incorporated into the Nupe kingdom, strongly maintained that they were Nupe, while the Nupe by extraction would refer to these newcomers disparagingly by their original tribal name and refuse to regard them as of equal status with themselves. The ambiguous nomenclature, the conflicting theory, and the uncertain boundaries of this widest group—a State growing by conquest and the absorption of alien peoples— thus all go together.

Finally, the users of names may themselves provoke the conflict. For they also meddle with the theory of names when it suits their book. People will say that the 'nation' must be protected against criminals, as though the criminals were not citizens of the nation; or that politicians of a certain persuasion are not 'true' Britons, Americans, Frenchmen, or whatever the case may be, even though, by the accepted criteria of group membership (birth, extraction, a passport), they have an undoubted title to that name. Yet the accusers would use the name so as to brand the accused as not-belonging, and the refusal to accord them the group name would indicate at least the inclination to refuse them the respective rights. Here, then, a group protects its believed-in norms through twisting the pointers that lie in names. Yet the accusers might be self-appointed or speak only for a section of the group, so that the clash of meanings reflects a struggle for supremacy, for the right to lay down what is 'normal' and what is not, and words become weapons wilfully used. Whether this is a case of a group *versus* its dissenters, or of groups changing their inclusiveness, or of groups divided—this can be decided only on the grounds of the attributes which any group must possess to be described as such.

We can now attempt to define them. They are (1) the principles whereby any group renews its human material, that is, whereby it is 'recruited'; (2) the contexts of institutional activity through which groups operate and are visible; (3) the factors making for the cohesion and endurance of groups; (4) the 'internal order' of groups, that is, the arrangement of relationships within them; and (5) the 'external order' of groups—the way in which groups are related with one another. When we describe groups, we describe all these features; together, excepting only the contexts of activity, they constitute the *structure* of groups.[1] In addition, we must also describe the prerequisite material conditions of group existence, namely, the numerical size of groups; their physical environment; and, more particularly, that sector of the environment in which the group habitually acts, that is, its 'locale'.

Little can· be said purely descriptively and in general terms about the material conditions of group existence. Their interrelation with the group structure, however, poses two special problems, which may here be briefly stated. The first concerns the relation between the endurance of groups and their numerical size, which appears to be such that there is an optimum size for groups of a given structure. If this optimum is exceeded or not attained, the group will cease to operate adequately; in the first case, it will be forced to subdivide in order to maintain its operations, while in the second it will be absorbed by another group or simply disappear as an effective unit. The progressive subdivision of lineages, clans or tribes, or the absorption and extinction of these and similar groups, are too familiar instances to need illustration. The second problem concerns the relation between the 'locale' of groups and their structure or, expressed differently, between their physical concentration and their 'social density' (Durkheim); it will be more convenient to deal with this point in a different context.

---

[1] The contexts of activity, bearing as they do on qualitatively defined purposes, cannot be included among the structural features if by 'structure' we mean an arrangement or pattern valid apart from qualitative data.

2. RECRUITMENT

All forms of groups are based upon some principle of recruitment whereby individuals are made members, that is, are made to assume the implicit rights and obligations. For the individual, then, these follow from his recruitment, both logically and as expected consequences. It is by this principle that groups maintain and renew themselves, and by this principle too, that individuals change into persons or add new 'roles' to those they already hold.

Groups form and renew themselves in the following manner. They may operate with *open* recruitment, so that individuals can join at will, for the purpose of participating in the group activities, as one joins a club or profession. Or groups may be *closed* in some degree, imposing conditions of entry, either special qualifications or at least some proof of the would-be member's ability to engage in the group activities.[1] We note that in open recruitment individuals are accepted *qua* individuals; while in closed recruitment the would-be member might be accepted only because he already is a 'person' in some other respect and hence the member of some other group—he might have to be a married man, a father, or belong to some profession, and so forth. Differently expressed, admission into a group would imply some pre-existing 'pointer relation'.[2] But in either case the admission itself will always be bound up with some 'pointer event', demonstrating that henceforth so-and-so is a member of the new group. This event may take the form of some ceremonial of admission or a simple obligation such as the payment of a fee; but this pointer event may be more than just this, namely, a consequence of the 'closedness' of groups, if the initiation is also a test, and ability to pay the fee a condition of entry.

Completely closed groups, in which the desire to join would play no part, are also *compulsory*, individuals who satisfy certain conditions being automatically recruited or drafted into the group, as one is born into a family or clan or conscripted into an army or age set. Completely open groups are rare. Most groups are more or less closed, and this difference of degree also enters into the conditions of admittance they entail. For these may either require *vested* qualifications, that is, attributes which the individual cannot alter, such

[1] Max Weber speaks in a similar context of 'open' and 'closed' relationships (1947), p. 127.

[2] See above p. 98.

as descent, sex, age, or other somatic properties (e.g. able-bodiedness), and partly residence; or they may rest on *contingent* qualifications, attributes that can be acquired, such as occupational skills, financial resources, aptitudes, or particular experiences. To some extent the division is fluid; residence can be changed; physical fitness may be acquired; groups based on descent may yet accept fictitious or spurious pedigrees; the required age will eventually be reached by everyone. Conversely, great wealth or some special aptitude might not be attainable by all. Even so, it is clear that the vested qualifications contribute to the 'closedness' of groups, while the contingent qualifications keep recruitment relatively 'open'. Fully closed groups mostly also operate with vested qualifications, but there are exceptions. The so-called Secret Societies of West Africa are often compulsory for any person (male and sometimes female) who disposes of certain financial resources; membership of craft guilds is compulsory even though the profession itself can be joined voluntarily. The 'closed shop' in our own society seems to represent an analogous case.

It is probably true to say that simpler societies lean towards compulsory, and complex societies towards voluntary, recruitment, which lends to the former their more static nature, and to the latter their greater mobility. Equally, primitive societies give wider scope to vested qualifications, especially to those of descent and age, than to contingent ones, while in modern societies the opposite is true.[1]

Although we listed common residence as a criterion of recruitment among others, it stands apart in several respects. To begin with, it is as ubiquitous as recruitment by descent, and as 'natural'. It is a truism to say that people always live in some form of local aggregation. The possibility to recruit them on such grounds is thus simply there. What is more important, certain kinds of co-activity presuppose a more or less permanent living-together, as family life presupposes a household; or follow from it, as collective self-defence follows from aggregation in a locality. Here, then, recruitment by residence is simply an implicit feature of the co-activity, one entailing the other.

Furthermore, common residence implies other things besides being a condition of group membership. For in the sense that

---

[1] Expressed somewhat differently, this point is made by Linton (1936), pp. 115 ff.

living-together in an area involves access to its resources, it amounts to a vital prerogative vested in the group. Groups defined by residence are thus also groups which exploit or occupy a territory by right; and the principle whereby they are recruited is also one of the purposes for which they are organized.

Finally, common residence in a sense also makes a group. Individuals living in proximity are by this very fact welded into some form of unity; they are bound to come into frequent contacts and to be faced with a variety of common tasks and problems of life, so that among them the awareness of belonging together, mutual familiarity, and mutual adjustment of behaviour will tend to arise spontaneously. Any such human aggregate thus forms a potential or emergent group, and we mean this emergent group character when we speak of communities or local communities.[1] When therefore living-together also forms a criterion of recruitment, a group-like arrangement is being acknowledged and utilized, rather than a group created e nihilo. It is 'acknowledged and utilized', that is, institutionalized, when the collection of individuals in the locality, in virtue of belonging to the same locality, also stands under rules of co-activity—economic, political, religious, and the like. It must be added that institutionalized groups, though they may not draw their members from some pre-existing local grouping, may shape them into one by causing them to live together in a defined locality, as craft guilds live in wards of their own in West African towns or age regiments are housed in special military kraals among the Zulu. Here living-together is not strictly a principle of recruitment, but an obligation following from it; even so, the spontaneously emerging group-like arrangement is utilized in building up the institutionalized group, that is, is added to the other forms of 'togetherness' which the group entails.

All these statements are true only within certain limits. When we spoke of living together in an area we assumed a human aggregation sufficiently close and compact to call forth regular collective contacts, the 'face-to-face' relations of which sociologists speak, and all the other features of intensive community life. This is clearly a matter of degree. The spontaneously emerging community

---

[1] The term 'community' is, of course, applied much more widely, referring to the sort of unity entailed in common religion, language, or culture in general. Even so, it always refers to some such 'emergent' group character, unless 'community' is understood merely as a synonym for 'group' (see below, p. 186).

character must vary with the dimensions of the locale and with the size and density of its population; equally, it will vary with the uniformity or diversity of the human material, in language, interests, and cultural background in general. Now, societies institutionalize local groupings of widely varying dimensions and make-up, being themselves the widest groupings of this kind. Yet when the 'locale' corresponds to a large territory inhabited by a tribe or a nation, perhaps internally divided by language or culture, it will no longer produce that spontaneous community character, and recruitment by residence will create a local group which is not also a potential group.

Here, then, mechanisms of association must make up for the loss of community character; techniques of communication will make the wide-range coordination of behaviour possible; an administrative machinery will enforce it; and idea systems will sustain the awareness of belonging together which can no longer spring from proximity and familiarity. Needless to say, this is true of all modern societies, which, by sheer technological efficiency, have become capable of extending far beyond the boundaries of community life. But it is true also, in some measure, of primitive societies. Though they may not possess the technical means for wide-range communication, nor perhaps an adequate administrative machinery, they achieve the same end by different means—through emphasis on common descent irrespective of local dispersal; through some myth holding the widespread group together; and perhaps also through the classificatory kinship terminology, whose effectiveness as a 'wide-range' system of relationships has been emphasized by Radcliffe-Brown.[1] But there are limits beyond which these mechanisms seem unable to work. For we find that widespread groups, even if they are firmly bound together, will yet attempt to utilize also the spontaneous unity which springs from physical proximity. This will be brought into play, on a more or less collective scale, only intermittently and for a brief space of time; but there will be periodical gatherings of a religious or political kind, all-tribal games and festivities, and the like. Thus certain institutions will be so

[1] See (1941), p. 8. In this context Radcliffe-Brown refers only to the fact that the classificatory kinship terminology includes 'a very large number of near and distant relations' in a few categories. But he has also shown how, for example in Australia, the 'wide range' system in this logical sense helps to maintain effective relationships between kinsmen normally physically separated.

designed as to foster something like a community and to make regular collective contacts possible where otherwise contacts would be irregular as well as sporadic. And we find, too, that groups so grown or scattered that collective contacts and familiarity become difficult, will tend to split into smaller units which can preserve their community character. Often, this process of fission will be gradual and at first unacknowledged, the large, dispersed group remaining the theoretical group, still bearing the common name, while the locally more concentrated segments will become the effective units. This is not only a question of expediency, in the sense that certain cooperative tasks are less adequately performed by a scattered group; rather, the very readiness to perform them will weaken. Thus the locally dispersed sections of a clan often disregard the rules of exogamy, since they have become 'like strangers,' or the duty of blood revenge, since one feels bound to avenge only persons one has known or whose injury is before one's eyes.

One is tempted to speak here of two types of grouping, or two extremes on the scale of human aggregation—one which reaches its optimum size and scatter at the boundaries of the spontaneous community and is driven to fission beyond that; and another which can expand beyond this boundary, by mechanisms of ever widening 'association'. We have spoken of the part which the technology of communication must play; yet this is not the only factor at work. There seems to be another factor also, which cannot easily be isolated, and which operates through the whole structural arrangement of a society, being embodied in some basic intention to live in such-and-such aggregate, and in no other. This intention is no doubt habitual, the structure expressing the habit, and both can be changed. But at any given moment one is simply given with the other, with the weight of a total trend, and descriptively nothing further can be said. However this may be, when we speak of primitive as against non-primitive societies we often mean this extreme variation in the optimum size and scatter of societies.

Some such total trend or intention can be exhibited also in another way. We have so far spoken of the effect of the 'locale' upon the community character of groups as though it were essentially fortuitous, groups being simply forced into a particular local dispersal or concentration, the locale then doing the rest. To some extent this is no doubt a true picture; groups are forced into this or that kind of aggregation by their size, their technology, the suitability of the environment for subsistence and settlement, or the need for self-protection from enemies. Yet these are not the only determinants. For we find that societies in much the same physical environment, living on the same technological level, and facing the same problems of subsistence or self-protection, will in one case live loosely dispersed, and in another in close concentration, in compact settlements of the village or city type. Again, in some such societies there would be no compact group larger than the homestead, housing an elementary family, while in others expanding families or kin groups would stay together. Once more, then, we must accept an intentional factor, effective over and above utilitarian motives. It would seem that groups simply choose a locale congenial to them, that is, congenial with regard to the intensity of contacts and relationships they desire to maintain in all or in certain spheres of activity. I suggest that this desire is not further reducible, that it is part of the social structure and given with it. Perhaps indeed, the puzzling nomadic 'mentality' is only an extreme instance of the same thing. At some point utilitarian motives and necessities will probably overrule this 'given' desire, but within limits the physical concentration of groups reflects a trend of grouping alone, a purely 'social' trend, if you like, and is to that extent autonomous.[1]

3. GROUPS AND INSTITUTIONS

We have held that groups operate and become visible through institutions. This statement requires correction in one respect. Groups also become visible, in a preliminary but important sense, through modes of action which are not fully institutionalized but have the diffuse and fluid character of customs and mores. I am referring to the rules of etiquette which are incumbent upon group members in their dealings with each other or outsiders, and which materialize in greetings, forms of address, and other characteristic gestures indicative of social 'belonging'. Closely allied are forms of dress or other symbols and badges of group membership, which again indicate the latter and so point to, or foreshadow, the kind of

[1] This view corresponds in some respects to Durkheim's concept of a 'social density', which presupposes a given 'volume' and 'material density' of populations, but does not follow from these; rather is the 'material density' an index of some autonomous trend towards a particular 'condensation de la masse sociale' (1902, pp. 237–9, 243–4, 250).

behaviour that may be expected of persons so distinguished. These forms of behaviour are all signs, indicators, and have no aim beyond that; they have that 'pointer' quality of which we spoke earlier on, and will serve as such, not only for the actors, but also for the observer, at least when he first attempts to find his bearings. Here, moreover, mutually adjusted behaviour, co-activity in the strict sense of the word, becomes attenuated to uniform activity or behaviour. But this uniformity retains one crucial aspect; in observing the prescribed rules of etiquette or dress the people understand that, in doing so, they follow the code or statutes of their group, and that their behaviour is intended to be distinctive of group membership. In other words, these purely formal, distinctive modes of behaving are yet conceived of as rights and obligations. I have elsewhere called them *diacritical*, to distinguish them from the rights and obligations which involve co-activity proper, and which may thus be termed (if by a *tour de force*) *syncretic*.[1] The clan offers perhaps the best illustration; clan food taboos, the clan name, certain ritual observances incumbent upon individuals and varying from clan to clan, are its diacritical characteristics; the duty of bloodfeud, exogamy, a funeral rite performed by the clansfellows, its syncretic characteristics.

It must be noted, however, that under certain conditions institutional co-activities proper might equally represent diacritical characteristics. For if in any society different modes of co-activity are valid in different sections, being thought of as 'apportioned tasks' of these sections, then the varying modes of co-activity also serve as diacritical rights and obligations.[2] Syncretic rights and obligations may thus turn into diacritical ones according to the compass of the group considered. The collective funeral rites or other ceremonials of clans (being syncretic in that unit) often vary typically from clan to clan, so that they are diacritical in the tribe at large.

The distinction between 'diacritical' and 'syncretic' rights and obligations need not concern us further. We turn now to institutions in the full sense of the word and to the part they play in the make-up of groups. In the preceding chapter we examined the various ways in which institutions are 'valid' for groups of any

---

[1] See (1950) p. 337.

[2] This is in a sense a restatement, from the point of view of groupings, of the 'sectional validity' of institutions. See pp. 121-2.

L

kind. The groups themselves we took to be independently defined by some principle of recruitment. We now know how groups are recruited. There remains the question how groups are distinguished by their manner of 'possessing' institutions or operating through them as through rights and obligations.

In the simplest case group and institution stand in a one-to-one relationship; the group operates through a single institution only, the modes of action implied in the institution being all that the group possesses in the way of rights and obligations. The group, therefore, is merely the personnel of the institution, in whose contexts of activity the group is alone mobilized, and whose purpose is the only basis for its appearance and duration. The coincidence of group and institution makes it difficult to assign different names to each so that we often use one word for both. Think of such examples as the congregation of a church or of a religious cult, the army, a savings association, or a board of directors. It will be seen that the institution in question is of the 'associative' type, and that its personnel corresponds to the kind of group commonly known as *association*.[1] Associations may be both 'open' and 'closed', and voluntary or compulsory, though the distinction is not always rigid, as in the case of religious congregations into which one is born but which one can also voluntarily join or leave.[2] The constitution of the group, its purpose, and the activities realizing it, are expressed in a body of rules, in a code or in statutes of some kind. It is these statutes that are summarized in the familiar 'if-situations' of anthropological accounts, for example: 'Every year, on such and such occasions, initiates of the cult X assemble in order to perform certain sacrifices believed to safeguard the fertility of the land.'

I have here assumed that the cult association X acts in a coordinated fashion, that is, shows itself to be a group, on no other occasion and in no other context of activity; or—to change the example—that the soldiers of an army behave according to the code of their group only in military activities; that the behaviour of a board of directors outside their specific directorial tasks betrays in no way their membership of that association. This is clearly not always true. To begin with, the rules of etiquette and other dia-

[1] See above, p. 120.

[2] In this use of the term 'association' I depart from MacIver, for whom 'associations' are *ex definitione* voluntary (see 1924, pp. 23–4, 1931, pp. 12–13).

critical rights and obligations implied in group membership may be meant to be effective also *vis-à-vis* 'outsiders' and in contexts of activity other than those for which the association is organized. Moreover, the attitudes and interests fostered in these contexts may fortuitously extend beyond them, overflowing, as it were, to other contexts, so that the initiates of a cult, the soldiers, or the directors on a board will be distinguished in their general bearing from persons not belonging to these groups. But if groups show more than merely such a diffuse or fortuitous extension of effects; if their statutes stipulate regular modes of action in diverse contexts, then two consequences follow.

First, the institutionalized activities will be such that they can be activated by several groups, the manner of actuation being modified as different groups are involved, with which point we shall deal later. Second, the groups themselves are now of a different kind. For here the association operates through (or 'possesses') a series of different institutions, realizes a number of purposes, and functions in different capacities. The large majority of institutionalized groups belong to this category of 'multi-purposive' associations. We may find, for example, that soldiers are, after their period of service, settled on the land in special colonies, so that membership of the army indirectly entails these particular economic activities; that the soldiers stand under particular rules of marriage, so that the army operates through this institution also; or that the soldiers enjoy certain privileges with regard to legal rights or to taxation, or must settle legal disputes between themselves by different methods than do civilians. In many European countries before the First World War, for example, officers had to resort to duels when ordinary civilians would go to court. In a different way the family is an instance of such multi-purposive associations; so is the clan, which is effective in marriage (through exogamy), in the legal sphere (through bloodfeud), also in ritual matters and often in land tenure or economic services. The State is a multi-purposive association of very wide dimensions, or of the widest dimensions when it is taken to correspond to that all-embracing group, a 'society'. Here, however, this must be added. Whenever we speak of institutions we imply, of course, that they exist in a society, so that this widest group by definition operates through and 'possesses' them all (as its culture). But this ultimate locus of all institutions we may take for granted and for the moment disregard.

The multi-purposive associations are, once more, both compulsory and more or less open to voluntary enlistment; again, the former kind seems to preponderate in primitive societies—think of the clan, the tribe based on common descent, age sets, or political units into which one is born; the latter kind is exemplified in the modern State, in which one can become naturalized; in the family, into which one can marry or be adopted; or any club or fraternity with a mixed programme, say, recreational, political, and mutual-aid. There may be cases in which the varying contexts of activity could be classified both as part purposes of the same institution or as diverse institutions—a point which we have already discussed. However this may be, in as much as any association realizes a series of purposes, it assumes certain characteristics not present, or not present to the same degree, in the single-purpose association. To begin with, membership in the former case amounts to sharing in a series of rights and duties meant to be activated in diverse if-situations. We can appropriately speak of these rights and duties as of collective assets and liabilities, and hence of an *estate* vested in or 'possessed' by the group and corporately by all members.[1] Nor is a multi-purposive association likely to be as transient as the simple association, organized for one specific purpose, might well be. Furthermore, the diverse activities in which the group engages will also, for purely practical reasons, make for a division of labour. In other words, certain persons will, in certain situations, act on behalf of the rest. The same is no doubt true of single-purpose associations which are large and engage in activities requiring specialized interests or skills. But I would suggest that multi-purposive associations are by their very constitution bound to operate more fully with such a division of tasks, which may be *ad hoc* or permanent, and will turn certain members into 'representatives' of the group or into some kind of 'executive'. Finally, the need to ensure the adequate functioning of so complex an organization will similarly make for the creation of a special 'administrative staff'. From these various points of view, then, the multi-purposive associations correspond to what are commonly known as *corporate* groups, and might be called by that name.

---

[1] The term 'estate' is here taken to refer not only to strictly material possessions (which single-purpose associations might also have) but to a plurality of rights and obligations of any kind. In using 'estate' in this wider sense I follow Radcliffe-Brown (1935, pp. 288–9).

In the simplest case the corporate group would act collectively in all the various contexts of activity, the same human aggregate being visible in each. Thus the same family group may collaborate in some productive task, in its ancestor cult, or in educational activities; or age sets would work together on the land, appear in a body at ceremonies, or form a military regiment. Here, then, the corporate group is *mobilized* in the diverse institutional activities and on the appropriate occasions. But the activities through which the group operates need not be of this 'associative' kind; they may be 'parallel' or 'sectional', so that different individuals would be the actors on different occasions and only part of the corporate group would be mobilized on each. Yet the corporate group would always be *involved*, in the sense that the manner of acting of the individuals would be understood to follow from their membership in that group and from its code. The distinction between 'involvement' and 'mobilization', however, depends to some extent on the compass of the group considered. Any appointed 'executive' (a police force, a judiciary, the clergy) will also form a narrower association, organized for a particular purpose, within the wider corporate group (a county, the State, the Church); when the former acts in a body, it will itself be fully mobilized, while only 'involving' the wider unit. The widest effective group, the society as a whole, is in this sense always involved (though rarely mobilized) since all modes of action of its members are understood to follow from the norms which make up its culture. Furthermore, 'involvement' may shade over into 'mobilization'; for the group whose code is translated into action by an executive might not only tacitly endorse it, but also take some active part, however diffuse—as when the general public shows its sympathies with the soldiers fighting its wars. These various instances seem all exemplified in the clan duty of bloodfeud; here the members of the victim's clan must, on some collective scale, avenge the death of their fellow clansman. Now the clan might be mobilized *in toto*; or neighbours or close kinsmen might act on its behalf, fortuitously or through being specifically chosen; the whole local community, moreover, may endorse this mode of action, not only through tacit approval and non-interference, but through actively aiding in this self-help, for example, through ostracizing both the assailant's group and the tardy avenger.

The last example brings us back to a point raised earlier on, namely, the fact that the same institution may be activated, and activated in a different manner, by different groups. Occasionally, a corporate group may possess an exclusive title to a particular social task (as when some tribal sport is 'reserved' for a certain age set). More often, the first alternative will obtain. This is too familiar a case to need illustration; think, for example, of the institution of Sunday rest, which members of the Church will observe in one manner, while other people will observe it in another, in virtue of their citizenship in a country having this observance, or perhaps in virtue of being members of a professional organization which adopted the observance for other reasons. There are, however, these important variants.

Once the institution is activated, the involvement or mobilization of different groups may be such that each is apportioned a particular share in the institutionalized task, in accordance with its several part-purposes. In the event of marriage, for example, the clans of the spouses will be involved inasmuch as the marriage is exogamous; their kin groups will be mobilized inasmuch as the brideprice must be paid jointly or other mutual obligations be fulfilled; and a religious congregation will be both mobilized and involved inasmuch as the union must be solemnized. Marriage, as we know, is a contingent institution; furthermore, the contingency (or 'if-situation') which brings the institution into play, and hence involves the respective groups, applies generally throughout the society. Stated in simplest terms, whenever anyone reaches a certain age the given procedure will follow. But in other contingent institutions this threefold relation between if-situation, institutionalized procedure, and the involvement of groups, may be more complicated. The same kind of contingency will bring different institutions (and groups) into play, or cause the same institutionalized procedure to be modified, as that contingency happens to affect or involve different groups; so that we have a double involvement of groups, both in the if-situation, and in the institutional response to it. Think again of bloodfeud; if the homicide occurs between two clans of the same local community, the institution 'bloodfeud' will ensue, mobilizing the two clans (wholly or partly) and involving the local community (in the manner described); if, on the other hand the homicide occurs within one clan, the institution 'expiation' will come into play, mobilizing or involving the clan and perhaps some special cult association. Or consider the system of land tenure in a certain primitive community. Here, if the member of a local family desires more land, he will receive it, apportioned outright, from the head of his family or kin group; but if the land is required by a stranger, he will receive it only against payment of a tithe or rent, and must address himself to the chief of the village or tribe, that is, to the representative of that group.[1]

To summarize. The relations between institutions and corporate groups seem to take these main forms: (1) the institutional activity is 'reserved' for particular groups; (2) the institutional activity is valid for the whole society but is modified for different groups; (3) the institutional activity is uniformly valid for the whole society but involves different groups (by means of an 'apportionment' of tasks) in its actuation; (4) the institutional activity is valid for the whole society, but is modified and also involves different groups in accordance with the involvement of groups in the if-situation.

In conclusion, we may consider certain difficulties of nomenclature which arise in the description of corporate groups. Usually we pick out one particular group activity and use it as criterion, referring to the remaining activities as though they were additional features. For example, we choose productive activity, and say that the labour team is also a family group, a mutual-aid association, and a ritual congregation; or we express this plural purposiveness by saying the family unit has such and such economic and religious aspects. What is actually meant is that one corporate group is mobilized or involved in all these institutional activities. Frequently criteria of different logical order are used, and it is said, say, of a political unit that it coincides with the clan or with the local community. Strictly speaking a statement of this kind means that a corporate group operating in the political sphere (among others) is recruited on the basis of descent or residence.

This inaccuracy cannot be entirely avoided since we obviously must call the group something and, unless we want to call it A or B, must give it a descriptive name reflecting one or the other aspect

---

[1] Whether we take these two examples to show the coming into play of different institutions or only of the same institution modified, will largely depend on our definition of the institution in question. We might, for example, call all methods of settling homicide one institution—in which case 'bloodfeud' and 'expiation' represent only modified procedures. Conversely, we might regard 'outright apportionment' and 'lease' as different institutions, and not as variants of 'land tenure'.

of its composition or functions. In the case of groups based on 'closed' recruitment, by 'vested' qualifications, the problem is a simple one, for here the principles of recruitment offer convenient and basic criteria. Thus we may speak of a territorial group which becomes the land-owning unit, the religious congregation, and the political community; or of a descent group which supplies the political organization. But let us not forget that the principle of recruitment is a 'basic' criterion only in the sense that it bears on the foundations upon which groups appear to be constructed. Equally, it is we who select it, on the ground of this relevance, so as to give the group a name, which fact does not enhance the relevance of the criterion we use. This is obvious enough, but confusions of this kind yet tend to arise. They arise, above all, in the case of recruitment by descent. Because we discover that a politically united group is also a kinship unit, we sometimes take this to mean an *ipso facto* more effective political organization; conversely, the absence of any basis of descent would by itself seem to detract from the effectiveness of groups. Perhaps because it is practically ubiquitous, certainly because it is natural, being rooted in biological facts, recruitment by descent tends to assume some intrinsic faculty and force, almost as though it partook of the mystic 'bonds of blood' of popular novelists.

I do not wish to deny that, in given cultural conditions, certain types of recruitment appear to lead to more effective group unity than others. When speaking of the spontaneous community character of 'local groups', we assumed some such connection. Again, recruitment by descent may strengthen a political or economic unit while different principles of recruitment may fail to do so. Indeed, since the continuity of groups, as we shall see, is coterminous with group existence; and since descent itself produces continuity, in a physical or biological sense; recruitment by descent seems to sustain groups more effectively than does any other form of recruitment. Yet groups which do not fully utilize the descent principle, or which cannot do so because, like the Australian aborigines or Trobrianders, they are unaware of the physiological facts of paternity, sustain their cohesion and continuity as effectively, by means of other principles of recruitment. Moreover, recruitment by descent, which must lead to ever widening groups, may also interfere with their effectiveness, for example, in economic pursuits, or exceed their optimum size for efficient integration. In brief, the greater efficacy of particular forms of recruitment rests, not on anything unalterable in their nature, but on the fact that they offer certain potentialities which can be exploited, such as the frequency of contacts, the permanence of relationships, or their bearing on continuity.

4. COHESION AND ENDURANCE

Here we are touching upon the very essence of groups, and upon the very essence of society itself—on the attributes which make a group a group and a society a society. Without cohesion we should have only multitudes of individuals, and without endurance, only fleeting aggregates. Linguistically, this fundamental aspect of unification, of 'groupishness', commands a series of substantives, all synonyms save for shades of meaning—cohesion, solidarity, integration; permanence and continuity express the same thing in terms of time, and stability or equilibrium by a physical analogy. Integration, which may stand for all these concepts, means operationally the observable enduring disposition of individuals in any given group to coordinate their actions closely towards each other or in respect of each other. It is meaningless to speak of integration unless it is understood to exist in degrees, which must be measurable and definable in quantitative terms. These refer to the strength and permanence of the relationships and, since relationships are merely shorthand for forms of co-activity, to the frequency and certainty of actions in the group.

We may, then, note these quantitative features: (1) the number of diverse action patterns into which the members of the group enter; (2) their frequency and regularity in the life span of the group and its members; (3) the scatter of any type of activity through the group; and (4)—a corollary of (3)—the exclusiveness of group activities, that is, the degree to which a given group activity scatters beyond the group. Let me make this clear by an example taken from my own field, the hill tribes of the Nuba Mountains.

A certain Nuba clan entails the following institutionalized action patterns. There is, first, the clan meal, which periodically but irregularly unites the members of the clan so far as its local dispersal permits; this communal meal takes place whenever any household in the clan can dispose of meat in any quantity. Secondly, certain ritual events become the occasion for similar but more large-scale gatherings, the main instance being funeral feasts, which happen, of course, irregularly, but which are attended by all or nearly all clan members, irrespective of the local dispersal. Thirdly, there is the obligation of exogamy; it represents a contingent but repetitive obligation, materializing in every marriage. It is also, essentially, a negative obligation; we may put it this way —the marriage union and all that it entails has a negative 'scatter' in the group, being excluded from it. Yet it has also a positive aspect in that it links, if only irregularly, the members of one clan with those of others and initiates a series of mutual rights and obligations (through brideprice, concern with the fate of the marriage, concern in the offspring, etc.). Finally, there is the obligation of bloodfeud in the event of homicide between clans. This involves the approval or aid of the whole community and mobilizes, in the clans concerned, every male member, often irrespective of local dispersal. But this contingency is not a frequent one, and may in fact not arise in the lifetime of every person. Together, these contacts and co-activities build up that total readiness to coordinate behaviour which we call clan loyalty or clan cohesion, and which may well diffuse or 'overflow' into other spheres of activity as well.

Now, it is easy to see that mere quantitative statements on the frequency or duration of these contacts and co-activities would only inadequately define the degree of integration that emerges from them. A qualitative factor is also involved, namely, the different emotional responses implied in the varying contexts. It can be taken for granted that individuals who share in a certain activity and and go through the same experience together derive from it some more or less lasting bond, some more or less compelling predisposition to coordinate their behaviour also in other contexts. Just how much this is the case, depends on the nature of the common activity and experience. Men who have gone through the war together will be bound to each other emotionally much more strongly than men who work together in the same office. Thus the emotional effect of sharing a clan meal is obviously less than that of taking part in a communal ritual or in the stirring scenes of a funeral. By the same token the integrative effect of the bloodfeud, though it may happen only once in a lifetime, can obviously not be measured by the yardstick of frequency, which would make clan meals rank higher in this respect. In assessing group integration, therefore, we must make psychological assumptions and judge the efficacy of different forces of experiencing. With this aspect we shall deal more fully in a later context.

Another difficulty arises from this observation. All group activities both foster and presuppose integration; they contribute to the bonds uniting the group, and make demands upon them. The fact that individuals share the emotional experience of a ritual undergone together or of bloodfeuds jointly pursued must forge the sentiments of clan loyalty. Yet the readiness to undergo these experiences together or for one another also presupposes these sentiments; clan loyalty must overcome such considerations as the risks entailed in bloodfeud, or the expense in time, effort or property involved in the attendance of funerals. The balance between clan loyalty and the demands upon it clearly varies; in the clan meal integration is mostly fostered, in the bloodfeud it is mostly presupposed. But we note this circle: the clan meal, though it does not draw heavily on group loyalty, also adds little emotional weight, while the bloodfeud, drawing heavily on cohesion and the sentiments of loyalty, also strengthens them.

In practice, this circle partly disappears. For the fostering of group loyalties is also entrusted to distinct regulative mechanisms.[1] Voluntary associations are in this respect self-regulating, since here the acceptance of the common purpose implies all the cohesion which the group possesses or needs. Elsewhere we find special regulative action patterns designed to maintain the group and to create or revive group sentiments. We find, firstly, mechanisms operating with physical constraint and sanctions, often entrusted to selected agents of the society, which are meant to prevent or correct any transgression of the group code. Secondly, there are the regulative influences of idea systems and forms of teaching. Here codes of honour are formulated, and pride in 'belonging' is implanted in the minds of the individuals. Such idea systems will tend to bear on every aspect of the group statutes, and the principle of recruitment is often singled out for special emphasis; the compulsory recruitment by descent or common origin, especially, will be buttressed by religious teaching or made persuasive by myths or quasi-history.

The positive effect of group loyalty has its negative corollary in barriers of some kind. The stronger the integration of a group,

[1] See Chapter VI, Section 6.

the more will it be cut off from others. The deeper the in-group loyalty, the more alien becomes the stranger. In the extreme case strong internal loyalty means readiness to suspect or despise all those who 'do not belong'. And this is true of groups of any compass, that is, also of groups within groups; so that here a new problem arises, of preserving a wider unity over and above the separateness of narrower units. It has often been noted that such internal cleavages (of creed, class, or descent) tend to disappear when the wider group—a tribe or nation—is gathered for some collective effort against external threats, especially for war. The hostility or antagonism of sub-groups are then sunk in the hostility that animates the group at large. This effect has been called a weakening of 'internal group barriers' consequent upon the greater rigidity of the 'external group barriers'.[1] Yet what occurs is not, strictly speaking, a change in the validity of pre-existing barriers; rather, new ones become valid, that is, a different kind of grouping comes into play, being mobilized for a new purpose and by a different criterion of recruitment. The question remains, why the new grouping, though relatively rarely mobilized on this scale, should prove so effective. Partly, it is the force and cogency of this overriding purpose (as the people are made to see it) which will carry the grouping and tend to make it self-regulating. One understands that this is a case of first things first, of collective fate and survival as against the self-interest of particular sections. But partly, I think, it is also the nature of the activity, with its high emotional charge, which, as I put it, fosters loyalties and cohesion as much as it draws upon them, so that war and collective violent actions themselves strengthen the group by which they are executed.

As we shall see, in this task of overcoming the internal cleavages for the sake of some wider unity societies can utilize also certain new integrative mechanisms—of 'consociation', 'symbiosis', and of the transference of loyalties. Even so, one kind of cohesion must be balanced against another. That this is no easy task we know full well. Loyalty that shall not become intolerance; patriotism that shall not turn into contempt for other nations or races—these are only too often the tools of a sorcerer's apprentice.

[1] See J. F. Brown (1936), p. 76.

5. INTERNAL ORDER

We have so far dealt with the simple issue of 'belonging' and 'not-belonging', and of 'in-group' *versus* 'out-group'. We now turn to the varying positions occupied by group members relative to one another. This internal order of groups, then, is constituted by the differential rights and obligations of persons. They could be considered qualitatively, as such-and-such actions materializing between such-and-such persons. Kinship systems, for example, are often described in this manner—in terms of the concrete modes of behaviour valid between parents and children, between siblings, between blood relations and affinal relations, and so forth. This kind of approach gives us only an inventory, but not yet an 'order'. We arrive at the latter when we view the differential rights and obligations, not with regard to the concrete, qualitatively defined contexts of activity in which they materialize, but as mere 'positional values', fully abstracted from the former.[1] As a first step, we could consider only the mutual relationships of persons and express them in terms of the equal or unequal command two individuals have over each other's actions; here we might distinguish, with Radcliffe-Brown, between symmetrical and asymmetrical relationships. We can clearly go beyond pair-relationships and construct an order of this kind for the whole multiple network of relationships obtaining in any group, so that each group member would be seen to occupy a graded position in that order. Nor is it only we, the observers, who take this step; the actors equally view their groups as such embracing arrangements of positional values. We mean these when we speak of power, authority, status, rank, and prestige.

'Power' and 'authority' indicate once more an individual's command over the actions of others or, as a corollary, his own freedom of action. There is, however, a subtle distinction of meaning between the two terms. 'Power' might be taken to refer to an 'unexpected' command over the actions of others, that is, to a command not thought of as a right but rather as a *de facto* use of resources, of any kind—physical, economic, based on belief, and so forth; while 'authority' is always 'expected' and *de jure*. Status, rank, and prestige are not strictly co-terminous with power and authority. More precisely, status and so forth need not imply a

[1] See above, pp. 81–2.

greater (or lesser) amount of power or authority all round, so that individuals of superior status would, in their group, command more than they are commanded and have more numerous rights than they have obligations. Rather, status often rests on some specific command over the actions of others, which happens to be highly valued, or on some specific right, which may only signify access to enjoyments appreciated by all. Greater prestige, higher rank or status may even entail more numerous obligations and weightier responsibilities, and so lesser freedom of action, though these too would by common consent be desirable and worthwhile things. Finally, we shall normally count among these worthwhile things also greater social insight, the fuller knowledge of the working of society which is open to individuals in certain capacities, and which may or may not go hand in hand with actual command. Whenever we speak of status and the rest, then, we assume to begin with some such scale of worthwhileness; we accept the fact that different modes of action or experiences are differently valued and that the varying individual chances of participating in them are taken to mean an unequal access to existing benefits.

The situation is complicated by the fact that many of these benefits are symbolic, that is to say, that they only signify the entitlement of individuals to some other benefits, but do not convey them in fact. It is not easy to distinguish between 'symbolic' and 'real' or intrinsic benefits. The right to wear a certain kind of dress may be of the latter kind if in the group in question the dress has a certain aesthetic appeal or is considered to be particularly comfortable; yet the right to wear the dress may, like the right to expect a certain kind of salute, merely indicate that the individuals so entitled are also entitled to the obedience, loyalty, or the services of others on given occasions, or to some specified enjoyment not open to others. Again, once the sign nexus is established, the symbol will by itself be a source of enjoyment—for example, when we are respectfully greeted by others. Finally, the symbolic benefits might be acquired vicariously, *in lieu* of the 'real' benefits to which they point, the latter being less easily attainable. That people thus often take the shadow for the substance goes without saying; in other words, they strive for and parade 'diacritical' signs denoting a particular position in the internal order of groups without actually procuring it.

Now, status, prestige, and rank are almost household words and thus loosely used. Any sharper formulation is bound to be arbitrary in some respect. In support of the definitions here proposed I can only say that they seem to me to be the most consistent as well as useful. By status I shall mean the rights and obligations of any individual relative both to those of others and to the scale of worth-whileness valid in the group.[1] Like group membership as such, status is understood to be relatively enduring. But it may be more or less so according to the principle of recruitment on which status, like group membership, always rests. Thus recruitment to status may follow from vested qualifications such as descent, age, or sex, so that the status is more or less rigidly 'ascribed' to the individuals satisfying these conditions; or status may rest on contingent qualifications—aptitudes, achievement, experience—being 'achieved', and hence also changeable.[2] Equally, there are transitional forms of recruitment, as when a certain status, though not automatically ascribed to males or to individuals of a certain descent, is open to them only. Inasmuch as a group operates with ascribed status it is rigid and static; in the opposite case, it possesses mobility and implies competition.

'Rank' is a more highly formalized version of status. Here each step on the positional scale is sharply defined by formalities of admission and promotion, and the whole scale is made conspicuous by a series of 'diacritical' characteristics—titles and other symbols, rules of etiquette, and so forth. 'Prestige' I take to mean a more fluid version of status. Prestige is no doubt one of the vaguest terms used in sociological description. It always refers to some acquired preeminence of individuals over one another, and to some acquired command over one another's actions; but often one cannot help feeling that the term conveniently hides the writer's reluctance to commit himself as to the precise nature of this preeminence and command. The term is useful, however, if its vagueness is intended to reflect the vagueness of the social situation. For all societies make use of such unspecified forms of preeminence, voluntarily and

[1] It will be seen, I think, that 'status' so understood is not merely an unnecessary duplication of the term 'person'. Both terms mean the individual *cum* his rights and obligations; but they imply different viewpoints and levels of abstraction, 'person' referring to rights and obligations understood qualitatively, as such-and-such actions undertaken in such-and-such conditions, 'status' to rights and obligations compared and reduced to 'positional values'. As commonly used, 'status' implies both, e.g., married status, professional status, and superior or inferior status. Linton uses 'status' in this double sense (see p. 93 above).

[2] The terms 'ascribed' and 'achieved' status are borrowed from Linton (1936), p. 115.

diffusely accorded to individuals. Prestige, so understood, would be visible in the deference shown to an individual, in the readiness of others to support him in varying ways, to take his advice, imitate his example, or merely express their admiration or approval. Prestige is thus in a sense not-yet-status, being less formalized, perhaps more fortuitously acquired, and implying a more 'unexpected' command over the actions of others, that is, being less *de jure*. Prestige may operate in a supererogatory fashion, adding to (or detracting from) the preeminence implicit in status. We should say, for example, that a Kwakiutl noble gains prestige if he lavishly performs the 'privileged obligation' of potlach which goes with his status, though he would not by this act alter his 'statutory' privileges; or we should speak of a chief losing prestige through behaving in an unconventional manner. Through granting or withholding prestige, then, societies take care of variations in behaviour which are not important enough to cause changes in status. Again, prestige may be understood to go hand in hand with status, as when we speak of priests or old men having great prestige in this or that society. Always, however, we take it that the influence of prestige, unlike that of status, is not visible only in specific contexts of activity but, as it were, 'overflows' to others.

The scale of worthwhileness which underlies the grading of status and prestige may be said to have a zero point; in a sense, it also has its negative grades. They refer perhaps not so much to intrinsically objectionable actions as to the illegitimacy of their circumstances—to the behaviour of criminals or abnormals, and to all serious deviations from a group code. The individuals who act in this fashion do not place themselves outside society by their actions; nor are they necessarily excommunicated from the group against whose code they offend. They are and remain 'persons' (the offender, the criminal) in the sense that their manner of acting is expected and fitted into accepted relationships; but their behaviour is not 'trusted' to occur, and they are such 'persons' by default and not by any right or obligation. Measured against the position of others, theirs is a 'degraded' position in the strict sense of the word; and punishment, whatever the concrete deprivations it imposes upon the culprit, to a greater or lesser extent always also publicizes his degraded status. Equally, it may formalize it, through withdrawing from the culprit rights and prerogatives which would normally be his due.

There are, however, exceptions or borderline cases. For actions enjoined upon the members of one section of the society, as their rights and obligations, may be regarded as crimes by all others. Yet since that section and its code are constituted, and hence recognized, within the body of the society, the criminal actions are themselves recognized modes of action, that is, licensed or condoned in some way. Thus age sets are sometimes expected (and 'trusted') to be thieves, and young men or soldiers to be Lotharios; indeed, they may gain prestige by these actions, and though they would be punished if caught, this does not contradict the approval of illegitimacy. The punishment is still worthwhile, a price paid for preeminence, or at least a justifiable risk. That actions legitimate in one section of the society, by its code, might be illegitimate in another, needs no emphasis. Nor need we ask ourselves what advantages are balanced against what disadvantages when a society permits conflicting group codes of this kind. But there must be some such balancing, for in cultivating a particular *morale* or efficiency in one section of the society it may not be possible to prevent a clash with the interests of others. It is this conflict which is resolved or at least kept within workable limits through including even illegitimate actions in the scale of worthwhileness.

The negative or degraded status of offenders is clearly not confined to one particular group or context of behaviour, but spreads throughout the society in accordance with the severity of the offence; as I have suggested, this publicizing of infamy is one of the essential aspects of all forms of punishment. Of prestige, too, we have said that it 'overflows' from the context of activity in which it is acquired to others. Status and rank, however, we understood to be valid only in a given group and for the contexts of activity through which that group operates. Now, in the case of completely separate groups, whose human material does not overlap, the diverse status arrangements are simply not comparable; the 'superior' position of a family head and the 'inferior' position of a common soldier can plainly not be measured on the same scale, unless both persons belong to an embracing group in which they are assigned positions relative to one another. The same individual will often belong to different groups in which he holds different status, high in one and low in another; again, the two cannot be assessed in common terms, nor can we calculate a mean status, though it might be true that the high status in one group adds to the

M

prestige of the individual in the other. In corporate associations, operating through diverse contexts of activity, status may even vary with these. Thus in a village community which acts collectively also in religious ceremonies, the chief may be a leader in political matters but only one of the congregation in religious ones; and in an extended family the grandfather may have authority in religious affairs, while a younger man leads the labour team. Again, the prestige that goes with chieftainship or old age may 'overflow' into the other activities, so that the advice of these men will yet be asked and their judgment accepted.

The question arises if status does not equally 'overflow' in some way, so that we could speak also of a total or over-all status of individuals in their society. I doubt if this concept is useful, at least in complex and differentiated societies. Admittedly, we often refer to such a Status writ large; but we mean, in reality, not a sum total of statuses, or a resultant status, but status in the widest relevant group. And this is usually the politically effective corporation, so that Status means political status—an individual's command over political actions or privileges.

When a society is divided into large aggregates of individuals who share, in relevant respects, the same status and are marked off from other such aggregates by different status, we speak of social strata. When the uniform status in each stratum is rigidly ascribed on the grounds of descent, we speak of *castes*; where the uniform status is based on acquired qualifications, so that there is mobility between the strata, we speak of *social classes*. Let me explain the proviso 'in relevant respects' contained in the first sentence. Clearly, the various age groups in a society, or the two sexes, may also be collectively differentiated by status; yet we should not in that case speak of social strata. The relevant difference of status must therefore cut across physiological differences and attach to the species 'human being'. Nor are all the forms of behaviour in which status becomes visible equally significant. To begin with, the uniformity of status within the social stratum is only of a rough and approximate kind; in other words, we take a certain equality in rights and obligations to override other, less relevant, inequalities. The same is true of the unequal status of diverse strata. If, for example, all the people in the society have equal access to certain recreational activities, to aesthetic enjoyments, or to religious observances, but are unequally entitled to political command or legal protection, or unequally capable of safeguarding their subsistence, we should presumably consider the inequalities more relevant than the equalities. Often the various aspects of status will appear combined in some unequivocal fashion; yet if they are not, power and authority would seem to be more relevant criteria of social stratification than the varying access to other commonly valued benefits, so that political status and wealth would count above all.

Of the numerous questions bearing on class structure I propose to examine only this—when and how far do social classes represent institutionalized groups? Social classes satisfy the conditions of institutionalized groups if they involve some co-activity mobilizing all members (and predominantly only members)—such as intermarriage, economic collaboration of a certain kind not occurring between the classes, religious duties or privileges and so forth. Social classes are still institutionalized groups, even in the absence of co-activity proper, if the manners of acting in the different classes are understood to be typically and intentionally different, that is, if they represent for the actors 'diacritical' rights and obligations; and these may take various forms—of occupations, customary pursuits, standards of living, or of diffuse conventions of etiquette.[1] If on the other hand the diverse manners of acting in the social classes merely reflect fortuitous capabilities or shortcomings, and are not part of a conscious code, then the social classes are only 'quasi-groups', however clearly the differential behaviour is understood as a graded access to generally valued benefits.

The emphasis is on 'graded access'; for not all the differential modes of behaviour present in society are of this kind. A good many are observed without such implication, merely as different manners of acting which happen to obtain in one section and not in others— such as food habits, fashions of dress, or customary recreations. The 'high tea' of the lower middle classes, the 'Sunday best' of peasants, or the different public of 'soccer' and 'rugger' are instances familiar from English society. If only this kind of differential behaviour is present, we have no longer social classes, but merely cultural divisions within the society. Expressed differently, such cultural differences form the basis of social classes only when

---

[1] It will be seen that castes are in this sense always institutionalized groups since the rigid recruitment by descent imposes at least one embracing co-activity—endogamy or near-endogamy—and since here 'diacritical' behaviour is strongly pronounced.

the actors are conscious of them as of unequal rights and obligations, resented and perhaps assailed by the lower strata and
jealously defended by the higher. Thus the dual aspect, 'subjective'
as well as 'objective', of all social phenomena holds good here also.
However, one viewpoint may obtrude upon the other. For the graded
access to existing benefits is often merely inferred by the observer
on the grounds of some 'objective' scale of this kind. He might, for
example, assess different standards of living in the society in terms
of the unequal chances of comfort, ease, or security they seem to
offer, and accordingly speak of social classes; yet subjectively, no
such conception might exist—at least at the time. Whether under
such conditions a true class structure is not potentially present or
in an incipient stage, I will not decide.

6. External Order

Social strata, on their graded levels, merge in an embracing
group—the nation or tribe, or whatever the nature of that entity,
the 'society as a whole'. So do 'sections' or 'segments' on the same,
as it were, 'horizontal' plane. All groups exist in a similar order of
inclusiveness (or 'compass'), narrower groups merging in wider
ones. If, then, we mean by the 'external order' of groups the order
or pattern exhibited by their interrelations, we seem to be throwing
together at least two different things—relations between groups of
widest compass, that is, 'societies', and relations between groups of
narrower compass, that is, 'sub-groups' of some kind. But as we
shall see, the interrelation of societies takes in many respects the
same form as that of sub-groups; moreover, the large majority of
inter-group relations occurs within societies; and finally, the interrelation of sub-groups cannot be examined without reference to the
wider or widest group within which they occur. So much for the
appropriateness of this section heading. We are, however, guilty
of a terminological inaccuracy; for the 'external order' of sub-groups
might well be called the 'internal order' of the embracing group;
but this inaccuracy is unlikely to lead to confusion.

If we pick sub-groups at random, they might well turn out to be
disparate groups, differing in compass, in their methods of recruitment, as in their contexts of activity, such as the army, a golf club, a
religious congregation, or a board of directors. Between such groups
there may be no relations, save the one that they all merge some-

how, once more in random fashion, in an embracing wider or widest group. If these sub-groups share the same human material, they do so accidentally. On the other hand, sub-groups of dissimilar compass, recruitment, and activities may yet be so planned that their human material overlaps in some definite fashion, so that they are in this sense interrelated. We shall presently discuss this 'planned' overlapping—e.g. of age sets meant to cut across families or clans, or of cult associations meant to unite local communities. Yet other sub-groups are similar in compass, based on the same principle of recruitment, and concerned with the same kind of activities; they are, as it were, different species of the same *genus*. Such groups are mostly mutually exclusive as regards their human material—such as the different clans or craft guilds which exist in a tribe, the religious orders or sects of a church, or the castes and social classes of a stratified society. We must add that this mutual exclusiveness may be true only at a given moment, and that individuals might be able to change their membership, moving from one group to another, in accordance with given rules of adoption and mobility.

There are probably a great many other ways in which sub-groups can be compared and placed in some order. But we shall be concerned only with the last category of comparable and mutually exclusive groups. For they exhibit a special feature, which bears relevantly on the nature of social solidarity. They do not simply merge in a wider group, least of all in the society as such, but help to build it up. Often, too, they reach that widest compass by means of a hierarchical structure, being arranged in an order of progressive inclusiveness, as lineages, for example, build up clans, and clans build up a tribe, or as several village communities form a district, and several districts the State. This process, however, of building up the wider group may be more or less complete. Certain of the sub-groups mentioned *combine* to form the next wider unit in the sense that the latter contains no human material other than that recruited in its component groups; thus clans make up a tribe, sects a church, castes a society, and village communities a district. In other words, these are subdivisions which are not only mutually exclusive but also exhaustive. Craft guilds, on the other hand, do not make up a tribe, but are merely of it; religious orders do not make up a church, whose compass is much wider; even social classes might not 'combine' to form the stratified society if there are

also persons or groups of persons of indefinite status. It seems expedient to distinguish these two kinds of subdivisions by calling
those which are exhaustive 'segments', and those which are not,
more non-committally, 'sections'.[1]

Now, the interrelation (or 'external order') of sections or segments appears to take three main forms. (1) The sub-groups
simply co-exist, in a repetitive fashion, within the embracing group.
Think, for example, of a tribe divided into a number of sub-tribes
or extended families; these àll duplicate each other, both in their
structure and their modes of action; each is relatively self-contained,
and such relations as obtain between them (intermarriage, economic cooperation, and so forth) do not follow from their constitution
(their 'statutes'), but are contingent upon circumstances and outside interests. Though such segments may in fact 'combine' to
form the society at large, they could exist without each other
and in any number; one could add to or subtract from it without affecting the working either of each segment or of the
embracing group. We might, with Durkheim, call this a 'segmentary structure', and the solidarity it possesses a 'mechanical
solidarity'.[2]

(2) The segments or sections are coordinated in a determinate
fashion, duplicating each other only in their structure, while their
modes of action differ characteristically, being more or less complementary to one another. That is to say, the relations between
them are conceived of as necessary and even as preordained, and
their respective activities as tasks so-and-so apportioned for the
common weal. One cannot add to or subtract from the number of
segments without endangering the carefully balanced coordination
and interdependence. This is Durkheim's 'organized' structure,
leading to 'organic solidarity'.[3] There are, of course, degrees of
this coordination; any division of labour or any series of age sets
exhibits it in some measure. But let us here consider only its most
intensive form, in which the interdependence has some character
of compulsion or of a believed-in necessity, and in which the

---

[1] The same kind of sub-group may be a segment in one society and a section
in another. In tribes where every individual permanently belongs to one or the
other age set (e.g. among the Kikuyu), the age sets correspond to segments. In
tribes where adults cease to belong to the age sets (e.g. in Nupe), these correspond
to sections.

[2] (1902), pp. 85–98.

[3] Ibid., Chap. VI *et passim*.

interdependent sub-groups represent segments, dividing the whole society. Clan exogamy combined with tribal endogamy, which makes each clan dependent upon all others with regard to marriage and hence biological continuity, is an approximation to this 'organic' solidarity; it is fully attained in forms of exogamy which also include marriage classes or moieties. It is visible, too, in the Pueblo and other clan systems entailing close ritual interdependence, religious beliefs providing here the background of compulsion. The organic solidarity appears combined with social stratification where caste divisions similarly rest on apportioned rights and obligations, all of which are conceived of as vital to the existence or well-being of the society.

In a different context I introduced the term 'symbiotic' to express this close, subjectively absolute and unalterable, interdependence which causes 'every section, as section, to assume specific duties (religious, political, etc.) on behalf of the community at large, i.e. on behalf of every other section.[1] Let me here comment on the relation between symbiotic and diacritical behaviour. As we have said, any 'apportionment' of tasks to the group segments also may be diacritical in that it serves to mark them off from one another.[2] But it must be stressed that purely formal differences in behaviour between segments shade over into differences which have symbiotic importance. Thus the Nuba clans are distinguished by the varying ritual procedures which they must follow, e.g. at funerals; each clan, moreover, stands under particular food taboos, which vary from clan to clan. These, then, are clearly 'diacritical' characteristics, and in some instances they are no more. Yet certain of these observances are also thought to involve the well-being of the whole tribe, so that their neglect would cause disaster, while their faithful performance would contribute to the common weal. Indeed, the whole universe is thought of as being controlled by the segments severally, that is, by the behaviour apportioned to, as well as distinctive of, the segments making up the society.[3]

Whether symbiotic arrangements are an outcome of internal differentiation or of the coalescence of diverse and possibly alien

---

[1] (1938), 85, and (1947), p. 9, n. 2. I should now say 'segments' instead of 'sections'.

[2] Equally, it may be 'syncretic', if the task apportioned to any one segment implies some coordinated action on its part—a communal ritual, a group dance, or some other cooperative effort (see above, p. 157).

[3] S. F. Nadel (1947), pp. 189-90, 207-8.

groups, is a moot question. They might well be either. We have, however, sufficient historical evidence to suggest that the latter process has often taken place. Social symbiosis, therefore, is also a mechanism for overcoming heterogeneity through recognizing it and for balancing divergent and even antagonistic interests through embodying them in an 'apportionment' of sectional tasks.[1] Which brings us to our next point.

(3) The segments or sections, finally, may oppose each other in some form of regular conflict, antagonism, or competition. Thus the sects of a church are rarely self-contained groups, content with side-by-side existence, but would each claim an exclusive title to the true creed; kin groups such as dynasties will compete for political power; social classes compete almost *ex hypothesi* for the rights and obligations existing in the society at large. This uncertain, dynamic relationship may be just that—a struggle of sections for supremacy, that is, for the power to dictate the character of the embracing group; and this struggle may be decided by force, or suppressed by means of force and sanctions (as in the 'power state'). Yet equally, these conflicts may be absorbed, more or less successfully, in the embracing group; at least, there will always be efforts on the part of that wider group to maintain its unity by means more subtle (and less expensive) than coercion. In some measure, as we know, all groups of wide compass must face problems of this kind since their component groups, themselves possessed of internal solidarity, will tend towards mutual estrangement and perhaps antagonism. Thus specific regulative mechanisms will aim at establishing some overriding common purpose (say, patriotism) over and above the purposes animating the sections (say, the class struggle). Or groups differently recruited will bridge the cleavages between segments; age sets will cut across families, ritual associations across local communities, affinal relationships across clans. No society is without this kind of bridgework whereby a human aggregate broken up into certain groups is brought together in others. Again, there may be mechanisms aiming, not at spiriting away the antagonism, but at controlling and stabilizing it. Let me mention only one instance, familiar from many primitive societies —the 'privileged insults' implied in the so-called joking relationship. It is utilized mainly between classes of kinship relations between which for various reasons tension and antagonism are

---

[1] I described a development of this kind in (1949), pp. 183–6.

likely to arise; but it serves also to 'ally' or 'consociate' potentially hostile yet interdependent communities, or political factions within the same community.[1] The problem of 'consociation' may finally be resolved through the suggestion (or simulation) of a symbiotic relationship that would absorb the sectional conflicts. Suggestion and reality must here flow into each other; for an interdependence believed in is an interdependence effective; what counts is the persuasiveness of the belief. Plato, the prophet of a 'closed society', spoke of the 'noble falsehood' which the founders of his ideal State must invent so that its citizens, rulers and ruled, shall be content with their place in life and see in it a supreme necessity, a division of tasks willed by the gods.[2] Many societies, primitive and modern, live by some such myth or ideology.

We have spoken of these integrative efforts as though they belonged in some peculiar way to the embracing group, as opposed to its sections or segments. This was clearly a loose way of speaking; for the embracing group, or the 'whole society', cannot be anything more than the sections and segments which build it up. The question therefore arises: Where do these efforts at unity reside? Often, we meet with a special governing body disposing of the means of force and administering the regulative mechanisms; and this may consist of a separately recruited group section claiming authority over and responsibility for the embracing group—a ruling class, some form of social *élite*, or some college of political Platonists. Or such governing bodies may be composed of individuals coming from the various sections or segments, who would occupy their official positions without ceasing to be members of the component groups—elders, councillors, or other appointed spokesmen. Here, then, the embracing group maintains itself through persons who are at once representatives of the sections and agents of the embracing group, and who possess that wider social insight of which we spoke on previous occasions. Nor need that wider social insight pertain only to appointed persons; it may be diffused through the sections, being merely the knowledge of their constitution as it is embodied in codes and statutes. The separateness of the sections

---

[1] See A. R. Radcliffe-Brown (1940); the terms 'alliance' and 'consociation' are borrowed from that paper (p. 207); M. Griaulle (1948); S. F. Nadel (1939), pp. 396–7.

[2] *Republic*, Book III, 414.

and the identity of the wider group would both be accounted for in these codes and statutes, and in them alone. Every person would be an agent of both; it is his awareness of 'belonging' and his belief in the appropriateness of the social arrangement (its 'symbiosis' or 'consociation') that would make the embracing group.

Let me for a moment return to the merging of narrower in wider groups. In the case of coordinated or antagonistic groups this process remains in a sense incomplete; for the group of narrow compass will preserve its identity, and individuals will be expected to fit into the framework of the embracing group still as members of the narrower group. Thus a clansman will act as such in a great many tribal activities; the members of a religious sect will remain separated in the body of the church; and social classes are at least often accused of acting from class interest even on national issues. In the case of other groups, comparable or disparate, the merging may amount to absorption; the narrower group loses its identity completely and the individual enters the wider group as an individual, or as a new person. Thus families or professional groups are absorbed in the nation, as are certain age sets in the tribe. It is probably true to say that primitive societies tend to carry the segmentation through the whole social structure while our society leans towards complete absorption. However this may be, inasmuch as groups merge into one another, and so share their human material, they can utilize an important mechanism of social integration, namely, the transference of loyalties, loyalties formed between individuals in the narrower group remaining effective in the wider group. Thus people who have passed through the same age sets, who are bound together by kinship ties, or belong to the same religious congregation or the same social class, will preserve the loyalties fostered there when acting as members of the embracing group, say, the tribe or nation. Often, these transferred loyalties establish only random zones of 'belonging', irregularly dispersed through the wider group. Or they may be utilized more specifically, as when the military bodies of a tribe are recruited from age sets, clans, or some other pre-existing association, or when a bureaucracy is recruited from the same social class.

The transference of loyalties is not merely an integrative mechanism discovered and named by the student of the society; that it is present also to the actors is shown by the fact that they themselves employ suggestions of this kind. Thus it will be claimed that the State is rooted in the family, or that it is a model of the family, headed by a 'father' who paternally rules over men who are all 'like brothers'. This is a play on the similarity of loyalties rather than their transference in the sense here understood. Yet some transference there is, if only of concepts and of ways of looking at things. Undoubtedly, certain relationships and disciplines valid in the family can be held up as akin to those effective, or desired to be effective, in the State, and the awareness of one can be made to merge with the awareness of the other. In this sense, and perhaps in this sense only, is it true to say, as so many have said, that the State or nation rests on the family.

Here, then, the concept of loyalty as such, the very consciousness of group membership, is susceptible of 'transference'. And this process also operates, almost automatically, in another sense. The individual who is strongly aware of the disciplines and aims imposed upon him through his group membership (of any kind) will project the same awareness upon all other individuals he meets. They will be to him, not Tom, Dick and Harry, but members of a particular group, a faction or class, and exponents of the modes of behaviour valid in these groups. Within the same society, where the overlap of human material and the chances of contact play across group barriers, this identification of individuals with their group remains incomplete; on the boundaries of the widest group, where such links might well cease, it is absolute. As a society, a self-conscious class, a party, creed or nation, impress upon their members the paramountcy of group existence, so they induce them to view individuals outside in a similar light. The corollary of in-group solidarity, estrangement from all who do not 'belong', merges with the ready equation individual-group. Together they throw up the conventional stereotypes, the summary statements on national character, and summary falsehoods about group mentality, which are the blinkers of individuals and the weapons of the group.

7. Society as a Whole

We turn to our final questions: What is the nature of that widest group, referred to at every step, which we call a 'society', a 'whole community', or the 'group at large'? And where lie its boundaries? Paradoxically, though every anthropologist (or sociologist or historian) starts with a more or less definite idea about the society or societies he proposes to study, it is extremely difficult to state precisely, in general terms, what constitutes a society. For all practical purposes this difficulty may seem negligible, if it exists at all. Thus in the case of small island communities or peoples in some other fashion physically separated from their neighbours the extent of their societies will hardly be in doubt. In other situations we could at least set out with some rough and ready criterion, say, common language or political allegiance, planning to refine it as we go along. Or we might perhaps follow some existing convention of calling a certain population, known by a certain name, a 'people' or 'tribe', and equate these terms expediently with 'society'. Yet when we attempt to analyze our terms and to give them a validity not depending on chance conditions or expediency, the obviousness of societies soon disappears.

Like all assessments of group existence that of 'widest groups' must be true both 'subjectively' and 'objectively'. We must imply the people's awareness of belonging, as it is expressed, above all, in names and verbal statements on being 'one' people, tribe, nation, and so forth; so that the widest group must be a group proclaimed. And we must imply also the practical consequences of group existence—its visibility in behaviour; so that the widest group would equal the widest range of regular and permanent relationships, and so of co-activity. Now, neither criterion is by itself sufficient; yet even when they are combined their ambiguity does not cancel out.

To begin with, people proclaim their unity on widely varying grounds—on the grounds of descent and common origin (and we might speak of 'tribes'); of political allegiance (a 'nation'); of common language, or common religion (the Christian world, the Islamic brotherhood of nations). Sometimes the diverse criteria are used as alternatives, circumscribing from different angles the same population. More often, they circumscribe varying and overlapping populations, each of which regards itself as 'one' in this or that sense. Surely, we cannot simply measure which is numerically the largest, and call this the 'society'; perhaps indeed there are several 'widest' groups of different construction, or societies within societies, or societies overlapping. However this may be, we should speak of societies only where this varying awareness of belonging-together pertains to *actors*, who intentionally act from it. Expressed differently, we must be certain that we are here dealing with true groups, and not merely with *quasi-groups* (to borrow Professor Ginsberg's term).[1]

Take the familiar claim of common descent—whether understood literally, in the narrow genealogical sense, or more loosely, referring to the (roughly) undisturbed continuation of descent lines somehow established. Whether the claim happens to be historically justified or not is irrelevant in this context; we know that genealogies may be falsified and pedigrees produced *ad hoc*. What counts is the accepted belief or theory. Our problem, then, is to discover how far the consciousness of one-ness so stated is correlated with effective relationships of the same compass. If no such correlation exists, we have an ideology supporting nothing, a putative principle of recruitment, but no rights and obligations built upon it. In other words, we have a borderline case in which only one of the conditions of institutionalized groups is satisfied, and hence a quasi-group. Yet it is doubtful if such an ideology is ever without practical consequences. Some rights and obligations, however diffuse or infrequently practised, will probably always correspond to the believed-in unity, such as the right to visit unmolested each other's territory, rules of intermarriage, or mutual aid in emergencies. These relationships may not be sufficiently effective to make us speak of a 'society' rather than a quasi-group; but they will blur the boundary between the two. Furthermore, situations of this kind may well be the results of historical processes, an originally effective group having undergone fission and progressive weakening until its widest unit survived only in beliefs or in the symbolism of a common name.

In the case of common language, religion, and customs our problem lies in distinguishing groups proper from another spurious group, the 'cultural group' so-called; for behaviour which happens to be uniform in a given population, and which the people concerned know to be uniform, is easily confused with behaviour which is intentionally coordinated.[2] The very word 'common' is misleading, referring as it does both to 'like' or 'uniform' behaviour

[1] M. Ginsberg (1947), pp. 12–13.

[2] We are, of course, only considering groups which are aware of their uniform culture; groups which are culturally uniform only in an 'objective' sense, having been discovered to be so by the observer, are only so many uniformly coloured areas on a map, and sociologically irrelevant.

patterns and to norms of behaviour intentionally shared. Once more our question will be: Is there some co-activity between all individuals and sections in the alleged or apparent group? If all, for example, knowingly practise the same marriage system, is this enforced by a common (and not merely identical) legal machinery? If it is not, we have again a quasi-group, conscious of their uniform behaviour without coordinating it planfully. We note this difference, however, between the 'ideological' group based on beliefs in common origin and the quasi-group resting on a consciously uniform culture. If the former is often a past group, the latter is always a potential group; for it owns a prerequisite for the emergence of co-activity, namely, the awareness of identical, and hence predictable, modes of action. This, I think, is meant by MacIver when he says 'one of the great processes of society is . . . that whereby the common is built out of the like, common interests growing out of what were at first sight merely like interests'.[1] Needless to say, when common culture means also common language, this potential group-character is infinitely strengthened since communication is even more of a prerequisite for any planned coordination of behaviour.

The ambiguity of names and other claims to unity is therefore only partly corrected by the evidence of co-activity. More importantly, this is itself inconclusive and indeed leads us into contradictions. Thus we had to say that any effective group of widest compass extends as far as do the regular relationships and co-activities of the population. But it surely also makes sense to say that whole societies maintain regular relations with one another (intermarriage, economic collaboration, political alliances); so that relationships and co-activity would both cease and continue at the boundaries of a society.

Purely practically, this ambiguity can be corrected by referring back to the linguistic evidence; for the relationships in question would be shown to be external or otherwise by the names of the populations involved and by their own statements on being separate or 'one'. Yet this expedient does not remove the self-contradiction in our definition of society.[2] We could, of course, easily avoid it if

---

[1] (1931), p. 8.

[2] Also, as we know, names may exist both for the several 'societies' which maintain such external relations and for the population (perhaps a quasi-group) embracing them all.

we maintained only that the relationships within a society are of a different kind from those obtaining without, more effective and perhaps more numerous. But then we should also admit that there is no absolute solution to this problem of boundaries. And indeed, there is no alternative. It seems to me impossible to define a society except as the *relatively widest effective* group, regarding a certain kind of effectiveness as crucial. In doing so we assess two factors— the quantitative range of institutional activities entered into by the group, that is, the range of its corporate functions, and the nature and general relevance of these activities. In either case the political unit will nearly always prove to be the one combining greatest effectiveness with relatively widest compass. There is general agreement on the nature of the 'political group'; it corresponds to the aggregate of human beings who coordinate their efforts for the employment of force against others and for the elimination of force between them, and who usually count as their principal estate the possession and utilization of a territory. Normally, no larger group exists which acts through a similarly wide range of contexts, operative or regulative; equally, the politically active group also bears on what we must consider to be the most vital contexts of activity—those ensuring physical survival. Mostly, then, when we look for a society we find the political unit, and when speaking of the former we mean in effect the latter.[1] Whatever other modes of action we ascribe to a society, they would happen within the ring drawn by that widest co-activity; when we say that a society 'possesses' such and such institutions, we mean that they materialize within a State, a nation, or any group organized defensively and offensively.

Admittedly, it is we who select these criteria, tacitly or otherwise, and some arbitrariness, some scope for alternative criteria, is unavoidable. If the somewhat Hegelian view here expressed meets with criticism, I can quote in support the similar, and even more uncompromising, statements of prominent scholars. "The great number and variety of mutually related groups within the State

---

[1] It may seem that we argue in a circle when identifying societies with politically active groups. For if we now say that a society is a group engaged in political activities, we have previously defined political activities as being intended to maintain a society (see above p. 141). But this circle disappears when we analyze our terms. We are in fact merely saying that, when we look for the widest population most effectively held together in a group, we find that it is the population held together by the employment of force (apart from other things); and the employment of force which is so effective we call 'political'.

considered as a whole is called society in contrast with the State. In this wider sense society is not different from the State; it is the same thing viewed from another point.'[1] And again: 'Where we speak simply of society, we have in mind the forces of masses already constrained by the framework of the State.'[2] Confirmation comes, finally, also from a different camp: 'We will briefly raise here the question of the objective existence of groups. It is our conviction that this notion is one of the greatest illusions of social science. There is nothing more real, however, than political life. It possesses as much objectivity as any part of the world can possess, and at the same time embraces . . . every phase of human experience and behaviour.'[3]

8. RESIDUAL CATEGORIES

Like institutions, institutionalized groups have their residual categories. We have spoken of some—of 'ideological' groups, 'quasi-groups', and 'potential groups'—and among the latter we included both the 'cultural group' just discussed and the 'community' referred to in an earlier context. It is interesting to examine the analogies between the two. Both furnish something in the nature of raw material for the building of societies, and both also set barriers to their expansion. But as the boundaries of community life can be overcome and in some measure moved outward by expanding societies, so the boundaries of language and culture are only relative barriers. Again, societies have expanded beyond them, mainly by political means such as conquests, probably more rarely by fusion or affiliation, and in the course of such expansions language and culture have often themselves become unified. The processes involved still await fuller analysis; basically, however,

---

[1] L. Gumplovicz (1899), p. 136.   [2] F. Oppenheimer (1922), p. 394.

[3] C. Murchinson (1929), p. 9. The passages quoted suggest the identity of political organization (of any form) with the State. This is not my own view, though the definition of the State must share the arbitrariness of all definitions of groupings or institutions. I would myself speak of 'State' only in the case of politically effective groups which correspond in their organization to the historical (or modern) instances which we have come to call States. And these all exhibit certain specific features over and above the mere organization of a population for 'offence and defence', namely, (1) territorial sovereignty; (2) a centralized machinery of government; and (3) a specialized privileged ruling group or class, separated in training, status, and recruitment from the body of the population. I have elaborated this definition elsewhere and have nothing to add (see 1942, pp. 69–70).

they must correspond to something like the pull of two forces. On the one side, there is the impetus of a society built, or to be built, out of coordination of action without any support from a pre-existing potential group and its spontaneous awareness of unity; on the other, the pull of these forms of togetherness. To win through, the expanding society must clearly realize purposes and bring into play integrative mechanisms sufficiently forceful and persuasive to hold their own until the barriers of language and culture become unimportant or disappear altogether. Equally, these purposes and integrative efforts must be sufficiently enduring; for whatever other conditions may account for their failure, we know that many unifications have broken down because the unifiers failed to last or stay the pace.

I would add two further 'residual categories', the fleeting aggregate of the crowd and the 'sympathy groups'. Here recruitment proper, defined by rules and statutes, is replaced by the spontaneous aggregation of individuals guided by emotions and suggestibility. The cohesion of such groups lasts as long as do these stimuli, and the purposiveness of behaviour is undefined save by the limits within which the emotional reactions hold sway. The quasi-group with largest personnel and weakest endurance is the crowd; the group with smallest personnel (possibly reduced to a pair) and relatively greatest endurance, the 'sympathy group' formed by friends or lovers.

That in most societies there are prescribed relationships for lovers, we know. Anthropologists know, too, that friendship may equally be institutionalized, having its prescribed recruitment and range of activities.[1] In blood-brothership institutionalized friendship is rendered more intimate and permanent through being assimilated to relationship by consanguinity.[2] Let us remember also that the crowd is often embodied in the 'personnel' of institutions. Thus a court session is expected to be attended by all manner of people; a religious ritual may imply chance attendance over and above the fixed congregation. But even if the personnel of institutions is more rigidly prescribed (as in 'associative' institutions), it yet takes the form of a crowd, and the mode of action is so calculated that crowd behaviour, the spontaneous inter-stimulation of individuals in proximity, can be exploited for its aims and tasks.

[1] See M. J. Herskovits (1948), pp. 305–6.
[2] See, for example, S. F. Nadel (1947), pp. 108–9.

There is no need to emphasize the converse case, where institutionalized groups enter into non-institutionalized actions (a professional army into war, a political faction into a rebellion). Nor need we dwell on the coincidence of non-institutionalized groups with non-institutionalized actions, as in a rioting mob or in lynch law. What is important is that both the action and its personnel are susceptible òf gradual fixation. When war becomes institutionalized (in the Crusades, or in the Holy War of Islam), chance participants and campfollowers may turn into an army; when a religious belief, spontaneously arisen, becomes standardized and its rituals recurrent, the mass of believers will shape into a congregation, with rules of recruitment, a code of behaviour, and the consciousness of group identity. Of such developments the history of all societies is full.

Nor is this process of 'becoming' absent from the internal order of groups and from the relationships between persons. Here, too, novel events and spontaneous achievements can refashion the positions of individuals and their command over one another's actions. Indeed, societies might be characterized by an internal order of this dynamic kind, that is, by mobility, competition, efforts at self-advancement. But let us distinguish two situations of this kind. In one, these efforts are in the nature of a regulated career; they are implied in the social *persons*, their recruitment and tasks, and hence fully belong to the given structure of society; in the other, they re-structure society; the efforts now pertain to *individuals* who, as it were, create their own, novel persons and unpredictably acquire command over others. Clearly, the society would fall apart if every individual had this liberty. But a few, or one exceptional individual destined to leadership, might achieve it —and be permitted to achieve it. Paradoxically speaking, the society might expect and even idealize the unexpected achievement. This is Weber's 'charismatic' authority, emerging without 'ordered procedure' or 'regulated career'.[1] And since 'by its very nature it is not an institutional and permanent structure', it still stands on the borderline of ordered social existence. But it can be absorbed back into that existence; for societies will 'routinize' the charismatic efforts, that is, once more institutionalize the 'non-institutional'.

[1] Max Weber, (1948) pp. 246, 248.

CHAPTER VIII

Explanation

1. ANTHROPOLOGY AND NATURAL SCIENCE

The thesis of this chapter has already been stated. Anthropology is a science in so far as it explains; and, unlike the historian, who explains a given event as the particular consequent of a particular antecedent, the anthropologist attempts to model his explanation on the natural sciences, that is, he attempts to subsume particular facts or events under general rules or laws.

Perhaps the word 'model' is misleading. It might be taken to imply that the anthropologist, or some anthropologists, having looked round for the most congenial method, decided on trying that of natural science. But we are not offered a free choice of this kind; nor is the method of natural science one among several that are available for our use. There is only one method of science, though it is practised with varying rigour and consistency, Physics and Chemistry marking in this respect the peaks of achievement.[1] Any research is bound to this method, and no other is conceivable, if it starts from the postulate that the world of phenomena to be examined is a world governed by repetitiveness and recurrence. This is the world of natural science; and this, as has here been held, is also the world of social facts as conceived by the anthropologist.

I am fully aware that many scholars of great authority hold an opposite view and sharply distinguish the methods (and postulates) of natural science from those valid in the universe of man, human thought, and human culture. One cannot argue about fundamental assumptions, and those who would divide human knowledge in this sense will not be convinced by whatever I might be able to add to the controversy. Moreover, I confess to a great reluctance to argue the case for the unity of science on *a priori* grounds. It will prove

[1] An explanation of scientific character 'consists in deducing (a statement) from the law of the same form as physical laws, i.e. from a general formula for inferring singular statements of the kind specified'. R. Carnap (1934), pp. 98–9.

itself (or not) by the adequacy of its results, which proof has by no means been so disappointing as to prejudge the whole issue.

To say it again, the methods of science as applied in different disciplines vary in rigour and consistency. The study of society and culture ranks low in this respect, but it does not perhaps rank as low as it is sometimes thought. Admittedly, the postulate of a world whose phenomena are repetitive and recurrent in turn implies that these phenomena are comparable and reducible to common denominators; and this ultimate common denominator seems to lie in quantity. This world of 'pure measurement', which is the world of natural science, is unattainable by anthropology; it is so to-day; whether it ever will be attainable I will not venture to discuss. The facts of anthropology cannot be conceived of without the aspect of quality, at least without a large residue of quality. There have been one or two attempts to reduce sociological or anthropological facts to basic units from which, by quantitative or quasi-quantitative combinations, the universe of culture and society can be built up.[1] Brave though these attempts are, their hopelessness is, I think, only all too evident. But we need not worry overmuch about the limits thus set to anthropology, and perhaps to all the 'human' sciences. Let me quote from Bertrand Russell: 'The part played by measurement and quantity in science is very great, but is, I think, sometimes overestimated. . . . Qualitative laws can be as scientific as quantitative ones.'[2]

In the field of social facts the postulate of a world governed by repetitiveness and recurrence is restricted also in another sense. The facts observed by the student of society are created facts—the results of historical processes and events, arrested, at the moment of observation, in the midst of such processes. Thus, over and above repetitiveness and recurrence, we must also accept the uniqueness of events; and over and above the 'common denominators', the nexus between particular antecedents and particular consequents. Does this peculiarity of the social field disqualify anthropology from being a science? Anthropology, we are told, refers 'directly to historically determined events or occurrences, and not to a series of quantitatively conceived observations as such.

---

[1] I am thinking here of the Social Field Theory and its 'forces' and 'vectors', which will be discussed later on; and of Chapple and Coon's *Principles of Anthropology*, which similarly employ a quantifiable basic unit, viz. 'interaction'.

[2] (1931), pp. 67–8.

... And since the scientific character of anthropology is an illusion, we must conclude that it is history or nothing. Any attempt to find in it, or to make of it, an historico-scientific world of ideas must always fail.'[1]

We have already argued that no scientific discipline can be assessed or defined on the ground of its subject matter. The crucial criterion lies in the aims of the discipline and the aspect under which it approaches its subject matter. Biology deals with organisms which are the result, or represent phases, of evolution, which is nothing but an infinite historical process. Economics (which Oakeshott admits among the sciences) examines historically created systems of human actions and incentives. Yet both also, like anthropology, view their subject matter *sub specie repetitionis*, and hence under the aspect of general rules, timelessly valid.

Furthermore, the uniqueness of historical events or sequences only limits the field of anthropological generalizations but does not eliminate it. This field is given where the comparative method is given. The comparative method may (in Oakeshott's words) not be a method at all 'which unites science and history; it dismisses history and never achieves the full condition of science'.[2] Anthropology, wedded to the comparative method, may be eternally condemned to remain an incomplete or hybrid science. If so, its incompleteness and dubious ancestry stem from the world which it attempts to embrace; for cultural and social facts can only be conceived of as hybrids born of repetitiveness *and* uniqueness. Uniqueness, that is, the appearance of characteristics which are not absorbed in regularities nor reducible to any determinate combination of conditions, is merely another word for accident or chance. In the world of cultural and social facts, then, we must be prepared to allow for chance as well as law. How far our expanding knowledge will press back the zone still given over to uniqueness and chance, no one will venture to predict. Even the paradigm of all sciences, physics, to-day admits a zone of indeterminacy, where chance must be acknowledged. The part played by indeterminacy in physics, where it is restricted to nuclear phenomena and

---

[1] M. Oakeshott (1933), pp. 165–7. The author is considering the anthropology of Frazer, Tylor and Haddon. Though the material upon which he bases his judgment is old-fashioned, the argument as such would seem to hold good for any form of anthropological enquiry.

[2] Op. cit., p. 167.

countered by calculations of probability, bears, of course, no comparison with the wide range of social phenomena which exhibit uniqueness and chance. But the analogy at least teaches us not to exaggerate the insufficiencies of our discipline.

Moreover, the 'true' scientific experience (which anthropology cannot fully attain) is a 'defective experience'; it falls short of the totality óf experience; scientific knowledge is abstract, conditional, incomplete, 'self-contained but not self-sufficient'.[1] Anthropology, I would say, touches upon that 'totality of experience', it reaches out to where the 'incomplete' scientific knowledge cannot reach. If anthropological knowledge is not strict scientific knowledge but something else, the something else has its own justification. If in the following pages we shall continue to speak of the science of anthropology, we shall do so with full awareness of what this means, or rather, of what it does not mean.

2. Explanation and Common Sense

One often speaks of 'facts' which have been explained or need explaining. Strictly speaking, this is incorrect. A fact simply is or happens. Explanation presupposes a problem, and this is furnished when objects appear in some (as yet not understood) conjunction or events occur in some (puzzling) context of time or space. Explaining is always the explaining of a state of affairs, that is, of relations between facts; explanation means showing that their conjunction is what it is 'by right' and in conformity with some order of things or law of occurrences; if this order and law appear to their students convincing, so that their curiosity is satisfied, they will agree that the state of affairs has been 'explained'.

By common sense standards, at least, this statement adequately sums up the position. For common sense accepts a sharp and self-evident distinction between description and explanation. There is a definite step from one to the other, which carries with it the experience of something new that has not been there before—of some suddenly achieved illumination. There is no need to emphasize that for the scientist this step is far from definite. As we know, even the description of single facts presupposes some preliminary ordering of the context in which they appear and some pre-existing explanatory knowledge. And as we shall see presently, the dis-

---

[1] M. Oakeshott, op. cit., p. 243.

covery of the 'right' by which things are such as they are might be
taken to lie merely in their complete description. Indeed, the
sharp distinction which common sense places between description
and explanation would seem to be true only of the sort of explanation which common sense itself has to offer.

Now, doubtless scientific knowledge is not just 'organized
common sense'; scientific knowledge describes a world of knowledge which begins to exist only when common sense and all its
postulates have been forgotten and rejected.[1] Even a cursory
acquaintance with modern natural science shows how wide the gap
may become. It is a gap between the apparent reality and one
methodically ascertained; between phenomena in their concreteness and particularity, and facts stripped of all that is tangible and
individual so that they may be fitted into some all-embracing
regularity. Russell's 'plain man' who thinks that matter is solid
while to the physicist it is 'a wave of probability undulating in
nothingness'[2] would perhaps feel less out of place among students
of society. But there, too, a gap exists. The plain man may think
that people go to war because they hate each other or seek an outlet
for over-population: the student of society (some students of
society) will prove that people go to war because, when they were
children, their erotic drives were frustrated, or because of some
compulsion inherent in economic processes. To common sense a
'society' or 'group' are tangible facts; sexual jealousy or social
ambition universal human incentives: scientifically, a 'society' or
'group' is extremely difficult to define, and jealousy or social
ambition are tendencies thrown up by a complex interplay of
social factors.

Yet it is not difficult to break a lance for common sense. In the
human sciences (and here I would include psychology) it does not
seem to lose its respectability so quickly; it certainly remains more
closely linked with scientific enquiry. To begin with, the human
sciences do not press their analysis very far beyond the 'apparent'
reality and into an order of things where waves of probability undulating in nothingness offer the ultimate common denominators.
For better or for worse, the human sciences are concerned with the
phenomenal surface of reality; if they discarded it entirely, they
would destroy their subject matter. Moreover, common sense and

[1] M. Oakeshott (op. cit.), p. 171.
[2] Bertrand Russell (1931), p. 76.

behaviour dictated by it belong to that subject matter. The products of common sense, the false or foolish rationalizations produced by all races at all times, are items of human study. We must, then, use Beelzebub to drive out the devil, and invoke common sense to understand its vagaries. Finally, though it is overcome in the end result of scientific enquiry, common sense stimulates the initial approach and guides the first steps. In some measure at least this must also be true of natural science. For if all science starts with problems, it is common sense that first produces them. Common sense also shows their first solution; the very fact that common sense, like science, attempts explanation proves that the two spring from the same root and follow from the same prompting.[1]

My thesis is that common-sense explanations are true models of explanation in form and aim; they fail only where their limitations are ignored. Common-sense explanation does what in essence scientific explanation also does, transforms observed particular phenomena into instances of some general law or regularity. Both kinds of explanation convey the same sense of novelty—of facts suddenly 'falling into place' and exhibiting their legitimacy. But common sense is more easily satisfied and accepts finality too readily. The explanations of common sense represent the simplest and most restricted kind of scientific explanation. They do no more than point out the analogy between what is being explored and what is already known; they merely attempt to classify, to put a name to some observed object or event, and so to subsume it under an order of things already assured. Common-sense explanations are derived or *deductive* explanations, and proceed by analogy and *diagnosis*.

There are, of course, many deductive explanations which do not rest on common sense. Diagnosis, the identification of a state of affairs as exemplifying some assured regularity, plays a vital part in all forms of scientific enquiry. But here the deductive explanation is only the counterpart, the descending arc, as it were, of an explanation previously evolved inductively from the analysis of analogous phenomena. Moreover, the analogy between the state of

[1] 'Scientific subject matter and procedures grow out of the direct problems and methods of common sense' (John Dewey, 1938, p. 66). And again: 'Scientific knowledge and the knowledge of common sense have the same origin, and for long periods of time in the history of any subject they go together and are nearly indistinguishable' (C. C. Pratt, 1939, p. 167).

affairs already framed in assured knowledge and the one newly explored may not lie on the surface; the analogy must itself be explored through analysis so that, in attempting to apply the derived explanation, we partly retrace the processes that led to it. For common sense, there is no awareness of the steps that led to the assured knowledge; it is simply given and intuitively used. The assurance of common sense is the assurance that goes with obviousness and with the assumption of common agreement. It is this that makes common-sense explanations so eminently satisfactory, as well as dangerous. Their danger lies not so much in the risk of using false knowledge (which could easily enough be checked) as in the temptation to use true knowledge uncritically, to take analogies for granted, and hence to cut short analysis. Yet in social enquiry we cannot do without some guidance from common sense. In searching for the rational motives of people, for consistency in action, or for some gratification and utility behind regular behaviour, we are applying the canons of common sense and judge from the ready analogy with self-knowledge and the familiar, everyday world around us. Nor is this surprising; for the reality we study—man and behaviour—is itself analogous to the reality that is ourselves and our lives. The caution that must be voiced is a trite one, not to stop at surface analogies and not to rest content with a diagnosis offering itself too readily.

But we must add that common sense also employs scientific knowledge, being to some extent a storehouse for scientific facts grown so familiar that they have acquired the seeming self-evidence of common-sense truths. Sometimes they are tenets since discarded by science, like the theory of instincts which survives in popular literature, the 'economic man' of early economic theory, or the *clichés* of early Darwinism—survival of the fittest, struggle for existence, and the like. Occasionally new theories capture the imagination so rapidly that they acquire the hallmark of self-evidence; the psychoanalyst's identification of aggressive behaviour with frustration or of religious beliefs with wish-fulfilment has almost attained the status of common-sense truths. Common sense is thus not constant; rather does it change through 'the infiltration and incorporation of scientific conclusions and methods into itself'.[1]

Now the evolutionary theory in anthropology made a fetish of

[1] J. Dewey (1938), p. 75.

common-sense explanations.[1] Diffusionist anthropology at least takes its lead from common sense; the plausibilities which it argues —that people adopt new cultural items because they 'fill a gap' or meet a pre-existing want—mean nothing else. But it is more interesting to consider another province of anthropological explanations, where the promptings of common sense are more subtle as well as insidious. Many a pseudo-'need' formulated by anthropologists seems to belong in this province. Here the promptings of common sense even tempt us to invent *ad hoc* the 'assured regularities' under which an observed situation might be subsumed, so that its explanation, though it is no longer 'deductive', is yet made to look like it. To be sure, the assured regularities are not entirely invented, and the explanation conforms to some pre-existing knowledge. But it conforms only to vague self-knowledge or perhaps to some deeply ingrained habitual way of looking at things; while the obviousness of the explanation rests only on the persuasiveness of the words in which we choose to express it.

Thus we observe a certain widespread, perhaps universal, mode of behaviour, say, that people everywhere consult oracles; we postulate (from self-knowledge or a 'habitual way of looking at things') that such a uniformity must correspond to something that requires it, to some demand-like agency, which we call a 'need'; hence we invent an appropriate species of need and make it responsible for the behaviour from the observation of which it is derived. In other words, we do not merely say, 'people generally consult oracles in this as in other instances'; but 'there is a need of self-assurance, and the observed cases are instances of it'. In a sense, we pile one regularity upon another, one that is observed upon one we assume to be working behind it. The 'need' is both, a summary of the observed regular mode of behaviour and a machine invented to account for it. This is, of course, a circular argument, but the circularity as such is harmless—it is typical of many analytical (i.e. non-deductive) explanations. It is misleading only if it is taken for a deductive explanation, as though we had independent knowledge of the particular 'machine' and its effi-

---

[1] It seems characteristic that Tylor recommended the study of anthropology on the grounds that it did in its own field what other disciplines often omit to do in theirs, namely, to show to the scholars 'first the practical common-sense starting point' (1930, vol. I, p. xi). And again, Tylor held that 'the true philosophy of history lies in extending and improving the methods of the plain people...' (1913, vol. I, p. 2).

ciency, and had merely identified (not invented) its presence in an analogous situation. As we shall see, the confusion between invention and identification by analogy is often difficult to avoid; and even the exact sciences make use of such models of machines—and thus admit common sense; for a machine behind the observed regularity of phenomena is the most complete answer to the promptings of common sense. The motions of a round-about are puzzling only until we lift the trapdoor and discover a well known engine driving the thing. Common sense always urges us to look for such trapdoors.

3. EXPLANATION AND ANALYSIS

When we know of no assured order of things under which the observed phenomena can readily be subsumed, diagnosis turns into a different kind of explanation, which is best called *inductive* or *analytical*. For here the 'order' or 'regularity' after which we strive comes to mean a rule specifically evolved through the analysis of the observed facts. And this in turn involves the twofold procedure of hypothesis (which foreshadows the rule, or some rule), and verification (which tests its validity by other, not yet examined facts). The latter always, the former often, rests on experiment, that is, on the variation of all facts between which relevant relations are suspected. The result is the discovery of *invariant relations* underlying the fortuitous relations which pose the problem. Schematically expressed, our problem starts with the presence of A among B, C, D . . . (if A, B, C, D . . . be different facts or aspects of facts). We ask: Why should it be so? The final answer is, say, that A is there because of D (but not because of B or C); in other words, A and D are shown to stand in significant, invariant relations. Once more, objects or events become instances of a general, assured regularity, order, or law, though now not one that is independently established, but one that is merely refined from the initially given coincidences.

From this view on the nature of scientific explanations (on which there is general agreement) two things appear to follow. First, that no explanation can exist in isolation; and second, that explanation is, in essence, nothing but complete description. The first consequence may be stated more fully as follows. Explanation 'connects any given incident with the scheme of reality at large by exhibiting it as one instance of relations holding universally.' Yet 'while we can always hope to explain a particular fact as the outcome of some combination of data . . . we do not explain the combination itself'. We can only trace it 'to some anterior combination'.[1] Let me disregard the somewhat ambiguous word 'anterior'. What is clearly meant is that any ascertained regularity, while accounting for the particular facts subsumed in it, poses, in a wider scheme of things, once more the problem of the right by which it appears in that scheme. There are, then, ever widening circles of explanatory hypotheses. But this continuity comes to an end somewhere; somewhere it reaches a range of facts beyond which there is no 'anterior combination of data', and hence can be no wider explanatory hypothesis. The final step, if one cares to make it, is one of postulates, or of faith (according to temperament), and always beyond the grasp of verification.

The science of society no less than natural science has already been driven, here and there, against this ultimate boundary of empirical knowledge. It is easily lost to sight in the investigation of particular problems; here practical relevance and current interests define the narrower provinces of worth-while enquiry. But though these particular enquiries may break up the continuous chain of explanations, the validity of the enquiries will depend on their fitting as links into the chain. But 'chain' must obviously be in the plural. For the starting points for explanations are as numerous as are the interests which guide our enquiry. In the study of any social fact these (and more) are such possible starting points—the physiological constitution of man, his mental life, the physical environment surrounding him, and the conditions of his social existence. The first three are, for the student of society, extraneous starting points, and only the last lies fully within his province. Yet that all explanations, from whichever point they start, should converge, that they should be compatible and build up the 'scheme of reality at large'—this is the ideal (and postulate) of scientific understanding. Its achievement presupposes one thing: the absolute commutability of all discovered regularities. They must be capable of being translated from the order of existence in which they are first found or explored into any other order of existence. In other words, my sociological 'law' must be translatable into the laws obtaining for physiology, psychology, biology, and so forth.

[1] L. T. Hobhouse (1927), pp. 409, 410.

That social enquiries cannot possibly hope to attain this ideal needs no emphasis. But should they attempt to attain it, in however limited a fashion? The transmutability of all facts in the universe may be philosophically desirable; but is it desirable for the student of society, and would it illuminate the sort of problems with which he is faced? A great thinker gives the answer in no uncertain terms: 'Social phenomena cannot be understood except as there is prior understanding of physical conditions and the laws of their inter-action. Social phenomena cannot be attacked, *qua* social, directly.'[1] This is surely a fundamental question, bearing as it does on the claim of social enquiry to be itself, and nothing else, and entitled to disregard all 'extraneous' explanations. We need not answer this question now since it will reappear in the discussion that follows.

We turn now to the second consequence apparently entailed in the nature of analytical explanations, namely, the coincidence of explaining and describing. Since explaining in the sense here understood involves the analysis of all the relations in which objects or events appear, explanation seems indeed to equal full description. Scientists and logicians, as well as humble anthropologists, have found this conclusion inescapable, and coined for it the phrase 'descriptive explanation'.[2] But this seems to me unwarranted. The step between describing and explaining may be blurred; but a step it is nevertheless. Stebbing has called explanation 'constructive description'.[3] Explanation, then, is description 'plus'. It 'con-structs'; it adds something that is not found in description. What precisely does it add? Two answers, I think, are possible.

First, if explanation were only complete description, it would be longer and more complicated than any particular description. Precisely the opposite is true, however. The 'law' which constitutes the explanation is an abbreviated statement and a summary (of a special kind, as we shall see). Moreover, complete description, which would imply also complete observation, is an illusion.

---

[1] John Dewey (1938), p. 492.

[2] Bertrand Russell speaks of the 'descriptive view' of modern physics (1926, p. 220). A. Wolf says that science is concerned with the 'how', not the 'why' of events and is therefore 'perhaps only description' (1928, p. 118). And Golden-weiser, when discussing whether anthropological facts can be 'explained' in psychological terms, points to the 'descriptive explanations' of modern science (1933, pp. 60–1, n.).

[3] L. S. Stebbing (1930), p. 392.

Observation and description always remain partial and incomplete.[1] Nor do the observable facts force themselves upon our attention in a form ready-made for us to generalize from; we correct experience as well as generalize it (Poincaré). The data from which we ultimately derive significant regularities nowhere exist in the form in which we make use of them—whether they concern the frictionless momentum of classical physics, the pure sensations of psychology, or that fictitious but necessary entity, a society round which we can draw precise boundaries. All these are ideal data. The 'plus' of description when it is constructed into laws or regularities thus lies in the 'simplifying, schematizing, idealizing of the facts'—facts which can 'never be perfectly found in reality'.[2]

Secondly, the invariant relations discovered between facts, even in this idealized form, are as yet without the character of finality which explanation connotes. Whatever field of enquiry we consider, explanation means the assertion of a state of affairs in terms so satisfying that, with the assertion, our curiosity is satisfied.[3] The mere discovery of the state of affairs does not yet satisfy this condition; the mere statement (or 'law') describing the discovered regular relations between facts is as yet without this added convincingness. Consider that the discovery of such regularities is the more fruitful the more novel and unexpected are the relations between the facts; for it enables us to bring order into a sphere not hitherto betraying the presence of order and system. But it is precisely this character of novelty which requires the additional step that shall leave us convinced and satisfied; without it, we merely record a striking and unexpected coincidence. The coincidence becomes convincing and meaningful, it can be 'understood' and taken as an 'explanation', only when the relations between the facts are stated in terms implying some intrinsic requiredness or fitness. Often, the discovery of the invariant relations is not entirely novel but expected, some definite suspicion having guided our search. But this suspicion is, once more, that of some intrinsic

---

[1] No serious student of scientific method has ever doubted this. Let me quote this one statement by a physicist. In our description we include 'nothing that is unobservable, but a great deal that is actually unobserved ... "Complete description" must be understood with these limitations' (Arthur Eddington, 1928, p. 227).

[2] Ernst Mach (1920), p. 455.

[3] A similar view of the nature of explanation is given by G. A. Lundberg 1939), p. 6.

fitness of the phenomena for being so related. The 'plus' of explanation, then, lies in the formulation of some *fitness* or *requiredness* in
the discovered regularities.

We cannot avoid the subjectivity of such terms as fitness, convincingness, or meaning; it is precisely by an appeal of this kind to
our intellectual faculties, which cannot be expressed otherwise,
that the explanation is lifted above the level of ordinary statements
and assertions. We can, however, specify the processes whereby we
impart meaning to the relations between phenomena or express the
fitness of the laws governing them. We do so by *conceptualizing* the
relations, that is, by constructing for them a single summarizing
concept and its appropriate linguistic (or other symbolic) expression. As will readily be seen, this is essentially a circular process;
for though this conceptualization merely 'summarizes' and expresses the observed relations between phenomena, these are, by
this very fact, taken to be satisfactorily accounted for or 'explained'.
The weight of that satisfying 'appeal' to our intellect is therefore
borne by the formulation and logical construction of the summarizing concept; and indeed, the laws of natural science are
paramount instances of analytical explanations which are such in
virtue of this naming and conceptualizing, and not through being
full statements on discovered regularities.

Certain scholars have clearly formulated this 'plus', which is
explanation. Henri Poincaré calls it the 'principle', as opposed to
the ordinary or rudimentary 'law'. 'The rudimentary law (*la loi
primitive*) announces the relation between two crude facts, A and
B; one introduces between these two crude facts an intermediary C,
more or less fictitious in nature (e.g. the intangible entity of gravi-
tation). And now we have a relation . . . which we suppose to be
rigorous and which is the *principle*.'[1] The psychologists Lewin
and Tolman speak in a similar sense of 'intervening concepts'
and 'intervening variables',[2] and the philosopher Cohen of
'concepts'.[3]

The kind of appeal utilized in framing the 'principles' or 'intervening concepts' varies widely with the nature of the scientific

[1] H. Poincaré (1935), p. 239.
[2] K. Lewin (1938), pp. 11–12; E. C. Tolman (1938 b), p. 229.
[3] 'Concepts are signs pointing to invariant relations. . . . Significant concepts,
therefore, enable us to arrange in order and hold together diverse phenomena,
. . . They point to relations and operations which really unify diverse phenomena
and reveal unexpected characteristics' (M. R. Cohen, 1946, pp. 71–2).

discipline and its historical stage. Science started with the elementary appeal of self-knowledge, reading an anthropomorphous 'fitness' into the phenomena of the universe. The elements 'desired' to be true to their nature, there were 'sympathies' between substances, and a *horror vacui* in nature. Though now banished from science, this early appeal survives in the scientific vocabulary in such terms as force, energy, attraction and repulsion. But now 'forces' and the like intervene only in the sense of mathematical functions linking the phenomena. Thus, at the other end of the scale, stands the mathematical symbolism of modern physics, whose expression of the 'fitness' and 'meaning' of the natural laws has only the appeal of logical consistency within a given framework of reference.

What, we may now ask, is the 'appeal to our intellect' utilized in the explanatory concepts of social enquiry? Social enquiry in this respect seems to be in a peculiar position. For it has evolved few concepts which are strictly its own and summarize the regularities observable in social phenomena in terms of that framework of reference. I would number among such concepts Radcliffe-Brown's 'social integration'; Durkheim's 'mechanic and organic solidarity'; the concept of 'social adjustment'; the principle of an 'optimum' size and scatter of societies previously stated; Tylor's 'cultural adhesions'; MacIver's use of 'differentiation' as an aspect of social evolution; and one or two other explanatory concepts which will be mentioned in later chapters. Mostly, however, the explanatory concepts of social enquiry seem to come from other frameworks of reference, that is, from other disciplines; and here social enquiry seems to look in two directions. On one side, it is drawn towards the concepts evolved by psychology, physiology, or biology— the 'drives', 'needs,' or 'psychological forces' attributed to the human organism; on the other, it is drawn towards the abstract, quasi-mathematical concepts of natural science, so that anthropologists speak of equilibrium, stability, cohesion, or of a social 'field of forces'. In either case, apparently, the unification of diverse explanatory principles of which we spoke before represents, in social enquiry, not an ultimate goal, but something this enquiry cannot do without; so that John Dewey's warning, that 'social phenomena cannot be attacked, *qua* social, directly', would seem to be in some measure justified.[1]

[1] See above, p. 201.

As regards the psychological or physiological concepts utilized in social explanation, we now mean, not 'pseudo-needs' invented *ad hoc*, but needs, or drives, or similar 'forces', independently established by these other disciplines and as it were borrowed by social enquiry for its 'intervening concepts'. The 'pseudo-needs' themselves would represent fully analytical explanations, evolved within social enquiry; and the ambiguity of meaning might in certain cases be avoided by speaking more specifically of 'social needs' (as Durkheim, for example, speaks of *besoins socials*). I myself do not see any particular advantage in this anthropomorphous nomenclature, which only leads us to confuse the names by which we express the 'requiredness' of phenomena with the diagnosis of a 'machine' behind the phenomena, known to us from independent sources. However this may be, when we refer to true needs, drives, and so forth, we imply precisely this diagnosis. We deliberately make use of the findings of the sister disciplines; more precisely, we adopt the mechanism discovered and named in these disciplines, so as to indicate that their efficacy in fact 'intervenes' between social phenomena. Of these literally 'intervening concepts' we shall speak a great deal in the following discussion, and we need say here only that they cut short the analytical explanations of social enquiry, turning them, at some point, into deductive ones, that is, into identifications and diagnoses. The test is a simple one; for when we in this sense speak of needs, drives, forces, and so forth, we imply that the efficacies so named can be verified in social phenomena by the same procedures which made the psychologist or biologist formulate these principles. So far, then, John Dewey is right.

But in the case of such concepts as equilibrium or cohesion it would seem that only the names are borrowed and their appeal is used vicariously. For clearly we do not claim that our kind of equilibrium or cohesion can be verified by the normal procedure of physics or chemistry. Applied to the social phenomena, the words are convincing because they name something that is analogous here and in the other disciplines, and because they name it with the weight of authority which the words acquired in the disciplines where they have citizenship. But the words only help us to express a requiredness or fitness which we independently perceived in our phenomena. We do not import extraneous mechanisms, but merely point to a general analogy in the situations, and on these grounds

o

borrow the appropriate formula. The analogy itself is vague, and may once more lead to confusion. But it would seem that we have no choice in the matter; for this course is forced upon us by the poverty of our language and the ruts of our thought. The science of society, one feels tempted to say, has come on the scene too late. If I wish to express a state of affairs in which' recurrent modes of behaviour, after being disturbed, are re-established, I have no other words than 'equilibrium' or 'stability'; if I wish to indicate that social groups persist and hang together, I must talk about 'cohesion'; and if I wish to express the fact that human behaviour follows a determinate course in spite of distractions and alternate possibilities, I seem unable to think of any word more adequate than 'forces'.

To sum up. These explanatory concepts are fully 'invented', and only in the last step of naming does the invention merge with something like a diagnosis or identification by analogy; but this is no more than an incidental and often unwitting trespass in nomenclature. Even so, it has been taken to imply more, namely, a precise analogy between social explanations and the concepts of modern physics, which it is desirable to pursue and develop (as in Spencer's day it seemed desirable to develop the analogy with biology and the laws of 'organisms'). A universe of discourse is envisaged in which ultimately 'physics [would be] building "up" and "out" ... towards the inclusion of society, man-society building "down" and "in" towards the inclusion of physics'.[1] The statement is ambiguous since it does not make it clear which of the two is meant—a true diagnosis of identical (i.e. physical) mechanisms in social situations and in the natural world, or the naming of analogous situations. The former is no doubt possible, though as we shall see irrelevant; that the latter would relevantly contribute to the unification of the sciences seems to me doubtful.

In this discussion we were in a sense anticipating; for we were considering already the final act of naming the explanatory principles in social enquiry before having examined their nature and varieties. As I have suggested, all explanatory principles indicate some 'requiredness' or 'fitness' in the observed regularities of phenomena. In social regularities we seem able to perceive three kinds of 'fitness', which appeal to our intellect and satisfy our

[1] A. F. Bentley (1926), p. 208. A similar viewpoint is implied by G. A. Lundberg (1939), p. 131, N.20.

curiosity in different ways. They are, the fitness of logical consistency; that of purpose and means-to-end relations; and that of mechanical causality. We need not at the moment concern ourselves more closely with the first two. This, however, can at once be seen. These two kinds of 'fitness' involve no extraneous verification. They remain essentially within the range of social facts, that is, of modes of action which, by definition, are purposive and have a content or meaning that can be named and treated logically. The 'intervening concepts' expressing these two kinds of fitness are 'invented' concepts, and are always linked with the phenomena by the circular argument of which we have spoken. If the intervening concept is supported by any extraneous analogy, it is only the inevitable, elementary analogy with self-knowledge or an analogy forced upon us by the poverty of language.

The third principle, causality, tends to involve an extraneous verification; here we often invoke mechanisms established by other disciplines and base ourselves on analogies with their findings. Causal explanations, moreover, seem capable of breaking the circle of mere conceptualization. Here, then, the question of method previously touched upon once more arises: How far should we, or must we, go beyond the range of social enquiry to illuminate the problems encountered in that enquiry?

4. CAUSALITY

It is meaningless to ask whether causal explanations are more important or adequate than explanations in terms of logical and purposive connections. I hold, and hope to show, that in social enquiry the three must co-exist. But it is true to say that these other explanations always imply also the concept of causality, though often in a sense so basic or general that it may simply be taken for granted. For if we discover a logically compelling correspondence between certain social facts (that is, certain intentional modes of action) we must assume that the attainment of this correspondence is caused by the mental organization of the actors; and if we formulate a nexus of means-and-ends between one action and another, then the end or purpose must itself be assumed to have a cause, and the means employed for its attainment some causal adequacy. Causality, then, is the most pervasive intervening concept which social enquiry can apply.

Equally, it is peculiarly satisfying. Why this should be so is a question which philosophers might answer. The curiosity for causes certainly dominates common sense and its search for explanatory 'machines'. This may well be an impurity of thinking, reflecting that residue of anthropomorphous thought, that analogy with the human machinery of volition, which our mind overcomes only with difficulty.[1] Yet since J. S. Mill and Mach, scientists have prided themselves on asking only 'how', not 'why', and it has become fashionable to say that the causal explanation 'is confined to the early stages of a science; it is satisfactory only at the level of organized common sense knowledge'.[2] Causality thus seems destined to give way to the more cautious but less exhaustive statement of mere invariant relations; less exhaustive since in causal explanations we predicate these additional features—an irreversible sequence of time; the appearance of novelty in identity, so that one combination of facts is seen to be transformed into another; and the element of compulsion peculiar to this process.

It is no good pretending that a full-blooded causal explanation is not more satisfactory than the emaciated version. We may have to be content with the latter, but this is only bowing to the (for the moment) inevitable. I am speaking for the students of society. In natural science the promptings of common sense are more easily silenced, and we are assured that modern physicists 'have been doing valid thinking' without the 'assumption of the principle of causality'.[3] However that may be, it seems significant that, in surveying the field of natural science, we meet with two different types of theories. In one—in the 'physical' theories—the explanation of observed phenomena is in terms of an 'easily imagined hidden mechanism'; in the other, explanation is focused upon 'relations abstracted from phenomena' and leads to 'mathematical or abstractive' theories of the universe.[4] This may be the result of individual preference and attraction; but it is a preference for or attraction by principles which do or do not bear a close relation to the promptings of common sense. The *human* sciences will, by their very nature, always gravitate towards the 'physical' theories.

[1] See Bertrand Russell (1926), p. 229; also Cohen and Nagel (1947), p. 136.
[2] L. S. Stebbing (1930), p. 393.
[3] P. W. Bridgman (1938), p. 345.
[4] Cohen and Nagel (1947), pp. 234-6.

Now, the search for 'hidden mechanisms' appears to be most successful along the divisions which separate the various scientific disciplines. I may, for example, as a psychologist analyse the various conditions under which human beings evince fear. I can frame the regularities discoverable in such situations in concepts belonging fully to my discipline, and talk about 'stimuli and responses', or innate instincts, and the like. But if I am able to refer also to the findings of other disciplines, namely physiology or biochemistry, to the fact that adrenalin is discharged into the blood whenever fear is felt, I seem to have got hold of a more cogent explanation and a somehow fuller causality. To some extent this is no doubt due to the fact that here I have amplified my knowledge by including in my analysis a wider range of relations; I have, in other words, gone some way towards that unification of explanatory principles after which we are always striving. But partly the greater satisfaction offered by such extraneous explanations lies merely in their extraneousness; for here we seem to have laid bare a 'hidden mechanism', and common sense has found the expected trapdoor. Is this all an illusion? Certain arguments indeed seem to make it so.

5. THE HIERARCHY OF SCIENCES

Empirical science is arranged, fortuitously or otherwise, in a hierarchy of disciplines each representing a level of analysis, which proceeds to a certain point and no further. Social enquiry has its place in that hierarchy, being placed above psychology, which in turn is placed above physiology, chemistry, and physics.[1] In this general hierarchy the analytical levels stand in the relationship of progressive inclusiveness so that any phenomenon taken to define a unit on one level may be broken down to components which are the unit phenomena on the next lower level. In every phenomenon visible on the higher level, then, phenomena open to a lower-level analysis must be implicit, and all formulations of unit phenomena on the higher level constitute a 'shorthand' as compared with the 'longhand' of lower-level analysis. Furthermore, any statement of the regularities discovered on the higher level

[1] For the purpose of this argument we will consider this hierarchy in a simplified form, disregarding specialized disciplines which either occupy the same level though pursuing different interests (e.g. biology as compared with physiology), or represent additional, intermediate levels (e.g. biochemistry).

must 'bracket' regularities discovered or discoverable on the lower level; these are taken for granted and assumed to be established (at least potentially) by that deeper-going analysis. I have used the word 'must', for all this is indeed a basic postulate of our understanding. We cannot conceive of the kind of nature in which, say, physical laws would be inapplicable to chemical processes or the bloodstream of the organism would not obey the laws governing the behaviour of fluids.

In the natural sciences this seems to be all. Their field of observation is homogeneous and only conveniently divided between different disciplines, each of which merely defines the level of complexity in the phenomena to which, by common agreement, analysis is to penetrate. The human sciences, too, appear at first sight to embrace a homogeneous field, divided fortuitously and conveniently into different levels of analysis: man is the same whether he is studied by sociology, psychology or physiology, and reveals different aspects of his being only in conformity with the agreed depth of analysis. Thus every social fact, that is, every human action in respect of other humans is, *at any given moment*, a complex of psychological processes (by which I mean mental events, such as seeing, hearing, thinking, desiring), physiological processes (movements, muscle-tensions, innervations), and innumerable other processes discoverable on yet deeper levels of analysis, and can be broken down to these events and processes. It is merely convenient to handle the phenomena and their relations, on a given level, in the less completely analyzed form and to frame them in the corresponding 'shorthand' concepts. Economy alone would forbid the breaking-up of, say, 'marriage' or 'war' into their mental and physiological components; the description of any social fact would fill volumes if it had to be expressed in the longhand of the more complete analysis. Yet 'marriage' and 'war' *are* all these implicit facts, and nothing really new. In applying the more far-reaching analysis we merely *repeat*, in more detailed and copious language, all that can be discovered in the less fully analyzed phenomena.[1] Thus it has been said that 'mind' is only a 'short-cut

---

[1] A perfect model of this three-level approach will be found in E. C. Tolman (1938 b). He chooses, in fact, the same example, marriage, to show how the sociological data of 'group conduct' (i.e. the institution 'marriage') can be broken down to the psychological data of individual behaviour ('X going to the wedding'), and these in turn to physiological activities, neural and biochemical processes, etc. Tolman, however, emphasizes that the psychological data 'are

expression' for physiological observations;[1] and that the concepts referring to social behaviour only summarize the facts open to the lower-level analysis of psychology.[2]

Now if this were all, the step to a lower level of analysis would not help us to understand the problems encountered on the higher level. More precisely, such a step would widen our knowledge, but only in the sense of unfolding the 'inside' of any phenomenon we study. If we were to name the regularities discovered in social enquiry (e.g. the interdependence of war and economic factors) in terms of psychology or physiology, we should indeed be 'diagnosing' independently established facts—the efficacy of feelings, acts of volition, thoughts, or of muscular strain, locomotion, and of the processes of metabolism. But 'independently established' would only mean 'studied by different methods'. We should discover no causes, only correlates, and no hidden machines driving the things we first perceived, but only the things themselves, looked at, as it were, from underneath.

Obviously, this is not true, or not entirely true. The criteria of scientific convenience and economy cannot therefore exhaust the relations between the levels of analysis in the human sciences. I propose to show that the analogy with the natural sciences breaks down on closer inspection for three reasons. It breaks down, first, because in the human sciences the transition from level to level involves what I propose to call a 'phenomenal regression'; secondly, because social and psychological phenomena are incapable of completely independent definition; and thirdly, because social and psychological phenomena also 'interact' (to use for the moment the conventional phraseology). It is this last fact which turns the hierarchy of levels into true causal relations between the levels.

(1) Each level of analysis has its own 'current character of importance' (to borrow Whitehead's phrase). By this I mean that the phenomenal complexes—the complexes of facts given to our experience—are, on any given level, important and interesting as such. The relations that can be pursued between facts of the given

---

not in a final sense independent and absolute'; rather are they always immersed in a 'field' constituted by the 'culture pattern', i.e. by data definable only on the sociological level (p. 235). This view essentially accords with the one developed further on.

[1] C. C. Pratt (1939), p. 26.
[2] F. W. H. Rivers (1926), p. 14.

phenomenal complexity have their peculiar relevance, which cannot simply be replaced by that of relations discovered on a different level of analysis. In progressive analysis precisely this occurs. The phenomenal properties of facts given on one level disappear on the next lower level. The peculiar qualities of solids or liquids are no longer visible when chemistry is replaced by physics; the irritation of nerve ends is no longer itself, but something else, when the physiologist hands over to the biochemist. This phenomenal regression matters little in the natural sciences, which reduce the qualities of phenomena to mere 'pointer-readings' on indicators and the whole phenomenal world to one of pure measurement.[1] In the human sciences, which remain attached to the phenomenal side of things, it matters a great deal. Man is still the same for the physiologist, psychologist, and anthropologist. But the fact that man's fears, considered physiologically, become something else, or that his culture and society, broken down to psycho-physical processes, disappear as phenomenal entities, means that the subject matter of these disciplines itself disappears. Thus, between one level of analysis and the next there is a break, a relevant discontinuity—not merely a conventional and fortuitous division. In the field of human phenomena therefore the hierarchy of sciences appears broken up into a series of separate and self-contained disciplines. We now understand why the transition from one to the other appears to be more than merely a deepening of analysis; it gives at least the illusion of stepping into another order of existence, governed by regularities peculiar to it and only there established.

(2) At the same time, the current character of importance of any given level may spread to the other levels. Although I know that in any social action certain mental events are implicit I may be interested in rendering them explicit. In the simplest case this is only a question of the extent to which general knowledge concerning these implicit events can be taken for granted and tacitly assumed. Clearly, I shall not bother to mention the knowledge concerning vision, hearing, or memory which psychologists have accumulated, nor the physiologist's knowledge of muscle tensions and innervations, though all these processes must operate in the movements and perceptions which go to make up any social action. But occasionally this specialist knowledge requires to be expressed

[1] Sir Arthur Eddington (1928), p. 252.

in so many words or at least referred to, as it were, in a footnote. For certain social actions have the result (intended or not) of producing or utilizing particular mental states or physiological processes. Think of religious cults or dances inducing mental dissociation and hysteria, of alleged cures of disease, customary ways of securing physical fitness, and the like. As a student of society I wish to be reassured that I have correctly diagnosed these phenomena, which are not really my field; perhaps, too, I wish to learn more about them since this amplified knowledge might lead me to relevant connections I should otherwise overlook. This sort of situation poses no problem of method but only bears on practical considerations. Nor is it peculiar to the human sciences; the study of electric currents in nerve-physiology or of the surface tension of liquids in chemistry represents the same amplification of knowledge in terms of lower-level analysis.

But in the human sciences this amplification is more pervasive and is entailed in the very definition of our subject matter. For in any statement about social events we must *name* at least one species of the implicit lower-level events. We cannot define action except as intended behaviour, and hence must specifically refer to the mental functions underlying or carrying the intention—the desires, aims, motives, and so forth. But let me emphasize that this reference is descriptive, not explanatory; we do not establish a novel and causal relation between a specific action and the intention carrying it, but merely amplify our statement that such-and-such is an 'action' by indicating that, with deeper analysis, we should find in it intentions (as well as other mental events).[1]

(3) Yet it surely also makes sense to say that social facts exist and arise *because* the actors have had certain intentions or felt the efficacy of certain mental events, and that they have intentions and other mental events *because* certain social facts happen to exist. The social fact thus entails psychological (or psycho-physical) processes not only as part of its texture but also as something that exists outside and apart from it, namely, as its cause or antecedent and as its effect or consequent. It is a matter of common agreement that the social field is pervaded throughout by relations of this causal and

[1] As we shall see, this analysis does not completely reduce social facts to mental events; for the latter always contain an implicit reference to 'objects', some of which are again social **facts**, i.e. the results of social actions or such actions themselves (see below, pp. 291 ff.).

circular kind. In other words, we take it for granted that social facts are not merely the 'outside' to which psycho-physical facts are the 'inside', but that the two also affect and condition each other, that is, 'interact'.

In accepting this co-existence of implicitness and interaction we are faced with certain logical difficulties. For we predicate some mutual influence between a datum visible on one level of analysis and the same datum analyzed more deeply; between a 'short-hand' standing for certain phenomena and the phenomena themselves. This sounds paradoxical; and, indeed, in natural science this would mean, for example, that the chemical properties of a fluid interact with the molecular structure underlying the chemical properties; or that the irritation of nerve ends influences, and is influenced by, the biochemical processes which are the 'long-hand' for the physiological data. This is obviously nonsense. But, in the human field, precisely this is true. (The old controversy over psycho-physical interaction proves that in psychology such propositions are not nonsensical.) In sociology and anthropology, as I have presumed, no one will quarrel with the assumption that social facts 'act' upon mental facts and *vice versa*.

The paradox is resolved when we realize that we do not arbitrarily adopt the 'shorthand' which is the social fact, but that it is forced upon us, upon our way of perceiving and understanding, by the organization of the data themselves. The unity for which the 'shorthand' stands—marriage, the family, a ceremonial, a legal procedure, or whatever the mode of action may be—is phenomenally there; it palpably attaches to the combination of psycho-physical elements—the sensations, thoughts, motions, and the like—which make up the given mode of action. Call this phenomenal unity a 'pattern', or a recognizable 'type' of action, or—more correctly—a 'norm'; for we always understand this combination of diverse elements to be of a required kind, that is, to exemplify a rule of conduct. Furthermore, this combination of elements is effective *as a whole*; it exercises its peculiar influence upon the same elements not so combined or organized—upon other sensations, thoughts, motions in the environment, and is in turn subject to the influences coming from them. For a convenient illustration we may contrast the actors in any mode of action, say, a ceremonial or legal procedure, with the spectators or onlookers, with a public of some kind. While the sensations, thoughts, and motions of the actors would combine to make up the unitary phenomenon, the particular ceremonial or legal procedure, the spectators would react to the phenomenon as such, and under the influence of its occurrence, with their own, separate sensations, thoughts, and motions. But this is too simplified a picture. The reactions of a public also form part of the total social fact as we, the observers, understand it; while each actor, apart from contributing to the make-up of the social fact, also sees it as such a total combination, made up of the behaviour of all other actors and exemplifying a norm of conduct; indeed his own sensations, thoughts, and motions are reactions to that totality, that is, thoughts about the ceremonial or procedure, likes and dislikes with regard to its rules, intentions to join in or to keep away, and so forth.[1] The valid distinction between 'actions' and 'reactions' lies elsewhere. For the behaviour of any individual involved in the efficacy of a social fact, whether as onlooker or participant, can be of two kinds. It may only occur under the influence of, and be absorbed in, the normal course of events, simply falling within the given 'pattern', 'type,' or 'norm'; alternatively, his behaviour may relevantly influence the course of events, affecting its end results, or the particular form it takes, or even the future validity of the 'norm'; so that his sensations, thoughts, and motions will add some novel feature to the combination of psycho-physical processes as it now eventuates.

The organization of psycho-physical processes into that phenomenal unit we call a social fact thus has at any moment, and for any organism involved in it, an 'outside' and an 'inside', whose frontiers may move at any subsequent moment. More generally speaking, the combination of psycho-physical processes which is the social fact has a past and a future. It shapes its own future whenever it eventuates; for though it is produced in a particular form at a point in time, its effectiveness lasts beyond this point. And it has a past when it cannot yet have occurred in this particular form, or cannot have occurred at all; for at some stage this combination has been produced for a first time, that is, has been created. It is produced and created by individuals out of their psycho-physical

---

[1] Max Weber similarly pointed out that the 'empirical reality' of any social fact includes both the numerous actions, intentions, and 'actual relationships' of the individuals concerned, and certain ideas *about* the obtaining norms of behaviour present in varying degrees of clarity in the actors' minds. While the 'conceptualization' of the social fact, carried out by the student of the society, must always rest on a synthesis of both these aspects (see 1904, pp. 71–4).

resources; but these individuals and others must be conceived of as existing both before and after that stage, so that at any given moment they (or their psycho-physical processes) are both creative of social facts and subject to their effectiveness. Social facts are unthinkable without this genetic or, in the widest sense, historical aspect. Once we grasp this, we also grasp the final consequence, that something that is not yet a social fact, but only an event in a mind or organism, can become that repetitive, patterned, standardized complex of events in numerous minds and organisms which we call a mode of action or a social fact, and can go on involving more minds in its effectiveness. Thus, though the social fact is made up of psycho-physical processes it can also be understood to result from them and to initiate or cause such processes, as though it were a thing extraneous to them.

For this process of 'becoming' which underlies all social and psychological 'interaction' certain scholars have found the name *emergence*. By this is meant a 'novelty of behaviour arising from the specific . . . organization of a number of elements, whether inorganic, organic, or mental, which thereby constitute a whole, as distinguished from their mere sum, or resultant'.[1] Emergence is thus a 'synthetic event'; it is 'creative of real novelty, of some new quality or property of a type that did not exist before the emergence'; and this 'new quality or property has causal efficiency, (making) a difference to the further course of events'.[2] 'Emergence' so understood seems to hold good in the whole field of organic life and evolution; these implications I will not venture to discuss. But I would hold, with the defenders of 'emergent evolution', that social facts are 'emergents' from the orders of things which we call psychological and organic. To the relation of *implicitness* between the phenomena analyzed on different levels we must thus add this other relation, of *emergence* from level to level.

Let me stress that there is nothing fictitious or metaphysical, nor purely metaphorical, about emergent properties in the field of social phenomena. Nor are they unfamiliar. A thought or experience expressed, a gesture performed, in so far as they sub-

---

[1] W. M. Wheeler (1928), p. 14.

[2] W. McDougall (1934), pp. 120–1, *et passim*. Similar statements will be found in the writings of Lloyd Morgan and C. D. Broad. See also Talcott Parson (1937), p. 749.

sequently influence other events in the environment of thought and action, are instances of rudimentary emergence. A book in which thoughts are perpetuated, a lasting monument or work of art, a code of law or morals, or an act of authority accepted or resented by others, are emergents in the full sense of the word. If we call such things and events 'social' or 'cultural', and not psychophysical, we do so precisely because they possess the peculiar efficacy of emergents.

We must, however, enlarge a little upon the conditions necessary for emergence to take place. I have said that something that is an event in a mind or organism at one moment may, at the next, become a social fact. Now, this is possible only under two conditions: first, the mental and organic events materializing in the action of an individual must be capable of being *experienced by others*; and secondly, this experiencing by others must *once more evoke action*. Expressed differently, the mental event-become-action must add to the environment of objects in which all experiences and actions take place. We assume therefore that, once the initial action materializes, it is there to be perceived, remembered, perhaps felt, and responded to; it thus, in some measure, delimits the random experiences of others, and hence their random behaviour, providing 'objects' for the former and models, goals, or constraints for the latter. If the objects and models endure, and if they are uniformly responded to, the resulting novel combination of events in many minds and organisms is the social fact 'emerged'. Yet no mental or organic event occurs in a vacuum. Any 'initial' mental event I posit can be such an event only in a relative sense; so far as my empirical knowledge goes, it must already have occurred in a given environment of objects, models, goals, and constraints. The mental event, then, which materializes in novel action must also, at some preceding moment, have been provoked or shaped by the experiencing of a given environment. This is little better than a truism; if a book has been written which changes the outlook and behaviour of other people, or a person acts in some novel way which serves others as model or warning, the writer or actor has clearly himself been influenced by the books or actions of others; and as he adds to the environment, so this 'addition' of his is in some measure also a response to the pre-existing environment. Stated more generally, the 'initial' mental event *causes* social action to run a novel course, and the modes of social action existing at any moment *cause* mental events to be of a certain kind. This circular relationship can be expressed in the following diagram:

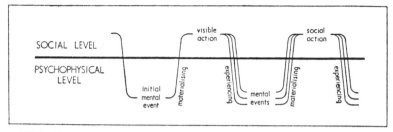

This double causality is not, of course, complete or rigid. For not all mental events materialize in action, or in actions of sufficient magnitude and novelty to add significantly to the environment; nor does the environment of pre-existing modes of action fully and uniformly delimit the random experiences and responses of the individuals within it. If this were so, the two forms of causality would cancel out; for the former would lead to a world re-made in every action and the latter to a world where no novel action ever takes place. In reality, there is some permanence and some novelty in this world of ours. Can we at least say this: If we knew all the conditions under which mental events materialize in novel actions, as well as all the conditions under which 'objects' in the environment evoke mental events of a uniform kind, we should know the machinery which, ultimately, moves our world? It is doubtful if we can say as much, for we cannot exclude some randomness that evades any statement in terms of conditions and their effects. Even so, this 'machinery' exists and is analyzable, if only incompletely; it exists in the psycho-physical make-up of man and the regularities governing it.

In any closed system, in any culture or society free from outside influences, this knowledge must, if you like, lead us in a circle; but to resolve it we need not go back to hypothetical beginnings.[1] The circle is resolved by the principle of emergence, which is as continuous as the existence of society and culture. Sometimes, as we have seen, the circle appears broken up into conspicuous beginnings—whenever mental events materialize in actions capable

[1] Goldenweiser calls the relationship between culture and the individual mind, whereby one springs from the other, yet is also determined by it, 'superficially paradoxical', adding that, if our knowledge were 'infinitely expanded', it would finally derive culture from the individual mind (1933, p. 59).

of significantly altering the environment. I shall later speak of this kind of emergence as of the *genesis* of social facts. More often, the emergence is not fully creative, but, as it were, re-creative or repetitive, peopling the environment with permanent and familiar models, goals, and constraints of behaviour. As I shall try to show, this 'repetitive' emergence of social from psycho-physical facts accounts for the *linkage* of social facts. Whether emergence is one or the other, it exhibits that novel relation between the different levels of analysis to which I referred before. Once more we draw this lesson: In the human sciences the transition from one to the other assumes the significance of a step into a different order of existence. And now this is more than an illusion; for the different order fully means different, 'independently established' facts and their regularities which, viewed from the higher level, must appear both as causal determinants and as 'hidden mechanisms'.

6. CONCLUSIONS

We conclude that one range of problems posed by social enquiry, namely that of finding a mechanical-causal 'requiredness' or 'fitness' in the social phenomena, can in fact be illuminated by a move to other, lower levels of analysis, and that the respective explanatory concepts can fruitfully be constructed in the extraneous terms which have citizenship on the lower levels. These, so far as they are relevant for social enquiry, are given in the disciplines dealing with the human organism—psychology, physiology, and biology. The levels of analysis lower down in the hierarchy of disciplines—chemistry or physics—are irrelevant in a twofold sense. Here the 'phenomenal regression' goes too far and dissolves too completely the kind of facts upon which our interest is centred; and here, too, emergence seems to disappear, leaving only the progressive inclusiveness of phenomena completely reducible to each other.

The question of the fruitfulness and legitimacy of such extraneous explanations in social enquiry has not been uniformly answered in this positive sense; and not a few scholars prefer not to raise it at all but to proceed by what I am tempted to call rule of thumb. That the question, where it has been raised, is mostly applied only to the relationship between the two adjacent levels, social enquiry and psychology, is no accident; for these two levels clearly interpenetrate most fully. Thus Rivers and Allport have held that all explanations of social phenomena must be in psychological terms;[1] and many anthropologists and sociologists, especially those influenced by Freudian.teaching, proceed as though this reduction of social to psychological enquiry were a foregone conclusion. Yet there are also the defenders of a 'pure', autonomous, sociology—Durkheim, Simmel, A. F. Bentley, Radcliffe-Brown, and others. Admittedly, certain of these scholars would banish 'individual' psychology only, while they graciously offer a niche to 'social psychology'. But since the distinction between these two kinds of psychology is little better than a fallacy, I will here disregard this compromise.[2]

The contrast between the views for and against the inclusion of psychological principles can be put even more sharply; for while the 'pure sociologist' would condemn all explanation in non-social terms, he freely admits psychology in description. To quote but one example, Durkheim's writings are full of descriptive psychological statements, and you can read hardly a single page without finding on it such words as sentiments, emotions, desires, fears, excitement, and a great many others denoting mental states. Conversely, one scholar at least admits a purely sociological description and classification of social facts, though no ultimate explanation save in terms of psychology.[3] Clearly, where views are so strikingly contradictory, the true answer is likely to lie midway, and we may expect to find the reason for the discrepancy in some confusion of thought. I have suggested how this may have arisen. It is, first, a confusion between the different kinds of explanation possible in social enquiry, only one of which (explanation in terms of causality) entails a move to lower levels of analysis; and it is, secondly, a confusion between the two kinds of relation linking social enquiry with the lower levels of analysis—the relation of implicitness (offering only a spurious causality), and that of 'emergence' (offering true causality).

---

[1] F. W. H. Rivers (1926), p. 5; F. H. Allport (1924), p. 10.

[2] I find myself in almost complete agreement with A. F. Bentley's summary dismissal of social psychology, of which 'the less said the better' (1935, p. 326). However, as social psychology has come to play so large a part in modern literature, I propose to say a little more about it in a later context (see below Chap. XI, sec. 2).

[3] F. W. H. Rivers (1926), p. 5.—If I understand Allport correctly, he holds a similar view (1924), pp. 10–11.

One question, however, remains. This whole discussion revolved upon the discovery of invariant relations between phenomena, which in turn rests upon the experimental method: yet in social enquiry we cannot easily experiment. Can we then employ some alternative but equally adequate method of discovery and verification? This question shall form the subject of the next chapter.

CHAPTER IX

Experimental Anthropology

1. THE COMPARATIVE METHOD

It is true enough that 'Social Anthropology cannot experiment'. But the same limitation is shared by certain branches of natural science, such as astronomy or geology. Here as in the human sciences the artificial induction of variations in phenomena is replaced by the observation of variable phenomena. We study variations, found and looked for in the data of observation, and correlate them so that from them general regularities may emerge.

This equivalent of the experiment in the study of society is usually called, somewhat loosely, the comparative method.[1] For comparison as such is only the handling of material which might yield relevant knowledge. Comparison needs further refinement— planned selection and rigorous checks or controls—to approach the accuracy of a quasi-experimental method. This refinement is offered in the study of 'concomitant variations', formulated by J. S. Mill as one of the methods of inductive enquiry,[2] and elevated by Durkheim to a paramount principle in sociological research.[3] It means, in essence, the analysis of social situations which are at first sight already comparable, that is, which appear to share certain features (modes of action, relationships) while differing in others, or to share their common features with some degree of difference. This first-sight impression will be rendered more precise by demonstrating the extent to which uniformities or differences in any one feature are accompanied by, or 'correlated' with, uniformities or differences in others. Hence we are able, finally, to isolate the invariant relations between facts upon which all scientific explanations must rest. The concomitant variations (or co-variations for

---

[1] 'The Experiment is . . . nothing but the comparative method where the cases to be compared are produced to order and under controlled conditions' (Talcott Parsons, 1937, p. 743).

[2] J. S. Mill (1875), vol. I.   [3] E. Durkheim (1927), pp. 163 ff.

short) thus lead us to some such formula as: If A, then B, for in situations s^1, s^2, s^3 . . . there are A and B; and in situations s^4, s^5, s^6 . . . there are A-changed and B-changed.[1]

The concomitant variations do not mean quite the same thing in J. S. Mill's *Logic* and in Durkheim's sociological treatise. For Mill, they provide the *quantitative* precision lacking in his other 'experimental' methods—the methods of Agreement and Difference—which only demonstrate the occurrence or non-occurrence of a particular phenomenon in conformity with the occurrence or non-occurrence of others; while Durkheim also includes variations of the latter kind, that is, *qualitative* changes in the situation. Occasionally Durkheim's method comes as close to purely quantitative variations as is possible in social enquiry, for example, in his classical study of suicide, where he correlates the frequency of suicide (among other things) with the prevalence, in the given societies, of different denominations.[2] But often Durkheim's method is quantitative only in its preliminaries, in the collection and assessment of the data, but qualitative in its end results. We cannot otherwise interpret the kind of studies he envisages—studies concerned with the changes that occur, in different societies or historical phases, in the make-up of the family, in practices of marriage, in norms of morality or religious creeds, and so forth. Here, then, it is a question of demonstrating the invariant 'agreement' (or the opposite) between the social phenomenon investigated and the circumstances in which it appears, disappears, or appears in a particular form.

It can be argued, I think, that this extended meaning of 'concomitant variations' is legitimate, and that Mill's 'qualitative' methods in fact only amount to a special, if perhaps cruder, application of the 'quantitative' approach; for the occurrence or non-occurrence of phenomena may be taken to constitute once more quantitative variations, though they are here, as it were, at a maximum or minimum, and of an all-or-none kind. However this may be, it seems clear that in social enquiry the two cannot be separated. For one thing, we cannot do without the 'cruder' experiment, and

---

[1] In order to distinguish these empirically established 'invariant relations' from logical ones (i.e., from relations of implication or entailment) we might phrase our formula more carefully, thus: Where A, there B. But in the present context a confusion of this kind is unlikely to arise.

[2] E. Durkheim (1897), pp. 154–9.

must as often consider the presence, absence, or changes of particular social facts (institutions, forms of grouping, and the like) as the frequency, prevalence, or certainty with which modes of action appear. And for another, when we speak of the 'presence' of an institution or form of grouping we speak implicitly of the prevalence of the respective modes of action; so that our qualitative variations always conceal quantitative ones, though it is unnecessary to state them in this form, if not impossible to do so with any precision. We shall therefore in the following discussion understand the 'concomitant variations' in the wider sense; also, we shall mostly frame our correlations in that all-or-none fashion, disregarding the quantitative alternative.

Now, the method of co-variations presupposes three things. First, in a technical sense, it presupposes some preliminary hypothesis or suspicion as to the kind of correlation likely to prove relevant. We have already stressed the part played by such anticipations of relevance in all forms of scientific enquiry, and we might here add that the series of co-variations we propose to examine may or may not verify these anticipations; also, we shall mostly start out with several such possibilities in mind; but without some such anticipations our experimental method would be committed to that 'complete observation' of all facts which is both futile and impossible.[1] Secondly, the method of co-variations implies the general postulate that social situations are not made up of random items, but of facts which hang together by some meaningful nexus or intrinsic fitness; for unless this is so, it is clearly useless to search for any concomitance in the variations which social facts may undergo.

My third point concerns the fact that the study of co-variations is bound up with judgments on the identity and difference of social facts. These judgments, moreover, must be such that there can be general agreement about them, lest the study of co-variations be reduced to the private computations of individual observers. That we can make such judgments, unaided by the test tubes or indicators of the natural scientist, no one will deny; that we also make mistakes or fail to agree, we must admit. But this is not quite all. The study of co-variations is bound up, more specifically, with judgments on similarity and partial identity, the very concept of

---

[1] This important qualification of J. S. Mill's 'experimental methods' has been emphasized by Cohen and Nagel (1939), pp. 143, 147, 153.

variations implying a sameness of facts which yet permits of some measure of difference. Now, judgments on 'full identity' are much more convincing and more satisfactory to handle than are judgments on similarity. Needless to say, even 'full identity' is only an approximation, valid on a given level of analysis and adequate only for 'all practical purposes', that is, the purposes the observers have in mind; even so, it will leave less scope for disagreement than the sort of appearance which all observers at the outset admit to imply only partial identity (i.e. similarity). For here the question at once arises whether the things and events which duplicate each other in some respects but not in others do so in relevant respects, so that we can in fact speak of an 'essential' identity. Clearly, according to my criteria of relevance I might consider the similar phenomena to be the same thing varied, while you might regard them as 'essentially' different. The boundaries of any presumed 'essential' identity are, of course, prescribed by the concepts we construct for classes of phenomena and the names we give to them; thus, if we agree to call certain similar phenomena by the same name—say, 'marriage,' or 'law', or a 'medium of exchange'—we should also agree, by implication, that their relevant features have remained unvaried. Yet only too often it is argued that these two agreements need not coincide and that the presumed essential identity of the phenomena is an identity 'in name only'.

The issue involved is clearly one of classification, with which we have dealt at length. Let me only add this. Identity in name is a relevant identity, however limited it may be; at least, unless the common name has been bestowed or is used arbitrarily, it stands for some aspect in the phenomena which we have come to consider sufficiently crucial to generalize from it to the essence or meaning of the whole phenomenon and make it a basis for the common name. Ultimately, it is we who judge that relevance, as it is the history of our discipline which guides or forces our judgments; and though this history has often been haphazard, it has also produced far-reaching agreement. There may well be uncertainties of nomenclature; but there is also, as we know, one crucial test to correct any such ambiguity, namely, the reference to the 'operations'—observational and intellectual—which go into the making of our concepts and their names.[1] And in this sense marriage is 'marriage' in whatever varied forms it appears if the term is used with its

[1] See above, p. 134.

operational (and agreed) meaning of an enduring relationship between man and woman, implying sexual intimacy and care for offspring; the things we call a 'medium of exchange' or a system of 'law' are always and everywhere modes of behaviour identical in relevant features if these terms have any operational meaning at all.

Assuming then, that we can with reasonable accuracy proceed with an analysis so bound up with judgments on identity and similarity, it is clear that we can follow different lines of attack. We may, with Durkheim, distinguish these three applications of the method of co-variations.[1] (1) We could consider a single society at a given time and analyze the broad variations in particular modes of action or relationships occurring in that society.[2] (2) We could consider several societies of generally similar nature which differ in certain modes of action or relationships; more precisely, we could here compare either different and perhaps contemporaneous societies, or the same society at different periods, if these exhibit some limited cultural change. (3) We could compare several, perhaps numerous, societies of widely different nature yet sharing some identical feature; or different periods, showing radical change, in the life of the same society. The 'identical' feature might be a specific mode of action or relationship, so that we can search for concomitantly identical circumstances in the diverse situations (as when we compare, say, the craft guilds in a West African State with the craft guilds of medieval Europe); or it might be one of the ubiquitous facts of social existence, which is only 'essentially' identical, so that we should attempt to correlate its varying forms with the varied circumstances in which it appears (as when we trace the institution of marriage through diverse ages or cultures).

These are differences in approach and in scope of interest, and in practice we could concentrate on one or the other. But the three applications of the method of co-variation cannot, I think, be regarded as separate and independent lines of enquiry. It is true that the third, most far-flung, approach is sometimes taken to constitute the field of a special discipline, which Durkheim, Weber,

---

[1] E. Durkheim (1927), p. 167.

[2] The emphasis is on 'broad' variations; for we mean here major divergences in group behaviour, whether this is institutionalized or not (e.g. incidence of crimes or suicide, the distribution of poverty and wealth, diverse social practices, political and religious movements, etc.). We do not mean the individual variability of behaviour which still falls within the 'normal curve' of distribution. The part played by the latter will be examined later.

and Radcliffe-Brown have called 'comparative sociology'.[1] I would not myself adopt this distinction; rather should I regard the field of 'comparative sociology' as the typical field of social enquiry, and the three approaches as phases or steps in it. Even if we are initially concerned only with a single society and the appearance in it of a particular social fact (which we wish to 'explain'), our search for co-variations capable of illuminating our problem will often lead us beyond that society to others, similar or diverse, since the given society may not offer an adequate range of variations. Also, the regularities which we can extract from narrow-range comparisons are themselves of narrow applicability; they would exhibit specific phenomena present only in a limited number of societies—such as marriage concluded by payment of brideprice, homicide settled by means of bloodfeud; or age sets organizing adolescence. While in the far-flung comparisons we deal with the ubiquitous classes of social facts, which are features of human society writ large—marriage as such, law as such, the organization of adolescence as such. As we shall see, these far-flung comparisons offer a shortcut to the laws or regularities we are after. Yet whatever general laws we might discover in this way, they will clearly embrace the kind of facts discoverable through the narrower variations; so that in this sense the third approach in the method of co-variations represents the synthesis of the evidence obtained by the first and second.

Whether or not we press our study towards that synthesis depends, as I have suggested, on the scope of our interest. But it can readily be seen that for such far-flung enquiries the subject matter of anthropology—primitive society—itself presents a set of data for comparison and one of the varying situations in which social facts may appear. It is, too, a particularly fruitful and convenient situation. For one thing, the comparison of advanced with primitive societies offers the suggestive combination of extreme differences with 'essentially' identical features. Moreover, on the level of primitive societies one of the main technical difficulties besetting the study of co-variations is greatly reduced, namely, the difficulty of pursuing the variations in a multitude of co-existing facts. In primitive societies, where groups are relatively small, modes of living less complex, and where no varied history has left its agglomerations of cultural possessions, the field of social facts is

---

[1] Cf. E. Durkheim (1927), p. 167; Max Weber (1947), p. 88; A. R. Radcliffe-Brown (1931), p. 17.

more easily surveyed. Thus the comparison with primitive societies may throw into relief salient features which, in advanced societies, are often obscured, and suggest hypotheses of correlations otherwise not as readily seen. No wonder, then, that anthropology has become almost a laboratory for the quasi-experimental approach to social phenomena, which all students of society have been ready to utilize.[1]

Yet warnings are not lacking either that such far-flung comparisons involve a dangerous lack of accuracy. This is the familiar argument that social facts must not be torn from their context, and that they become meaningless if so treated. This means, apparently, that if we examined social facts in the artificial isolation entailed in any comparison and increasing with its range, we could not intelligently speak about them, since something unique, which pertains to them in their given context alone, would be lost in the process. If this were true, and if therefore 'comparative sociology' were methodologically unsound, social explanations as we understand them would be impossible. Optimism about the limits set to a scientific enquiry is, of course, not an adequate ground for assuming its validity. But I am convinced (as are many others) that our standpoint is assured by more than optimism. On the contrary, the sceptics might be accused of defeatism and of overplaying purely technical obstacles. The anthropologist (or any scientist) whose motto is 'never depart from contexts' ignores that we possess intellectual means for isolating elements from their settings without disastrous loss of meaning. Some loss there may well be; this follows from our postulate that social facts 'hang together by some meaningful nexus'. But we also know that this nexus is not all-embracing, and that not all connections are of equal relevance, so that some can be disregarded in the study of any one fact. The context of the room in which I write, of the street and town in which I live, is clearly unique, and different from the context in which other writers have written much the same thing; but the ideas we express bear comparison in spite of this. And indeed, since each context is built into a wider one, the assumption that context and setting are all-powerful would mean that everything is unique, and that there could be no isolation of facts anywhere; yet

[1] The comparison between the anthropological field and a 'laboratory' for social enquiry has frequently been drawn; cf. e.g. D. Forde (1947), p. 1; M. J. Herskovits (1948), p. 79.

clearly, we can stop short of the boundaries of the universe. There is an obvious fallacy in the intellectual attitude which, to quote from Cohen, conceives of all facts only as 'determined by the contexts in which they occur, and thus tends to arrive at the logical conclusion that it is the whole universe that is the real subject of every significant proposition'; for this view 'systematically under-values the importance of abstraction, and does scant justice to the relative independence of the various parts of the world'.[1]

2. TECHNIQUE

The basic formula, 'If A, then B,' at which all experimental methods aim, will emerge from co-variations of two different kinds. In the first, the presence or absence of one social fact will determine the presence or absence respectively of the other, so that we can extract a straight or parallel correlation; in the second, the presence of one fact will determine the absence of the other, so that the correlation is inverse. It must be noted, however, that it might only be a matter of viewpoint or convenience whether we state a correlation in parallel or inverse form, since the 'absence' of a particular social fact can often be stated positively, as the 'presence' of the opposite fact (e.g. instead of saying that the presence of a national emergency goes together with the absence of internal conflicts, we might say it goes together with increased social solidarity). Schematically expressed, in 'all-or-none' form, we obtain these two formulae (the index ° meaning the absence of the fact in question):

A ... with (XYZ) ... with B   A ... with (XYZ) ... with B°
A° ... with (XYZ) ... with B°   A° ... with (XYZ) ... with B

These correlations are over-simplified, not only because they operate with two co-variants only, but because they leave undefined the 'setting', the surrounding circumstances, in which the co-variations occur. The main difficulty involved in our experimental technique lies precisely in defining these surrounding circumstances and their bearing on the correlations we extract. In the simplest case the surrounding circumstances will be identical, as will be the case if we choose the first and second approach mentioned before. Instead of

A ... with (XYZ) ... with B

[1] M. Cohen (1946), p. 79.

we shall then specify

A . . . with (PQR) . . . with B

Here, then, we have a clear-cut distinction between 'background features' (which remain unchanged) and the relevant factors (the 'co-variants'). But let me stress again that it is we who produce this identical setting for the sake of convenience, so that our initial hypothesis may be verified with relative ease, and perhaps so that some such hypothesis may readily suggest itself. We cannot assume that the 'background features' are in fact irrelevant for our correlation; we only choose our conditions so that these additional features can be disregarded. This is the familiar condition of *ceteris paribus* which, though it simplifies analysis, may also hide unsuspected co-variants, and thus limit the validity of our correlations.

Assuming we find in the primitive society which we initially study that male age sets appear together with regular tribal warfare. This would strike us as a meaningful connection; for an efficient organization for war implies rigid discipline and a strong *esprit de corps*, which the age sets in fact provide. There is, then, a 'fit' between the two, and we shall assume that the co existence of these two features is likely to prove an invariant relation. We shall probably not find the required negative evidence in the same society, and we turn therefore to similar ones (on the same technological level, sharing the same kinship organization, and so forth) where it can be found. Assuming that our hypothesis is borne out in all cases examined, then it would still be assured only for these similar conditions. If we aim at a correlation of wider validity we must widen our scope of enquiry over societies in which the 'background features', too, appear varied; and here we might (or might not) find that, as the technological level or the kinship system changes, our correlation fails to hold. It might be, for example, that the societies initially examined all possessed rigidly segmented clan systems, and that in societies only loosely divided into clans, age sets and war no longer go together. In other words, the clan system would prove to be a co-variant, so that our simple one-to-one correlation must be replaced by a multiple one.

We should be forced to review the background features also in another case, namely, where the co-variations fail to confirm our initial hypothesis. This may of course only mean that we were

wrong in making that assumption. Yet if we are only unable to
verify our assumption as *widely* as we expected (or if we strongly
believe in our hypothesis), we should re-examine the facts whose
identity we took for granted; for we might have relied on too super-
ficial an identity or minimized the importance of some dissimilarity.
For example, we might have considered the societies examined to
be essentially identical since they all involve a division into clans;
as it now turns out, we should have distinguished between rigid
clan segmentation and the less sharply pronounced variety, the
failure of our correlation being explained by this omission. And if
we pursued this new, once more multiple, correlation further, we
might find that age sets go together with rigid clan segmentation
even in the absence of regular warfare.

In the terms of our example, and expressed schematically for
three co-variants, these two groups of multiple correlations may in
principle occur:

$$A \ldots \text{with P} \ldots \text{with B}$$
$$A° \ldots \text{with P°} \ldots \text{with B}$$
$$A° \ldots \text{with P} \ldots \text{with B°}$$

$$A \ldots \text{with P°} \ldots \text{with B}$$
$$A \ldots \text{with P} \ldots \text{with B°}$$
$$A^+ \ldots \text{with P} \ldots \text{with B}$$

The first three formulae indicate that age sets (A) occur only if
both other factors (P, B)—rigid clan segmentation and warfare—
are present, and do not occur if only one is present. The two
factors are therefore *complementary* determinants of the fact under
investigation. The second group of formulae indicates that age sets
occur when either of the two factors is present, so that these appear
as *alternative* determinants. In the latter case it is possible that in
the presence of both alternative determinants the fact under investigation reflects this double nexus, being more strongly pronounced than when only one determinant is present; for example,
the age sets may in this case exhibit a more rigorous organization;
this possibility is expressed by the plus sign in the last formula.

I am here using 'determinant' in a somewhat inaccurate sense.
Assuming that age sets never occur without tribal warfare, while
the latter can occur without age sets, then we shall clearly call war a
determinant of the presence of age sets. If on the other hand the
two facts always occur together (*ceteris paribus*), then they would

appear to determinè each other, being simply interdependent. And if we still called war the determinant and age sets the thing determined (as we shall probably do), then this interpretation would be derived from knowledge we possess independently of the situations analyzed, namely, from the general knowledge that war is likely to be in some way the primary factor, the thing that requires, and age sets the thing that meets the requirement. But this question bears on a wider one, namely the possibility of interpreting relations of interdependence in terms of causality.

Now, we might wish to pursue our multiple correlations much further and to examine the kind of thing into which age sets change in societies not operating with clan segmentation, belonging to a different level of technology, and perhaps no longer organized for war or a particular kind of war. Ultimately, we should arrive at the far-flung regularities we spoke of before, which govern not the species 'age sets', but the genus 'organization of adolescence' in widely different cultures and even in Society writ large. But, as I have suggested, there is a short-cut. For we can disregard the diverse settings, concerning ourselves only with two things—the social fact whose variations we wish to trace, and that other feature or set of features which we presume to be its correlate. Here the XYZ of our original formula means literally XYZ, that is, unknown 'surrounding features'; all we know is that they differ in the different instances we examine. We can therefore no longer *ab initio* distinguish between unchanged background features and co-variants, and must fully rely on our initial hypothesis or suspicion.

The fact that we leave the diverse surrounding features unanalyzed does not as such detract from the validity of the correlations we extract. On the contrary, it is because the correlation is established for a series of undefined situations that we can expect it to hold also for numerous others, and perhaps for 'society at large'. The only condition that must be satisfied is that the instances we presume to be diverse should not conceal some unsuspected uniformity. Paradoxically speaking, our co-variations presuppose the condition of *ceteris imparibus*. For example, if I examined the correlation between population pressure and emigration I must clearly exclude the possibility that all instances of population pressure are instances also, say, of a subsistence economy, or of a family organization based on primogeniture, barring younger brothers from inheritance and so inducing them to emigrate. It is unlikely, however, that we should overlook such additional determinants; for if they in fact occurred, they would probably limit the validity of our correlation, and we should find instances of population pressure which do not go together with emigration. Also, this source of error, such as it is, is avoided by random sampling, that is, by precisely that choice of instances from everywhere and anywhere which is (at least often) implied in our far-flung comparisons.[1] But obviously the correlation we suspect may still not hold in all the cases examined, thus revealing the presence of additional determinants. Nor perhaps shall we ignore this possibility when framing our initial hypothesis. In other words, we shall again be prepared to delimit or to re-examine the XYZ of our formula and to operate with multiple correlations.

In the foregoing discussion we spoke of correlations being established for 'all cases examined'. This is a somewhat loose way of speaking. In effect, we do not mean *all known* cases of a particular kind (nor, of course, all cases that occur or are possible), but only those of which we happen to have adequate knowledge. Even so, our correlations will often prove true only in a numerically significant proportion of instances. Yet if these are sufficiently numerous, we can claim to have established the statistically valid probability that the correlation will hold also in cases not examined, or not analyzed with equal thoroughness, *if these are of the stipulated kind*. Now in anthropological research we can at the moment specify the 'stipulated kind' only roughly on the grounds of such analyses as we have found adequate. New discoveries, or the re-examination of already known instances, may well call this adequacy in question. Social situations not hitherto encountered or examined may contradict the regularities we established and force us to search for additional determinants not previously suspected or isolated. Some such tentativeness is of course typical of every growing science. But in social enquiry this is less a question of widening and deepening our knowledge than of handling it when it has been so expanded.

[1] This is not always so. If our far-flung comparisons concern different phases in the history of one society, the instances are clearly not random, however extensive the cultural change; and if we, as anthropologists, take our instances from primitive societies we include at least one unchanged background feature—the 'primitivity' of the culture (whatever is meant by the term), in which case the validity of the correlations is limited by the presence of these potential additional determinants.

In anthropology we are only just beginning to marshal our facts for analysis; we are still operating with limited regularities established for narrow and disconnected collections of 'cases examined'. These limited and disconnected regularities must be unified and built into embracing ones, though we cannot as yet foresee the end result. We can foresee one thing, however. With every widening and deepening of our analysis simple correlations will change into multiple ones, and these might become so complicated that they can no longer be adequately handled or indeed conceived.[1] Shall we, then, be compelled to go on employing limited and crude correlations rather than regularities more widely valid and more fully refined? This is, at the moment, our practice. We prefer to state our correlations in a simple one-to-one form and to qualify them by means of provisos and exceptions rather than to embody these in our formulae; or we limit the validity of our correlations by saying that they hold, say, only in primitive societies; or again, we liberally use that 'exculpating phrase of sociologists—other things being equal'.[2] As I shall later suggest, we cannot hope to exclude provisos and exceptions altogether from the field of social enquiry. But need our technique and formulation remain so crude and clumsy? We can probably look forward to some advance in our technique of expressing multiple correlations and of constructing concepts which should hold together the complicated interconnections. These new concepts would have to be of even greater abstractness than some we already use—such as social integration, social stability, or the concept of an optimum size of groups. Yet their very generality would empty them of all the particular references which seem to us important if we are at all to visualize the kinds of situation they stand for. Thus we should have to think along new lines; we must not only widen our knowledge but also learn to frame it in a new way, leaving concreteness and features that can be visualized far behind. How far or when this will become possible, can once more not be foreseen.

Let me, in conclusion, illustrate the technique of enquiry here discussed by a concrete example. It concerns the important relationship between intermittent generations in the family, to which

---

[1] It is interesting to quote this comment on the comparable difficulties encountered in physiological analysis: 'The mind, so-to-speak, often fails to keep pace with the tremendous activity of interrelations' (J. P. Pavlov, 1927, p. 378).

[2] Robert S. Lynd (1939), p. 16.

Radcliffe-Brown has drawn attention.[1] In many primitive societies grandfather and grandchild stand in an especially intimate relationship, which is friendly and of equal footing, and implies that familiarity and privileged disrespect which anthropologists call 'joking relationship'. Between grandfather and grandchild there is none of the disciplinarian attitude and demand for respect which characterizes the relationship between a father and his boy and their respective generations. On the grounds of general knowledge we suspect where the relevant conditions for this state of affairs may lie. They would seem to lie in the fact that the grandfather stands, by his age, on the borderline of social usefulness and, by his generation, on the border of the effective family group. He does not need to exact the respect of the growing generation, while the father, who directs the family and the education of the young, must do so. The grandfather-grandchild relationship would therefore seem to offer a relief from the sterner atmosphere of authority which otherwise dominates the relationship between the child and the adults of his family.

Now, in a study of a number of Nuba communities I discovered that this hypothesis is borne out by the co-variations which I was able to establish. In nine out of the ten tribes examined the people live in small household groups, each comprising an elementary family of which the grandfather forms no part; physically and socially, he is outside this living unit. In all nine cases the father, the head of the household, is also the disciplinarian, while grandfather and grandson stand in joking relationship. In the tenth case, the people live in a large, joint family group the head of which is the grandfather (or a man of the grandfather generation); and here the grandfather appears as the disciplinarian, as the authoritarian family head, and no joking relationship exists between him and his grandchildren. The father, not being the head of the household, is also without the aloofness of authority, and he and his children freely joke together and behave with a familiarity unknown in the other tribes. So far, the joking relationship between intermittent generations appears clearly correlated (in 'inverse' fashion) with the assumption of authority in the family group. In two different tribes, however, among the Nupe and Gbari of West Africa, I found the same joint family organization, headed by the grandfather, combined with joking relationship between their intermittent genera-

[1] (1940b), pp. 201–2; (1941), p. 13.

tions. But here this additional feature also appears: among the Nupe and Gbari the grandson is believed to be the reincarnation of a deceased grandfather; he is given the same name and is even expected to marry his widowed grandmother in nominal marriage. Grandson and living grandfather treat one another as equals, for such—in a mystic sense—they are, and the boy behaves towards the old man in the same jocular manner as he does towards his age-mates and, more particularly, his parallel cousins, whose widows he is equally expected to marry. The joking relationship, then, though not correlated with family organization and distribution of authority, appears linked with the 'alternative' determinants of the belief in reincarnation and the practice of a modified levirate. We may tabulate the results of our brief enquiry thus (plus signs indicating the presence, and minus signs the absence of the features in question)—

Joint family organization	Grandfather disciplinarian	Father disciplinarian	Reincarnation, modified Levirate	Joking Relationship	
				Grandfather Grandsons	Father Sons
−	−	+	−	+	−
+	+	−	−	−	+
+	+	−	+	+	−

Let me add that the correlation established for the nine Nuba tribes holds good both in patrilineal and matrilineal kinship systems, though in the latter the kinship degrees involved differ somewhat (the mother-brother replacing the biological father, and the mother's mother-brother being included among the 'grandfathers'). Nor do other social conditions affect the correlation, such as absence or presence of chieftainship, the particular religious system (apart from the belief in reincarnation), or economic organization. In other words, these conditions represent the XYZ of our first formula, or at least, they do so for the societies considered; their possible relevance in other 'settings' must here be disregarded.

3. The Limitations of the Method

The method of co-variations is applicable only within certain limits, which are to some extent self-evident. Social facts which are unique (so far as our knowledge goes) are plainly outside these limits; so are universal cultural features. In either case no further situations exist in which the facts examined would reappear or appear in varied form. But we should, more precisely, speak of social facts 'inasmuch as they are' unique or universal; for the uniqueness and universality depend on the level of abstraction on which they are considered. I may call the persecution of the Jews a unique fact; but the class of facts to which it belongs—the persecution of 'racial' minorities—is represented in numerous instances. Several eminent sociologists have analyzed the relations between Calvinism and capitalism, though Calvinism, at least, is a 'unique' historical datum; yet it can also be viewed as an instance of a wider class of facts, namely, belief in predestination. Again, marriage or law as we defined it are universal features of societies, but their special forms are not. Inasmuch, then, as a social fact is considered in its unique or universal aspects, it cannot be 'explained', at least not by the method here discussed.

Nor can we be certain that all non-unique and non-universal social facts enter into co-variations. There are always, in any social context, random features, accidental additions to the network of interrelations. It is impossible to state in general terms when or where we shall meet with such random features; they are merely features which elude our explanatory efforts. When we invoke 'accident' and fortuitous cases we do not at the outset define a particular range of facts and say: Here, and not there, accidents play a part; rather do we only name the residue of explanation. More precisely, we name the residue of explanations within a given frame of reference; for if we changed or extended our framework of reference, the 'accident' might cease to be one. Thus in studying any mode of action, its purposive content will suggest some nexus with other purposes and admit of this approach through co-variations; but the details of execution characteristic of this social task, the form or style of its performance, will not be susceptible of an analysis so oriented. Think of the layout of a settlement, which may be conspicuously correlated with political or kinship organization, as against the shape or style of the buildings;

Q

or of a class and rank system as against the particular ranks which exist and the symbols and forms of etiquette that go with them. In the latter case it will often seem as though the society in question had selected at random from a number of possibilities, all equally suitable for the given task. Yet if we extend our frame of reference to include also psychological factors, the apparently fortuitous selection might itself prove an instance of this kind of regularity. I have suggested before that this extension or shifting of our frame of reference is ultimately limited by our interests and the 'current character of importance' which things have for us. Let me now add that, as I see it, even the widest frame of reference possible in social enquiry will not eliminate the residue of accident. But of this we shall speak again.

The method of co-variations is more seriously limited by the fact that the required situations may simply not exist or not be known to exist. Here we are often tempted to construct ourselves the non-existing co-variations, that is, to carry out 'imaginary experiments'. Let me quote this passage from Max Weber. Outlining the scope of 'comparative sociology' he says: 'Often, unfortunately, there is available only the dangerous and uncertain procedure of the "imaginary experiment", which consists in thinking away certain elements and working out probable consequences.'[1] Dangerous and uncertain though this procedure may be, it is warranted in certain marginal situations; by this I mean situations where the possible variations in the conditions are so limited and their consequences so well known that these can indeed be calculated with reasonable certainty. This limitation of variability applies especially to physical circumstances and to the human responses to them where the latter are of so elementary an order that they can be predicted from assured general knowledge. This is true, above all, of negative predictions, expressing the certainty that certain variations are impossible.[2] Thus I may safely say that all systems of inheritance must in some measure do justice to sex differences since a girl can never fully exploit the state or status she might inherit from her father, nor a boy that of his mother; so that societies based on matrilineal descent *must* operate with the vicarious male

---

[1] (1947), p. 88.

[2] Cf. Max Weber: The connection between actions has sometimes appeared to the observer as 'inevitable, when no other way (of action) was open to the actors since, given the ends, no other means were available' (op. cit., p. 98).

succession, especially by the sister's son.[1] Or I might predicate that societies without machine technology and depending on co-operative work of a physically strenuous nature *must* specially organize their medium age groups for this task since it cannot be left either to the very old or the very young.

But let us realize that the general knowledge from which we argue might be of so basic a kind that our conclusions will amount merely to truisms. It is clearly self-evident and hardly worth stating that societies *must* reckon descent either in the paternal or in the maternal line, or in both combined, and that there is no other possibility. Conversely, where this general knowledge is less assured, the imaginary experiments might easily lead us astray. The further we move away from elementary physical conditions the more fully shall we be committed to arguing from plausibilities, that is, merely from some assumption how 'average man' would behave in the imagined circumstances. Thus I might argue that societies in which the male birth or survival rate greatly outweighs the female one cannot have polygyny. Yet it is by no means impossible that this marriage practice should obtain even under such conditions, either through letting men remain bachelors or through importing women from outside. Though I cannot think of a primitive society exemplifying the former solution, there is some evidence of the latter.[2]

The following example, illustrating once more the dangers of the imaginary experiment, is taken from Chapple and Coon, who link the cultural achievement of 'true division of labour' (i.e. full-time specialization of craftsmen) with the amount of surplus that can be produced on a certain level of technology.[3] As such specialization is absent in arctic and sub-arctic areas, the authors argue that, when the environment precludes the accumulation of surplus as well as easy transport and exchange, specialization is impossible; presumably, then, under conditions of living which do not permit the food-producing individual to collect food above his minimum needs, he cannot spare enough for a specialist who would not himself be a producer. In other words, if these arctic communities

[1] See A. R. Radcliffe-Brown (1935), p. 292.

[2] S. F. Nadel (1942), pp. 8–9. The sex ratio in question refers to the child population of Bida Town, where large-scale polygyny is the practice. Though the number of boys does not 'heavily outweigh' that of girls, the ratio is yet significant, the proportion of female to male children being 0.8: 1.

[3] (1942), p. 271.

maintained full-time specialists (an imaginary situation), they could not maintain themselves; hence, according to the argument, they cannot have full-time specialists. Now the conclusions are fully valid in an empirical sense, to the extent to which they bear upon observed data; the 'cannot' in the argument, however, we must, I think, reject. The argument holds good only if the precarious balance between total productivity in the community and its minimum subsistence cannot be redressed by any other means —means not here considered. But it is conceivable that the community might rid itself of other non-producers, the aged and ailing, or an excessive number of infants, in order to maintain the specialist. We certainly know from societies living on higher technological levels that full-time specialists, such as an idle priesthood, are often maintained in spite of the inadequacy of subsistence. Though these conditions do not apply to the arctic communities examined, they belong to the realm of possibilities, and so limit the validity of the 'imaginary experiment'.

The impossibility of observing co-variations may also be true in a more limited sense. If the scope of our enquiry is restricted to a single society we might well be unable to observe the required varied situations or at least to observe them on an adequate scale. The very fact of institutionalization precludes the non-occurrence or the greatly varied occurrence of the modes of action or relationships we study. Thus it has been argued that, while 'the study of a single society may . . . afford occasion for hypotheses, which then need to be tested by reference to other societies, it cannot give demonstrated results'.[1] Though this conclusion undoubtedly often holds, I do not think that it applies invariably. Thus, if we include time perspective and cultural change in our enquiry, the necessary co-variations will be available. They will be available, too, in societies sufficiently differentiated to exhibit the 'broad' variations in the behaviour of different group sections we spoke of before. Furthermore, in any society we also meet with narrower and, as it were, 'internal' variations which will lead us to 'demonstrated results'. For inasmuch as cultural elements 'hang together' in their own institutional setting, they do so by means of co-variations: the standardized, predictable patterns of behaviour which are the elements of social existence mean nothing else. This predictability means not only that, if A does a certain thing (or has certain

[1] A. R. Radcliffe-Brown (1940a), p. 5.

attributes), B will respond in a specific fashion, but also that between action and response there is some measure of variability, and that at a given point the varied action entails a corresponding varied response.

Let me make this clear by the example of marriage and brideprice. In certain primitive societies the amount of brideprice increases with the physical attractiveness of the bride; brideprice, then, is correlated with sexual attraction and so reveals its meaning as an 'appreciation' of the latter. Again, we may find that the brideprice is refunded upon the dissolution of marriage, less certain deductions made for offspring, or when the marriage remains barren; here the brideprice connotes an emphasis on fecundity and reveals itself as a 'price' paid for the offspring born by the woman. Finally, we might find that the brideprice is relatively high, its accumulation entailing a serious economic strain, that it is contributed by and distributed among numerous relatives on the man's and woman's side; and that it must be refunded in the event of divorce before the wife can legally remarry. We should observe, too, that the relations who are expected to refund the brideprice make great efforts to avoid this by trying to reconcile man and wife; while the husband who, for economic reasons, is unable to remarry until he has recovered the brideprice, will be only too willing to take back a runaway wife. The payment and distribution of brideprice thus place obstacles in the way of an easy dissolution of the union and appear as a safeguard of enduring marriage.

In all these examples the single element, brideprice, could be 'explained', that is, could be demonstrated to be present 'by right', or by some 'intrinsic fitness', on the grounds of the concomitant variability of other elements in the institution. Any institution presents the same picture, even if we only consider variability within the range of normalcy. Where variability exceeds this range and turns into deviations from the norm, into abnormal or criminal behaviour, the position is once more the same, provided only that the deviation is of sufficient recurrence, and not of the order of unique events.

Needless to say, such explanations on the grounds of 'internal' co-variations are valid for the given contexts alone and applicable to others only *ceteris paribus*. Nor can we take them to be self-sufficient and to stand apart from explanations based on wider evidence. Yet anthropologists sometimes seem to hold such a view and to imply, if they do not say so openly, that all they are interested in is to explain the facts of the one society or culture with which they happen to be concerned. This makes no sense. It reminds one of the joke about the painter who says that he is interested only in painting pictures and not in art. If this restricted explanation is an explanation at all (and not only a common-sense description), then it must fit as an instance into the explanations derived from more far-flung co-variations; and if the student of any particular society declines to view his facts in that wider perspective, then he simply declines to put his theories to a test. Clearly, there cannot be two kinds of scientific truth, one for the special case, and another for the general state of affairs.

Our admission of 'internal' co-variations, however, has also another consequence. For if the co-variations can in this fashion be carried into the very make-up of social actions, their significance must far exceed that of a mere method of enquiry. If early in this book we have defined the subject matter of social analysis as 'coordinated behaviour', we could now rephrase it as 'co-varying behaviour'. The co-variations thus come to mean both a tool of analysis and the fabric of the phenomena analyzed. Indeed it cannot be otherwise; for if our subject matter is to yield understanding, it must be of such a nature that it can be handled by the method whereby we attain understanding. When Mill or Durkheim formulated the method of concomitant variations they also implied this postulate of a correspondence between subject matter and enquiry, which correspondence can be stated thus—we can only understand the world around us inasmuch as it is a world governed by concomitant variations; or, more generally,—the world is, *ex hypothesi*, a world which can be elucidated by scientific methods.[1]

This correspondence of subject matter and enquiry poses a final technical problem. Since both are governed by co-variations the question arises when their analysis will reveal merely the descriptive characteristics of social facts, and when it will amount to the significant discovery of invariant relations between them. In the preceding discussion we spoke, very generally, of co-variations between social 'facts' or 'phenomena'; we implied that co-

[1] I have here paraphrased a passage from M. Oakeshott which states this postulate somewhat more specifically, viz., 'Nature is, *ex hypothesi*, a world which can be elucidated by statistical generalization' (1933, pp. 210–11). Similar formulations are of course familiar from logical positivist philosophy.

variations could profitably be studied between social facts and events of any kind or magnitude—between self-contained action patterns as well as features of action patterns or elements within them. Yet in the latter case we might be dealing merely with characteristics constituting the particular action pattern we describe; so that the explanations derived from such 'internal' co-variations, or from any co-variations between social facts which are not self-contained, would be spurious explanations; they would offer no significant *novel* knowledge of invariant relations, but would merely demonstrate what we observe to be the character of the given facts or events.

Since our whole enquiry aims at the discovery of connections where previously none were apparent, we must clearly start with some evidence for the unconnectedness of the phenomena. It has, in fact, been pointed out that the comparative (or experimental) method is sterile unless it deals with instances 'which are demonstrably separate'.[1] Now, I am not sure that I know what this means. We can obviously say of a great many things that they are 'demonstrably separate':

> Of shoes, and ships, and sealing wax,
> Of cabbages and kings.

They are so conspicuously separate since they are undoubtedly independently variable. But in this form we can do nothing with them; they are disparate and random entities, whose co-existence must forever remain meaningless. We can do something with these facts only when we suspect that their co-existence is not random but hides invariant relations. Yet if this can be said of these facts, then they are no longer independently variable or 'demonstrably separate', so that the comparative method would be reduced to sterility at the precise moment when the comparison begins to make sense.

To avoid this impasse let me define the separateness of phenomena differently. It holds between facts or features of facts which can be described without positing one another; in other words, the 'separate' phenomena must be capable of being 'thought apart'. If

---

[1] M. Oakeshott (1933), p. 166. Cf. also H. Poincaré: The experimental method is intended to 'reveal unsuspected relations between . . . facts, long since known, but wrongly believed to be unrelated to each other. Among the combinations we choose the most fruitful are often those which are formed of elements borrowed from widely separated domains' (1914), p. 51.

they cannot be separated in thought but hang together by some inevitable mutual requiredness, then the invariant relations between them do not amount to a true discovery, and our enquiry remains sterile. This mutual requiredness can be of two kinds. It may, firstly, be of a logical nature, in the sense that it is implicit in our definition of any given social fact and in the meaning of the word we use for it. Thus, if I take chieftainship to mean an enduring exercise of authority by one person over others, this feature is simply required to make up chieftainship as I choose to know it, and there is clearly no sense in showing that the two always appear and disappear together. What I should show is that chieftainship changes, perhaps into a different kind of leadership, concomitantly with some other social fact, which must not be one of the characteristics stipulated in my use of the word 'chieftainship'. In this example it is difficult to see what other meaning we could give to it, so that the element of choice in the definition is obscured. But when speaking, say, of clans I could both include or omit exogamy as a required characteristic, and it will depend on this decision whether or not there is any sense in studying the co-variations between the two phenomena. Secondly, the mutual requiredness may come from some general empirical knowledge which I possess at the outset and which tells me that the absence of certain facts other than the one examined would make the whole situation highly improbable or even absurd. Brideprice, for example, must in this sense always be accompanied by productive efforts producing the required commodities; witchcraft beliefs can hardly be imagined without certain fear complexes among the people holding the belief; and in a strongly competitive society jealousy among the people seems inevitable (though here the presence of jealousy might already be implicit in the meaning of 'strongly competitive').

In the case of logical requiredness, the study of co-variations merely exposes the kind of observations that went into my definition and affords no novel knowledge that things do in fact hang together.[1] In the case of empirical requiredness, the study of co-variations (if it is at all possible) might render my descriptive account more complete, but would afford no worthwhile novel

---

[1] This holds good only where the implications of the terms and concepts we use are fully given to our awareness. Where this is not so, as is often the case when we operate with very general and basic concepts, this exposing of implicit meanings does afford 'novel' knowledge (see below, p. 253).

knowledge of this kind; for it would obviously be absurd to imagine situations in which the things in question do not hang together— where the brideprice commodities would fall from heaven like manna or the belief in evil powers of witches would cause no fear.

Only this remains to be said. Definitions are not static; and the way we think about things and events is less static still. To begin with, we do not always start our enquiries with sharp definitions of the facts whose relations with others we propose to examine; mostly we start with some vaguely conceived 'separate' object or event, whose precise definition only emerges gradually from our observations of the invariant characteristics it exhibits in different circumstances. Yet even if, at some stage of our enquiry, we already have a formulated definition of our facts, we constantly discover new things about their relations with others—about the behaviour of objects in varying conditions, or about the occurrence of events in connection with other events; and these observations add to the characteristics of the objects and events as we now think about them—and as we should now define them. 'Laws' then (stating invariant relations between facts), and definitions (stating the characteristics of facts) turn into one another.[1] That water boils at sea level at 100°C.; that a dog withdraws its paw from an electric shock; or that (let us assume) groups always subdivide when they reach a certain size—these observations can clearly be represented as statements on invariant relations between the things I call water and temperature; between the nervous system of dogs and a physical stimulus; or between the cohesion and the size of groups. Yet equally the substance of these observations will also enter, if not into our formal definitions, at least into our way of thinking about water, nervous systems, or social groups.

The 'separateness' of social (or other) facts is thus relative to the stage of our knowledge and to the meaning we give to our terms. What can be 'thought apart' at one stage becomes subsequently incapable of being so separated. This is no longer an impasse, since our comparative analysis is at an end when the 'separate' facts are understood to be in fact connected. Yet the question remains, how far this new way of 'thinking about' them shall be stipulated semantically, in a formal definition. Now in social enquiry, as we know, this issue is mostly settled by the gradual hardening of

[1] In a more general context this point is made by H. Poincaré (1935), pp. 235–6, and K. Britton (1939), p. 179.

linguistic usage rather than by *ad hoc* decisions. But this much may be said in general terms. Sheer economy of thought seems to forbid that our definitions should be made to absorb all that we know about the behaviour of things or the variability of events. It seems most advantageous to operate with definitions which remain as far as possible unaltered by subsequent discoveries, that is, with *minimum definitions*. Thus we tend to embody in our definition of a phenomenon only such characteristics as it exhibits under all known circumstances, and assign its variations under specific conditions to statements on the invariant relations between this phenomenon and others. Perhaps its characteristics 'under all known circumstances' will themselves only be gradually discovered; and undoubtedly the history of science shows that even minimum definitions may be revised. However this may be, at some stage of our enquiry we tend to bar any further encroachment of definitions upon 'laws', even though we may bar it only temporarily; and in doing so we reestablish the distinction between invariant relations worth exploring and stating, and others which are required (or 'posited') by our use of words.

4. The Nature of Sociological Laws

Let me return to a point made previously, namely, that the invariant relations between social facts—and hence the 'regularities' or 'laws' governing them—have only statistical validity. We argue from a regularity observed in a number of instances to one taken to hold in all similar instances; we predict that the regularity will be verifiable in the stipulated instances, and we also invite further verification. But, as in all statistical arguments, we only pronounce upon an expected state of affairs, that is, upon a probability. From this two things seem to follow. First, in any such argument we imply that instances of the stipulated kind do in fact occur outside the series of instances we have examined; and second, the probability we predicate must be assumed to vary with the number of instances we have examined, increasing in proportion.

The first point bears on our fundamental postulate that the world of social phenomena is a world exhibiting repetitiveness and uniformities, which we need not discuss further. But here a technical issue is also involved. It seems clear that an insufficient analysis of the observed instances, which does not enable us to specify the conditions in which the presumed regularity may be expected to hold, must vitiate both our prediction and its verification. Yet it must also be conceded that the interrelations of social facts are of such complexity that we may not, at the moment, be capable of carrying our analysis sufficiently far and, above all, of adequately formulating its results. Shall we therefore throw overboard all our tentative and often vague generalizations? I think not. Lowie thinks otherwise—hence his severe criticism of Radcliffe-Brown's 'universal sociological law' which holds, 'though it is not yet possible to formulate precisely its scope, . . . that in certain specific conditions a society has need to provide itself with a segmentary organization.' With much reason on his side, Lowie asks: 'Whoever heard of a universal law with an as yet undefinable scope, of a law that works in certain specific *but unspecified* conditions?'[1] Admittedly Radcliffe-Brown's 'law' would correspond to a statement such as: 'All fluids have a boiling point, though we cannot precisely state the conditions under which they reach it.' But Lowie does not only question the precision of the statement, but makes it seem absurd altogether.

Yet is this vague 'sociological law' so absurd? As Lowie points out, Radcliffe-Brown asserts, in essence, that some societies have a segmentary organization, and others have not; and so far, this is still crude, unrefined observation. But Radcliffe-Brown also asserts that the segmentary organization is not random, but subject to conditions; and this is surely something worthwhile asserting, namely, that societies do not grow infinitely as homogeneous entities, but subdivide. We can, in fact, outline some of the conditions underlying this process, as we did when we spoke, only a little less vaguely than Radcliffe-Brown, of the 'optimum point' in the growth of societies. If we cannot enumerate all conditions or specify them more accurately, this is due to the immensely complicated interrelation of conditions in the social field. Radcliffe-Brown's statement predicates, on the grounds of certain analyses, that the dependence on conditions suggested by these analyses also holds elsewhere, and universally. This is, perhaps, not yet a 'law'— only the prediction or suspicion of one, that is, a hypothesis; it is, too, an unprecise hypothesis. But it is not useless; it does not preclude verification, though it requires to be rendered more specific in the process. Furthermore, even in natural science the borderline

[1] R. Lowie (1937), pp. 224–5.

between hypothesis and law is a fluid one; nor are unprecise hypotheses absent in certain stages of its development. It is perhaps unwise to measure social enquiry against the infinitely more homogeneous fields of physics or chemistry and the precise regularities there formulated. But many 'laws' stipulated by biology seem as tentative and unprecise as some of our sociological laws will have to be for a long time to come.

My second point, that the probability of regularities increases with the number of instances observed, is often taken as an axiom. In certain respects it undoubtedly has this weight. We mean, of course, not just any instances, but significant instances, that is to say, instances which have been adequately analyzed and whose representative character is reasonably assured. But 'adequate' and 'reasonably' are relative terms, so that the repetition of observations is necessary if only to make certain that we have not overlooked anything. How far, however, is our 'axiom' valid beyond the measure of control and correction it affords? We must, to begin with, distinguish between two kinds of probability. One rests on our belief or expectation concerning the likelihood of particular events or states of affairs, which comes from our general knowledge, from previous experiences, and from habitual modes of thinking; this is a 'non-numerical' or 'non-technical' probability, which requires verification. The other probability is 'numerical' and 'technical' in that it rests on the demonstrated frequency of the events or states of affairs; this probability is itself a verification, which can be strengthened through extending the demonstration of that frequency.[1] The two kinds of probability hang together and are combined in most, perhaps all, scientific statements; for the suspicion and anticipation of some 'fitness' in the observed facts with which all enquiries into regularities start express the first kind of probability; and this is confirmed (or otherwise) by the second. Now, though the assurance afforded by the second probability depends on the frequency of confirmatory observations, does it not also depend on the strength of the initial, 'non-numerical', probability? In other words, do we not curtail our statistical evidence if our belief in this initially perceived 'fitness' is very strong? I have no doubts that in practice this is so. If I start from a situation which

[1] See A. Eddington (1935), pp. 115-16. Bertrand Russell, much in the same sense, speaks of 'degree of credibility', as against 'mathematical probability' (1948, pp. 359-60).

convincingly and unambiguously 'makes sense', I shall require less confirmatory evidence than if I have doubts about the 'fitness' suggested by my original data; and if I were to stumble on a puzzling correlation, say, between suicide rate and the length of skirts worn by women, I should look for confirmation in thousands of cases before accepting the correlation and venturing to pronounce on its fitness. Now my point is that this happens not only usually, in practice, but inevitably. For it is not the intensity of believing as such which makes the initial probability, but the nature of the things in regard to which we believe—'the content of what is asserted'.[1] And this comes to us from previous knowledge which, however roughly, approximates to some numerical assessment of observed regularities. We are always guided by some pre-existing knowledge which is of the same kind as the knowledge we wish to attain, namely, about the possible independence or connection of phenomena. If therefore the process of establishing the numerical probability only gives definiteness to tacit knowledge, the weight and suggestiveness of the latter cannot but affect our readiness to trust the former.

Conversely, this trust need not be proportionate to the frequency of confirmatory observations. Indeed, it is extremely difficult to say just how large their number must be (provided we take all the prescribed precautions) to afford adequate confirmation. Assuming I observe that fathers beat their children more often than do mothers, in two societies, in a dozen, in 100, and in 1000; assuming also, for the sake of simplicity, that I observe no contrary cases and that the societies I examine are, to the best of my knowledge, of diverse nature. When can I speak of a statistically valid regularity? Surely not if I examine only two societies; but need I examine 100 or 1000? Considering the practically infinite number of societies in which fathers may or may not beat their children, a dozen observations, or 100, or 1000 all seem equally good or bad. It is true that 1000 observations assure more fully the random nature of my sample; but by this I mean only the exclusion of possibly concealed uniformities, for example, that all the societies examined have the same kinship system or hold the same religious belief that fathers— but not mothers—shall not spare the rod. In other words, I consider it unlikely that such uniformities *as I can think of* will occur

[1] M. Cohen (1946), p. 117.

in 1000 cases, while they might in 12 or 100. This is, of course, arguing from an initial, rough and 'subjective' probability. But more importantly, if I can think of these sources of error I might also eliminate them in a dozen cases if these are sufficiently well analyzed. (If I cannot think of them, 1000 cases would seem to be as much a shot in the dark as 12.) Now we shall probably accept a dozen observations and certainly a hundred as significant, while we shall not accept two (however well analyzed). Why? Surely not because 12 or 100 instances out of God knows how many are more convincing than two. We accept them because of some unexpressed conviction that this 'cannot be accident'. And if we put our conviction into words we should admit, first, that we believe in some uniformity in this world of ours, of which we have now caught a glimpse; and secondly, that by all the criteria afforded by our pre-existing knowledge the observed cases exhibit some 'fitness' or 'meaning', which we should not attribute to the opposite state of affairs.

The question just discussed entails a preliminary one, namely, how many observations are required in any one society to enable us to say that a certain state of affairs—say, the treatment of children by their parents—is in fact typical of that society.[1] Here the issue may seem to be simpler; for we can now calculate the proportion of cases examined (and found to be positive or negative) to the total number of possible cases (i.e. the total family population) and hence assess the validity of our observations more accurately. But we might still ask—what percentage is required, say, 2, 10, or 75 per cent? Clearly, the purely quantitative issue once more cannot be settled with any precision; and we shall again be guided by some pre-existing knowledge, now referring to the uniformity of conditions likely to obtain in the given society; which knowledge we should have acquired through observations other than those we are concerned with at the moment. We might know, for example, that families all tend to be of equal size, that fathers mostly have the same profession or follow the same religion, or perhaps only that in primitive societies of the kind examined uniform behaviour is usually strongly insisted on. We should then expect the treatment of children to be similarly uniform, and in

[1] Expressed differently, the question concerns the number of observations required for the construction of the 'normal curve of error' which we took to demonstrate any 'normal' or 'typical' mode of behaviour. (See pp. 113–4.)

consequence accept a relatively small number of instances as convincing. Thus, in the assessment of 'typical' modes of behaviour no less than in that of regularities valid for numerous societies, we inevitably argue in some measure from *a priori* knowledge or assumptions.

I am fully aware of the inadequacy of my pronouncements on one of the most difficult problems of scientific method. But perhaps I may, in support of my arguments, quote this passage from Cohen's *Preface to Logic*: 'Reasoning on matters of probability involves a remarkable amount of reliance on *a priori* considerations,' if by *a priori* we mean 'general principles which are not based on the observation of the course of events' in question.[1] We may take it that the same holds good for the frequency of observations intended to sustain this reasoning. And we can also, I think, agree that the analyses of limited series of cases, on which anthropologists must mostly rely, are not quite valueless, nor their statements futile that social phenomena 'tend' to be of a certain kind or occur 'mostly' or 'often', clumsily though they indicate the weight of numbers.

Social regularities, then, being merely observed and statistical, predicate nothing about a necessity of things being as they are; nor can statements about 'invariant relations' between social facts contain a 'must'. Yet this 'must' does occur in social enquiry, and there are, in fact, two exceptions to this rule. The first applies in the imaginary experiments previously discussed. Here our general knowledge of the physical nature of the world and the psycho-physical nature of man makes certain unobserved combinations of phenomena unthinkable, so that the phenomena actually observed together 'posit' each other in an empirical sense. The second exception applies when the different statements we make about certain states of affairs posit each other in an analytical or logical sense (as 'being a society' posits 'having a population'). The first exception amounts only to a pseudo-necessity. That is to say, though our knowledge of the physical or psycho-physical laws may rule out certain variations in the observed conditions as impossible and unthinkable, these are only actually impossible and unthinkable, given the state of our empirical knowledge. And this knowledge refers to conditions which are what they are from no inner necessity, and to laws which, in the language of philosophers,

[1] M. Cohen (1946), p. 114.

are only 'contingent'. The second exception alone amounts to a true necessity—for 'there is only *logical* necessity'.[1] It obtains whenever what we think and say in one form is entailed in what we think and say in another, as a particular consequence (e.g. 'X has a population') is entailed in the meaning we lay into words and assertions (e.g. 'X is a society').[2]

Now, in social enquiry we rarely start with analyzing some concept or assertion previously formulated, exposing all that it entails, and then look round for exemplifying instances. Mostly we start with the latter, that is, we start with observing and stating what we take to be invariant relations or 'laws' governing separate facts, and impute to them necessity only when closer inspection reveals our statements to be logically connected. The part played by this closer inspection is sometimes ignored, so that the logical necessity is treated as though it were factual and empirical. But it can easily be shown that it comes only from the concepts and words we use to represent the empirical phenomena, and perhaps ultimately from our intellectual equipment which makes us conceive of them in the given fashion. Previous chapters included a few instances of this kind. Thus we have stated that, the greater the cohesion of a group, the sharper must be its alienation from individuals outside the group; but in this 'law' we merely rendered explicit a consequence implicit in the concept 'cohesion', namely, that the inward orientation of group members is inevitably a separation from outside. The familiar 'laws' asserting the interdependence of organisms and their environment conceal a similar logical nexus; for we cannot think of an 'organism' save as existing in an environment. And when anthropologists speak of what a society 'must' do or a culture 'cannot' do, they again express such logical necessities (if they are necessities at all), implicit in the current meaning of 'society' and 'culture'.[3]

---

[1] L. Wittgenstein (1922), sec. 6. 37.

[2] I suspect that the two kinds of necessity sometimes coincide, at least in social enquiry. For we do not operate with a rigid logical calculus, at every step exposing the significance we lay into our terms. Often our knowledge about practical possibilities or impossibilities will tacitly enter into the meaning of the words we use, so that empirical and semantic (or logical) evidence will fuse. E.g. we cannot imagine a situation in which the whole human population forms one group and one group only; hence certain consequences will appear to follow with logical necessity from the accepted meaning of 'group'—viz. that there must be several groups in the world and that for every 'in-group' there must be 'out-groups'.

[3] It might be added that when anthropologists attribute a certain character to *all* social facts, a 'must' is concealed in their statements. Thus when Malinowski

Yet if in all this we are merely 'exhibiting relations of implication' (as logicians would say), then our findings would seem to be sterile tautologies. We produce no truly additional or novel knowledge, and the facts stated to be necessarily related cannot really be several related facts, but must be the same fact, differently apprehended and expressed. The modern study of scientific method, however, has amply shown that such seeming tautologies are far from sterile; for not every implication of the assertions or concepts we formulate is at once given to our awareness, so that their inspection and analysis does afford novelty, if only a 'psychological' novelty. In other words, in demonstrating the implications of our assertions or concepts, though we do not produce strictly novel or additional knowledge, we yet expose hitherto hidden knowledge.[1] And this is true whether we start with the logical analysis of a given concept and then turn back to the phenomena with a new awareness of their order, or from the observation of the phenomena and afterwards come to understand their place in the conceptual order. As we shall see, one or the other procedure is inevitable whenever we touch upon the basic concepts of social existence—'cohesion', 'integration', or 'society' as such. Yet the share of such logical demonstrations in social enquiry is limited. The 'laws' which we can hope to formulate are largely empirical and without necessity. And in this they conform to the laws of natural science; though physics, like the analysis of society, also operates with some laws that are compulsory in that they are logical in origin, that is, come from our intellect alone—from something in our capacity to apprehend and state facts and to collect them into concepts.[2]

Perhaps this whole discussion has been over-elaborate. But I spoke at such length about the nature of sociological laws since this

holds that every cultural fact 'has a function', he really means since no one can conceivably have examined 'every' fact—that it *must* have a 'function', whether it is examined or not; which implication has either a logical validity (the concept 'cultural fact' entailing the possession of a 'function'), or none at all.

[1] See Cohen and Nagel (1939), pp. 65-7. Cf. Wittgenstein, 'In philosophy the question "Why do we really use that word, that proposition?" constantly leads to valuable results' (1922, sec. 6. 211).

[2] This is the view of Eddington, who speaks of the 'epistemological' laws in physics, which are 'compulsory' because they are 'subjective' and only reflect 'the observer's sensory and intellectual equipment in the knowledge obtained through such equipment'. All other laws of nature are non-compulsory, and constitute the 'vast amount of special knowledge about the particular objects surrounding us'. (1939, pp. 20, 104.)

R

is often misunderstood and the search for laws in social enquiry dismissed as futile, either because it cannot produce 'necessary' laws, or because such necessary laws as it can produce are simply self-evident.[1] I have tried to show that both criticisms are unfounded, or at least, that they would apply equally to all forms of science. Undoubtedly, however, social enquiry is much less advanced than natural science; and for this as well as other reasons the parallel with natural science must not be driven too far. Though the natural laws are mainly empirical and 'contingent', they are also universal and admit of no exceptions. It is true that on the borderline of empirical knowledge even physics to-day admits only probabilities and statistical regularities. But for an immense range of facts its probabilities amount to practical certainties. If by any chance there were a single instance of apples rising instead of falling, of moving bodies unaccountably stopping in their tracks, or heat flowing from a colder to a warmer body, then the whole explanatory system of physics would have to be revised.[2] In the human or social sciences we deal with probabilities of a much cruder sort. A single or infrequent event going counter to any formulated 'law' cannot contradict it since its validity is only statistical and does not hold for individual cases; and frequent deviations will only force us to admit exceptions or alternative possibilities. Thus we can speak only of events or states of affairs 'tending' to be of a certain kind; we conceive of the realm of social phenomena as of one where more or less likely, or even alternative, possibilities hold, and where the uniqueness of events, chance, accident, and hence indeterminacy, have at least some play.

Shall we then, in this final context, admit that the regularities we can announce for the realm of social or human phenomena are so

[1] Thus Boas emphasizes the 'lack of necessary connections between the various aspects of culture', and goes on to say: 'The phenomena of our science are so individualized, so exposed to outer accident, that no set of laws could explain them.' The laws that *can* be found 'will be necessarily vague and, we might almost say, so self-evident that they are of little help to a real understanding'. (1948, pp. 256–8.)

[2] Many scholars deny that the explanatory system of natural science would be called in question by a single contradictory event; even if all errors of observation had been adequately excluded, and the contradiction remained a contradiction, the explanatory system would only be adjusted *ad hoc* rather than completely revised (see e.g. M. Cohen, 1946, p. 135). However this may be, we may take it that the laws governing the gross phenomena of nature are of this universal and practically absolute kind.

limited only because our knowledge is limited, not permitting us to reckon with the totality of relations pervading the human universe? So that, if we only knew more about the experiences to which individuals have been subjected, about their heredity and psycho-physical make-up, and about hundreds of things besides, we should not be compelled to accept accidents, unique events, or alternative possibilities? Perhaps this is so; though we cannot possibly put any meaning to the 'more' that would be required. Above all, any extension of our knowledge over wider and wider domains will add to the complexity of phenomena, of whose immensity we are already fully aware. Indeed, we might reach a stage, and perhaps we have reached it already, when we can no longer hold this complexity together in thought and calculation. Thus, though the admission of chance may only be an admission of ignorance, it is certainly also forced upon us by the vast number of facts about which we do know and with which we always reckon. I believe it was Poincaré who said that chance is merely another word for complexity. And since 'the scientist's brain, which is only a corner of the universe, will never be able to contain the whole universe, . . . it follows that, of the innumerable facts offered by nature, we shall leave some aside and retain others'.[1] In the study of things human at least, this 'leaving aside' is partly also leaving to be accounted for by accident. Whether there are or are not 'true' accidents in this world of ours, apart from those entailed in our capacity of understanding, is, I suspect, a meaningless question.

[1] H. Poincaré (1914), p. 26.

CHAPTER X

Experimental Anthropology (*continued*)

1. THE CATEGORIES OF SOCIAL UNDERSTANDING

Let me refer once more to the empirical and contingent nature of the regularities or laws discoverable in social phenomena. Being without necessity, these regularities are also without immediate persuasiveness; they are not as such meaningful and self-explanatory, but still indicate a just-so state of affairs. They acquire meaning and explanatory weight only when they yield, that is, when we read into them, that additional datum which I have called their *fitness* or *requiredness*. I have enumerated three categories of this 'fitness'—logical consistency; mechanical causality; and purpose. And it now remains to be shown that only these, and no others, satisfy our desire to understand.

Let A and B be two co-varying action patterns; then, as they refer to the intentional behaviour of individuals, and thus to behaviour initiated by minds, their co-variation must remain a meaningless coincidence, exhibiting no intrinsic 'fitness', unless it can be understood to have a counterpart in the minds of individuals; more precisely, the mental events implicit in A and B must be understood to be *connected in individual minds*. This presupposes another, more elementary condition. If I find that in a given society the action patterns A and B appear in co-variation, the co-variation would again be meaningless unless the individuals acting in the sense of A as well as B are either the same individuals, or stand in such communication or physical contact that they can influence each other. Any genuine social co-variation (or 'correlation') satisfies these two conditions; in fact, it usually satisfies them so fully and self-evidently that we are apt to take all this for granted. Take the familiar correlation between rising standards of living and birth restriction. At the risk of stating the obvious I might point out that this correlation only makes sense, first, if the people who live in greater comfort are also the same who decide not to have too many children, or at least stand under the influence of others who hold that view; and secondly, if the mental event, desire for comfort, is understood to become connected in the respective minds with the decision to restrict birth.

This particular form of 'connection in the mind' corresponds to one of the three categories of fitness I have postulated, namely, to that of purpose. Here I understand the action A to fit the action B in the same way as a means (reducing expenditure on children) fits a desired end (achievement of greater comfort). But an action A may also be seen to fit an action B in the logical sense in which two statements are seen to agree (to be 'consistent') when one repeats or brings out what the other implies, or in which any statement is consistent with the state of affairs it describes.[1] Or finally, an action A may be understood to fit an action B in the way a cause corresponds to the effect it produces. Expressed differently, we have these three situations: (1) The intention to achieve a certain state or mode of behaviour (the end) becomes a rational motivation for another mode of behaviour (the means); (2) a thought or meaning, underlying one mode of behaviour, leads to further (logically consistent) modes of behaviour expressing the same thought or meaning; (3) an experience, arising in some context of behaviour, produces another mode of behaviour by means of some psychophysical mechanism. I hold that these three 'connections in the mind' are necessary, and sufficient, for our understanding of the 'fitness' in social regularities.

I also hold that they are independent and not reducible to one another, though, as we shall later see, they may coexist in the same nexus of action. Here I need defend only the separateness of the two categories of explanation, purpose and causality. The idea of causality, as I have admitted, is never absent from explanation, and many purposive connections we shall quote may at first sight appear to be causal ones. Yet this ubiquitous causality is of too general and unspecific a nature to exhaust the whole of our explanation. It is true that in every rational application of means (say, tools of any kind) to particular ends material causality plays a part, since here causes are utilized and the effects anticipated; but the

[1] Means-to-end relations could of course also be called 'logical' and 'consistent'. But this consistency is of a practical kind, demonstrable by means of material consequences, while the 'logical consistency' as here understood refers to agreements of meaning, demonstrable by the proof of non-contradiction.

causality operating in cases of this kind only constitutes the general empirical knowledge of the actors without which they could not act *purposively*. It is true also that in any purposive connection between two actions (as when I earn money to maintain my family) the aim of one action brings about or 'causes' the performance of the other; but it is still one *purpose* that produces another, and a conscious end that causes the mind to apply or find the adequate means. If this is still causality, it is one upon which purposes have been super-imposed, or a causality *a tergo*, where the end (the effect) determines the means (which cause the effect). This transformation of an underlying general causality must clearly be especially named, so that here the 'purpose' effecting the transformation becomes the operative concept. Equally, this transformed causality must be distinguished from the nothing-but-causality we meet with in other situations, where it exhausts all we can say by way of explanation; and this is no longer the ubiquitous general causality we always think about, but is of a specific kind, namely, the causality implicit in psycho-physical mechanisms, which we have made a separate category of explanation.

This distinction may be illustrated by the example quoted before. I should normally regard the correlation between birth re-striction and rising standards of living as one expressing a nexus of purpose; for the underlying linkage of cause-and-effect—the smaller size of the family facilitating the production of surplus—appears transformed into one of means (reduction of the size of the family) employed for definite ends (better conditions of living). But I may also construe this purposive relation into one of 'nothing-but-causality'. I should then have to assume (needless to say, on insufficient evidence) that 'softer' living weakens sexual desires or the faculty of procreation, so that the kind of behaviour responsible for the lower birthrate would follow quasi-mechanically, that is, by some psycho-physical mechanism, from behaviour aiming at greater comfort.

2. LOGICAL CONSISTENCY

Let me, to begin with, point out the difference between this category of 'fitness' read into social facts and the logical necessity that characterizes certain relations between facts. It is, in brief, the difference between mere consistency and inevitable entailment, and between a cognitive operation I impute to the actors and one that is my, the observer's, doing. The operation I impute to the actors consists in some judgment on their part that, acting in a certain manner in one context, they should act in a consistent sense in another; which consistency, as we shall see, may be both one of content and one of form. The nexus so established is not a necessary one; it only so happens that the actors feel moved to make this judgment in a particular case, and hence accompany one action pattern with another, consistent with it, or adjust different action patterns to one another. I cannot conceive of this step being inevitable, though my general experience and self-knowledge assure me that people do in fact tend to introduce some measure of consistency into the variety of their modes of acting. Nor can I assume that the underlying judgment is present in their minds whenever they act in the consistent manner; but I assume that it was effective when the respective behaviour patterns crystallized and became habitual. And it is because I can perceive the nexus of consistency in the actually happening behaviour patterns that I recognize the 'fitness' in them. In assuming that people 'feel moved' to produce such logically consistent connection I introduce, of course, the other, or one of the other, explanatory categories—of purpose or of psycho-physical causality. This lack of self-containedness seems to characterize all explanations in terms of logical consistency. We can hardly think of them save as serving some particular purpose or resulting from some psycho-physical mechanism. This seems to be one of the reasons why we can quote only few instances of a purely logical consistency in action, not also supported by purposive or causal relations.

Another reason appears to be this. Though logical consistency undoubtedly pervades a wide range of social actions it is recognized with such immediacy and ease that many connections of this kind never strike us as having been specifically recognized and interpreted. And again, when they are so interpreted, the interpretation usually stops short of full analysis. The fact that such connections occur, seems sufficiently convincing, so that we do not subject them to the test of co-variations but take the conditions under which they occur for granted. If, for example, we find that people whose main material interests centre upon cattle also have songs and stories about cattle and elaborate the same theme in their mythology and art, this consistency in their interests seems self-explanatory; we note it, and our curiosity rests. Yet it is clear that this diffusion of an interest through diverse spheres of behaviour occurs in certain cases and not in others. And if we desired to specify the conditions, we should search for them in some relevant purpose which 'moves' the people to express the same theme in different ways, or perhaps in some psycho-physical mechanism which makes them project outward a deeply stirring thought.

We can, I think, distinguish three types of logical consistency in behaviour, each of which affords an explanatory principle.

(1) The above example illustrates the first type. It consists in the diffusion of the same thought, topic, interest, or 'motif', through diverse spheres of behaviour. We might say that a particular content of behaviour is *reduplicated* or *multiplied* in different settings, and we might visualize this process as one in which people, having evolved a particular mode of action, evolve or modify further modes of action so that they express the same content. Thus when people believe in hell or paradise, that theme will be elaborated also in legends, stories, pictures, which have no intrinsic connection with the body of belief; and when a people organizes its political life in a rigid system of ranks, some such grading of status may also reappear in the way they picture deities or in activities not connected with political life, such as activities of a playful and recreational nature. In other words, the same thought is being spun out in consistent fashion; and though it might be argued that the mythological 'reduplication' of a paramount political interest also serves as a 'charter', that is, serves the purpose of buttressing the political practice, it does so by means of the consistent diffusion of the same thought; and this is as such, and immediately, meaningful, irrespective of its implications of purpose.

This diffusion need not refer to features of content only—to a topic, or interest, or motif in the strict sense of the word; it can also apply to formal traits, to some organizing principle underlying the modes of expressing diverse contents. The division is a fluid one; where rank scales are reduplicated in the manner just described, it is as much an organizing principle as a 'motif' or interest that is reduplicated; and where we find a culture operating with the conception of polarity in many spheres of behaviour—in social organization, religion, and cosmology—we could see in this the diffusion both of a particular thought or topic, and of a formal schema of thoughts and topics. There are, however, a few instances of a purely formal consistency, as when the belief in anthropomorphous deities goes hand in hand with realism in art; or when the same style pervades the whole field of art; or perhaps when the same keynote of display pervades the spheres of economic, political, and aesthetic behaviour.

(2) The second type of consistency is represented in a 'reduplication' of a particular kind, namely, in *symbolic behaviour*. By this I mean modes of action so constructed that they 'stand for' or 'signify' other modes of action or events. And this implies that the arrangement and use of the signifying modes of action is in some manner consistent with the arrangement and occurrence of the facts signified. In the extreme case, there will be a one-to-one correspondence, any unit symbol being consistent with the thing it stands for; in which case, too, the correspondence is as it were 'natural' and at once visible to the observer. This seems to be true under three conditions. It is true when the symbols are 'iconic', that is, when they exhibit some perceptible similarity with the things symbolized[1]—as when the sculptural representation of an animal serves as the emblem of a totemic group. It is true, further, when the symbol is at the same time a 'sign', that is, some event or property commonly found together with the thing signified[2]—as when gestures spontaneously performed in a state of sadness are employed to indicate mourning in a drama or play. A final nexus of this 'natural' kind comes from the 'physiognomic character' of certain objects or situations, which resides in their 'look' (in shapes and contours, in the pattern of colours, in the motion of melodies) and conveys directly some dynamic expressiveness, of tension or calm, or of some emotional state.[3] The expressiveness of music offers perhaps the clearest illustration; or think of darkness used to symbolize mystery or, conversely, of glaring light or colours, which could not 'naturally' signify a calm or subdued state. The 'physiognomic character', however, is difficult to isolate; for it often blends with the sign character of things, as in expressive gestures, in the rising and falling of the voice, or in the case of objects which acquire their signifying capacity because they have been experienced

[1] Charles Morris (1946), pp. 191–2.   [2] See above, pp. 65 ff., n. 1.

[3] See K. Koffka (1935), pp. 358–60. This is a brief statement of a problem demanding much fuller analysis. Let me only add that the same spontaneous 'ascription of dynamic characteristics' (Köhler), where it refers to observed behaviour, gestures and the like, has also been taken to account for the immediacy of the 'you-experience', of which we spoke in an earlier context. (See p. 64.)

in connection with the things signified (as when darkness becomes the symbol of secrecy because secret activities are usually carried out in darkness).

The correspondence between symbols and the things signified is not at once visible when the former are 'artificial', having been constructed and invested with meaning by some arbitrary and merely conventional rule, as is the case in nearly all linguistic symbols. Here the correspondence attaches, not to the single 'reduplication' of an event or situation in its symbol, but to the set of symbols as a whole, that is, to its systematic arrangement and rules of usage. But having learned these rules and being able to understand the significance of the symbols, we also understand that one set of modes of behaving (operating as symbols) reduplicates another (the things symbolized) in consistent fashion.

Let me now briefly outline the main forms of symbolic behaviour, the fuller analysis of which I must leave for another occasion. We meet with symbolic behaviour whenever emblems or badges or any other 'diacritical' signs are employed to indicate social relationships or group membership. Whether these emblems are material objects or themselves forms of behaviour (gestures, or 'diacritical' observances), their display indicates that such-and-such 'real' behaviour may be expected of the persons displaying them. Again, we meet with symbolic behaviour in all forms of social nomenclature, which similarly indicate relationships and modes of action expected to occur in conformity with the nomenclature. The classificatory kinship terminology is a typical example; classes of relatives between or of whom particular behaviour patterns are expected are here grouped together under the same name, so that the arrangement of kinship names runs to that extent parallel with the arrangement of behaviour patterns. We meet, finally, with symbolic behaviour in the 'dramatizations' which far-reachingly pervade primitive cultures. Thus events or courses of action important for the community are represented in dramatic form in ritual contexts, the theme or plot of the ritual drama mirroring (or 'reduplicating') the social events in some conspicuous manner.[1] Van Gennep's analysis of *rites de passage* clearly illustrates this point; he could show how the change in social relationships, accompanying, for example, adolescence and puberty, reappears in the arrangement of the ritual, often in a close phase-

[1] See above, p. 138.

by-phase correspondence, the ritual illustrating successively each of the phases of the social metamorphosis—the separation of the adolescent from the group to which he first belonged; his marginal place as someone who no longer belongs to one group without having as yet been incorporated in the other; and his final reintegration, in a new capacity, in the adult society.

These comments, however, are necessary. The logical consistency here assumed does not preclude the intervention also of a purposive and utilitarian nexus. The emblems and badges of group membership are undoubtedly also adequate means for the practical requirement that group membership should be rendered conspicuous; the classificatory kinship terminology, as we have previously stated, also operates as a 'wide-range' system of communication, which is again a means to an end;[1] and the dramatizations, being concerned with 'important' events or courses of action, also serve to throw into relief or sustain the social purposes which have this importance. What concerns us here is that in each case this end is achieved by means of a 'reduplication' of behaviour patterns. We could perhaps imagine a society where changes in group membership and social relations are effected merely by verbal instruction, such as, 'from now on you will behave in this way and not in that towards these named individuals, or towards all individuals older than you, or towards all individuals living in this community,' and so forth. Whether or not this would be practicable we need not discuss. The point is, that this method is nowhere the only one; always, there is also symbolic behaviour.

Furthermore, we must note that the 'reduplications' in symbolic behaviour give varying scope to our first type of logical consistency. Apart from the mutual consistency which obtains between the connected sets of behaviour as such, the internal arrangement of the symbolic behaviour patterns may itself vary in consistency, in the sense that the same 'motif' may be diffused more or less widely. For example, the diacritical emblems of group membership may all be derived from the animal world, or inconsistently selected from diverse sources (as is the case in some totemic clan systems). The dramatizations may (or may not) employ the same theme throughout the ritual drama, say, in *rites de passage*, the theme of a visit to the nether world, of the intervention of spirits, or of death and rebirth. Again this 'diffusion' may concern, not the

[1] See above, p. 154.

content of what is expressed, but the formal or organizing principles which govern the expression. Thus a classificatory kinship terminology may operate consistently (or not) with the criterion of generation differences and consistently ignore sex differences; it may even consistently operate with the same principle of word-formation, expressing all generation differences by means of the attributes 'great', 'small', and so forth. These two consistencies, one obtaining between the symbol system and the set of things symbolized, and the other within the symbol system, mostly diverge at some point. Thus a classificatory kinship terminology operating consistently with the generation principle will often express distinctions which are not practically important or leave unexpressed differences which are so important. This merely indicates something that common sense also tells us, namely, that consistency cannot be made to prevail all round.[1] But it also indicates that the inducement to organize some field of behaviour consistently may, on occasion, operate independently of utilitarian and purposive considerations.

(3) Finally, whenever we speak of 'values' in a society or culture we admit also the effectiveness of logical consistency. For by a 'value' is meant an idea of worthwhileness governing a class of actions and imparting to each the index 'good' or 'bad', or 'desirable' and 'undesirable', as the case may be. We shall, for example, call patriotism a 'value', or love of parents, or display of wealth. And when we take the respective forms of behaviour to be instances of a 'value', we understand that here such-and-such an idea of worthwhileness is consistently applied to the various occasions of acting. Mostly, there is little advantage in isolating the sheer logical consistency in this nexus of behaviour since it is implicit in our very statement that a set of values exists in the society. But this isolation proves useful under certain conditions. The

---

[1] The modes of behaviour which are to be symbolized will clearly often lend themselves to different arrangements on the grounds of different criteria, so that several consistent symbol arrangements are in principle possible. The relative practical importance of the various criteria may well be decisive. But it need not be of one kind only. If, for example, in a kinship system generation is important for certain rights and obligations, sex for others, paternal or maternal descent for yet others, a symbol system operating with the same 'organizing principle' will to that extent fail to be consistent with the arrangement to which it refers, while a symbol system consistent with the latter will fail to be internally consistent. Most, if not all, kinship terminologies and symbol systems of similar practical import present the picture of a more or less successful compromise.

values might be specifically formulated in crucial contexts, such as a religious creed or a body of ethical doctrine, so that the extent of their consistent application to other, practical, contexts becomes a legitimate problem. Equally, this 'diffusion' (or 'transference', as we previously called it) of an idea of worthwhileness may proceed in the opposite direction, from practical interests to a body of doctrine which comes to express and endorse them. Above all, the consistency between the two might not lie on the surface; only through isolating it can we demonstrate the 'fitness' uniting the respective modes of action and make their observed co-existence intelligible. The oft-quoted nexus between Protestantism and the rise of Capitalism is a case in point. 'What is sometimes suggested . . . is not merely a coincidence of religious and economic movements, but a logical connection between changes in economic organization and changes in religious doctrines.'[1] And this connection can indeed be traced or analyzed out. Thus Calvinism, in preaching rigid predestination, in which efforts at individual salvation count for nought and every opportunity falling to man is part of God's design, made the pursuit of wealth and economic success consistent with spiritual grace; so that diligence, thrift, and business spirit rather than contempt for material goods became the virtues of the true Christian.[2] Similarly, it is said of the Puritan sects that, upholding a methodical, rational way of life and requiring of their members that they 'prove' themselves through success of this kind before God as well as their fellow believers, they 'helped to deliver the spirit of modern capitalism'.[3] These examples may seem to illustrate only a consistency spreading from the doctrine to a practice encouraged by it, rather than from the practice to the doctrine legitimizing it; but the distinction or merging of the two processes is irrelevant in this context.

3. PURPOSE

Here we at once face this difficulty: Which purpose shall we mean in our explanations—the purpose in the minds of the actors, or the purpose which we, the observers, find exemplified in the given nexus? Shall we base ourselves on the actors' conception that a particular mode of behaviour is an adequate means for achieving the desired end, or are we free to bring our own judgment to bear

[1] R. H. Tawney (1936), p. 83.   [2] Ibid., pp. 108–11.
[3] Max Weber (1948), p. 321.

and to assess the observed facts by our criteria of adequate means-
to-end relationships? In our paradigm, the correlation between
standards of living and birth restriction, this difficulty does not
arise; for here actors and observers share the same cultural background, and the motives and considerations of the former are also
those of the latter, or are at least readily intelligible to them. But in
the anthropological field many instances can be quoted where this
is not so. When early anthropologists spoke with emphasis of
primitive cultures as baffling to our way of thinking they obviously
did not mean that the people were acting without any conscious
purpose at all, but merely that the people were acting in a seem-
ingly irrational fashion in which we, the observers, could discern no
rhyme or reason—nothing that we could identify as adequate
means for intelligible ends. Of modern anthropology precisely the
opposite seems to be true; for to-day the observer readily discovers
the meaning of primitive behaviour in the 'needs' which it satisfies
or the 'functions' it fulfils, that is, in an 'objective' means-to-end
relationship visible to him, and not presumed to be consciously
pursued by the actors.

To consider only the 'subjective' purpose of the actors and their
conception of one mode of action as a 'means', and of another as the
'end', will clearly not do; for however convincing this assessment of
the situation may be for the actors, it need not satisfy us as to the
'right' by which this nexus of behaviour does in fact occur. To
construe, on the other hand, an ulterior purpose of which the
actors are unaware, constitutes an explanatory principle of a more
indirect and remote order, with which we are not at the moment
concerned. I suggest, then, that the explanatory category of purpose is primarily applicable to relations between actions in which
the nexus of subjective intentions coincides with that of an
'objective' purpose intelligible to the observer. In other words,
we are here concerned with *rational* relations between modes of
action.

The concept of rationality, much used in sociological and
anthropological literature, requires some comment. It is here taken
to mean purposiveness plus something else, namely, the fact that
the steps taken to achieve the purposive appear by their nature
appropriate and empirically sound. We ascribe rationality to
sequences of behaviour if they are analyzable in terms of means and
ends, more precisely, in terms of an intrinsic appropriateness of

means to ends of which the actors are aware and which the observer, drawing on his empirical knowledge, can discern and verify.[1] Pareto speaks in the same sense—with a somewhat unhappy choice of terms—of 'logical' actions, that is, actions 'logically' united towards an end from the point of view of the actor as well as the observer and his wider knowledge.[2] No other definition of rationality is adequate; for if we considered only the 'subjectively' assessed appropriateness of means to ends, nearly all forms of human behaviour would have to be called rational (save those produced by reflexes or by some other involuntary compulsion); and if we considered only the 'objective' appropriateness, rationality would merely reflect the knowledge and understanding of which the observer is capable.

Let us note that in referring to the empirical knowledge in any assessment of rational behaviour we refer to the knowledge of the causal efficacy of actions or materials used in actions, which is possessed both by the actors and the observer. Of this ubiquitous causality, which underlies also such connections of purpose, we have already spoken. But let us note further that the observer's knowledge must be wider than that of the actors, lest his whole enquiry become nonsensical; for unless the observer's knowledge were the wider, he could not assess when means are being appropriately used, and when the actors act with an insufficient or wrong understanding of the situation. In fact, the 'wider knowledge' of the observer must be taken to mean (as Parsons has pointed out) the widest knowledge available to his civilization and to his class of humanity—that of the scientist.

The empirical knowledge with which we must credit the actors poses a more complicated problem. As we are concerned with societies and cultures, we can clearly not rely on the fortuitous knowledge possessed by this or that individual. Yet we cannot rely either on the fullest knowledge available in the society since this might not represent the kind of awareness which guides the actions of the average person. The persecution of minorities might well represent a rational mode of action on the part of the leaders or of some sections of the population who, by this means, get rid of competitors or secure some desired benefit; but the masses of the people may join in the movement and in fact carry it to success

---

[1] Talcott Parsons (1937), pp. 187, 430
[2] Quoted from op. cit. (1937), p. 187.

without having so calculated means against ends. Conversely, the irrational obedience of a population to myths and supernatural beliefs might yet be utilized by the Platos or other purveyors of 'noble falsehoods', as a means whose efficacy has been empirically tested, serving an end whose worthwhileness has been carefully assessed. It would seem, therefore, that we must consider separately the knowledge available in each relevant class of people, so that we shall have to distinguish between the old and the young; between the social *élite* and the mass; between leaders and their followers; and perhaps between men (who mostly hold the positions of influence) and women. Yet if we consider society as a whole, including both subjects and leaders, shall we not assess the rationality of its modes of behaviour on the grounds of the fullest knowledge possessed by those who in fact control it? We shall probably do so, with the necessary provisos. That is, we shall not reckon with 'ideal types', nor yet with simple averages; but with differential levels of knowledge, one of which we shall take—and explicitly justify—as representative.

To return to the rational nexus of actions. Now, we must not think of it too narrowly, as one between two intimately connected modes of behaviour bearing upon one another with the same directness and exclusiveness with which a tool bears on the task for which it is fitted. Rather must we think of the nexus as of one between relatively self-contained patterns of behaviour, each governed by its own purpose, and leading to the other only ultimately, often indirectly and by several steps. We are, in other words, dealing with a *mutual adjustment of purposes in a total situation*, and all that our criterion requires is that in this adjustment a means-to-end relationship should be discernible. Nor is one mode of behaviour invariably the means, and the other the end for which this particular means is employed; rather both may represent means to an identical end, whether this is explicitly stated or tacitly assumed. The modes of behaviour may support each other, as in parallel co-variations; when, for example, we find that the organization of young men in age regiments goes hand in hand with rules of celibacy, the two modes of behaviour appear as complementary means towards the same end—the creation of an efficient military force, adequately trained as well as unencumbered by marital or quasi-marital ties. Again, the two modes of behaviour may appear inversely correlated, and thus reveal themselves as alternative means, one valid where the other is invalid; thus strong kinship obligations of mutual aid and specific credit associations achieve each in their own way the same desired end—insurance against the risks of production; economic success and property offences may similarly replace each other as alternative means for securing the necessities of life. This correlation of alternatives figures prominently in social analysis. We are forever on the look-out for purposes which must somehow be realized and which account for the varying modes of behaviour as for so many means appropriate in different circumstances.

Finally, the mutual adjustment of purposes need not always be expressed in positive terms, as an agreement of purposes appropriate to one another. Often it is more adequate to speak, negatively, of an incompatibility of purposes, and to say of one mode of action that it precludes another desirable and expected one. The organization of male adolescents is an instance where fighting regiments or similar age sets appear correlated with celibacy or late marriage; here, in fact, the people themselves may express this nexus in such negative terms, as do certain Nuba tribes when they say that you cannot keep men in fighting trim and let them marry, though marriage is yet considered generally desirable. If situations of this kind are expressed in the formula—if the end A is to be achieved, the end B cannot also be achieved (and B' must be substituted), we equally meet with correlations implying, as it were, a double negative, thus: Since the end A cannot be achieved, because the respective mode of behaviour has failed in its purpose, B cannot be achieved either, and B' is substituted. Here A and B stand for 'normal', that is, expected, behaviour, and B' for a mode of action consciously departing from a norm no longer compatible with the situation. The classical correlation between rising prices of bread and increase in theft is a case in point, as is any similar correlation between economic stress and crime; for economic stress means the failure of productive activities to achieve their end—the procurement of the necessities of life; hence the 'normal' respect for law and property is no longer pursued as a worthwhile end, and the consciously 'abnormal' mode of acting—crime—comes to replace it.

As I have suggested, it is often a matter of choice whether to state the observed rational nexus of behaviour positively, in terms of an agreement of purposes, or negatively, in terms of their incom-

s

patibility; in cases of this kind one kind of statement is transformed into the other simply by the appropriate choice of words. For example, I might state the correlation between efficient organization for war and celibacy of the young men as such, positively, rather than say that the former prevents early marriage; or I might say that rising standards of living go together with a lower birth-rate, rather than that they conflict with the raising of large families. But it will readily be seen that these two ways of stating our facts are only superficially the same; for they imply definite, and in a sense contrasting, assumptions as to the normality or desirability of the behaviour in question. When choosing the positive statement we represent the observed nexus of behaviour non-committally, as a matter of fact, without evaluating it; while the negative statement represents it as an instance of some maladjustment—some failure to achieve a state of affairs of which we tacitly approve. Now, we may have no choice in the matter and be unable to change the negative import of our statements. It clearly makes no difference whether we say of a certain mode of behaviour that it is correlated (negatively) with the weakening of law and order, or (positively) with an increase in crime; in either case there is the implication of maladjustment, failure, or abnormality. Perhaps this is true even of the examples previously quoted; for the terms 'celibacy' and 'birth restriction' are not quite non-committal but imply, at least for observers with the background of our civilization, some suggestion of abnormality. However this may be, it would seem that we are justified in expressing it only where the actors equally assess the situation in this negative sense.

Often, this will be the case. The actors may, in fact, openly regard the 'abnormal' solution as the only one practicable in the circumstances—as it were, as the lesser evil; to wit, the Nuba tribe which enforces celibacy for the sake of military efficiency. I suspect that much the same is true of societies on a marginal level of subsistence (like the Eskimos or the Chinese peasants) which practise infanticide in spite of their love of children and their desire for progeny. These are still cases of rational choice which present no problem of understanding. But again, there may be no question of choice; the actually occurring correlation of social facts may be unequivocally regarded as undesirable and as amounting to failures in no way planned or expected. Thus no society intends to have poverty, famines, unemployment, crime, and all the other aspects of 'social pathology'. Yet these phenomena occur in regular co-variation with other, intentional, modes of behaviour, intended to operate as appropriate means for the achievement of some beneficial end. Here, then, the 'subjective' purpose bears upon desired ends which are not, or not fully, achieved; while 'objectively' there is a connection between modes of behaviour which is not intended.

Can we, in this case, still speak of rational means-to-end relations? Or should we not rather relegate this whole field of phenomena to the realm of irrational action and of unreason in society? I have no doubts myself that we understand even such connections in terms of rationality; we still see in them a choice of appropriate means for the attainment of desired ends, though somewhere in this nexus effects not calculated by the actors must have come into play. More precisely, in these connections several means-to-end relations operate in chain fashion. The actors can calculate only the adjacent links in the chain but not the end links, which, for them, are unexpected or at least unintended. In social enquiry, the end links stand out, as co-varying phenomena, and the 'fit' which we, the observers, find in them is still the fit of means leading to ends, though, as I put it before, leading to them indirectly and by many steps. The actors, in other words, act rationally but with insufficient insight into or control over the total situation.[1]

In the simplest case our knowledge, wider and more unbiased than that of the actors, may permit us to lay our finger on some concrete error in the calculation, and on the spot where things begin to go wrong. Thus we might be able to show that the failure of a simple farming economy is due, say, to a system of inheritance implying an excessive fragmentation of the land; or that instability of marriage is bound up with a rigid kinship system which does not permit of the adoption of wives into the husband's kin group; or that an increase in criminality is a by-product of rapid and uncontrolled industrial development, entailing large-scale re-distributions of population, and repeated crises and waves of unemployment. But clearly our knowledge is not always as assured, or definitely wider and more reliable than that of the actors; nor is it

---

[1] Max Weber refers to situations of this kind when he speaks of forms of action which are 'purposive-rational' without being 'correctly rational' (*Richtigkeitsrational*), i.e. which are not also oriented on some 'objectively valid' type of correctness (1913, pp. 409–10).

unchanging. It is itself relative, changing with the times and with the general outlook of our civilization. In the early days of our triumphant technological progress it would have been heresy to doubt that we were on the threshold to Utopia and to suggest that crime, poverty, and unemployment were somehow bound up with this progress.

Above all, there is the problem on what grounds to judge the normality or abnormality of a situation and to make out a case for things having 'gone wrong'. We have so far assumed that actors and observers both assess the situation in the same negative sense. Obviously, this need not be the case; and if it is not, then we must either refrain from all such evaluative statements or realize that we claim to be judges of the value of the actions we observe, of the utility of the ends for which the people strive, and of their worth-whileness when measured against the means whereby they are achieved. It seems difficult to avoid doing the latter. If we find that a people devotes all its energies, even successfully, to war and con-quest at the cost of numerous lives and the stability of families; or that an economic system efficiently based on ruthless competition is maintained at the cost of widespread poverty and social iniqui-ties, we are tempted to speak once more of 'failure' and, if not of 'irrational' aims, at least of aims achieved iniquitously. Indeed, even without committing ourselves as fully, our choice of words will often betray us; for when we speak (as we often do) of ends achieved 'at a cost' we already express judgments of this kind. Yet if the actors have no sense of the cost of their professed aims, must we not resist this temptation, even to the extent of pruning our vocabulary and making it truly non-committal? If we do not, we shall be accused of going beyond the legitimate scope of social enquiry. For it will probably be argued that it is not our business to consider the worthwhileness of ends or means, but only to assess the appropriateness of the latter, taking the former as given. Cer-tainly, the criterion of rationality is no longer applicable when we consider actions as ends in themselves; they are neither rational nor irrational, but merely desirable or not, good or bad, that is, they conform or do not conform to values in which we believe. If we analyze and assess also these, we do so as social philosophers, and not as enquirers plodding to understand the discoverable con-nections between ways of acting.

For a wide range of social facts this argument undoubtedly holds.

But let me say again that it does not hold for the whole realm of things social. At some stage in his analysis the social enquirer inevitably turns into a philosopher and must posit absolute aims or purposes, and some self-reliant worthwhileness of actions, since without these assumptions his subject matter simply makes no sense; so that he cannot but read success and failure into the modes of action—or certain modes of action—he describes. But this widest perspective of our enquiry we may for the moment disregard.

It might seem that the category of actions formulated above, which are 'incorrectly' rational, that is, are carried out with 'insufficient insight' into the situation, includes also all forms of behaviour usually described as magic or religious, and as aiming at the supernatural control of nature. The difference, however, seems clear. In the case of incorrectly rational actions the professed purpose of the actors (material prosperity, the stability of marriage, and so forth) is empirically possible and the means employed (a system of inheritance, a technique of production, a kinship organization) are intrinsically capable of achieving it, though the same kinds of means could be made more efficient if they were modified in some manner. In the case of supernatural aims the professed purpose is either not capable of being empirically achieved at all, or not capable of being achieved by the kind of means actually employed. In other words, the actors do not merely act from insufficient knowledge but act in contradiction to all empirical knowledge, unless indeed our own knowledge is all wrong. Yet undoubtedly the actors do act purposively and employ what are, for them, appropriate means. This raises the wider issue: How are we to deal with connections between modes of action which are only 'subjectively' rational but 'objectively' irrational or (in Pareto's phraseology) non-logical? More precisely, how are we to understand situations in the case of which the observer cannot accept the actors' view that here particular means are appropriately used for desired ends?

It must be said, first of all, that we can do nothing with a nexus of behaviour which in this way makes sense for the actors but fails to make any sense for us; it simply remains unintelligible, although, as we shall see, this contingency is unlikely to arise. What does happen, however, is that we, the observers, find a different kind of sense in the nexus of behaviour—some fit or appropriateness of which the actors are unaware. Firstly, we might discern a causal nexus in what the actors take to be a nexus of means to ends. This is true of all rationalizations (or 'super-rationalizations', if this term might be coined) offered by the people for causal connections which they do not comprehend. Think, for example, of certain magic or religious cures which are nevertheless effective; for the people, they represent modes of behaviour appropriate to secure some supernatural intervention and hence the desired benefits, while we might be able to demonstrate that the beneficial results are due to the operation of some therapeutic mechanism set in motion by the would-be magic activity.

Secondly, we might discern a different, 'objective', kind of rationality in actions whose subjective purposiveness we must dismiss as empirically impossible. Once more, religious and magic practices offer typical examples. Thus we find in many primitive peasant communities rigid rules permitting the harvesting and consumption of first-fruits only after certain sacrifices or rituals have been performed. The professed purpose of these rules is the perpetuation of the fertility of the land which, it is believed, would be endangered if these taboos were broken. From our general knowledge we can substitute an empirical appropriateness for the professed mystic one; for we should argue that the taboos in question enable men with expert knowledge to control these important activities, so that labour will be efficiently coordinated, the premature dissipation of food-stocks prevented, and perhaps also the danger to health obviated which might be caused by eating unripe crops.

Thirdly, we might superimpose an 'objective' rational purpose upon the subjective one, not because the latter is false, but because, crudely speaking, we think that there is more in the situation than the actors appreciate. This is true of a vast number of instances in which the professed purpose is merely the proximal purpose of obeying a custom not further questioned and of behaving in accordance with a tradition more or less blindly accepted. If here we feel compelled to go beyond the overt purpose guiding the actors we do so because it inadequately expresses the outcome of their actions, that is, because it does not satisfactorily account for the correlation between modes of behaviour we actually observe.

Whether we disregard the professed aim because of its empirical falsity (as in our first two examples) or because of its inadequacy (as in the third), in either case we are abandoning the explanatory category of purpose as we originally defined it. We no longer rely on the coincidence of 'subjective' and 'objective' purpose, but ourselves read the purpose (or rationality) into the observed nexus of actions; we impute to them a utility which the actors do not consciously seek, and an efficacy which they only unwittingly realize. We might put it this way: We make society and culture think for the people, and customs or habits carry means-to-end relations which transcend individual awareness or capacity of understanding. Here we are dealing with a new kind of explanatory concept, namely, with ulterior social purposes or (as we usually say) *functions*.[1] Modern anthropological literature is full of such purposes or functions read into the facts, though they differ widely in abstractness and thus in their capacity of being empirically demonstrated and verified. If the practical usefulness of the first-fruit rituals is placed at one end of this scale of abstractness, at the other end we meet with interpretations such as these: that religion maintains the 'sense of dependence' of the individual upon his society; that exogamy protects the unity of the clan from 'the open working of sex'; or that witchcraft 'provides means for displacing hostile impulses against relatives' and 'objectifies anxiety' in a socially advantageous way.[2] We can see that a limited practical utility, readily demonstrable in specified circumstances, shades over into one valid in an absolute sense, measured on the yardstick of social solidarity or group survival, and involving assumptions which seem to evade verification save by imaginary experiments.

Of this yardstick and the assumptions on which it is constructed I shall have to say more in a later chapter. Here we need consider only this final question: How are we to picture the genesis of situations of this kind when society or culture appear to 'think for' the individuals and to make them pursue worthwhile ends by appro-

[1] Certain American anthropologists have suggested that means-to-end relations of this ulterior kind should be termed 'latent functions', as against the 'motivations stimulating the individual', which would represent 'manifest functions' (C. Kluckhohn, 1944, p. 46). Though I would draw the same kind of distinction I cannot see that the suggested terminology is an improvement. Even the 'latent' function, if it can at all be handled by the observer, must be 'manifest' in some manner and for him; also, it seems to me to go against the accepted usage of 'function' to extend the term to consciously held purposes and aims.

[2] These (greatly condensed) quotations are taken respectively from A. R. Radcliffe-Brown (1945), p. 11; B. Malinowski (1931), p. 630; and C. Kluckhohn (1944), pp. 56, 61.

priate means under the guise of 'false' purposes and 'irrational' means? In choosing the metaphor of culture 'thinking for' the individual I mean to imply no collective unconscious or group mind or any similar metaphysical construction. The metaphor is meant to represent conditions as they exist at the moment of observation. If it were possible to trace these back to their first emergence, they would be traced back also to innovations, discoveries, or inventions produced by individuals, by chance or design, and perpetuated by others for their actual utility. But to appreciate the usefulness of end results is one thing; to understand its why's and wherefore's, quite another. The nexus of cause and effect or of means and ends might well have been misunderstood by the inventors or their successors, since they could only draw upon the obtaining knowledge; or the nexus might have been intentionally misinterpreted to make it.acceptable to the way of thinking of the time and place. Thus the actions of a more enlightened *élite* become the cultural possession of a wider group, disguised by 'noble falsehoods' or by the rationalizations of what passed at the time for common sense.

4. CAUSALITY

The point I wish to make can best be illustrated by a fictitious example, though it is not as far-fetched as it might seem. In Book III of the *Republic*, Plato recommends that certain musical scales should be made *de rigueur* for composers in his ideal State, while others should be banished; for as Plato claims to have observed, the latter, of Asiatic origin, are detrimental to morality and martial virtues. (A similar idea inspired Tolstoi's 'Kreutzer-Sonata'). Now Plato clearly assumes that the individuals who practise and listen to music would also be the citizens and soldiers of the State, or would at least be in contact with them and capable of influencing their behaviour. In this respect his theory (or speculation) satisfies our crucial condition, that the correlated modes of behaviour must come into contact in the minds of the actors. Plato further assumes that listening to such music has a lasting psychological effect, weakening or strengthening, as the case may be, certain personality traits. For Plato the observed correlation (assuming he did observe it) between musical scales and morality was significant since it was backed by a theory of the psychological efficacy of music generally held since Pythagoras; for us, it would amount to more than coincidence only if we shared Plato's (or similar) ideas about psychology. Yet if we had good reason to share them, then this would be a precise instance of the mechanical psycho-physical causality which serves us as an explanatory or 'intervening' concept.

We conceive of one mode of behaviour or experience (the musical practice) as producing, vaguely speaking, a mental state, which in turn produces the correlated mode of behaviour (the *morale* of citizens or soldiers). More precisely, we understand the co-varying phenomena through placing between them some mechanism which turns one mode of behaviour and experience into another. And this mechanism is visible on a level of analysis deeper than that on which the co-varying phenomena themselves are examined, namely, on the level of psychology or physiology. It is a mechanism in the full sense of the word; for its effectiveness does not, basically, depend on the actors' intentions or awareness. The mechanism does throw up intentions, conscious desires, needs, and the like; but these are the end results of processes which themselves are unconscious or at least involuntary. While in the case of logical consistency and purpose we assume that the correlated modes of behaviour become connected in the awareness of the actors and through the agency of their intellect, we now make no such as-sumption. We merely diagnose, from our knowledge of the disci-plines in question, a stimulus and a response, some psycho-physical process and its external symptoms, and name the con-necting 'hidden machine'. To say it again, we accept that this may work unconsciously, so that our understanding of psycho-physical causality, unlike that of logical consistency or purpose, has no 'subjective' counterpart.

In our fictitious example the causal explanation of the presumed coincidence of musical style and civic morale might seem absurd: but it is absurd only because the underlying psychological know-ledge is unsound or inadequately verified. Yet as even the soundest knowledge of this kind belongs to a discipline other than social enquiry, it may well at some stage be unfamiliar to many students of society and, when used in social explanations, strike them as equally far-fetched and even abstruse. I do not think that this point needs special proof; the first reaction of many anthropologists to the findings of psychoanalysis is sufficient evidence. We shall later examine the usefulness and soundness of psychoanalytical and other psycho-physical explanations of social phenomena. My point here is that we must always rely on these neighbouring disciplines and be prepared for such 'far-fetched' explanations. No doubt this fact is often obscured. Anthropologists also seem able to offer causal explanations of social phenomena which, far from being 'far-fetched', are at once intelligible and appear to involve no such reliance on the special findings of psychology or physiology. Yet this does not mean that the anthropologist really dispenses with such borrowed knowledge, but only that this knowledge is so fully familiar that it is simply taken for granted. Whether it is so familiar because it is borne out by the self-knowledge every observer possesses or because it has become widely disseminated, we may disregard. In either case the knowledge has become common sense. It is thus that we immediately understand the correlation, say, between prolonged wars and the breakdown of morality; for it is our general and perhaps tacit psychological knowledge which makes us here see a connection of cause-and-effect, between the frustration and suppression of normal needs and desires on the one side, and their break-through and uncontrolled indulgence on the other (though psychoanalysis would probably go further and demonstrate also another causal nexus, namely, between sexuality and aggression). And when Durkheim correlates 'anomic' suicide with sudden readjustments forced upon the society, we equally readily and by the same intellectual process grasp the link between such disturbances of the stability and security of life and the readiness of individuals to seek escape in suicide.

As in the explanations in terms of purpose, then, we again base ourselves on empirical knowledge which changes and progresses. It can legitimately be said that causal connections between modes of behaviour unperceived until a short time ago are to-day understood, and this process is likely to be repeated in the future as our insight into psycho-physical mechanisms deepens and becomes more assured. I am speaking here of connections 'unperceived', not of connections perceived but not at once intelligible. For we do not normally proceed from a stage when we can demonstrate co-variations between social phenomena without as yet grasping their 'fitness' or meaning, to one when psychology or physiology have provided us with the missing cue. To say it once more, we always start with a suspicion or theory of significant connections, and not with the random search for co-variations which might prove significant. It is true that social psychologists often stress the importance for their work of anthropological observations, as posing problems for which psychology must find the solution. But what happens here is that certain descriptive data suggest to the psychologist the presence of some important psychological mechanism, which he will analyze and attempt to isolate, and formulate as an explanatory principle; the anthropologist's search for co-variations in the social field will then be guided by this new knowledge, whether it is already assured or only tentatively put forth. It is therefore unlikely that the discovery of regularities in social behaviour precedes their understanding in the terms of psychological theories. This disposes of a question previously touched upon, namely, whether there are any social correlations which, at the time of their discovery, remain unintelligible. This question, as we now see, does not really arise.

5. Rules of Application

The preceding discussion has left the interrelation of our three explanatory categories largely undefined. To some extent we anticipated that they cannot always be kept apart as though each would apply only to its own peculiar province of social phenomena. In the case of logical consistency, at least, we noted that all three categories of explanation might seem applicable to the same social situation. As we shall see, the same kind of overlap is also true of explanations in terms of purpose and of psycho-physical causality. The question then arises whether it is possible to formulate some rule governing the application of our explanatory concepts and laying down when or where each is appropriate or relevant.

It is tempting to answer in the affirmative and to formulate at least a rule of precedence. We might argue that, where a nexus of behaviour is intelligible in terms of logical consistency or rational purpose, we have already grasped its relevant 'fitness' and meaning, and need go no farther; while, where these two categories are inapplicable, that is, in the field of 'irrational' or 'non-logical' actions, explanations in terms of psycho-physical causality are required and appropriate. This is, in essence, the view of Max Weber and Pareto.[1] It might seem that we can carry this viewpoint even

---

[1] Certain psychologists argue in much the same sense. Kardiner, for example, considers that rational and logical modes of action—'institutions of purely

further. For since social behaviour is *ex definitione* purposive, any visible purposive nexus which might overlap with a logical one would overrule the latter and have priority. Logical consistency would thus become a residual category, as it were, of the first degree, and psycho-physical causality one of the second degree; which rule of precedence would, incidentally, satisfy the philosopher's Law of Parsimony. Equally, it would answer the question raised previously, as to the claims of a self-contained, 'pure' sociology. Its field would seem to extend as far as do the explanations in terms of logical consistency and rational purpose—explanations, that is, which involve no borrowing of concepts from other disciplines. And only where such explanations fail should we be compelled to admit the extraneous, borrowed concepts, rely upon lower levels of analysis, and invoke the 'hidden machines' of psycho-physical mechanisms.

I fear no such simple canon is possible. At least two of our categories of explanation—rationality and psycho-physical causality—often appear inseparable in the same nexus of behaviour, the different kinds of 'fitness' striking us as equally relevant and convincing. This is true, to begin with, of all connections of behaviour which are rationally directed towards the attainment of some psycho-physical satisfaction; for here we understand the rationality of the behaviour, that is, we understand the professed aims to be true aims, and the means employed to be appropriate means, only because we understand also the psycho-physical mechanisms involved. Take the familiar connection between everyday routine and the recreative institutions of holidays or feasts. All societies operate with some regular alternation of this kind, and we clearly understand its rational purpose—to obviate the boredom or fatigue of prolonged routine and the consequent drop in efficiency, and so to enable routine to be efficiently maintained. Yet we accept this link of purpose only because we know certain things about the working of the organism; we know that the uninterrupted application to routine tasks does cause boredom and fatigue; that these provoke the desire for change and relaxation; and that the stimulation offered by the latter facilitates the resumption of the routine work. It may well seem unnecessary specifically to mention this causal nexus underlying a purposive one; but it is

rational origin'—do not concern the psychologist and do not belong to the subject matter of his analysis (1939), pp. 1, 485.

unnecessary only because we take it for granted. The 'pure' sociological explanation is thus 'pure' only insamuch as the 'hidden machine' is too widely known to be explicitly referred to; and once we do refer to it explicitly we operate with extraneous and borrowed concepts.

But there are also instances of such linked xplanations in which the reference to psycho-physical mechanisms is not obscured by their familiarity. Think of the well known correlation between economic stress and hostility to aliens or racial minorities. Again, we may point to a wholly rational motive—the desire to reduce or eliminate competition; but we must also reckon with the possibility that the same reaction is caused by the unconsciously operating mechanisms which psychoanalysis has demonstrated, of frustration-aggression and scapegoat-hunting. Perhaps, indeed, the professed rational purpose of eliminating competition will prove to be not a true purpose at all, but merely one of those rationalizations against which we must always be on guard. Let me quote finally an example in which all three categories of explanation are combined. We mentioned before the correlation between wars and moral laxity as an instance of psycho-physical causality. Now this nexus may be purposive-rational at the same time; for the actors will often act purposively on a maxim whose appropriateness we readily understand—'let us enjoy ourselves while we can, for to-morrow we may die'; also, the society may consciously condone this self-indulgence, as a means to achieve a definite end, namely, sustained further efforts. Furthermore, the principle of logical consistency may be joined to the others; for in ignoring the conventions of morality the people may also be moved by the desire or compulsion to extend the mode of thinking entailed in war—that normal morality and discipline are suspended—to the contexts of peaceful living.

If, then, our simple canon of precedence is inapplicable and the Law of Parsimony offers no guidance, it is impossible to predict from general considerations when 'pure' sociological explanations are legitimate, and when the extraneous, psycho-physical explanations must be admitted, instead of, or in addition to, the former. In practice, this means that we shall often have to explain the connection of social phenomena in terms of 'partly this' and 'partly that'. I can see no way out of this difficulty—if this absence of neatness is considered a difficulty. When this will be the case will depend on the extent to which psychology can account for the nexus of phenomena we observe in the social field. Thus, if we wish to judge the claims of pure sociology we must start, not from an examination of what it can do, but rather from the opposite end, from an examination of what the other forms of analysis can do. In other words, we must proceed purely pragmatically and by way of elimination. Delimiting the efficiency of non-sociological, that is, 'extraneous,' explanations, we shall be delimiting also the autonomy that can be ascribed to 'purely' social laws or regularities.

This shall be the programme of the following chapter. For purely practical reasons, however, I propose to curtail it considerably. Though we have in this discussion dealt with one kind of extraneous explanations only, in terms of psychology, their scope is of course much wider. As we have previously stated, it would include explanations in terms of biological regularities and of purely physiological mechanisms, and would thus rest also on the study of genetics, heredity and race, and of the influence of the physical environment upon the human organism through climate, nutrition, and the like. All these problems I propose to disregard, for these reasons. The influence of heredity, race, and of the physical environment on social behaviour has been amply and expertly examined by other scholars, and there is little that can be usefully added to what they have said. Also, they are in far-reaching agreement. Few scholars will deny to-day that the factors of heredity, environment and so forth cannot fully account for the regularities of behaviour which we call 'social' or 'cultural', and that the realm of society and culture retains some autonomy, irreducible by this kind of extraneous approach. Indeed, even when this approach indicates some such extraneous determinacy of human behaviour, this is not only restricted but also often dubious, permitting us in the present stage of our knowledge to speak only vaguely and non-committally of possible or plausible causes and effects. Above all, these extraneous influences, so far as they exist, do not compel the human organism purely mechanically to behave in a certain way; rather do they exercise this compulsion by way of the psycho-physical organization, that is, through the medium of human drives, needs, desires, motives of some kind. So that our analysis of that organization will elucidate the relevant end phase of the extraneous influences, wherever they may start—in the effectiveness of climate or nutrition, or in genes and chromosomes.

The issue of the autonomy or otherwise of social regularities shall thus be dealt with as an issue between anthropology and psychology.

Before we embark upon this task, however, another, theoretical, consequence of the overlap of our explanatory categories must be considered. The point I wish to make is that this overlap often makes it impossible to identify the components of any nexus of behaviour as antecedent and consequent respectively. Now, whichever explanatory concept we adopt, we predicate a relation of this kind. In the case of psycho-physical causality this is obvious; in the case of logical consistency, when we speak of certain ideas, values, or organizing principles being 'diffused' through diverse contexts of activity, we imply at least the possibility of demonstrating some such antecedence; and when we speak of means-to-end relations, we definitely visualize a causality *a tergo*, that is, we visualize the end being given first and then determining the choice or fashioning of the means. In each case we assign to one of the correlated facts the role of a determinant, and to the other that of the thing determined. In other words, we back one kind of 'fitness' (logical, purposive) visible in the facts by another, namely, by that most satisfying fitness or requiredness—causality understood in its most general sense.

I am here speaking of 'antecedent' and 'consequent' in a double sense, equating a concrete time sequence between the correlated phenomena with their causal interdependence. Nor can it be otherwise; for we cannot intelligently speak about one thing determining or causing the other without assuming that one also follows upon the other. It is true, however, that we might not be able to observe this time sequence, as would be the case in co-variations occurring simultaneously at the moment of observation. For example, in establishing the correlation between falling birthrate and rising standards of living, we should probably observe the two processes together and be unable to show that the former occurs for such-and-such time before the latter becomes effective. Even so, if we understand the nexus at all, we understand it as one between an antecedent and consequent projected, however vaguely or speculatively, on a time scale.

Let me leave this point for the moment and turn to the question: What kind of evidence does allow us to assess our facts in this sense? It seems to me that we use three criteria, singly or in combination. First, we may actually observe the time sequence in which the correlated phenomena follow upon each other. This may be on a semi-historical and collective scale, the correlated events or modes of behaviour occurring in successive periods of group life, as when we observe the breakdown of morality as an aftermath of war or at least as a phase in group life setting in when the other phase, warfare, has lasted for some time. Or the time sequence may be of narrow range and on an individual scale, the correlated events or modes of behaviour occurring simultaneously in the group but succeeding each other in the lives of individuals. Thus, in the correlation between warlike organization and age sets in primitive societies we do not observe one social fact as such succeeding the other; but we observe individuals entering age sets first, and afterwards engaging in military tasks. If it were not so, and the time-order were reversed, we should clearly not conclude warlike efficiency to be the desired 'end' and age set organization the prerequisite 'means'.

Secondly, where the time sequence is unobservable, the statistical distribution of the co-variations may yet indicate which is the determinant and which the thing determined.[1] Thirdly, our general empirical knowledge will often compel us to accept one relation of this kind rather than another, since a different reading of our facts would strike us as unlikely or even absurd. This general knowledge is difficult to define; it includes all our previous experiences of time sequences, co-variations, or causal mechanism valid in similar situations, as it also includes our awareness of connections stretching beyond the nexus actually examined. Together, these items of knowledge build up an *a priori* certainty that the facts examined can only hang together in this way, and not in that. Thus, when we discover that juvenile delinquency appears conspicuously correlated with low income levels, we shall have no doubts as to which is the antecedent and which the consequent; and when, again, we demonstrate the correlation between age set organization and regular warfare we shall hardly consider the latter to be caused by the former.

The guidance offered by these three criteria is likely to be absent only in the case of logical consistency; here we may indeed be unable, at least at the time of observation, to assess the observed nexus in terms of antecedent and consequent, so that we can only state the existence and extent of the nexus. Thus, when we dis-

---

[1] See above, p. 231.

cover that the same values dominate the religious beliefs and the political life of a certain society on whose history we have no evidence, we cannot say more than that the two modes of behaviour are interdependent; and when we observe that the same organizing principle, say, matrilineal affiliation, governs the inheritance of land, the succession to titles or offices, kinship terminology, marriage prohibitions, and religious observances, we cannot point to the sphere of behaviour where the principle first emerged, as against others to which it has 'diffused'; though from general considerations we shall probably argue that a kinship terminology cannot have preceded the actual occurrence of the relationships it tabulates or (less convincingly) that the modes of behaviour concerned with subsistence needs must be assigned primacy over all others. Now, the same difficulty of identifying antecedent and consequent also arises in social situations which are open to the double explanation in terms both of purpose and psycho-physical causality; and the difficulty arises, not because the conditions enabling us to identify this relation are absent, but because they in a sense cancel out.

Let me make this clear by an example previously quoted. Speaking of the alternation of routine work and institutionalized relaxations, we said that here a rational-purposive nexus implies a psycho-physical, causal one. We note, however, that the two do not coincide squarely but, as it were, in a transposed time sequence. For if in the relevant psycho-physical nexus the chance of relaxation (the cause) precedes the maintained efficiency of routine work (the effect), in the purposive nexus the effect is anticipated as the desired end, and the cause introduced as the means employed to achieve the end. This may be graphically expressed in this curve meant to represent the rhythm of routine and relaxation:

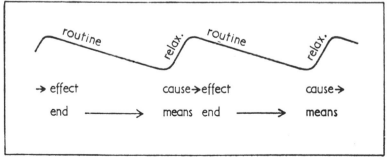

T

The causal and purposive connections, then, do not simply duplicate each other; the former is *utilized* by the latter and fitted into it.
As social existence rests on the regular recurrence of modes of
action, and thus on the possibility of securing the mental or
physical states conducive to such a recurrence, this 'transposed'
sequence must be widely typical of all explanations combining
purposive and psycho-physical understanding. And in such
situations we cannot pronounce upon any unequivocal relation of antecedents and consequents; all we can pronounce upon
with safety is the reciprocal interdependence of the phenomena
in question.

We must go a step further. For the same difficulty also arises in
situations which are open to purposive understanding alone. More
precisely, it arises when we consider means-to-end relations from
the viewpoint of the material causality involved in the effectiveness
of the means. As I have suggested, in any purposive nexus we take
the actors' conception of the end to precede their fashioning or
choice of the means; yet purely empirically, the use of the means
must at least once have preceded its effects before the actors can
have judged it to be appropriate. If a small family is indeed an
appropriate means to improve one's standard of living, the improvement must be an aim in the minds of the actors before they decide
to restrict the size of their families; but equally, they must have had
a chance of discovering that one thing does actually lead to the
other, if only by means of an imaginary experiment. If age sets are
in fact an appropriate means to achieve military efficiency, the
latter intention must have come before the organization of adolescence in this fashion; but equally this organization must have
existed before the military exploits, or its efficiency for that purpose
could not have been assessed nor the nexus between the two intentionally maintained. At least, the actors must have realized how
badly off they were without this organization of adolescence,
which they would then evolve by rational argument or by trial and
error. I am not suggesting that we should indulge in speculations
of this kind. But I do suggest that these are possibilities always
implied, if only tacitly, in all purposive explanations. Nor is this
conflicting time sequence paradoxical; for we can readily visualize
the double relationship of means-and-ends and cause-and-effect as
a gradual process in which, step by step, one becomes adjusted to
the other; that is, an end is anticipated, however vaguely; causal

effects are observed which suggest a suitable means, until the means has been fully tested and fitted to the desired end.

Sometimes, indeed, we can isolate a crucial phase in this process. I described elsewhere how in a Nuba tribe recently dispersed over a wide area a new custom made its appearance, consciously meant to bind together the scattered sections.[1] In this tribe annual wrestling tournaments, staged between the different local sections, used to link the whole population in this collective activity. Lately the sections living far apart also agreed to exchange bulls on this occasion, the home team presenting the visitors with this gift. The people openly state that the new custom is meant as an inducement to keep the traditional practice alive in spite of the local dispersal, as they also state that 'there is no need' to do the same in the case of close-by sections. Here, then, an 'end' is clearly anticipated, and the appropriate 'means' produced; also, the effectiveness of the means has already been known, since the exchange of bulls was copied from a neighbouring Arab tribe. Above all, we can observe the gradualness of the process, for this new expedient failed to work in some cases after a number of years; so that, if the 'end' in question is still desired, some new, more efficient, means will have to be found and tested.

Often, however, we observe only the final phase of this process. And this we can define only in terms of a reciprocal interdependence between modes of action or events co-varying simultaneously. Thus we can do little with the concepts of antecedent and consequent. Their relevance does not disappear altogether; we still think of the ends as causing the means. But this relation can no longer be translated into a concrete time sequence, nor into an unequivocal nexus between determinants and things determined. Modern anthropologists are well aware of this ambiguity and, like the physicists, and partly for the same reason, tend to abandon the old irreversible nexus of cause-and-effect for the reversible and reciprocal relation of mere 'functional' interdependence.[2] But it

---

[1] (1947), p. 234.

[2] The concept of 'function' represents 'the interdependence of elements more completely and precisely' than does the concept of cause-and-effect since many forms of physical interdependence are 'simultaneous and reciprocal' rather than irreversible in time (E. Mach, 1920, pp. 278–9). It is unfortunate that the term *function* has come to be used with at least two different meanings, standing for 'interdependence' as well as for 'ulterior purpose' (see p. 275). This ambiguity, however, cannot be avoided, and all we can do is to specify on each occasion in which sense the term is being used (see also below, p. 368).

seemed important to point out that it is not the category of causality which is inapplicable or useless in social enquiry. Rather is it the merging of causal and purposive aspects in the same pattern of co-varying phenomena which blurs the time sequence, and hence the irreversibility, of antecedent and consequent.

CHAPTER XI

Psychological Explanations: Mental Energy

---

1. PRELIMINARIES

I embark on this discussion with considerable hesitation. The relationship of psychology and anthropology presents so complex and controversial a problem that I can hardly hope to deal with it adequately in the course of a chapter or two. Indeed, the hazards of such an enquiry show already in the widely divergent views held by various scholars. Is this then a thankless task? And perhaps a redundant one? It might well seem so. In a great many respects the psychologist and anthropologist approach an identical subject matter—human behaviour—by different roads; and in cases of this kind it is tempting to say: Let each go ahead and borrow from the other if need be, without worrying too much about the theory of the thing; the different lines of attack, so one trusts, will enrich our knowledge even if the respective roads are not charted in advance or barred against trespass. Certainly, a prolific literature testifies to the vitality of this combined approach to culture and society, insensible though its exponents may be of methodological scruples.

If I here pay more attention to these scruples, this follows from the tenor of this book. But let me also say that, unless the relations between social and psychological enquiry are precisely stated, certain dangers, all-too-evident in anthropological and psychological literature, will never be banished. Psychologists will overstate their claims and produce, by valid psychological methods, spurious sociological explanations; or the student of society, while officially disregarding psychology, will smuggle it in by the backdoor; or he may assign to psychology merely the residue of his enquiry—all the facts with which his own methods seem incapable of dealing. Not infrequently, then, the anthropologist or sociologist is apt to treat psychology (whether he accepts it openly or not) as a stopgap rather than a discipline whose potentialities he has carefully assessed. His is often the emaciated, non-committal everyman's psychology, or some conventional psychology which he can adapt as it is expedient.[1] Conversely, he will credit psychology with a convenient omniscience, and burden it with tasks which that science is incapable of executing.[2]

To some extent, these accusations are unfair. The anthropologist who wishes in all consciousness to use psychology finds unhappily not *one* agreed system, but is faced with numerous and often conflicting theories. Like anthropology, psychology is still a young science, rapidly growing and changing. The anthropologist is compelled to select, and select what appears to him the most suitable version. Here again, only the analysis of the relations between the two disciplines will resolve or at least reduce the dilemma. Once we know in what form psychological problems become relevant for the explanation of social facts, the kind of psychology needed will suggest itself.

2. SOCIAL PSYCHOLOGY

Perhaps I may here deviate a little and examine the position of Social Psychology so-called. For it might be thought that the kind of psychology helpful or necessary for social enquiry already exists in this separate and suggestively named discipline. I have previously dismissed social psychology somewhat summarily; let me now briefly defend my attitude.

If social psychology represents a separate field of enquiry, then it must either be concerned with a range of phenomena not accounted for by the other branches of psychology, or approach phenomena common to all branches under a special aspect. In the sense of the first alternative social psychology is commonly contrasted with individual psychology. This distinction would be meaningful only if individual psychology could be said to examine mental events peculiar to isolated individuals—thoughts or emotions which live, in unique form, in the minds of selected persons but disappear or change into something else in man in the

[1] Cf. A. F. Bentley: The sociologist tends to choose a psychological presentation 'conventional or convenient to him, and goes ahead' (1935, p. 326, N.).

[2] To quote again from Bentley: There is a widespread 'lingering feeling that psychology must face the task of being a guarantee of all knowledge' (op. cit., p. 340).

aggregate. This seems to me absurd.[1] Apart perhaps from personality studies or psycho-pathological case-histories, 'individual'
psychology is concerned, not with *one* individual, or a few selected
ones, but with *the* individual; it aims at the discovery of regularities valid, with whatever variations, for man at large. Everything,
then, that individual psychology records is true also of the human
beings who live in and make up society; and the individual whose
perceptions, memory or thought processes are examined in the
laboratory sustains, by these same mental faculties, his social
behaviour.

It is true that the psychological reactions of individuals are sometimes modified in contact situations, for example, in the crowd,
and that certain reactions are only visible when individuals act
together or in institutional groups; such are the responses of sympathy and antipathy, the manifold reactions of imitation, the psychological factors operating in respect, authority, love, aesthetic
appreciation, religious worship, and the rest. But these 'social'
responses equally exist, as capabilities and potentialities, in the
individual mind, much as do seeing or hearing, which equally presuppose an object outside the individual. To assume that there can
be a special psychology bent on studying the human mind *in vacuo*
is wholly unwarranted. Nor indeed can we, whether we are
psychologists or anything else, conceive of the individual except
as existing with others and organized for life in society, as he is
organized also for life in a world of things.

If thus everything that is discoverable in the mind of the individual enters into his social responses, the social contexts in which
he exists also enter into almost every individual mental event. Let
me explain this more fully. It was one of the fundamental advances
in psychology when Brentano pointed out that all psychological
processes and functions bear upon *objects*—things, events, states of
affairs—that is, upon some material palpably different from the
mental 'act' itself. Consciousness is always consciousness of something; and every mental function, save perhaps vague states of
feeling ('pathic states,' as they have been called) entails an 'object-
reference'. This elemental quality of mental events has not been
uniformly formulated by psychologists, perhaps because it is so

---

[1] The most extreme views of this kind—the theories of a 'collective consciousness' or 'unconscious', or of a 'group mind'—represent either picturesque
metaphors or meaningless assumptions.

elemental and thus difficult to define.[1] But this difficulty need not concern us. What is important for us is that there is such an 'object-reference', and that it means, at any given moment, a reference to things existing, not only in nature, but also in society and culture. For, clearly, the realm of 'objects' must embrace also instances of the latter kind. When Pierre Janet, in his analysis of the 'primary acts of intelligence', distinguishes between 'perceptual' and 'intellectual' objects he seems to mean precisely this; for his description of the latter is a description of objects created and having meaning for man living in a particular society and culture. 'In the world there are, not only fruits or rocks or lions, but also the road, the public place, the door, the tool, the portrait, the basket, the part of a cake, the drawers of a cupboard, the flag, the word. To understand these peculiar objects, which patently have not been created by nature but by man, to see their relations to the behaviour which gave them birth, this is the best way to understand elementary intelligence.'[2] Perhaps even the sharp distinction between natural and social objects is at fault; and human responses are always addressed, not to 'natural' objects existing with the autonomy of unambiguous and neutral things, but to objects already in some measure interpreted in the sense of cultural norms and values. More importantly, among the social objects we must reckon, not only the things 'created by man', as the end results of his behaviour, but this behaviour itself in all its aspects and phases, that is, any visible mode of action, and any intention, thought, feeling, or demand visible in it.

It is thus surely true to say that the 'things' referred to in our perceptions, thoughts or memories, the aims laid into our actions, and the objects of our feelings and fancies, come to us at least partly from the culture that surrounds us. The psychologist examining any mental mechanism therefore examines of necessity a mechanism normally operating with material given in society and culture. I said 'normally'; for admittedly the psychologist in his laboratory often studies the mechanism, the mental function as

---

[1] Brentano terms it 'intentionality'; Lloyd Morgan 'object reference' or 'projicience' (1923); Driesch speaks of 'objects' or 'material had consciously' (1925); Bartlett contrasts 'psychological functions' and 'psychological material' (1932, p. 290); Spearman speaks of the 'transitiveness' of perception and cognition, and contrasts the 'matter of fact regarded' with the 'way of regarding' (1937, vol. I, pp. 267, 449).

[2] Pierre Janet (1935), pp. 31–2.

such, neutralizing the influence of the 'given things' by various expedients, such as the use of meaningless syllables in memory experiments or of artificial models in intelligence tests. But these are merely steps in an analysis, not intentionally set limits. No one can seriously maintain that there is one psychology whose universe is peopled with meaningless syllables, formboards or measuring scales, and another concerned with the living contents of perceptions, thoughts, or emotions. Moreover, these living contents are effective, in an indirect fashion, even in the artificial isolation of the experiment. For the habitual material of the mental functions also affects their manner of operating, so that they exhibit a certain selectiveness or bias in whatever context they are stimulated. Bartlett has demonstrated this for the field of remembering, and other psychologists for a great many other mental activities.[1] There is, then, no justification for separating a 'social' from a 'non-social' psychology, each dealing with a different order of phenomena. I can do no better than quote this passage from Bartlett. He considers social psychology to be concerned 'with the modifications of human experience and conduct which are due to social grouping', and so with 'reactions which are specific to groups, found in them, and not found outside them'. Yet he has to admit that this definition is 'troublesome'; for it makes almost everything in psychology material also for social psychology.[2]

There is, however, the second interpretation of social psychology, which holds that this branch of psychology approaches the phenomena of the mind from a specific viewpoint. Social psychology is thus contrasted, not with 'individual', but with 'general' psychology, and is understood to be concerned with psychological data in so far as they are effective in (or affected by) social and cultural phenomena. In other words, it is psychology viewed under the aspect of its social relevance. This is an unexceptionable definition. Not even the most extravagant defender of the psychological interpretation of culture will maintain that everything psychological must be adduced for this purpose. Somewhere, then, a line of relevance must be drawn; and this is precisely our

[1] F. C. Bartlett (1935), pp. 255 ff.; for a general discussion of the relation between laboratory psychology and 'social frames of reference' see Murphy and Newcomb (1937), pp. 220 ff.

[2] F. C. Bartlett, op. cit., pp. 241, 243. See also Murphy and Newcomb, op. cit., p. 222: 'The separation of individual and social psychology is shown to be artificial and misleading.'

problem. All I can say is that I do not feel that the social psychologists have solved it for us. Often, in fact, they have shelved it. Many studies in social psychology, excellent as descriptive efforts, are only just this; they differ little, save perhaps in their vocabulary, from such descriptions as any anthropologist, well-read in psychology, might produce. Others touch upon the problem of the explanatory relevance of psychological as against social factors; but they treat it in a non-committal, on-the-one-hand-on-the-other-hand fashion, which I for one find unsatisfying. This does not mean that the borderland of psychology and social enquiry has never yet been systematically explored. A number of studies of this kind stand out brilliantly, such as the writings of Kurt Lewin, Kardiner, or Fromm, and, needless to say, the pioneer work of Freud. Few of these studies, incidentally, bear the label 'social psychology', which is, perhaps, no accident.

3. OBJECT AND FUNCTION LANGUAGE

In an earlier chapter I spoke of the implicitness of psychological in social facts to denote a first, ubiquitous, relationship between the two. I have held that every behaviour pattern (or 'social fact') implies or 'brackets' a pattern of psychological order, that is, mental processes integrated in some fashion—as it further implies also a pattern of physiological order, made up of such processes as nerve synapses, muscle actions, and so forth. So understood, social and psycho-physical facts are one and the same thing, examined on different levels of analysis, and any statements about the former merely 'shorthand' for the 'longhand' description in psycho-physical terms.[1]

To this relationship we have now added another, similar one, operating in the opposite sense; for we also hold that all psychological processes bear an 'object-reference', and that among these 'objects' must be reckoned forms of social behaviour. Social data thus seem as much implicit in psychological ones as these are implicit in the former. But the implicitness is not of the same order. Psychological facts are implicit in any mode of behaviour in the sense that they represent *underlying* events, to which the mode of behaviour can be broken down by the lower-level analysis. The 'social object', on the other hand, belongs to the mental event, as it

[1] See above, pp. 210–11.

were, as its content, and hence is only part of it; for the mental event consists, besides, of the psychological processes conveying or carrying this content—of the psychological 'function' as against the psychological 'material' (Bartlett), or the 'way of regarding' as against the 'matter of fact regarded' (Spearman). And this latter content, whichever name we give it, is found in the mental event without any breaking down, on the same level of analysis on which the mental event itself is visible. This means that the lower-level analysis of any mode of action does not break it down completely to psychological processes; for the latter will still bear their reference to 'social objects', which will, in some measure, be the very mode of action analyzed. If, for example, I tried to demonstrate the mental events implicit in the behaviour pattern 'bloodfeud', I should find that at least some of the psychological processes—perceiving, thinking, feeling, remembering, and so forth—are once more about 'bloodfeud'; so that we obtain this kind of interpenetration:

Social level	Modes of behaviour making up	Bloodfeud
Psychological level	Perceiving, thinking . . . with object	

Inasmuch, therefore, as the psychological analysis pays attention to the content of mental events rather than to the processes involved it will only duplicate the findings of the social enquiry. This becomes important where the object-reference of mental processes is not, or not directly, to concrete things or events (such as modes of behaviour), but to thoughts or beliefs about things and events. These, too, are among the 'objects' referred to in mental processes or functions; for if the term object-reference has any value at all, it must clearly be taken to include also such conceptual material as expectations, imaginary states of affairs, moral convictions, or ideas about truth and falsity. Now we know that precisely such material is also inevitably encountered in social enquiry, whenever we touch upon idea systems and the like. I have regarded ideas, beliefs, or convictions current and expressed in a society fully as social facts, visible on that particular level of analysis. But whether one agrees with this view or would rather consider these data to be of a psychological order, interpenetrating with the social data, does not matter; what matters is that at this point the social analysis (dealing with idea systems) and the psychological analysis (dealing with 'objects' of this kind) coincide and can only reveal the same things.

Generally speaking, then, a psychological approach concerned only or predominantly with the content side of mental events—with ideas, beliefs, convictions, moral values—will add nothing relevant to the knowledge we acquire in social analysis. This seems to me to apply to a good many efforts of social psychology, and also to the whole school of the German 'verstehende Psychologie' and its followers. Clearly, if the psychological enquiries are to add relevant, novel knowledge, which social enquiry cannot attain, they must relate the things visible in the latter with things and factors not so visible, that is, with the *modus operandi* of the psychological processes.

This is, essentially, the field of experimental (and partly clinical) psychology. As I see it, it is primarily concerned with mental processes and mechanisms, and with the regularities governing them. This approach does not cancel or neutralize the world of objects reached and conveyed by the various psychological processes. But psychology treats only of this conveying and reaching, that is, of the object-reference, and not of the objects considered in themselves. It treats, for example, of the 'psychological space', and not of the space as it may exist apart from experiencing; or of the 'behavioural' environment, as it is perceived, understood, and reacted to, not of the 'geographical' environment.[1] These are still natural objects (or object worlds), which appear as simply given, and not yet social 'objects', which are fashioned and created, or have 'emerged' from mental events. But whether they are one thing or the other, the objects are regarded merely as occasions for the functioning of the psychological processes and as so many instances of their *modus operandi*. In other words, psychology as here understood states its findings, not in *object language*, but essentially in *function language*.[2]

By the same token we, in social enquiry, use predominantly 'object language'.[3] We sometimes resort to the other language,

[1] K. Koffka (1935), pp. 30 ff.

[2] The latter term is unsatisfactory in many ways. The thing I mean would more accurately be called '*modus operandi* language', or 'mechanism language'; neither term, however, recommends itself for practical use.

[3] For the world of 'natural' objects, the physicist, geographer, and so forth would be the users of 'object language'.

when we explicitly state that the actors involved in any mode of behaviour perceive, think, experience desires or emotions, and so forth. This rendering explicit of implicit psychological (or perhaps physiological) processes is clearly to some extent inevitable; and the processes or mechanisms to which we refer may be so simple or familiar that we hardly think of our statements as involving another, lower, level of analysis. But the question arises whether we are not also on occasion compelled to employ function language of a less commonplace nature and to refer to more specific or intricate assumptions about psycho-physical mechanisms. This is indeed the case in one important respect.

Consider that the social behaviour patterns are intentional and task-like. Now, any task reveals on psychological analysis an inherent tension set up by it and carrying its execution.[1] Every social behaviour pattern, therefore, contains a dynamic component, something in the nature of an energy, which holds it together and accounts for its actuation. Since social behaviour patterns are also recurrent, the recurrence is equally carried by this energy, which must be available somehow and translatable into action upon a given stimulus. Here, then, we invoke a first specific psychological assumption; in every statement on intentional behaviour we presuppose the operation of mental energy, and thus definite regularities governing the dynamic 'functioning' of psychological processes. Occasionally, we shall do so tacitly; for the mental energy which carries the social task varies with the latter both in intensity and conspicuousness. An action pattern like hospitality may well be completely described without the use of such 'function' language, and indeed without the use of any psychological term (save those referring to simple acts of perception). If, on the other hand, we describe marriage, where we cannot help mentioning the presence (or absence) of affection and sexual attraction; or bloodfeud, where we cannot help mentioning emotions or emotional tension; or any other mode of behaviour 'motivated' by such-and-such sentiments or thoughts, we are using terms meaningless without such an assumption of mental energy.

But let us note that the reference to this kind of motive has only descriptive, and not yet explanatory significance; it adds no novel knowledge and does not express an invariant relation between 'demonstrably separate' facts as we understand the term.[2] The

---

[1] See K. Koffka (1935), pp. 333–4.   [2] See above, pp. 211, 243 ff.

psychological processes concerned are still implicit in the behaviour pattern and cannot be thought apart, though they are here
specifically named; they are *of* the behaviour pattern and its
actuation, as energy is *of* a moving body and visible in its motions.
The failure to recognize the nature of this relationship easily leads
to confusion. Let me illustrate this by the argument, a classical
argument almost, which arose between Rivers and Westermarck
over the explanation of bloodfeud. While Westermarck held that
bloodfeud must be explained in terms of the emotion or sentiment
of revenge, Rivers maintained that the only legitimate explanation
must be in social terms, derived from the interrelation between this
institution and other social facts.[1] We must side with Rivers since,
with him, we speak of explanations only when relations *between*
facts are meant. That these are here of a social kind is, I think,
correct, though this is not the point. The point is, rather, that
Westermarck's 'psychological explanation' is not based on any such
relation at all. He refers to something that is inherent in the mode
of behaviour in question and occurring whenever this occurs,
namely, to that emotional tension or motive power which we call
'desire for revenge'. In other words, Westermarck only describes
the psychological implications of bloodfeud and names the mental
energy which carries the behaviour pattern.

4. MENTAL ENERGY

The concept of mental energy is well established in modern
psychology, and the analogy with physics (more particularly with
classical physics) is indeed precise.[2] To begin with, in physics
energy means 'capacity for work': it is not an engine pushing a body
from behind, but a property of the moving body. So is mental
energy only capacity for action, not some extraneous entity causing

[1] W. H. R. Rivers (1926), pp. 8–9.

[2] Thus McDougall devotes a whole book to this topic (1935). Spearman formu-
lates a number of laws governing mental energy (1937, vol. II, Chap. XXXII).
Köhler carefully analyzes the analogy between physical and mental energy
(1938, pp. 317–20). Cf. also Morton Prince: 'Without the concept of energy of
some kind behaviour cannot be explained' (1928, p. 165). Other psychologists
speak in the same sense of 'forces'. E.g. Koffka regards all forms of action as
'requiring forces' (1935, p. 333). Köhler and Lewin also speak of 'vectors', i.e.
directed quantities in a field of forces (W. Köhler, 1947, pp. 299–301); see also
below, p. 304 ff.

the action to become action.[1] Again, energy in physics is conceived of as both kinetic and latent. Similarly the mental energy operating in the social field must be conceived of as existing both within the activated action pattern and before it is so activated. This is an important point. Since social action is recurrent action, social mechanisms must be in existence to render the energy available for the time and situation when it will be activated. Moreover, since social action is always predictable action, the society must have subjective certainty as to this availability. The mental energy, then, is discoverable not only as an attribute inherent in action, but also as a distinct social objective, as a capacity cultivated and fostered purposively (though not necessarily with the knowledge possessed by a psychologically trained observer). When we speak of societies implanting sentiments of love or loyalty or of incentives for any kind of effort, we mean this rendering-available of mental energy.

Furthermore, in physics energy is understood to be expended and dissipated; so are incentives, sentiments, drives, even that weak form of mental energy which is merely directed consciousness—attention. All these impulses diminish with continued actuation and must be recreated or replenished lest the modes of action they are meant to carry themselves disappear. In any short-range observation this recreation of mental energy presents no great problem; either the human organism by itself renews its store of energy, or this is replenished with the help of the social mechanisms of which we have spoken. In the perspective of long-range developments or ultimate states, the recreation of mental energy turns into a problem incapable of empirical treatment. In physics, the energies of any isolated system, and ultimately of the universe, are conceived of as draining away through continued action and conversion, becoming more and more disorganized, and tending towards an equilibrium in which 'no further work can be done'. The recovery of this loss of energy by some molecular redistribution would be pure chance, and its probability nil (or almost nil).[2] Does, then, the analogy between mental and physical energy stretch that far? Philosophers who visualize ageing societies,

---

[1] Cf. Janet, who uses the concept of 'force' and defines it as 'capacity for action' (1925, Chap. III). Among sociologists Lundberg operates most consistently with the analogous concept of 'societal energy', which is once more defined as the 'potential capacity of a group to act' (1939, p. 202).

[2] Sir Arthur Eddington (1935), p. 57.

historians who speak of civilizations as weakening and losing their creative or sustaining impetus, come close to speculations about the running down of energy in the social universe. Nor are anthropologists unfamiliar with the disintegration of cultures and the weakening of all forces which once sustained them. There are, too, the few instances of a reputed loss of the 'will to live' in primitive communities. As often, however, we meet, not with the 'running down' of isolated social systems, but with their absorption in other systems; and we encounter, not a loss of creative or sustaining energy, but its redirection under the impact of novel cultural aims. The human world, then, seems full of accidents which reorganize the flow of energies. Whether we can say more than this and intelligently discuss the chances of an entropy for the universe of human action, I will leave undecided.

Finally, both the energy of physics and mental energy are subject to transformation and conversion. Energy becomes action, and action creates energy. We meet with action patterns which are carried by their energy (as patriotic conduct is carried by sentiments of loyalty), as well as with others which 'store up' energy (as education for citizenship implants loyalty to one's country). Also, one kind of energy changes into another; love for one's country becomes hatred for the enemy, and feelings of injury, desire for revenge. This transformation of mental energy can probably be traced further, to its sources in the physical energy generated in the organism. Undoubtedly, some such ultimate conversion of energy must be assumed. The energy entering into social action is itself partly of a physical, organic nature, 'ultimately acquired through metabolic processes'; but even when it is purely psychological—a felt tension pressing to be relieved, an intention sustaining behaviour—it may be considered an 'output' of forces generated by organic mechanisms.[1] Moreover, a definite quantitative relationship seems to link organic and mental energy, so that a great expenditure of the former reduces the availability of the latter.[2] For the purpose of this discussion, this ultimate derivation of mental energy may be disregarded. But here an important question arises: Does this far-reaching conversion imply that, like

[1] G. A. Lundberg (1939), pp. 206–7.

[2] Cf. for example, the correlation between growth (implying an expenditure of physical energy) and the intellectual efforts of children (implying an expenditure of mental energy), which has been analyzed by E. Claparède (1946, vol. I, pp. 111–12).

the energy of physics, the energy within thought and action is essentially unspecific and indeterminate? If this is so, then all the specific qualitative aims which govern human action are merely so many particular kinds of 'work' which an identical form of energy is made to carry; and this energy would exhibit no quality, but only varying measures of impetus. Yet it is also possible to assume that, unlike the energy of physics, mental energy is qualitatively differentiated, so that, in the field of human action, we find, not *one* energy, but a number of forces each bearing a determinate relationship to a particular kind of action. The answer to this question will follow from another question and answer, concerning the place of mental energy within that total organization of mental events which we call (however ineptly) the mind.

Classical psychology solved this problem by assigning the creation and actuation of mental energy to specific faculties of the mind, from which the various forms of mental energy would also derive such qualitative features as they seem to possess. These faculties were found in the instincts, in the will, and partly in the emotions, which seemed to stand apart from the other, non-dynamic faculties (sensations, perceptions, memory, thought). Modern psychology has largely abandoned this splitting-up of the mind into distinct compartments. The instincts are still mentioned, though their status has for other reasons become dubious; but the will has almost disappeared from psychological textbooks; and the things we used to call emotions are now treated as total states of the mind[1] or as mere dynamic aspects visible in certain psycho-physical processes.[2] Nor yet can perception, memory or thought be sharply isolated from each other or from the dynamic components of consciousness. It seems, then, that the classical division of psychological processes—into perception, emotion, cognition, and conation— may be retained only for the purpose of convenient but inaccurate illustration, so that the whole organization of the mind must be redefined. Let me therefore trespass a little longer upon psychology proper. The following synopsis may not be acceptable to every psychologist, nor can I present it but in a tentative fashion; but it does not, I think, seriously misrepresent the present state of knowledge in psychology—at least among psychologists of my persuasion.

[1] R. H. Thouless (1937), p. 74.   [2] K. Koffka (1935), p. 401.

5. The Dynamic Properties of Mental Events

In any report about mental events three kinds of facts will always be stated. By 'mental event', incidentally, I mean simply something that happens in or to our awareness, that is, an act of experiencing. First, the mental event is about something. It has an 'object-reference' or, as we might also say, a presentational aspect; for the mental event *presents* certain objects or contents to our awareness with a character or, as Driesch would say, with 'accents' varying with the psychological processes involved. Secondly, the mental event is always *my* event; it implies an 'I-reference' or 'Ego-relatedness' (Koffka)—what Claparède calls its *moi-ité* ('me-ness' in Maccurdy's paraphrase).[1] Thirdly, there is that which connects the two in a given, particular fashion—the *mode* of experiencing, which we can name and distinguish from other modes, establishing the same connection in a different fashion. This is Spearman's 'way of regarding'; Bartlett's psychological 'function'; and the 'psychological process' of textbooks.

Now this triadic relationship—I-experience-something—may be heavily weighted in the sense of the object-reference, so that the mental event appears to be fully exhausted by the presentation of objects to the Self. In naïve analysis the objects appear as the causes or starting points of the process 'presenting' them, and the Self as the recipient. When we speak of 'pure' perception or cognition we mean this kind of awareness; it describes the field of just-so-existence, in which the objects appear with varying character or with varying 'accents'. These are—the accents of 'suchness' (as in sense qualities); of time and space (as in actual perception, and in memory or anticipation); of order and meaning (when a state of affairs is 'understood'); of truth (when things are 'right', known, or have finality); of degrees of reality (as in actual perception against thought and imagination); and perhaps also the accents of moderate feeling tone (as in slight pleasures or discomforts felt, in a detached way, by the Person).[2] It must be emphasized

---

[1] J. T. Maccurdy (1928), pp. 113–16.—The definition of this aspect is complicated by the fact that the 'Me' enters awareness both as a reference point, and as an 'object', i.e. as the body and all that happens within or to it. It is convenient to distinguish in this sense between the Self or Ego, and the Body or Person (see W. Köhler, 1947, pp. 211, 297–8).

[2] This is essentially Driesch's list of 'accents' (1925, pp. 16–34). It can probably be improved; the term 'accent', in particular, is somewhat unsatis-

that these accents overlap widely. Two in particular are never absent save in the most fleeting mental events. The first is the accent on degrees of reality. The second that of order and meaning; for almost every mental event also carries the awareness either of a causal nexus stretching backwards and forwards from the given object, or of a sign nexus, whereby the given object stands for others or signals their presence, or at least of some general order into which the objects are understood to 'fit' or 'belong'.

In other mental events I-reference and object-reference are evenly weighted, or the former outweighs the latter. Here our triadic relationship assumes an additional, dynamic aspect. It is no longer a tacit Me that perceives, feels, or understands, but one that is more or less deeply *concerned*. The objects appear not only as starting points of the mental processes but as their goal points, so that they assume, over and above the 'presentational' accents, also that of a *demand* upon the Self—to approach or avoid, or generally to do something about the state of things. The Self becomes the seat of tensions and urges, a starting point for movements and efforts, and the Person the instrument for their execution. Intensive feeling tones, thought dominated by task consciousness, and the excited perceptual or cognitive states we call emotions, exemplify this kind of awareness.

It is entirely absent only in pathological states. Only there is the Self confronted with a fully static, self-contained and just-so-existing world of objects. This is Janet's *état du vide*, in which the individual merely 'contemplates' reality as though it were a spectacle with which he has no concern and towards which he feels no urge of reacting. Objects and events provoke no aims or interest, and have neither beauty nor ugliness, only the neutral character of presence.[1] The other extreme, an exaggerated sense of concern, belongs once more to pathology. Here all items of awareness are emotionally charged and none is merely 'presented' to the Self. Rather, the Self is overwhelmed by demands requiring to be disposed of and helpless under the impact of urges to 'do something about' this dynamic world of things. At least, this is how I read the symptoms of neurotic anxiety

factory. But I found no better way of describing the 'givenness' of object awareness, at least in a brief outline like the present.

[1] P. Janet (1935), pp. 110–12.

and Freud's classical statement ȯn the relation between anxiety and helplessness.[1]

In normal states the re-structuring of the field of just-so-existence in this dynamic sense is intermittent, though rapid and ubiquitous. For this field is unstable and at any moment on the point of turning into a field of tensions, aims, and efforts. Gestalt psychologists speak, suggestively, of a 'field of forces'. In it, the Self and the objects represent the poles of a 'bi-polar organization', within which the psychological processes operate as 'vectors'. Let me quote this passage: 'Apart from states of lowest vitality, there is hardly a total field from which bi-polar organization is absent. The Self is virtually always directed towards something, or away from it. The most striking instances are intense emotions and motivations.'[2] This model of a 'field of forces' is somewhat over-simplified. The dynamic relationship between the Self and the object is not of a simple, one-to-one kind. The ˙door may be there for me to enter or to leave by; a tool, to be handled or discarded; a picture or story will hold my attention or frighten and disgust me. But the door and tool also imply that other objects are reached by their manipulation; and the things presented in the picture or story may become incentives, exhilarating or distressing, for behaviour concerned with other objects in my environment. In other words, the mental forces play between the Self and a whole sector of the world of objects, any one object leading to others, in the sense of *manipulanda* (Koffka) leading to the attainment of goals, or of signs leading to the behaviour signified, or merely in the sense of intermediate points or steps. Furthermore, this play of forces is not exhausted by the directedness of the Self upon given objects. The handling of a tool points beyond itself to the creation of other objects; signs may refer to existing things or events as much as to things or events requiring to be created or remodelled in some way. So that the 'field of forces' also implies its own re-structuring—some adding to or changing of the world of objects.

We must note, further, that these dynamic processes may be visible only in introspection, that is, may not extend beyond the handling of imaginary objects (as in the mental solving of problems). With this kind of situation we are not concerned. We are concerned only with the dynamic processes which project into

---

[1] S. Freud (1933), pp. 108–9; (1936), pp. 106–7, 161.
[2] W. Köhler (1947), p. 299.

physical behaviour and involve what Koffka calls the 'Executive' of the organism. But even where this is the case, we must still presuppose this inner-personal play of forces; and to describe and classify its forms is to enumerate the familiar vocabulary of 'dynamic psychology', which is neither economical nor very precise. Thus, when we understand the urges and tensions preceding action to be indeterminate and perhaps to erupt spontaneously into awareness, we speak of impulses; when we understand them to be determinate, that is, to vary with the kind of action they produce, we usually speak of drives or needs; when we understand this play of forces to be indeterminate but capable of being mobilized and employed in full awareness, we construe a will.[1] The phase anterior to the action itself, when the urges and tensions appear as conscious 'demands upon the Self', we know as motivation.[2] Any relatively permanent relationship between the experiencing of demands and particular classes of objects we call sentiments (emphasizing the feeling tone) or interests (emphasizing the cognitive aspect). While of the objects themselves we say that they operate as incentives or as values. The consummation, finally, of the 'demand upon the Self', that is, the end state towards which the urges and tensions are moving, we conceive of as satisfaction or gratification; perhaps the former term refers more specifically to organic end states (perceived through sensing and feeling), and the latter to end states of a cognitive nature (whose worthwhileness is 'understood').

We need, I think, a generic term to denote these tensions and pressures projecting into awareness and requiring to be 'relieved by action' (Koffka). I propose to speak here of *action potentials*, which term seems to me to have precisely that meaning. Now, the words 'tension' or 'pressure' merely describe mental energy from a subjective viewpoint; and 'action potential' means, so far, only energies mobilized and directed upon aims or goals. The energies as such, of course, are always generated within the organism, and on our level of analysis we need go no further. But the question arises how they come to be mobilized and invested with aim directions. Clearly, the action potentials must come from somewhere, and

[1] The essence of 'true willing' lies in the 'resolution', not merely in the 'striving', i.e. in the urges and tensions as such. The latter serve to 'carry out the willed operation' (F. Aveling, 1931, p. 91).

[2] 'Psychological forces do not carry a person forward mechanically but generally by way of motivation' (K. Lewin, 1938, p. 46).

there seem to be only three possibilities. The action potentials might as such be innate, in the manner of action patterns preformed in the organism and pressing for realization in specific modes of behaviour. Or they might come from the experiencing of external data, being generated in that act, so that every impetus to action would come from what Koffka calls the 'demand character of objects' and Lewin the 'valences' of environmental features.[1] Or finally, the action potentials might spring from both sources. I hold, and hope to show, that the last solution is alone acceptable.

The first view is that of the instinct theory in its classical, ambitious form, which sees in all modes of action the expression of specific innate drives.[2] These are taken to be the sources of every impetus or 'striving'; the 'will' and the whole conative sphere of the mind are nothing but a playground for the instincts; and emotions, sentiments, even the elementary pleasure-pain reactions, possess their dynamic properties, not in their own right, but because they are the concomitants of instinctive tendencies or propensities. 'Take away the instinctive dispositions with their powerful impulses, and the organism would become incapable of activity of any kind. . . . These impulses are the mental forces that maintain and shape all the life of individuals and societies, and in them we are confronted with the central mystery of life and mind and will.'[3] This, then, is a theory of action potentials which are not only energies in an active and directed state, but are themselves the source of all forms of energy; it is, too, a theory of multiple energies, each possessing its peculiar quality and aim direction, so that it might be said, with but little exaggeration, that there are only as many aims in human (or social) behaviour as there are innate drives or 'propensities' in the organism or combinations and permutations of these drives. That the instinct theory, at least in this sweeping form, has proved untenable, is widely known. We need at this stage only say that it breaks down over the definition of innateness; it both overrates the rigidity and uniformity of human behaviour and underrates the difficulties of verifying innate propensities.

---

[1] K. Koffka (1935), p. 354; K. Lewin (1935), p. 51.

[2] See W. McDougall (1912) and (1935).

[3] W. McDougall (1912), p. 44. We find an echo of this in the following passage from Freud: 'Men can do no more than set their instinctual impulses in motion' (1933, p. 229).

The second view would imply that everything in action is response, and nothing innate drive; the mental energy would be diffuse and indeterminate, without intrinsic aim direction, being mobilized and directed only by the act of experiencing; so that the impulses to action would be as varied and numerous as the 'objects' experienced in one way or other. This extreme position is not, so far as I know, taken by anyone. But a certain approximation to it exists in the 'social field theory' elaborated by Lewin and others.[1] This theory considers, in brief, all the 'forces controlling behaviour' to be the resultants both of energies existing 'within the Self', in the form of 'needs or need-like tensions', and of the 'valences' of the environment as it is given to perception, that is, of the property of perceptual objects to attract or repel, to serve as goals for behaviour, or generally, to combine with the subjective tensions in creating aimful behaviour.[2] The need-like tensions on one side, and the valences on the other, constitute the 'field of forces' which at any moment determines the way in which individuals aimfully act in their given environment—positively, through approach, or negatively, through withdrawal. Thus the energies 'within the Self' are 'steered' towards goals of action by the presence of valences. The energies within the Self have their strength—the strength of needs and need-like tensions; so have the valences; and a determinate relationship is assumed to exist between the two. But though it is true to say that 'whenever a negative or positive valence in the environment exists, there exists a system in tension within the person,' the opposite is not necessarily true, since needs might also refer to imaginary objects, or to objects not occurring in the perceived environment.[3] Expressed in simple language—if I am thirsty (a need), and if there is drink available in my environment, this may be said to contain a valence which steers my 'inner-personal tensions' (my desire to drink) towards the jug of water or whatever it is; again, if I am thirsty but have acquired a taste for wine, and both wine and water are available, my need-like tensions will be steered towards the former. If, on the other hand, I am thirsty but nothing drinkable exists in my environment, the force

---

[1] See K. Lewin (1935), (1938) and (1936); J. F. Brown (1936).

[2] 'A region (of the environment) which has a valence is defined as a region within the life space of an individual which attracts or repulses the individual' (K. Lewin, 1938, p. 88).

[3] K. Lewin (1938), p. 108.

of my thirst will have no such behavioural effects; while nothing will happen either, if wine or water are available but I feel no desire to drink. This is no doubt a true picture, though not perhaps a very impressive one. However this may be, in the course of the discussion this balance between the need-like tensions in the person and the valences of objects becomes unevenly weighted, the latter completely over-shadowing the former.

For the inner-personal tensions are said to be affected by the perception of valence-invested objects in two different ways. This perception may act upon, or 'steer', already existing tensions, which are then translated into aimful behaviour concerned with the object in question. Or the perception of objects may cause the formation of a 'tense psychical system' not previously existing in this form.[1] Furthermore, the pre-existing tensions may arise both from innate needs and from 'need-like' desires of different origin. Now, the innate needs are nowhere defined or enumerated, and only the most obvious one, hunger, is quoted from time to time. Nor do they seem to do more than press for the specific satisfactions peculiar to them—the momentary satiation of hunger and thirst, of the sex drive, or of whatever 'needs' there are. If the innate needs also tend to endow objects that help or hinder their satisfaction with the respective valences (as thirst would make water or a jug a desirable object), or to build up the need-like tensions which are not innate (as perhaps sexual desire may turn into a desire to protect the beloved), this process remains obscure.[2] We can only conclude that this contribution of the innate needs is small, and that the main 'forces' controlling behaviour come either from the objects as such, or from desires with no innate basis. And since the latter must also arise somewhere, we must conclude that this happens through some first contact with those valence-invested objects which can produce a novel 'tense psychical system'. This conception of a first contact with the existing valences of objects is puzzling; yet it seems unavoidable if we follow Lewin's argument. We may clearly ask: Since need-like tensions can be formed through the perception of some valence-invested object, what was

[1] K. Lewin (1935), p. 51.

[2] Koffka, on the other hand, allows for it. For he distinguishes a special 'functional' demand character of objects, which follows from previous experiences of the way in which they have 'functioned in behavioural acts' (1935, p. 392); and this 'functioning' must clearly also include situations when objects have helped or hindered an innate need or desire.

in their place before they were so formed? If I understand Lewin correctly, there always exists in the Self a 'reservoir' of latent and indeterminate energies, of mere directionless tensions, accumulated from various previous experiences and efforts and left over through being incompletely discharged.[1] It thus requires the perception of valence-invested objects to activate the latent energies and give them direction, the organism itself affording only a general readiness to act. Yet if this be the case, then the valences of objects must be credited with some autonomous and irreducible potency, as self-evident as the effect of notice boards saying 'Keep left' or 'Beware of Dogs', and as absolute as the properties of things *an sich*. I do not think that I am exaggerating the ontological bias of the Social Field Theory. It appears also in other statements, made in a different context, to wit: 'The valence which an object or activity possesses for a person at a given time depends upon the character and state of the person, and upon the perceived nature of the object or activity',[2] which would seem to mean that the valence of objects (which comes from their 'perceived nature') depends partly upon itself.

Surely, this cannot be meant. What can only be meant is that *at any given moment* valences appear to exist in this absolute manner, and that it may be convenient, as a heuristic device for assessing the mental forces active there and then, to treat certain objects in the environment *as though* they could by themselves evoke aims in a Self possessed only of a general readiness to act in any fashion. One might point to the hundred-and-one things which we have come to desire or hate for no readily discernible innate reason; the processes which must have preceded any such state of affairs—processes of learning, habituation, or conditioning—might then be seen as instances of something like a contact between indeterminate energies and given valences. Lewin, in fact, confesses to such a restricted viewpoint: any statement about valences 'merely indicates that, for whatever reason, at the present time, and for this specific individual, a tendency exists in the direction toward this [valence-invested] region or away from it'; such statements predicate nothing about the *origin* of the attractiveness or otherwise of the objects.[3] My point is that this proviso seriously restricts the value of the whole approach. Neither the Social Field Theorist nor

---

[1] (1935), pp. 51, 60.   [2] K. Lewin (1938), p. 107.
[3] K. Lewin, op. cit., p. 88.

anyone el: e will maintain that valences, the demand character of objects, and the like, remain unaltered. They change, are built up, emerge and disappear in the life of individuals as well as societies; for clearly, the things around us do not retain the same significance for ever. Yet with these changes the Social Field Theory cannot deal. Its equations have only two terms—the energies within the Self, and the valences of the environment; and if the former are indeterminate and directionless they cannot build up or alter the valences from which they are said to receive their directedness. These, then, must be taken to change autonomously, to gain or lose strength, to come and go unpredictably. If we correct the momentary given-ness of valences we arrive at their utter randomness.

So much for the Social Field Theory. If the Instinct Theory breaks down because it assumes a rigidity of innate aims which cannot be substantiated, the Social Field Theory fails because it assumes a randomness of aims which would block all further enquiries. I do not claim that this randomness is entirely reducible to regularities of some sort. But it can be made less of an accident of thought or a penalty for undue curiosity. The solution lies, as I have anticipated, in a synthesis of the two opposed theories. Let me briefly outline it.

Clearly, a wide field of social enquiry is concerned with behaviour at a given moment and thus with the search for regularities visible in the 'forces' and 'valences' or 'demand characters' effective there and then. Equally, we are concerned with the emergence of modes of behaviour, and thus with the appearance, disappearance, and change of the 'forces' and 'valences'. As regards the first problem, we remember that the energies mobilized and directed upon goals through the experiencing of objects need not be 'steered' back to the objects which are the starting points of the experiencing, but may flow into behaviour concerned with other objects; so that we reckon with (at least) two co-varying social contexts; in one, the context responsible for the experiencing, tensions are set up and impulses generated; in the other, in which the individuals appear as actors in a specific task, the tensions are released in the action and the impulses consummated. This, however, is still too simplified a model. Experiencing and acting may only be two aspects of the same situation; for the individuals will also experience while and because they act, that is, they will be exposed to new stimuli in the execution of behaviour patterns which are themselves the response to some experiencing.[1] Furthermore, the social task in which one kind of behaviour reaches its goal may be a starting point for a different kind of behaviour, and 'demands' gratified, or impulses consummated, will produce yet further demands or impulses. We must therefore re-phrase our statement. We still reckon with at least two co-varying social contexts (which are contexts of behaving-and-experiencing); in one, something happens to the energies involved in the actor's concern with that situation—with its demands and their realization; and what 'happens' there determines the way in which he becomes concerned with the other situation and its demands. It will be seen that we are in reality dealing with a triadic, not a dual, relation; for the *modus operandi* of the mental energy (what 'happens' to it) is literally taken to *intervene* between the two contexts and to link them together. In so far as we can define the regularities governing this *modus operandi*, we can also explain in terms of psychophysical causality the co-variations between the modes of behaviour in question. This, then, will be our first task. I shall speak here simply of (indeterminate) 'energy' and of laws governing its movement; and I shall take these laws to account for the *linkage* of social facts.[2]

As regards our second problem, I shall attempt to show that it can be solved through accepting the existence of certain innate action potentials, that is, of behaviour patterns preformed in the organism and pressing for realization, so that these innate pressures or urges account for the emergence of the appropriate modes of action. Furthermore, since the innate action potentials exhibit certain regular oscillations, they account also for the weakening and disappearance of modes of action. And since all modes of action are concerned in one way or another with objects in the environment, the action potentials responsible for the modes of action are responsible also for the endowment of the objects with their demand character—positive, if they offer congenial occasions for the consummation of the impulse, and negative, if they do not;

[1] In the simplest case this process corresponds to the 'proprio-reception' in physiology, whereby motor behaviour occurring in response to stimuli received also generates new stimuli in the organism.

[2] This principle of a psychological 'linkage' has already been stated by Rivers, who spoke of psychological facts being 'interpolated as links in a chain of causation connecting social antecedents with social consequents' (1914, p. 22).

and when no congenial objects are available in the environment, these may well be fashioned or created *ad hoc* by that impulse. Here we are, in principle, dealing with situations involving only one social context—that of the particular mode of action in which the action potentials are realized. The *modus operandi* of these innate action potentials constitutes an 'intervening' agency only in that it links the psycho-physical organization of man with certain regular modes of action, starting in the former and ending in the consummatory behaviour. If any co-variation is discoverable, it occurs between the presence or oscillation of innate drives, predispositions, urges, and the emergence of determinate modes of acting. The examination of this *modus operandi* represents our second task. I shall speak here specifically of action potentials, and shall take them to account for the *genesis* of social facts.

Together, *linkage* and *genesis* define all the social regularities which are psychologically intelligible. I have called the acceptance of mental energy the first specific psychological assumption which we, as students of society, must make. The efficacy of the psychological *linkage* is our second, and the efficacy of innate action potentials in the *genesis* of actions, our third assumption.

This division of our field of enquiry is primarily heuristic and probably not final; indeed it is clear that the states of affairs as they appear 'at a given moment' and the processes of emergence or genesis must penetrate each other. Even so, a great many psychologists admit, at least tacitly, the side-by-side existence of indeterminate energies, mobilized through some form of experiencing (perceptive, emotional, intellectual), and of innately directed ('instinctive') impulses for behaviour. The nature of the latter, however, seems to suggest that this dualism can at least be reduced. For certain of the innate action potentials prove to possess only a *generic* aim direction, not a *specific* one like that ascribed to the classical instincts. Furthermore, the innate action potentials must be understood to come into play in two ways—spontaneously, by their intrinsic pressure for realization in action; and through experiencing, that is, under the stimulus and influence of 'objects'. These, in turn, do not only activate a dormant drive, but may also modify, block, or deflect a drive already active, thus inhibiting or changing the aim direction with which it appears; so that all that remains visible of the drive is the push, the impulse—the mere actuation of energy. And in this form the innate action potentials can be made to account for a great many conditions which would seem to indicate the presence of indeterminate energy. In whichever way we describe the latter—as some tension requiring release; as a balance upset and re-established; as the pressure of tasks unfulfilled; or as a force furnished from some reservoir in the organism —we should be describing a *modus operandi* typical also of innate action potentials. Where there is so much coincidence, scientific economy would seem to demand that of the two possible interpretations one should be chosen; and since we cannot do without accepting innate drives, the choice is made for us.[1] I am not certain that all instances indicating the operation of indeterminate energy can be so reduced; this seems to apply especially to purely cognitive operations, to task consciousness of a rational nature, and to that difficult phenomenon, the 'will.' Nor shall I press this attempt at monism, though it underlies the analysis that follows. Apart from methodological neatness, it is of little consequence for our enquiry. It certainly does not relieve us of the double approach outlined above.

6. Psychological Linkage

The linkage of social facts through some operation of mental energy rests essentially on conversion mechanisms, that is, on mechanisms transforming experiencing into motives for behaviour. Such mechanisms must of course be taken to underlie all forms of action, including rational and logical behaviour. But in the latter case the linkage is at once and fully intelligible; the mechanisms involved are in a sense silent, exhibiting no features that must be specifically accounted for, and can be disregarded. When, on the other hand, we call actions irrational and illogical we mean that here we are no longer dealing with 'silent' mechanisms and self-evident linkages; and these specific mechanisms can be most satisfactorily isolated in the study of irrational behaviour *par excellence*, that is, in psycho-pathology. It is, then, from that discipline that we may hope to learn about the laws governing mental energy and its *modus operandi*.

---

[1] The position here taken has some affinity with the Freudian theory of instincts, which are similarly generic and subject to aim-inhibition or conversion. But I cannot follow the Freudian school when it attempts to reduce all the energies behind behaviour to the single source of a protean libido.

Psychoanalysis has worked out a great number of such conversion mechanisms—frustration, repression, projection, transference, displacement, compensation, sublimation. Non-psycho-
analytical psycho-pathology has equally formulated such principles of mental dynamics, though in slightly different terms. I am
thinking here, in particular, of Janet's work.[1] Though psychoanalysis has undoubtedly produced the richer system and has
penetrated much more deeply into the dynamics of the mind, it is
in some respects less adequate for our purpose than is, for example,
Janet's approach. To begin with, the focus upon sex and libido
restricts the Freudian view. So does the preoccupation with
'experiencing' of a traumatic kind, that is, with shocks, repression,
frustration, and the like (though no form of clinical psychology can
quite avoid this bias). Above all, psychoanalysis does not separate
the conversion mechanisms qua mechanisms from the aim contents
which they happen to handle. In other words, the explanations of
psychoanalysis are couched in mixed object and function language.
This ambiguity is avoided in a system like Janet's, which is concerned with the mechanisms as such, and admits the 'objects' only
as so many instances of the manner in which the mechanisms
operate. The analysis that follows will be largely based on Janet's
approach; where I refer to familiar psychoanalytical principles, I
shall understand them in the wider and, I think, more consistent
sense here advocated.

This is not applying (or misapplying) logical purism. Rather is it
a question of the relative usefulness of the two approaches.
Consider the basic formula of psychoanalysis. It states that repressed desires or drives reappear in the behaviour pattern that is
the symptom of the repression. Repression-and-reappearance
represents a pure mechanism; but in analyzing it we must also
make assumptions about certain qualitative changes—changes in
aim—which the desires and drives undergo in the process. If these
changes were subject to clear and simple rules, this would be ideal
for the anthropologist; for he would be enabled to identify
correlated action patterns, apparently disparate and irrational, at
once as 'cause' and 'symptom'. This, however, is rarely true. In the
simplest case, the repressed aim will retain its meaning; disap-
pearing from one sector of life, where the repressive influences
exercise control, it will simply reappear in another, not so con-

[1] See Pierre Janet (1925).

trolled (as, for example, impracticable desires reappear in day-dreaming or other forms of wish-fulfilment). More often, the aims themselves undergo conversion, and reappear in some disguise or other. There will be some thread of meaning linking the repressed aim with the aim disguised. But this disguise, as is well known, is far from easy to penetrate; the transformation is widely variable and complicated, subject to ambivalence and hence ambiguity, and involves devious symbolisms which may tax the ingenuity even of expert psychoanalysts.

Furthermore, this conversion of aims is to some extent independent of the psychological mechanisms and in this sense fortuitous. In clinical situations the repressed desire may well be displaced into modes of behaviour which are, as it were, nothing but symptoms, that is, conspicuously 'abnormal'. Yet equally, they may bear no such obvious label; rather will the repressed desire reappear in modes of behaviour sanctioned by society and culture and hence 'normal'. For the same agency which is responsible for the repression (call it Culture and Society or, with Freud, Super Ego)[1] may also offer a permissible congenial, if vicarious, outlet. This may accommodate the repressed desire itself, as when homosexual leanings, restrained as such, can be gratified in romantic youth movements or quasi-monastic orders. Or the outlet may at least absorb the effects of the repression, as when aggressive desires resulting from some repression or frustration can be legitimately gratified in war, racial persecutions, ruthless business practices, or cruel sports. In either case the repressed or deflected aims undergo something like an *assimilation*, namely, to the regular modes of behaviour which happen to exist, as 'normal' practices, in the society; so that the final form of the 'symptoms' depends on these fortuitous circumstances.

Now, this is precisely the kind of situation with which the student of society is mostly dealing. What he finds is 'normal' behaviour—behaviour that is regular, simply available in the society, and fitted into the network of other social tasks in a rational or logical manner. Thus the romantic youth movement may serve political interests; the quasi-monastic orders may be modelled on the religious organization; war, business practices, racial persecutions, or blood

[1] The identification of the Super Ego with the moral norms obtaining in the society is clearly expressed in Freud's later writings (see 1933, pp. 84–5, 90–2, et passim).

sports will similarly be intelligible in terms of purpose or logical consistency. If these modes of action are also symptoms of re-pressed and deflected desires, they are so only with part of their make-up. We cannot therefore rely on precise rules defining the conversion or deflection of aims and desires, since these become assimilated to the social tasks existing, for other reasons, in the society. Not every social task will, of course, be capable of ab-sorbing the repressed drive and harbouring its deflected satis-faction; there must be some fit between the two. But the crucial fact is not the link between the aims repressed and those appearing in the 'symptoms', since the latter do not derive solely and simply from the conversion mechanisms; the crucial fact is, rather, the *modus operandi* of the mental energy which renders one or the other available mode of action suitable to serve as 'symptom'. We should not, therefore, concern ourselves overmuch at this stage with the transformation of aim contents—a process definable only in 'object language'—but with the displacement and flow of energy, the rules of which can be defined in 'function language'.

Unlike the conversion of aim contents, the operation of mental energy yields fairly sharply defined laws. They rest on two presup-positions. The first, which is of a theoretical kind, implies that the locus of mental energy—the person or the mind—constitutes a *system*, so that the actions of energy in different sectors of be-haviour or experiencing are interrelated. We can, therefore, speak of energy patterns embracing a wide, or perhaps the total, field of behaviour. The second presupposition concerns a technical issue, namely, our ability to recognize and compare the intensities of energy employed and discharged in behaviour—the degrees of effort, the excitedness or otherwise of gestures, and the violence or restraint of physical motions. Since without this ability to judge effort and excitement half the range of 'psychological processes' would be unrecognizable, and since undoubtedly they are so recognizable, this presupposition need not be especially defended. We can, then, formulate two principles or laws, which I shall call the laws of *uneven* and of *even levels of mental energy*.

The first principle is perhaps the more familiar. It can be stated as follows: If in any one (or more) sectors of behaviour and experiencing energy is discharged at a high level, the level of energy in other sectors will be correspondingly lower. This is Janet's principle of 'psychic equilibrium', which presupposes a limited and to some extent constant quantity of energy (or 'psychic force') in the person, heavy expenditure in one sector entailing a corresponding reduction of the energy available for action in the rest. Conversely, low expenditure of energy in one sector will raise the level of energy available in others, as when physical weakening leads to more intensive mental efforts.[1] The second principle means the exact opposite. It implies that, if in any one (or more) sectors of behaviour and experiencing energy is discharged at a high level, the level of energy will be raised to the same height in all others; and if in one sector little energy is discharged, this will correspondingly lower the level of energy in the other sectors. We must, then, visualize a situation in which any intense stimulation of energy in one sector of the mind spreads to others, and any weak excitation exercises a lowering effect of this kind.[2] Thus some intensive or excited mode of behaviour will cause us to behave in an exhilarated or excited fashion also in other contexts, while the lassitude experienced in one will similarly diffuse to others. This is Janet's second principle, which he calls 'syntonization' and makes responsible for the 'unity of tone' visible in behaviour.[3]

A few comments are necessary. In accepting even as well as uneven levels of mental energy we are not both invoking and denying the assumption of a constant quantity of energy. For though the quantity of energy is constant in the person (at least for a given phase of life), it is clearly not uniform for all persons or types of persons. Thus the available quantity of energy may permit a continued high level in the case of one person, and force it down in the

---

[1] P. Janet (1925), pp. 233–5. Spearman similarly speaks of a 'Law of constant output' and of the 'constant limited sum of mental energy' (1937, vol. II, Chap. XXXII).

[2] Lewin would accept only the first part of this proposition. In his view the mind is characterized by the presence of numerous relatively independent 'tension systems', i.e. 'sub-systems' within the total system of the mind, between which there is generally little communication. Only very strong tensions extend over neighbouring fields (1935, pp. 60–1). I feel, however, that the complementary effect is equally well substantiated, as is also the case for the far-reaching, and even complete, communication between the 'sub-systems'. Indeed, Lewin himself seems to accept that certain crucial operations of mental energy (e.g. the movement of all mental processes in the direction of an equilibrium) are valid 'for the system as a whole' (op. cit., p. 59).

[3] Op. cit., pp. 236–9. Janet adds a third principle, that of the 'mobilization of forces' (p. 226), which merely expresses our basic assumption, that energy *is* made available or 'mobilized' for conversion into physical action.

x

case of another. After a deeply stirring experience I, for example, may 'have no emotions left', while you may be capable of yet further thrills. Primarily, however, even and uneven levels indicate a different distribution of energy, irrespective of its given quantity; so that my high and low levels may in this sense correspond to a moderate even level visible in someone else's behaviour. We may here suggest that the dualism of even and uneven levels is related to a polarity in personality types, which would lean towards one or the other energy pattern; and some such assumption would also account for the dualism in the even levels, which would be high or low, according to the quantity of energy available in the person.

However this may be, in the present context we are not concerned with the ultimate provenance of mental energy. Rather do we consider only its actual operations; and these we take to be set in motion by acts of experiencing and behaving, in response to what we have called the 'demand character' of objects or events. In other words, we are dealing with desires, aims, impulses, that is, with tensions of some kind, which appear with greater or lesser strength and accordingly press for realization in actions bearing the mark of this intensity. Now this would seem to mean that behaviour of an intensive kind is always sustained by strong desires and tensions, and behaviour exhibiting no marked intensity, by weak desires and low tensions. But though the first equation is probably always true, the second is not. The relation between expenditure of energy and tensions is complicated and partly obscure (as Janet has pointed out); but one such relation, implying a marked discrepancy between the two, is both relevant and familiar.

When behaviour involves a low expenditure of energy as well as low tensions, the level of energy would seem to form spontaneously, being low inasmuch as the act of experiencing is unexcited and weak tensions are alone provoked. Yet the expenditure of energy may be low only because it is restrained; that is to say, the 'demand character' of the situation would retain its power to excite desires, impulses, and tensions, but these would be inhibited from flowing into the appropriate or appropriately intensive behaviour. These tensions, unrelieved and perhaps heightened by the repression, will constitute potential energy, and as its discharge through the particular channels is blocked it will press for a compensatory outlet through others. Here, then, the law of uneven levels once more applies, though in a different sense. It refers, not to a spontaneous level formation and to the efficacy of a self-adjusting 'inner economy' (as Janet would say), but to the efficacy of repression and compensation. In other words, the low levels of energy indicate impulses frustrated and energies blocked; and the high levels, the break-through and displacement of the dammed-up energies.

It is with this version of the law of uneven levels that psychoanalysis almost entirely deals. Its crucial concepts—frustration, repression, displacement, compensation—mean nothing else. In closer analysis, however, two kinds of repression would have to be distinguished. One, external in nature (exemplified in social prohibitions of particular modes of behaviour), only cuts short the consummation of aims and desires, but leaves these in an active state, or in the 'phase of erection'.[1] The other, internalized (as in Freud's Super-Ego), would effectively repress the aims and desires themselves, so that they are kept in a 'phase of latency' (Janet) or, in the phraseology of psychoanalysis, confined to the unconscious. In the first case the impetus of the blocked aims and desires, strengthened by the effect of the blockage, provides that explosive potential energy which will eventually find some deflected release. In the second case the picture seems much more complicated; for here the impetus of the repressed aims and desires is held in check by pressures which the organism itself provides and hence by a constant expenditure of energy. More precisely, the repressed impulses are held in check by the creation of others, namely, aims and desires reinforcing 'the attitude which is the opposite of the . . . trend that has to be repressed'.[2] And since the energy sustaining these superimposed aims and desires must also be found in the person, we must assume, both that a high degree of tension is being maintained and that a deficit of energy is likely to occur in other sectors of the person. We have, then, an over-expenditure of energy (which consumes tensions) serving to uphold frustrations (which create tensions). We shall presently meet with another instance of this complicated and, I think, still obscure mechanism. Here we need only point out the peculiar 'thread of meaning' visible between cause and symptom: it links aims inhibited and frustrated with intensive modes of behaviour expressing the opposed aims.

[1] P. Janet (1935), p. 56.
[2] S. Freud (1936), p. 144. Freud speaks in this context of 'instinctual' trends. But the same mechanism would seem to apply to all deeply rooted desires and impulses, whatever their origin.

To turn to another point. I have said before that the two laws of energy express opposed principles. This need not be so; we could, for example, visualize a situation in which 'syntonization' operates in certain contexts of behaviour, while in others the 'psychic equilibrium' will take effect. The two laws, however, will conflict if syntonization is taken to affect the whole system which is the mind or the person; and this efficacy we shall, in fact, imply. For there is strong evidence that the 'unity of tone' extends over the whole life-span of the personality, and even to the whole life-span of societies composed of such personalities; there, all would be violence, aggression, excitement, or all serenity, calm, restraint. Psychoanalysis has little to say about this principle, either in its narrow or extended form. It is, on the other hand, clearly implied in the work of those anthropologists who study cultures as total entities and see in them conspicuous 'patterns' and the expression of the varying 'genius' or 'ethos' of peoples. The concept of a 'total' culture is a difficult one, and will occupy us later.[1] Let me here discuss only two technical points which arise when the level principle (of either kind) is applied to societies and cultures.

The first point concerns the human aggregate involved in such situations. Any statement about the energy levels typical of a group or culture makes sense only if it refers to modes of behaviour executed (or at least likely to be executed) by the same individuals.[2] It would clearly be meaningless to talk about even or uneven levels of mental energy if they are visible in the behaviour of separate human aggregates. I might, for example, compare the ecstatic mood of a Methodist revivalist meeting with the excitement of a football crowd; or I might contrast both with the calm atmosphere *de rigueur* among English cricket players. But if the people who become Methodists never play football or cricket, and the football enthusiasts or cricketers never attend revivalist meetings, it would be nonsense to regard the affinity of mood as evidence for 'syntonization', and the contrast of mood as evidence for the 'psychic equilibrium' underlying English culture. Fictitious though the example is, it refers to a real possibility; as we shall see, complex cultures at least are sometimes subdivided in this rigid fashion, into

---

[1] See Chap. XIV, Sec. 3.

[2] This is merely a re-statement of our first condition for the understanding of social correlations, namely, that these are meaningful only if the modes of behaviour so correlated can be shown to 'come into contact in minds' (see p. 256).

sectors involving disparate human aggregates. Whenever, then, in
the following discussion we shall speak of energy levels characterizing a whole group or culture we shall primarily mean situations
where the respective modes of behaviour are executed (actually or
potentially) by an identical population.

Even so, our statements refer to an ideal state of affairs. The even
or uneven levels of mental energy represent extremes on a scale
which, in the concrete case, are only approximately reached. For
there will always be instances contradicting our generalization.
There will always be individuals who are calm when everyone else
is excited, or react excitedly to situations which leave others calm;
so that we can indicate merely an over-all picture and base ourselves
only on frequency distributions. Perhaps, too, there will be whole
contexts of behaviour, valid for all individuals, which we shall take
to be exceptions. Thus, in speaking of a culture where 'all is calm',
or 'all is excitement', we shall probably ignore some modes of action
of which the opposite is true, regarding them as an oscillation of
the 'even level' rather than as an index of an uneven one. We shall
base ourselves on such considerations as the regularity with which
the exceptional modes of behaviour occur, their magnitude, and
their place in the total picture of the culture. We shall argue,
further, that certain modes of behaviour present in all cultures also
entail particular levels of energy. Thus technological routine
cannot be carried out in a state of constant excitement and great
tension; rather does it require some measure of calm and of
energies moderately expended, even should the general 'tone' of
behaviour reveal a high level of energy. Conversely, religious
activities cannot be without some thrill or excitement, even in a
culture generally calm and restrained. Since all cultures involve
these activities, they will also involve the corresponding spheres of
restraint or excitement, whatever the remaining energy pattern.
Yet we shall be able to judge how greatly and completely these
spheres are contrasted with behaviour in the other contexts of social
life; for technological routine may yet show tension and excitement
breaking through, and religious behaviour only the occasional
expression of intense fervour. Here, then, we shall judge the situations to signify even levels, disturbed only by oscillations. Admittedly our judgment will be neither very precise nor free from
subjective impressions. But it can be made more precise through
employing also the techniques of experimental or clinical psycho-

logy which directly attack the energy patterns underlying overt behaviour. The need for such a combined approach will in fact become apparent also in other ways.

To return to our laws of mental energy. If they imply two conflicting assumptions—of even and uneven levels—one of them also permits of two different interpretations, in the sense of spontaneous level formations, and of level formations owing to extraneous pressure. Now psychoanalysts, I imagine, would find it easy to resolve these conflicts. For one thing, they largely disregard the possibility of energy levels forming spontaneously; and for another, they would probably deny that true even levels of energy ever materialize. For they would hold that, at least in one sphere of human existence, unevenness is always introduced, namely, in the sphere of infantile experiences, where the growing libido, the source of all energy, tends to be inhibited or restrained. If the tensions generated by the libido could be freely released, a uniform, and presumably uniformly low, level of energy would be the result, representing, as it were, the natural state of affairs, made possible by the absence of repressions. But since the libido *is* repressed and its energy not allowed free play, this will be both dammed up and displaced, so that it breaks out in destructiveness and hostility, or finds some other compensatory outlet. And if this outlet, which may be in the realm of ideas or phantasies, shows no trace of the dammed-up energy, then this has been 'sublimated' or otherwise absorbed.

I do not propose to examine the evidence for or against the libido theory and the paramount importance it attaches to infantile frustrations; both have been called in question even by psychoanalysts, and I feel inclined to side with the critics.[1] Undoubtedly, however, some such processes of conversion and compensation are true, for all forms of mental energy. Even so, this does not dispose of the evidence for Janet's principle of syntonization and thus for the existence of even levels of energy, as it were, in their own right. Nor does it dispose of the existence of uneven levels, once more in their own right, that is, as the result of a self-adjusting 'inner economy'. We are thus left with ambiguous principles of

---

[1] Cf. K. Horney: '. . . it is to be concluded that the libido concept is unproved'; and, 'In Freud's theory frustration as such is supposed to arouse hostility. Actually, however, healthy persons—*children* as well as adults (my italics)—are well able to endure a considerable amount of frustration without any reaction of hostility' (pp. 52, 67, and Chap. III passim).

mental dynamics. And we are left, further, with a serious practical difficulty, namely, of distinguishing in any concrete case uneven levels forming spontaneously from uneven levels produced through repressions or inhibitions.

If, for example, a group exhibits calm and serenity in everyday life but indulges in violent phantasies in art or religion, or perhaps in aggressive behaviour in one restricted context of social life, this may indicate that its aggressive desires are blocked here and released or compensated there. But it may also indicate that the available energies are only strong enough to carry aggressiveness and violence in these contexts and on these occasions. Again, when violence and ruthlessness in war or in the treatment of adolescents go hand in hand with restraint in other spheres, in kinship life, sexual relations, or play, this may well be the result of energies suppressed and then offered release; yet equally, it may be the result of energies exhausted and overspent. In a sense, the two kinds of linkage may coincide; for such an over-expenditure of energy may itself represent a result of constraint, as when war or ruthlessness in the training of the young are forced upon the group, say, by its existence in a hostile environment; so that the calm obtaining elsewhere in the culture would reflect, not exhaustion, but the 'natural' mood of the people and a compensation for its forcible distortion. In other words, whenever we meet with such contrasted moods each may be both a 'natural' tendency suppressed and compensated in the other mood, and the natural tendency itself, the opposite mood being its enforced distortion.[1] Or, finally, the contrasting moods may only reflect the self-adjustment of the 'inner economy'.

7. ENERGY IN EXPLANATION

This is a confusing position. We can state the two mechanisms governing the flow of energy, repression-release and 'psychic economy', and we assume that they are visible both in individual and group behaviour; yet we are unable to identify and distinguish them clearly in the latter. To some extent this difficulty merely reflects the diverse techniques used by the anthropologist and psychiatrist or psychologist respectively. Certainly, the final test proving whether the psychiatrist has correctly interpreted

[1] This point was made by A. A. Roback (1927), p. 307.

the mental processes—the disappearance of the pathological symptom—is on the whole inaccessible to the anthropologist. But the psychiatrist diagnosing repression has also these three criteria to guide him. His anamnesis leads him to events more or less clearly identifiable as extraneous influences blocking or constraining the desires or drives of the individual at the time; the psychiatrist, then, can isolate the cause. He can, further, identify the symptom, not only by its abnormality but by its invariant appearance subsequent to the cause. Finally, the psychiatrist will also trace the thread of meaning from cause to symptom in the form of an open wish-fulfilment or of some symbolic disguise. Let us see how far these three criteria are applicable in anthropological enquiry.

The first criterion would mean that modes of action indicative of a low level of energy must not merely just exist, but must exist in consequence of some visible, socially planned constraint. The second criterion would mean one of two things: either the modes of action indicative of high levels of energy must occur in the form of reactions, that is, must follow upon the phase of constraint—as, for example, excited religious or aesthetic movements follow upon periods of frustration; or these modes of action must again be socially planned, in the form of concessions, of some licence or permissible outlet, meant to take care of the 'symptom'—as the break of holidays or feasts takes care of the desire for stimulation frustrated by prolonged routine. The third criterion speaks for itself. It implies that we must be able to trace the conversion of aims as well as of energy and so to identify the desire or drive restrained by the 'cause' in the appearance of the 'symptom'. And here, in the sphere of wish-fulfilments and symbolic satisfactions, this may well prove relatively easy. For the conversion of aims often tends to move from one plane of reality to the other, an 'unreal' satisfaction, a 'phantasy gratification' (Kardiner), being substituted for the barred 'real' one; so that we shall look for the 'thread of meaning' in legends, myths, in artistic creations, in the promises of religion, or in play.

The instances so far quoted refer only to the repression of energies below their natural level and their break-through in other contexts of behaviour. Though this is the more familiar situation, another linkage also occurs, namely, between the enforced over-expenditure of energy in one sphere of social life and the consequences visible in others. In the simplest case the consequence is exhaustion, the 'inner economy' adjusting itself in this extreme manner. But the over-expenditure of energy may also be balanced by the generation, once more through constraint, of new energy. In other words, energy will be dammed up planfully, so that it may be utilized for particular social tasks. Thus the energies needed to sustain regular warfare, ruthless economic competition, or an ecstatic visionary cult, might be provided through a training of adolescents or neophytes which operates with severe deprivations and cruel disciplines. Here we should no longer be able to rely on a conspicuous 'thread of meaning'; instead, we have a more obscure conversion of aims and desires, of the kind that turns frustration into aggression. Furthermore, the frustrations which are thus utilized as a source for aggressive energy may yet be felt as frustrations; the deprivations and disciplines may yet produce their own compensatory satisfactions; so that the picture would be further complicated by the appearance also of wish-fulfilments and phantasy gratifications—as when a calm art and religion, perhaps eulogizing a quiet and peaceful life, appear in a society organized for war and ruthless competition.

Now it might also be argued that any over-expenditure of energy is in itself already a frustration, since the concentration of effort upon one aim or desire must mean the blocking of others. And here we encounter a curious situation; for as the former feeds on energies, so the latter creates them (unless exhaustion has gone too far and the other desirable things lose their demand character). War, for example, implies expenditure of energy, that is, high tensions constantly turned into desire to act, as much as it implies deprivations and the frustrations of other desires, and hence the creation of new tensions. There is indeed something of the *perpetuum mobile* in social activities of such intense and concentrated impetus. But the tensions created by deprivations and frustrations are probably not infinitely convertible and capable of flowing into any aim, for any span of time. Certainly some deficit will sooner or later appear. We need not especially emphasize that all societies face this problem of a deficit, that is, the problem of preserving the energies meant to sustain some vital effort from the disruptive effects of its very single-mindedness.

To sum up. All depends on whether the anthropologist is in a position to apply the three criteria of the psychiatrist, and, more particularly, whether he can identify repression through identify ing the planned social constraint. If he cannot do so, the ambiguity of which I spoke before will remain. I do not think that I have over-complicated the issue. It certainly seems no accident that anthropologists have concentrated, perhaps overmuch, on situations to which our criteria are most readily applicable. A first instance, familiar from recent literature, concerns the causal nexus between infantile experiences and culturally standardized adult behaviour. The rearing of infants is held to mobilize energies and produce tensions which, later in life, press for expression in appropriate modes of behaviour. How these energies are mobilized and how the pathways of expression are formed or afforded, we need not discuss. Nor, as I have said, do I entirely accept the evidence adduced in support of this theory. All I wish to show by this example is the application of the method I have just outlined. The important point, then, is that here cause and symptom are taken to be clearly visible as antecedent and consequent. The cause, moreover, is one bearing the mark of constraint and of 'disciplines' (to use Kardiner's phrase), while the symptom is understood to represent a permitted cultural outlet or a planned social task.

My second example carries much greater conviction. It concerns societies whose norms of behaviour undergo some enforced radical change. What happens here is that customary aims and desires are suddenly blocked, while the inhibited energies and the tensions created by the inhibition are not at once offered a permissible outlet. Think of a long period of war suddenly ending, so that all the aggressive energies assiduously cultivated are denied expression; or of a society whose economic or social security has suddenly been destroyed; or of a primitive community whose political freedom, with its play of ambition, rivalries, and active enterprise, has been abolished or restrained by some new authority. The tensions arising from the blockage and, especially, the energies still pressing for the accustomed realization are thus forced to find their own outlet.[1] They become, as it were, free energy, visible in spontaneous and disoriented behaviour, or perhaps in neuroses and similar mental disturbances. Now in the case of individuals, conflicts of this kind may arise all the time since in no society can education, vocations, and all the various cultural tasks be ideally

---

[1] This effect of the interruption of aim-directed activities can be demonstrated experimentally in the closely analogous case of uncompleted tasks, which similarly leave a 'residue of tensions' (see K. Koffka, 1935, p. 334).

adjusted to every contingency of individual life. But one might argue that in societies such conflicts, if they affect every individual, cannot be allowed to persist, lest the society itself ceased to be. Thus the psychological effects will be neutralized or canalized by the creation of institutionalized outlets absorbing the 'free energy', the disturbed phase of change leading once more to one of permanency. And this will be characterized by the presence of action patterns, compensatory or syntonizing, which harbour the deflected energies. The war which ended might be permitted to live on in poetry or legends; the tensions caused by the collapsing security might spread to the sphere of religion and call forth beliefs in witchcraft or the wish-fulfilment of miracle cults; and the constrained political ambitions might flow into the make-believe of clubs or secret societies or find an outlet in some messianic cult like the North American Ghost Dance. These are only a few of the possible solutions, which are numerous and of great variety. Nor can it be otherwise. For as we anticipated, the conversion of aims and desires follows no simple rules. Rather is the range of modes of behaviour into which the deflected energy might be directed wide and uncertain; it is narrowed down only by the possible 'assimilation' of the blocked aim to some congenial aim available in the given social environment, and by the laws of levels of energy.

The instances just quoted fittingly conclude our discussion of the psychological linkage. For they exhibit the widest span within which the linkage operates and the one furthest removed from our paradigm—a linkage active 'at any given moment'. Also, our instances touch upon the emergence of new modes of behaviour and thus upon the 'genesis' of social facts. That the two kinds of processes overlap and interpenetrate, I have anticipated. The discussion that follows will define this overlap more precisely.

CHAPTER XII

Psychological Instincts: Action Potentials

---

1. INSTINCTS AND PSEUDO-INSTINCTS

'Innate action potentials' might seem to be only another, and perhaps clumsier, name for those impulses to behaviour which are taken to be innate in the human organism and are variously referred to as instincts, drives, urges, tendencies, needs, and the like. Of all these the instinct concept emphasizes most strongly the innate nature of the impulses and their relation to specific behaviour patterns. Unhappily, the term has a confused history and, to-day, a dubious value. If the innateness of instincts and their relation to specific modes of behaviour are understood in a rigid sense, as they sometimes are, then the instinct is either a 'blind unconscious mechanism' or nothing.[1] Its essential feature is that it is unlearned and not modifiable by learning. It belongs to the universals of human behaviour in the strictest sense of the word. It would thus make no sense to say that instincts vary in different groups, that they are altered or controlled by habit, and 'weakly' or 'strongly' developed in varying cultural conditions. Yet precisely this sort of plasticity is also imputed to instincts, at least in man and the higher animals, to wit: 'The lower animals inherit fixed instincts, they must take their "ready-mades" and wear them. The higher animals inherit less well-fixed instincts, better able to be fashioned to fit the life of the times.'[2]

It is this uncertainty in the first step of definition that led to the present confusion in the theory of instincts. Often it is a confusion about words. McDougall, for whom instincts were the 'mainsprings' of all behaviour, sometimes rigid and sometimes not, enumerated a large number of instincts, which together account for practically every kind of human action. More recently, Cattell followed suit with another all-embracing list of 'psycho-physical dispositions', or innate 'preferences', for specific modes of acting,

---

[1] L. L. Bernard (1924), pp. 452–3.   [2] G. H. Thomson (1924), p. 34.

which he calls *ergs*, changing the name but not the concept.[1] Bernard, who chooses the most rigid definition of 'instinct', as comprehensively demolishes every instinct that might be relevant for the understanding of human behaviour, demonstrating that the so-called instincts are largely acquired 'habit-complexes'. Yet after 500 pages of demolition he admits that there are hundreds or even thousands of instincts—though these are 'minute, vestigial remains', mere 'constituents' of the habit-complexes or overlaid 'by acquired habits'.[2] More sceptically, Knight Dunlap holds that it is impossible at present to distinguish instincts from habits.[3] Thomson considers it at least difficult, 'because in man all instinctive reactions are so rapidly and deeply covered by a cake or crust of custom'.[4] Allport, though not doubting either the relevance or the tangibility of instincts, relegates them to the status of 'prepotent reflexes'.[5] While for other scholars a few instincts at least retain their ill-defined but momentous existence. 'The theory of instincts', in Freud's words, 'is, as it were, our mythology.'[6] The instincts are mythical beings, superb in their indefiniteness. In our work we cannot overlook them, and yet we are never certain that we are seeing them clearly. Warnings from other camps are not lacking that the search for instincts or innate propensities in general is profitless and unconstructive. Rather should we concentrate on something else, namely, on the study of the effectiveness of 'specific cultural conditions' upon man's mind and personality[7] or on the 'interplay' between his innate characteristics and the social influences which impinge upon these characteristics.[8] Yet how can we study this 'interplay' if we are not certain about one of the two factors entering into it? And how can we, as students of culture, rest satisfied with accepting the influence of 'specific cultural conditions' as a final, not further reducible fact? The psychologist who does so, throws the ball at us; yet surely, we wish to know why specific cultural conditions are what they are, and whether they are not in some measure rooted in the organization of the mind. Shall we then throw the ball back at the psychologist, and so on, endlessly? I have already stated my conviction that we must, and can, explore the innate sources of behaviour. The

[1] R. B. Cattell (1944), p. 110 et passim.   [2] L. L. Bernard, op. cit., pp. 522–4.
[3] Quoted from C. Murchinson (1929), p. 160.   [4] Op. cit., p. 27.
[5] F. H. Allport (1924), pp. 43 ff.   [6] (1933), p. 124.
[7] K. Horney (1939), p. 119.   [8] J. Blackburn (1945), p. 124.

position has, in my view, been aptly summarized by Bogardus when he concludes that, in spite of the uncertain state of affairs, 'we cannot get away from inherited tendencies to action', whichever way they are described—as instincts, drives, basic tendencies, 'wishes', needs, and the like.[1]

Yet if we 'cannot get away from inherited tendencies to action', then it is not irrelevant how they are described and named. 'Instinct', with its confused connotation, may well have become useless. I have suggested another term instead—'innate action potentials', which means precisely what it says, namely, that there exist, in the human organism, quantities of energy, or measures of tension, pressing for release in behaviour.[2] Now, although these tensions are generated in the organism they can be raised to the level where they press for release in action both by internal and external conditions, which we normally call 'stimuli'. If the stimulus is visceral or in some other way internal (as in hunger, or the desire for sleep), the action potentials seem to operate as autonomous forces, independent of any act of experiencing. Also, their efficacy is subject to more or less definite cycles, which can be stated in the form of 'maintenance schedules'.[3] If the stimuli are external (the sight of appetizing food, a dull book which makes you sleepy), they merely appear to set a mechanism in motion. Even so, the stimulus only determines the occasion for the release of the action potential and its 'readiness-to-go-off' (Tolman), not its peculiar direction into modes of behaving.[4] Here, however, we must distinguish between two different kinds of action potentials. In one the tensions are such that they press for release in *specific* modes of behaviour; in the other, they only require release of a *generic* kind,

[1] (1939), p. 125.

[2] 'Innate action potentials' is a clumsy phrase; I shall therefore also speak of 'drives' or, occasionally, of 'needs'. I hesitate to use 'need' at this stage; for this concept implies, not only a felt imperative demand, but also an objective criterion whereby the given course of behaviour is judged to be 'needful'. Though the two meanings of 'need' are rarely separated, I prefer not to speak of 'needs' until such an objective criterion has been introduced, namely, that of physical survival (see p. 372 below).

[3] E. C. Tolman (1937), p. 159.

[4] It will be seen that I do not distinguish between 'drives' and 'mechanisms'. The two are one and the same thing, though in the case of internal stimulations the thing that sets the mechanism going may not be visible for an observer concerned with behaviour (if indeed it is visible or known at all). Here I follow roughly Lashley's view: 'Physiologically all drives are no more than expressions of the activity of specific (sensi-motor) mechanisms' (1938), p. 468.

being capable of flowing into a whole series or class of modes of behaviour.[1] The first kind, then, corresponds to behaviour patterns 'pre-formed' or 'ready-made' in the organism, with their direction upon specific goals, and hence to the 'instincts' re-defined.[2] Thus hunger cannot be satisfied save by physical satiation; fatigue, only by physical rest; the drive of sex, only by cohabitation (though this last aim direction can to some extent be 'converted', as psychoanalysis has amply shown).

Understood in the widest sense, the specific action potentials cover an immense range, from simple reflexes and Bernard's 'vestigial' instincts (such as blinking or scratching) to the more complex behaviour patterns just mentioned. The former, however, are largely irrelevant for our enquiry. The behaviour cycles they start are too minute and short-range, too rigid as well as self-contained, to add to the modes of social behaviour or indeed to qualify for the name 'behaviour patterns'. Above all, they operate automatically, that is, they run their course without involving consciousness or being modified by events in consciousness. Yet precisely this involvement of consciousness is predicated by the definition of our subject matter, which we took to be aimful, intentional behaviour. The action potentials, then, with which we are concerned start long-range behaviour cycles in that they admit of delayed consummation; and this may further entail planning and the manipulation of means found in the environment (while, in the case of reflexes, the means lie in the organism itself); so that the impulse becomes a 'drive' lasting through the behaviour cycle, and its consummation a consciously had 'need'. The whole behaviour cycle, finally, can be modelled and modified by learning, acquired preferences, and habit. It is because of their magnitude, plasticity, and dependence upon an environment of means that these action potentials are allowed for in the cultural make-up and institutionalized in a particular form. Yet though they can be so modified, delayed, and subjected to the modelling influences of institutionalization, they cannot be spirited away or made to flow into a consummation other than that peculiar to their nature. They retain their specific direction upon goals. If this is modified or constrained beyond its given plasticity, the effect is visible, immedi-

---

[1] See above, p. 312.

[2] Cf. K. Bühler's definition of instincts as 'ready-for-use' inherited modes of behaviour (1930), p. 4.

ately, in the signal of all interrupted drives—in emotions, and ultimately in some explosive release or conversion of the dammed-up energies.

Let me emphasize that the distinction here drawn, between innate action potentials which are relevant for social enquiry and others which are not, is a fluid one, and that the brief list given below must be understood in that sense. A typical transitional form which comes to my mind is the impulse to rhythmical motor behaviour, visible in play, marching, dancing, or in the routine of physical labour. The behaviour cycle involved is of small magnitude, largely automatic, highly independent of external means, yet of great plasticity. Equally, it is widely modelled by cultural influences and institutionalized. Another instance is defecation. Again, the behaviour cycle is automatic, short-range, fairly rigid, and so relatively unimportant; yet it is not without social relevance since it is sufficiently plastic to admit of control by habit, and since it is everywhere subjected to rules of etiquette, hygiene, and the like. According to psychoanalysis, the control or constraint of the urge even leads to a certain conversion of energy whose effects are visible in other spheres of behaviour. However this may be, no society acknowledges or utilizes these effects, nor yet those produced by a similar inhibition of the rhythmical impulse; while precisely this is true of other, more wide-range, action potentials. Here, in fact, we encounter an additional criterion for the selection of the socially relevant action potentials. The magnitude of their behaviour cycles must be such that the effects of any constraint will tend to be embodied in the institutional make-up of societies, be it in order to allow for the 'conversion of energy' or to utilize this dynamic source.

These, so far as I can judge, are the socially relevant specific action potentials arranged in order of rigidity and magnitude: pain-rejection ('pushing away noxious stimuli');[1] fatigue-sleep; hunger and thirst; and sex. Every society must, and does, allow for these behaviour mechanisms by offering standardized occasions for their realization. Yet the manner in which this is done clearly varies immensely; we need only think of the many different systems of morality, with their diverse ideals of physical endurance, continence, or love, or of any other 'cultural shaping of appetites' (to borrow Malinowski's phrase). Having said this, we have said very

[1] F. H. Allport (1924), p. 50.

nearly all that can be said on this heading. One more word about
the effects of the constraint or inhibition of the specific action
potentials. If such a constraint or inhibition does in fact regularly
occur, and if its effects are not allowed for in some institutional
manner, the dammed-up tensions would be forced to seek random
release. We note, however, that the different action potentials show
a different degree of resistance to inhibitions. Sleep or satiation
can obviously not be indefinitely delayed; only the most plastic
drive, sex, can be altogether deprived of its consummation and
offered a vicarious satisfaction. Now, why societies should tend to
avoid the random release of tensions dammed-up in this fashion,
we need not for the moment consider. As regards the reasons for
imposing the inhibitions, I may point to one only, which is bound
up with the very effect of the constraint. For this effect may not
only be acknowledged and allowed for, but may be aimed at. In
other words, societies also utilize the conversion and accretion of
mental energy which result from the constraint of aims and
desires—from prolonged fasts, sexual abstinence, or from the
inhibition of bodily movements under pain. The preparations of
priests or religious congregations, the rigid disciplines imposed
upon initiates, the various physical deprivations customarily
meant to lead to a heightened consciousness—all these, and more,
exemplify this inverse social acknowledgment of the innate action
potentials.

2. GENERIC ACTION POTENTIALS

A technical issue, unimportant in the case of the specific action
potentials, assumes considerable importance in the case of the
action potentials which I have termed 'generic', namely, the procedure whereby their innateness is established. The specific action
potentials are sufficiently constant under all conditions of human
existence and sufficiently clearly linked with the organism to be
identified as innate without much difficulty. This is obviously not
so in the case of a great many modes of behaviour, in which we
only suspect the efficacy of innate agencies. When we call any impulse, desire, need, or tendency innate we usually imply two
things. We imply that the mode of behaviour expressing it appears
with some degree of uniformity under all conditions of social
existence, that is, that it belongs to the 'universals' of human culture; and we imply further that the impulse must be observable in

Y

the human being in relative isolation or at least under conditions neutralizing the influence of his environment—learning of all kinds, social norms and models for behaviour, and the like. Though these two observations are interdependent, I shall take it that the second is the one we are after, in that here alone we can demonstrate the existence of the innate mechanisms; while the first refers to the state of affairs which makes us suspect the innate agencies as well as to the state of affairs 'explained' when these have been demonstrated.

In practice, the procedure of 'isolating' and 'neutralizing' corresponds to the normal technique of psychologists—the observation of infant behaviour, and of adult behaviour under specific experimental or clinical conditions. Yet under these conditions certain innate impulses might conceivably escape us; for they might only mature or become visible in social situations in the full sense of the word, that is, in situations which cannot be fully reproduced in nurseries or laboratories, and they might even hinge upon the kind of factors we should attempt to neutralize. Assuming, for example, that there is such a thing as an innate drive to worship the supernatural; it would clearly be unobservable in infants of a certain age, while in every adult who might fall into our hands it would already reflect learning and a given cultural background. We are, as it were, using a camera with a fixed focus, which will not reproduce details beyond a certain depth; whether or not they are details in which we are interested, we cannot tell from the picture. If, then, my list of innate action potentials is extremely brief, it may be so for this reason. The list includes, I believe, all the innate impulses which can be established with any certainty. There may be others; and they may be less vague and 'generic' than those I shall describe, but our methods seem inadequate to verify them.

Nor can we change the method. We cannot throw the camera overboard and trust our eyes instead, that is, seize upon the observable universal features in human culture and argue back to their innateness. If we did so, we should be arguing in a circle. Take, say, submissiveness and dominance (to rephrase more cautiously McDougall's familiar 'instincts' of self-assertion and self-abasement), or any other presumed universal mode of behaviour. If we held that, being universal, submissive and dominating behaviour must express an innate tendency to act in the respective fashion, we should be arguing in the manner of the medieval philosophers who accounted for the property of soporifics by assuming an inherent *vis dormitiva*.

There is this, too. If any mode of behaviour is really universal, it is only as universal as is the context in which it appears, namely, existence in society. Indeed, it may be implicit in our conception of social existence. This is surely true of submissiveness and dominance. Every social group implies these features as part of its internal order, and would not be a social group without them; for the intentional coordination of behaviour among a plurality of individuals (which makes the social group) simply *is* dominance of some and submissiveness of others, even if these attitudes are only temporary and discontinuous. Again, communication by means of signs (verbal or otherwise) simply *is* an aspect of social existence, and cannot be 'thought away' from it. Somewhat modified, the same argument also applies to that other standby of instinct and kindred theories—aggressiveness. Though undoubtedly there exist societies where overt behaviour shows little aggressiveness (I doubt if it ever shows none), no society seems to exist where people do not at least think about aggressiveness, that is, behaviour intentionally injurious to others, guard against it through laws and the like, and compose myths or stories describing such behaviour.[1] Now as they stand, these modes of behaviour are clearly unobservable in the individual isolated from his society, or as isolated as we can make him in fact or imagination. They are unobservable simply because they require an environment of other individuals in which to take place and find their aims and objects—some form of togetherness. And if these modes of behaviour can be provoked also in the artificial isolation of experimental conditions, this means that these conditions have been made to include at least models or prototypes of that togetherness. The appearance of these modes of behaviour, then, depends on the appearance of this particular environment, and the universality of the former goes hand in hand with that other universality, of social existence.

I therefore have no means of deciding whether the identical actions spring from the identity of their carrier, the human

[1] To some extent we can view religion or art from the same angle. Although there are, of course, normal individuals who live happily without religious beliefs or interest in art, no society exists where these modes of behaviour are not institutionalized; so that they are once more bound up with the existence of societies as we know it.

organism, or from the identical conditions under which they alone appear. For all we know, man may be possessed of specific innate impulses to submit or dominate, to communicate with others, to be aggressive, and the rest, which are latent in the isolated individual and materialize or mature only when men live in togetherness. If so, this could never be shown; for the appearance of these modes of behaviour might also mean that here some other innate impulse, visible also under conditions of isolation and sufficiently flexible or generic in nature, has been directed upon the aims and objects that go with existence in togetherness.[1] Indeed, if we could show the existence of innate impulses so flexible and generic in nature (as I think we can), this proof would seem to overrule the assumption of more specific impulses, which we should have to credit with the requisite latency and maturation. Finally, since existence in 'togetherness' does include submission, dominance, and the other modes of behaviour in question, the respective innate impulses which we might ascribe to man would simply be impulses to live in society. Strictly speaking, then, the assumption of 'social instincts' or any other innate propensity driving man to do all the things which are inseparable from social existence as we know it, can be neither confirmed nor refuted. Furthermore, it involves us in the meaningless argument about some innate tendency of man to live in society. McDougall, for one, has argued the case to the end by stipulating his 'gregarious' instinct, which cuts the Gordian knot. But all this amounts to is the gratuitous assumption that man, who does live in society and in no other way, does so impelled by his nature.

So much for the legitimacy of our approach. As for its success, I have anticipated certain of its limitations. Let me add, further, that the generic action potentials stand in an intricate and partly obscure interrelation, which makes their precise definition difficult. Also, all seem characterized by an inherent ambivalence and polarity. I shall enumerate three such pairs of drives: Pleasure-Displeasure, Equilibrium-Tension, and Conformity-Shame. There can be no doubt, I think, of their existence; but it is possible that they can all be derived from each other, though I will do no more than indicate this possibility. I propose to start with the analysis of

---

[1] An example that comes to my mind is Janet's assumption of an innate need for 'excitation' gratified, among other things, through submissive and dominant behaviour towards others (1926, pp. 124-5).

the most 'solid' action potential, or at least one widely treated as a solid, irreducible fact—the Pleasure Drive.

(i) *Pleasure-Displeasure*

This dual drive is visible in the tendency to perpetuate or repeat pleasurable experiences, and to avoid or discontinue displeasurable ones. Psychologists see in pleasure-displeasure the primary characteristics of emotional states or even the two dimensions of all experiences carrying a feeling tone. It is clear, however, that these impulses need not operate only in the excited atmosphere of emotional states. For pleasure and displeasure have a delayed as well as immediate effectiveness; and in the former case the pleasure drive operates through the cognitive sphere, which as such seems to generate impulses to a much smaller degree. In other words, the pleasure drive may also lend its impetus to cognitive processes. Thus I may anticipate pain and pleasure in thought and imagination, and hence act in a certain way in order to attain the eventual pleasure or freedom from pain. The intervening action (or avoidance of action) may be neutral as regards pain and pleasure, or may involve the opposite experience from the one anticipated. I may do unpleasant things for the sake of a final pleasure, or avoid pleasurable actions because I know them to lead to pain in the end. There is obviously some balance between the two, though its values cannot be stated in absolute terms. If I find that people avoid eating food they like because they anticipate painful indigestion afterwards, I must infer that the avoidance of pleasure is less displeasurable than the final pain; and if I find that people eat nice food in spite of such anticipations, then it was obviously 'worth it'. But this 'worth' is relative, both to the individual experiences in question and, above all, to the circumstances under which it occurs; for the pleasure (or pain) may be enhanced by time, place and occasion, and especially by the immediacy of the given experience as measured against the opposite experience in the future. It is, then, only from regularly observed behaviour under given conditions that we can infer this balance of pleasure values.

The difficulty of assessing the relative urgency or weight of pleasures and displeasures is not the only one. It is extremely difficult even to state in general terms what is pleasurable and what is not. The variety of judgments is such that we are easily forced into the extreme relativism of calling 'pleasure' whatever people want to go on doing, and 'displeasure' whatever they are trying not to do.[1] If so, we could not really speak of a drive to attain pleasure and avoid displeasure; the only drive element we could predicate would consist in the very twin tendency to 'go on doing' and to 'cease from doing', under unspecified conditions.[2] I do not think that this extreme relativism is wholly warranted. In certain cases, at least, we can go beyond it and specify the nature of the things— experiences, stimuli—which people find pleasurable (worth 'having more of') or otherwise. The drives, then, are towards and away from something, namely, towards and away from the occasions that convey these experiences and stimuli. Thus it seems that all sense experiences of great intensity are displeasurable or painful; that darkness is always displeasurable, that is, avoided; that pleasure tends to attach to all experiences implying rhythm, symmetry, order, or balance; and finally, that the unhindered play of any drive or desire is as such pleasurable while its inhibition is painful.[3] The first two of these four statements may or may not be universally true; I believe that they are, but this is merely a question of verification. But the last two statements (which, as we shall see, hang together), while undoubtedly true, both alter and complicate the conception of the pleasure drive.

In saying that the unimpeded consummation of any drive or desire (including hunger, sex, and the rest) produces pleasure and its inhibition displeasure, we have given a new meaning to the pleasure principle. So far, we have considered it to operate in its own right, as a tendency of the organism to seek out or avoid experiences of a certain kind. We are now assuming that aim-directed behaviour of any kind, carried by its own impulses, also involves pleasure-displeasure as a by-product, according to the way the former are allowed to function, unimpeded or not. In other words, the pleasure drive seems to occur, both as a primary or

---

[1] Cf., e.g., this statement: 'Pleasant . . . is what we normally seek'; 'the reaction [of approach or withdrawal] determines the pleasantness or unpleasantness of objects' (H. N. Peters, 1935, pp. 357, 380).

[2] This is, in fact, the conclusion reached by certain psychologists, who operate with the concepts of *adience* and *abience*, which terms denote the two tendencies of any organism, to have 'more and more of what it first gets' in the way of stimuli, and conversely, to have less and less (K. B. Holt, 1931, quoted from Murphy and Newcomb, 1937, p. 102).

[3] This is, essentially, McDougall's view (see 1923, pp. 269 et seq.).

'operational' action potential and as a secondary or 'functional' one. Now unless we can, with McDougall, produce a sizable list of impulses to behaviour—innate impulses, more particularly—which are simply there, being in themselves neutral with regard to pleasure and displeasure, the new viewpoint leads to some awkward questions—for example: Is the pleasurable experience we desire to attain by some course of action increased if our desire has free play? Or is the pain we wish to avoid by some course of action rendered more painful if our desire is blocked? But disregarding these (I suspect meaningless) questions, the new viewpoint is important, in this sense. Any drive or desire allowed free play means tensions released, and tensions can only exist in an equilibrium system as temporary states of unbalance. Thus the pleasure attaching to the free play of a drive attaches implicitly to the re-establishment of a state of equilibrium, while displeasure attaches to the state of disequilibrium; which links the 'functional' pleasure-pain drive with the intrinsic pleasure quality which we attributed to all 'balanced' experiences. We can go a step further; for it can be demonstrated that in perception regular, balanced and uncomplicated wholes form more readily than irregular and 'open wholes'.[1] In consequence, this ready and smooth perception of balanced, ordered, and symmetrical data will set up less tension than the perception of unordered, unbalanced, and asymmetrical data, so that the two are accompanied by pleasurable and displeasurable experiences respectively. Indeed, it has long been suggested that all 'medium experiences', (i.e. tensionless experiences) entail pleasure, and all 'excessive' experiences, displeasure or pain.[2] So far, then, our picture appears greatly simplified; we could at last define the *genus* of the satisfactions aimed at in the pleasure drive, though the drive itself seems to have lost its separate identity, 'pleasure' and 'displeasure' being merely different words for equilibrium and tension.

But this equation is not quite correct. Many conspicuously pleasurable modes of behaviour contain a pronounced element of tension, which is pleasurable as such, not only in its cessation. In aesthetic pleasure it is often the disturbance to our equanimity that counts rather than the latter; sexual gratification lies at least as much in the orgasm as in the satiation that follows it; even pain may have a pleasure component, that is, may be desired for the

---

[1] See W. Köhler (1947), p. 145.   [2] Th. Ribot (1897), p. 56.

sharp stimulation and tension it implies. Generally speaking, 'to be directed towards a goal, to have the tension or desire, already gives the experience of being alive, which is as important as the final satisfaction. It is erroneous to take satisfaction in isolation from the general attitude.'[1] Certainly, any sensory or cognitive processes that function in a strongly noticeable manner appear to have a tension value which is sought out and tends to be perpetuated, and must be assumed to be pleasurable. Bühler speaks in this connection of 'function pleasure', which resides in movements as such, in exertions and tensions, whether these occur in play, in the exercise of the body, or in the intellectual effort of grappling with problems. In other words, pleasure is not only a 'brake' (indicating satiation) but also a 'motor' (and thus tension continued).[2] The pleasure-displeasure values, then, are not simply absorbed in equilibrium and tension, but add something to these states. But what they add is ambivalent; for equilibrium, absence of tension, is both pleasurable and non-pleasurable; and so are disequilibrium and tension. The polarity of pleasure-displeasure, then, implies a reference to the polarity of our second action potential. We might say that the ambivalence of the pleasure drive derives from the fact that its two dimensions are crossed by another two-dimensional field—that constituted by the drives moving between equilibrium and tension. This can be illustrated by the following diagram, which shows the opposed pleasure values that may attach to each of the two contrasted situations—facing unfamiliar and strange things (involving tensions), and facing familiar, habitual things (implying freedom from tension or 'equilibrium').

	Equilibrium	*Tension*
Pleasure	Enjoyment of the familiar	Curiosity, enjoyment of novel experiences
Displeasure	Boredom with the familiar	Disturbance, suspicion of novel experiences

(ii) *Equilibrium-Tension*

The principle here referred to has often been expressed, always in this general sense: the organism behaves as a system or pattern

[1] P. Schilder (1942), pp. 15–16. [2] K. Bühler (1928), pp. 196–8.

of interrelated processes which tends to maintain itself under changing conditions, that is, as a system in stable equilibrium.[1] All mental processes, more particularly, move in the direction of an equilibrium, so that tensions within the system are kept 'stationary' and gradients of energy reduced to a level permitting the stable state.[2] All modes of behaviour springing from these mental processes may therefore be taken to preserve the equilibrium when it is established and to re-establish it when it is disturbed.

I shall presently attempt to show that this statement is one-sided and to that extent inaccurate. But let me here explore a little further this oft-quoted phrase, 'an organic or psychological equilibrium'. It is difficult to handle, combining as it does the meaning of 'equilibrium' as the term is used in physics (and which we must borrow from sheer poverty of our language) and a new connotation laid into it to make it fit organic or psychological processes. I am, incidentally, speaking deliberately only of equilibrium, and not of 'stable equilibrium', although the statements just quoted suggest this more specific meaning. By stable equilibrium we mean the tendency to conserve or re-establish an *identical* state. And though it is true that organisms, or the human mind, do sometimes strive to conserve a *status quo*, this conservation is only an apparent one. Even when we consciously return to a previous state after some 'disturbance', it is never strictly speaking the same state; for it always implies at least the memory of the experience that has intervened. In more general terms, the identity preserved by the organism is not 'the continued identity of inert things', but the 'unity of developing and changing forms'.[3] When the organism re-establishes its equilibrium it assumes a state which, though once more stable, is in a certain sense always novel; so that the organism is 'conservative and evolving at the same time'.[4]

Now, in physics equilibrium means the state of a system in which energies are stationary and no further internal rearrangements are likely to happen; while in the opposite state these are likely to go on happening, involving the actuation and expenditure of energies, until a final stable rearrangement is reached. The physicist thus speaks of 'steady states', which simply *are* or *happen*. Also, the probability of their occurrence and continuance depends on the

[1] This is Humphrey's much-quoted 'Law'. See G. Humphrey (1933), p. 41.
[2] K. Lewin (1935), pp. 51, 59.   [3] G. Humphrey, op. cit., p. 55.
[4] K. Koffka (1935), p. 309.

presence or absence of 'disturbing' external forces; for the 'steady state' is predictable only for systems in isolation, and the series of internal rearrangements only for systems exposed to 'disturbing' forces. None of these premises applies to mental (or organic) processes.

To begin with, the human organism is never even relatively isolated nor in a state when further rearrangements are unlikely. It is always exposed to stimulations and 'disturbances', and these arise both in the environment and internally, since tensions are constantly produced through acts of experiencing and new energies brought into play through the sheer process of living. An isolated and tensionless state is inconceivable—though the apathy of the psychopath may be an approximation, and the *nirvana* of Indian philosophy the ideal of such a complete equilibrium. The maintenance of an organic or psychological equilibrium thus means the distribution of fluctuating energies and the manipulation of constantly recurring tensions. We must think of it as of a 'dynamic' quasi-equilibrium maintained 'in spite of external fluctuations' and involving a 'perpetual expenditure of energy'.[1] Its paradigm is rhythm rather than rest. Thus it is not paradoxical to say that there is a drive to establish or re-establish equilibrium, which would seem to mean that tensions and energies are brought into play so that tensions (and hence gradients of energy) may be overcome; for these are simply always there, the organism merely manipulating them. Nor is it paradoxical to say that our mind seeks out experiences offering equilibrium; for we are perpetually meeting also with opposite experiences, and can react selectively.

Here we depart once more from the concept of a physical equilibrium. To make sense, the psychological equilibrium cannot be taken to apply to states which merely are or happen. Rather has it the additional meaning of states *experienced* and *intentionally brought about*.[2] We mean by it states felt to be calm, restful, permanent—states of 'quiescence', as against *felt* states of stress, restlessness, or tension; while the change from one to the other constitutes an aimful striving, whereby the energies available in the state of tension are directed towards achieving the desired end

[1] A. D. Ritchie (1936), p. 64.

[2] 'Living organisms are never in a state of equilibrium as long as they are alive. What has deceived people is the fact that living organisms often aim (the teleology is deliberate) at maintaining a steady state . . .' (A. D. Ritchie, ibid.).

state of quiescence. Equally, this process is set in motion also through the anticipation of the disturbances, for when we are aware of some threat to the *status quo* we do not merely shut out the disturbing awareness but make efforts and expend energy to safeguard or perpetuate the state of equilibrium.

Finally, unless we accepted this additional meaning of equilibrium, we could not speak of a special category of behaviour expressing this drive or tendency. The change from disequilibrium to equilibrium in the sense of physics represents a model for any kind of behaviour, since this means always a movement that comes to an end, states of tension that cease, energy activated and finally expended, whichever way you choose to describe it.[1] We mean something more than merely the ultimate completion of all behaviour cycles, namely, the existence of behaviour cycles which are intended to lead to an end state of felt and enjoyed quiescence.

The striving after equilibrium is realized in all experiences and actions—spontaneous or culturally stabilized—which bear the character of order, pattern, consistency, and rhythmical repetitiveness, as it is also behind habit formation and the preference for the familiar. Where the equilibrium is re-established through explosive discharges of energy, we have the modes of cathartic behaviour well known to psychologists and anthropologists alike. Like the pleasure drive, the tendency towards equilibrium operates both over the short range of direct responses and in indirect, long-range fashion, through the medium of anticipatory motivations. Equally, I think, it embraces the whole range of experiences, cognitive as well as sensory, so that its effectiveness can be seen in work, play, aesthetic and ritual activities as much as in idea systems, religious or philosophical, which emphasize conceptions of order, safety and predictability.

A word on catharsis. It is, as we implied, one of the mechanisms for the discharge of pent up tensions. It plays, however, so important a part that it should perhaps be given the status of an action potential in its own right. If I have not done this, it is because catharsis is essentially a 'functional' action potential, presupposing as it does the operation—the inhibited operation—of other drives.

---

[1] Chapple and Coon use the equilibrium concept in this sense (1942), pp. 14, 43 ff. Thus they merely show that all modes of behaviour are so constructed that they fit the physical model, without accounting for the far more important thing—the varying aim-directions of behaviour.

Though catharsis represents a direct and explosive discharge of energy, it yet exhibits degrees of both explosiveness and immediacy. In excited motor behaviour, in shouting, crying, or violent actions, catharsis is in a high degree explosive and immediate. In cultural life, however, an intermediate and more restrained form is more important. When psychologists speak of 'projection' they imply this second form of catharsis. It lies in the external expression, by means of some visible or oral symbolism, of the experiences that caused the tension to arise; and being so externalized the tension is also discharged or 'abreacted'. Culture is pervaded by certain 'reduplications' of behaviour patterns; they are, loosely speaking, the reduplications of mundane events in the sphere of art, ceremonial, or idea systems. Here the contexts involving powerful experiences are duplicated in their dramatizations or other external representations, which both affirm the weight of the experiences and remove their tension effects. We have already spoken of the logical framework within which these reduplications occur; we have now touched upon the impulses behind them.[1]

Now, it is clear that these modes of catharsis are socially important, not only because they discharge the tensions felt by an individual, but also because they do so in a manner visible to others. The impulse to project inner experiences outward is equally an impulse to express them for others to see, and all culturally standardized forms of catharsis imply this orientation upon a public. We need not examine how far this 'visibility for others' rests on meanings conveyed by language or other conventional symbols which listeners or spectators have learned to understand, or on the unlearned expressiveness of tension-fraught behaviour, which resides in the sign character of gestures or in the 'physiognomic character' of objects serving as vehicles for such expressions.[2] I would only add that in all culturally standardized forms of catharsis this 'immediate ascription of dynamic characteristics to the perceived data'[3] plays a paramount part. And I would add, further, that the response of spectators or audience to such intentionally expressive behaviour often entails more than merely a dispassionate 'ascription'. It entails also the re-living of the behaviour, though in a paler version, by the perceiving person. Any aesthetic act or dramatization requires this resonance or 'empathy',

[1] See pp. 262–3.   [2] See p. 261.   [3] W. Köhler (1947), p. 226.

lest the works of art 'leave us cold' and the drama 'fall flat'. Thus, finally, all cathartic projections betray, not only the drives and impulses swaying the actors, but also the capacity and desire of their public to be similarly swayed. It is on these grounds that we may regard the numerous dramatizations in every culture and the aesthetic or religious expressions of societies as revealing a psychological bent typical of the whole culture and society; for they are often enacted and produced only by the few, and merely perceived and understood by the rest of the people.

To return to our theme. Once more like the pleasure drive, the equilibrium drive is essentially ambivalent. For at a certain point the attractiveness of measured experiences weakens and gives way to the opposed striving for new stimulations, and so disequilibrium. In individual responses balance and order become stale, and excitement and uncertainty desirable; familiarity turns into boredom, reluctance to embrace the strange into exciting curiosity; tension acquires that pleasure value of which we have spoken, until the striving for it in turn loses force and swings back to the desire for quiescence. I have presented the ambivalence of this drive in the form of a pendulum swing. As such, in fact, it appears acknowledged in all cultural settings, being visible in the alternation of work and play, restraint and licence, everyday routine and the periodical thrills of religious or aesthetic excitement. Expressed in terms of subjective experiences, the pendulum swing appears as satiation and exhaustion, though we know little about the amplitude of these phases. The psychological study of satiation in general is still in its infancy;[1] it may well one day enable us to define the point at which the pendulum swing tends to occur. To suggest one possible, and perhaps probable, discovery in this field, we might find that the stability aspect of pleasure has a greater amplitude than its tension aspect, and that the direction of the human organism towards tension values is more quickly satiated than the direction towards experiences satisfying the equilibrium drive. Let us note, however, that when cultures offer different sectors of life for the realization of the two opposed tendencies, they acknowledge the permanent presence of both. Society anticipates the pendulum swing before satiation has reduced the equilibrium drive to nil or exhaustion emptied the tension drive, thus avoiding the random interplay and fortuitous

[1] See K. Lewin (1935), pp. 254–7.

satisfaction of the two tendencies. Another thing is hereby also ensured, namely, the adequate allocation of tension and stability to sectors of life requiring one or the other action potential. War or revenge can only materialize under great tension; utilitarian occupations or workaday routine require a stable and restrained flow of energy; religion, though it may involve thrill and excitement in its rituals, must also offer certainty and ultimate equilibrium. Society, then, not only acknowledges the two drives, but also canalizes and distributes them.

To some extent this must always be so if society is to exist as we know it. Yet this segmentation of cultural life into sectors or phases expressing equilibrium and tension respectively may appear obscured. Over and above this segmentation, the interplay of the two drives appears to crystallize also in a more autonomous form. It crystallizes, first, in the cyclical phases visible in the history of styles of art, of philosophy, religions, and perhaps of entire patterns of cultural existence, so that these phases exhibit, now love for the ordered and serene, and now love for thrill and excitement.[1] Here we are still thinking in terms of a 'pendulum swing'. But secondly, the two drives seem to define also opposed personality types, and thus opposed types of culture expressive of these types of personality. Here, of course, we are dealing with approximations and predominant trends, not with faithful descriptions of historical phases or cultural differences. Perhaps, too, the co-existence of opposed 'culture patterns' is true only at the moment of observation, and would turn into a cyclical succession in the perspective of time. Let us note, finally, that here the dichotomy of equilibrium and tension links up with the principle of 'even' and 'uneven' levels of energy previously formulated. The 'even' level now means that one or the other drive pervades the whole field of cultural action; the 'uneven' level, that the two are distributed over different sectors of the cultural field. The dichotomy of equilibrium-tension, then, seems to account for the ultimate ambiguity of our laws of mental dynamics.

The distribution of tension and non-tension over different sectors or phases of cultural life, however, poses a final problem.

[1] Among anthropologists, Goldenweiser has drawn attention to this historical 'pendulum swing' (1933, p. 19). Historians of art and philosophers have often attempted to demonstrate it in the succession of 'classical' and 'romantic' styles or in the dichotomy (to quote from Nietzsche) of 'Apollonian' and 'Dionysian' ethos.

For it might be asked if this segmentation does not merely imply the maintenance of equilibrium in a mental system of wider span, in which the peaks of tension only indicate fluctuations of energy or phases preceding its discharge. This is the view of Lewin and many others. I believe that it fails to do justice to the observable facts. What we find is that, in certain phases and activities, people desire not merely to relieve tension, but to experience and retain it; the potential of this kind of action is directed, not towards finally discharging energy, but towards creating its gradients. Thrill, fear, danger, excitement, shock experiences of various kinds—all these are desired as such, as experiences progressing in 'peaks' of tension and 'bursts' of energy. In accepting this autonomy of the tension drive we fully abandon the model of a physical equilibrium. For in physics the state of equilibrium is not merely one of two observable data, but a state of highest probability, towards which all aggregates of matter are tending.[1] Against this we assume, perhaps with hazardous logic, that the human system produces tension and instability from within by an innate action potential. We imply that gradients of energy are not invariably levelled out but are self-increasing; that energy is made available so that stimulation and tension (creative of new energy) may be sought out and maintained; and that energy discharged in 'bursts' yet raises its own potential. Yet psychologists have accepted this paradoxical mechanism. It underlies Janet's proposition that 'energetic acts' may stimulate the whole mind to higher tension and that heavy expenditure of 'psychic force' may raise the level of 'forces' at the mind's disposal.[2]

In my view, then, the striving for tension and stimulation, what Janet suggestively calls the *besoin d'excitation*,[3] must be accepted, not as an accidental fluctuation within a system tending towards equilibrium, but as a dynamic component in its own right. I am tempted to add that this 'right' is concomitant with life itself. For the maintenance of systems in a 'steady state' or their return to that state after disturbances is not yet life—or not fully life as we must understand it. Life means also an impetus beyond this mere con-

---

[1] See Sir Arthur Eddington (1928), pp. 70 ff.; W. Köhler (1938), pp. 304-5.

[2] (1925), pp. 236, 239. See also Köhler: 'Neither is the standard state of an organism a state of equilibrium in the common sense of the word, nor do organic processes in their totality generally tend to approach such an equilibrium' (1938), p. 317.

[3] P. Janet (1926), p. 124.

servation, call it what you will—the impetus of creative action, or 'creative evolution', *élan vital* or, with Freud, 'life-instinct'.[1]

(iii) *Conformity-Shame*

This action potential is presented with some reserve—not because its existence is uncertain, but because it partakes so strongly of the general conditions of social existence that its separation from them appears difficult and perhaps doubtful. Also, it extends into the sphere of mere reflex actions where the 'involvement' of consciousness is no longer visible and the cycles may be reduced to irrelevant magnitudes.[2]

By conformity I mean the tendency of individuals in proximity to conform spontaneously to each other's behaviour.[3] This tendency is conspicuously exhibited by infants between the fifth and seventh month, when the child 'simply reflects the positive or negative expression of the adult, i.e. repeats the movements of the adult'.[4] The imitative stage follows upon an earlier phase during which the infant is 'socially responsive' in an indeterminate fashion, that is, smiles at any kind of face or voice, and is in turn succeeded by a phase marked, no longer by an imitative response, but by the approach-withdrawal response of the pleasure principle.[5] The fact that imitation is subsequently replaced or obscured by another response mechanism merely indicates that, like many other infantile reactions, imitation is, as it were, explicitly exhibited at one point of individual development and thereafter remains fixed as a ready though latent pattern of behaviour. The efficacy of conformity in adults can be observed in various quasi-experimental situations. Thus factory workers working in proximity show a spontaneous (downward) assimilation of their physical efforts, even when their wages are calculated on the output of the whole group so that the greater effort of individuals would benefit all. Conversely, when the workers are separated, their efforts become unequal.[6] A spontaneous and fully reflexive type of conformity is visible in a wide range of everyday situations: we yawn when others yawn, we find that laughing is infectious, we notice in ourselves in-

[1] S. Freud (1933), pp. 137–9.   [2] See above, pp. 331–2.

[3] My terms are borrowed from Claparède, who speaks of an innate *recherche du conforme*, lying at the root of all imitative behaviour (1946), p. 161.

[4] K. Bühler (1930), p. 160.   [5] Ibid., pp. 160, 161.

[6] E. Farmer (1939), pp. 419–20.

cipient motions when watching some sporting event, and we are easily swayed by crowd behaviour. The extreme suggestibility of the hysteric marks the maximum end of the scale.

This tendency passes by various names. Often, one speaks of imitation and suggestibility; McDougall comprises all related symptoms under the heading of 'sympathy' or 'sympathetic induction of emotions'; Linton and others refer to the 'contagion of emotions'; Kimball Young emphasizes the close affinity between ideo-motoric suggestibility and the 'empathy' of classical psychology.[1] In essence, the phenomenon is one. Always, it marks a spontaneous reaction, and one that is generic in the sense that it operates widely irrespective of the particular kind of behaviour with regard to which conformity is sought or attained.

Lately it has been claimed that 'imitation' is not a given tendency of the organism, but is placed there by 'conditioning', that is, by learning under the influence of social situations; society 'rewards' imitation and punishes 'non-imitation', and nothing more basic or instinctive must be assumed. The older theories which hold that identical group behaviour springs ultimately from an 'instinct' of imitation have clearly overstated their case; but so have, in my view, the recent writers who in turn deny any innate tendency to imitation. Miller and Dollard, for example, constructed experiments, carried out on rats and children, to prove the derived nature of the tendency.[2] Neither the experiments nor the arguments put forth seem convincing.

Much is made of reward-and-punishment motives and of the 'prestige suggestion'. Thus behind that prototype of imitative behaviour, crowd-behaviour, is merely the learned reward that 'there is safety in numbers'; many individuals 'have been separately punished or not rewarded for doing acts with only one person as model' but rewarded for acting as do large numbers.[3]

[1] W. McDougall (1912), Chap. IV; R. Linton (1936), p. 93; Kimball Young (1946), p. 111.

[2] See N. E. Miller and John Dollard (1941). The animal experiments, incidentally, show an initial tendency to imitate before the learning process begins to be effective, while the experiments with children show that non-imitation as well as imitation can be conditioned. Which would seem to indicate that there *is* some unconditioned tendency to imitate, unless behaviour is innately random, being fortuitously sometimes one thing and sometimes the other. Characteristically the imitative phase of infants is dismissed in a footnote which merely states that the 'origin of this early imitative act is not clear' (p. 326).

[3] Op. cit., p. 223.

z

To some extent, I suppose, this is true; but even if it were fully true this statement would only tell us that a particular kind of imitation *can also* be learned. Moreover, this statement presupposes a generic tendency towards imitation; for as the authors obligingly explain, individuals are taught to ignore the single-person 'model' (that is, one form of imitation) in favour of mass-models. That particular forms of imitation can be taught and learned no one will dispute; that society rests on planfully cultivating conformity of behaviour in a wide sense, we know; which only means that society canalizes a drive already there. Nor does the 'prestige-suggestion' mean anything else. One imitates or follows an individual (more precisely, a social 'person') who is credited with possessing desirable qualities to a marked degree or who is in a position to dispense rewards; and one imitates behaviour bearing this mark of desirability. In other words, conscious value judgments and utilitarian motivations extend and guide the ready tendency to conform to perceived behaviour. Imitation is provoked and utilized, not created, by society.

I would ascribe to the action potential of conformity a very deep foundation in the mental sphere. I conceive it to be intimately linked with the mechanism of 'empathy', that is, with the spontaneous apprehension of dynamic (or 'physiognomic') features in objects—human or material—without which aesthetic experiences and perhaps the basic phenomenon of 'you-awareness' would remain unintelligible.[1] The striving for conformity, of course, implies, beyond the mere experiencing, also a definite response in behaviour, which must run its course and attain its end state of satisfaction. The nature of this satisfaction is difficult to define since our language only offers gradations of the pleasure concept. Inasmuch as behaving-in-conformity reflects a true drive operating through consciousness, and not merely an automatic reflex, its smooth operation must indeed be expected to have some pleasure quality, and its obstruction the quality of displeasure. Yet both seem to be of a special kind, distinct from other experiences of pleasure or displeasure. Consider that in conforming to the behaviour of others I am repeating some perceived act, and that this repetition can convey a satisfaction which the copied act itself might not entail—as when I copy others in taking strong drink or behaving in a boisterous fashion, even though I find no

[1] See above, pp. 261, 344.

pleasure in these actions as such. What I enjoy, then, is a peculiar satisfaction which is not simply pleasure, but pleasure of an ambiguous and superimposed kind.

Nor can this satisfaction be more readily related to equilibrium and tension. Some relation of this kind we should expect since acting in conformity with others adds to the order and regularity of events and brings the actor in harmony with his surroundings. Yet clearly, this relation is not always visible. Can we, for example, speak of a felt equilibrium when individuals are moved to behave uniformly in a crowd swayed by violent excitement, pleasurable or displeasurable? Perhaps there are traces of some such feeling tone even there; even such tense mass actions convey a sense of security, and hence stability, not derived from any rational calculation that 'safety lies in numbers', but arising spontaneously, as a sensation of comfort. And this is, once more, only superimposed upon, and merging with, the tensions felt in the mass action itself.

The striving for conformity is, in a sense, self-limiting. For the events and persons in our environment are too varied to permit more than a partial conformity, whose scope the individual must choose or is taught to choose. This scope is probably also circumscribed by the twofold operation of the equilibrium drive and its phases of satiation and new stimulation. Perhaps, there are, finally, also the ultimate limits set to conformity by the fear of that 'loss of the Self' emphasized by certain psychologists.[1] These various brakes seem to disappear only in pathological cases, especially in the pantomimic urge of the hysteric.

More importantly, the striving for conformity may also be frustrated and inhibited, being offered no congenial occasions for its realization. It may be blocked by the inability of deviant personality types to be like the rest or by the accidents of life which isolate persons from their fellow beings. Again, the effect of this inhibition is not simply displeasure or tension, but displeasure or tension of a special kind, namely, *shame*. Let me admit that here I am speaking very tentatively, since we lack experimental data to demonstrate this polarity. Yet I would suggest that in any inhibition of the desire to conform to the behaviour of others shame appears as a 'functional' action potential and leads, like 'functional' displeasure, to self-withdrawal. Mostly, of course, the conformity aimed at in behaviour is socially planned, being held up as some-

[1] E. Fromm (1942), pp. 177 ff.

thing desirable and perhaps rewarded; while the feeling of shame on the part of the individuals failing in this aim is not entirely spontaneous but again expected, meant to occur, and hence, if you like, 'conditioned'. But this conventionalizing does not detract from the innateness of the response. Like imitation, it is provoked and utilized, not imposed upon random chances of behaviour. Also, there exist a few instances suggestive of the spontaneousness of shame.

Thus a wealthy person among the poor is often ashamed of being 'different', and individuals with physical defects are ashamed among normal people. The embarrassment of the stranger among people quite unlike himself is a weak form of the same reaction. Sexual shame between the sexes belongs fully to this category; at least, observations on children seem to demonstrate that their first feeling of shame springs from the discovery of their bodily difference. In adult behaviour, and in sexual shame felt by individuals of the same sex, convention somewhat distorts the reaction; here the painful embarrassment which we call sexual shame accompanies the exhibition of bodily parts or of actions which, by cultural standards, must be 'private', that is, in regard to which the demonstration of conformity is inhibited. But once more, the disappearance of the inhibition means the disappearance of shame. In the primitive avoidances between 'in-laws' spontaneous shame and conventionalized sexual shame appear combined; for these cultural features express (and prevent) both the embarrassment between 'strangers' (in a kinship sense) who are thrown together by marriage, and the embarrassment that springs from the awareness of the sexual occasion responsible for this new relationship.[1]

We must add a final observation. The desire to be or act like others presupposes, of course, the presence of others. It is thus tempting to go a step further, to ascribe a particular emotional satisfaction, akin to the one entailed in conformity, to the very fact of being with others, and even to stipulate an innate impulse or need of this kind. It was William James, I believe, who first spoke of the dependence of man upon the emotional responses from and to fellow beings; among anthropologists Linton reckons it among the 'universal reactions' of man;[2] and recently Fromm, speaking as

---

[1] I have quoted instances in (1947), p. 104.

[2] (1936), p. 141. Linton, however, considers it possible that 'early conditioning' may be responsible for this 'need'.

psychologist as well as philosopher, has expressed the same thought.[1] The existence of this drive and its drive character cannot be doubted; equally, its inhibition has all the characteristics of true drive inhibition, producing the same displeasurable tensions and the same pressure to alter that state. We can even point to the fact that societies purposefully employ this striving for togetherness by institutionalizing its inhibition and utilizing the psychological effects. Thus seclusion and ostracism are in many societies sanctions for grave offences. Alternatively, the tensions arising from loneliness may be provoked and made to sustain particular required modes of behaviour, as when selected social persons— priests, rulers, visionaries, neophytes—are made to undergo periods of rigid seclusion in order that they may respond with a heightened consciousness or bring to their tasks an uncommon intensity and concentration.[2]

Yet though the drive character of the desire for togetherness is certain, its nature and its provenance from innate sources must remain dubious. For here we are clearly on dangerous ground. Some measure of physical togetherness is entailed in the very existence we call social, being simply given and habitual for every individual from earliest childhood; also, every rational mode of social action, whatever other intentions it may imply, also implies the intention to be and act with others, and to derive the expected benefits of co-activity. Loneliness thus means the repression of a habitual state as well as the deprivation of the normal and expected share in social life. The emotional response to loneliness probably cannot be reduced entirely to the rational awareness of this deprivation and loss. Yet if we derived it from the frustration of an innate need we should merely be saying that man habitually lives in the way he innately desires; which is not so very far removed from the acceptance of a 'gregarious instinct'. If I am right, and the perpetuation of habitual states also satisfies the equilibrium drive, the emotional reaction to their interruption would be accounted for without this gratuitous assumption. But 'habitual state' is a loose phrase. It implies that by some process, in some aggregate of human

[1] Thus Fromm speaks of man's 'need' to be 'related to the world outside' himself, and of the 'need to avoid loneliness'. Complete aloneness leads to 'mental disintegration', as starvation leads to physical disintegration (1942), p. 15.

[2] We note the parallel with the frustration of physiological 'needs' similarly employed (see above, p. 333).

beings, togetherness of a certain scope or intensity happened to arise and subsequently became the expected state of existence. Consequently the 'need' of togetherness, of physical contacts and propinquity, should vary widely. This is precisely what we find, and beyond this, I think, we cannot go.

3. The Limits of Psychological Understanding

Let me draw up a balance sheet. On its credit side belongs, above all, the 'genesis' (or 'emergence') of a multitude of social facts. If man is possessed of the innate action potentials we enumerated, specific or generic, then there *must* be, in society and culture, congenial occasions for their consummation. There must be occasions for pleasure and the escape from displeasure, for the realization of equilibrium or tensions, for catharsis, and for the enjoyment of conformity. The presence of institutionalized modes of action constituting such occasions is therefore accounted for; it is accounted for, more precisely, by something like a direct or *spontaneous* genesis. The 'must' in these sentences is in a sense conditional; these occasions must be offered in culture if the 'functional' effects of inhibitions are to be avoided. We cannot conceive of societies completely denying the innate demands, though all societies entail some measure of denial; but equally they exhibit, or allow for, the disturbing effects. Thus other modes of action will emerge which are symptoms of inhibitions and frustration. In this sense we may perhaps speak of a *contingent* genesis of social facts— contingent upon the presence of these frustrating modes of action.

Stated thus generally, these assertions have a purely theoretical value. We have no means of calculating the 'normal' strength of drives, nor of estimating whether, say, there is enough pleasure or excitement in social life, or how far these drives have been denied their fair measure of self-expression. Nor yet, as we know, are the symptoms of frustration unambiguous. We are, however, on safer ground when we consider the institutionalized occasions which bring the innate action potentials into play. Once such an occasion is offered, the generic drive so activated must also be assured the satisfaction peculiar to its genus. Once the pleasure impulse is built into a particular social task, say, political ambition, it must be given its chance of consummation. Once tension is shown a pathway, say, in culturally encouraged aggression, it must be allowed to run its course. This sounds like a truism—like saying that people who have been made to like liquor cannot be expected to welcome Prohibition. But precisely this sort of situation does happen. Societies constantly give with one hand what they take away with the other. They foster bellicose patriotism and preach that 'who taketh the sword shall perish by the sword'. They teach the young ambition and love for adventure and then shut them up in factories or offices which offer scope for neither. More generally speaking, societies constantly stimulate the various action potentials only to cut short their course or block their final satisfaction.[1] Here, then, where the impetus of a drive and its inhibition can be, if not measured, at least demonstrated and compared, it should be possible to trace the nexus between cause and symptom.

Let us note that here the 'contingent genesis' of social facts turns into ordinary 'linkage'. But in tracing the latter we profit little from our knowledge of the innate action potentials; rather must we rely on the assessment of mere energy levels. It might be argued that, if an action potential is stimulated but also blocked in one particular course, the society can overcome the effects by offering an equivalent satisfaction still of the same genus; in other words, pleasure inhibited would be balanced once more by pleasure, conformity frustrated would be offered some further scope, and so forth. Now where the inhibited drive and its vicarious satisfaction are linked by a clear 'thread of meaning', as is the case in overt wish-fulfilments, this kind of nexus can in fact be identified. Thus the Nupe, having made the rise to political rank a highly valued pleasure, appealing to everyone but gratified only in the case of a minority, also offer a vicarious gratification in the make-believe ranks of the young men's societies. Again, in many primitive communities, male homosexuals, who must fail to conform to the common ideal of manhood, are offered the chance of a different conformity in being allowed to dress and behave as women. Yet if the nexus of meaning is not of this obvious kind, there can be no certainty that, say, a particular pleasure does in fact represent an exchange and not merely another congenial expression of the same drive.

[1] Kardiner touches upon this point when he relates the presence or absence of stresses visible in social life to the extent to which 'the tension points . . . raised in the development of the individual' are afforded 'proper outlets' (1945, pp. 420 et passim).

Societies, as we know, overcome the effects of inhibitions also in another way, namely, by absorbing the tensions produced by the inhibitions in some appropriate action pattern, and hence by deflecting the inhibited drive into some new channel altogether. Here we are dealing fully with the conversion of energies and with the ambiguous issue of separating high energy levels due to suppression from those formed spontaneously. Our knowledge of innate action potentials enables us to reformulate the problem but not to solve it. It is now a problem of separating the 'functional' action potentials (implying tension, restlessness, aggressiveness, cathartic behaviour) from the direct and spontaneous expression of the tension drive.

We have so far assumed that societies tend to allow for and compensate the effects of inhibitions. If this is not the case, the inhibited action potentials turn into impulses without legitimate pathways, and their pent-up energies into 'free energy', flowing into general restlessness or tension, seeking random satisfaction, and finding it perhaps in the simulations of psycho-neuroses. Yet why should societies wish to prevent and forestall this free play of energies? Clearly, unless they do so in some measure they cease to be societies. Since social life is regulated life and rests upon the stability of given patterns of action, it rests also upon the existence of given pathways for the innate drives. Their erratic movements would jeopardize social existence as much as would the withdrawal of large numbers of individuals into the privacy of pathological illusions. That one or the other does happen, we know; but these are the phases of disturbance which precede some refashioning of the society, of unbalance which gives way to new stability—unless indeed they herald the very dissolution of the society.

Behind the question just asked there is another, logically antecedent one. Why should there be inhibitions? Why should the innate drives be blocked at all? The answer may seem banal. Since social existence means the ordered living-together of a multitude of individuals and the coordination of their behaviour, it surely cannot run its course without imposing some restraint upon the drives of the individuals so co-existing. But the strength of drives probably varies considerably with constitutional factors; and even if repressions and inhibitions were ubiquitous, they might yet be such that they can be overcome by the dispersed casual adjustments of individuals. We are concerned only with repressions grown to such dimensions that they will be visible in the cultural make-up. Now this will often happen owing to historical vicissitudes, to the uneven development of cultures and social structures, and to extraneous influences beyond the control of societies. But we can also point to certain potential sources of such far-reaching repressions which are implicit in the very conditions of social existence.

One such source lies in the interpenetration of the component groups which make up any society—families, clans, social classes, political factions, religious congregations, and so forth. Each is sustained by group consciousness and loyalties, that is, by energies directed towards particular pleasures and gratifications. As these component groups interpenetrate, so that the same individual acts now in one and now in the other role, so his loyalties are redirected and gratifications valid in one context are expected to give way in another, as it were on demand. Thus the family will build up emotional attachments between parents and children and husband and wife; clan solidarity, expressing itself in the segregation of clans, and perhaps in rivalry, blood revenge, and mutual suspicion, may alienate a man from his wife and mother (or father) and set him against their kin; while the closely knit life of local communities may cut across clans and families. Again, tribal loyalty will supersede both the tensions between clans and the self-containedness of local communities; while a religious sect may require its converts to forsake their families and country for a higher ideal. We spoke of this before when we predicated that the cohesion of any group entails some estrangement or hostility between groups. This is once more a matter of degree and of balances that can be worked out. But here lies, too, the danger of repressions and frustrations, which will increase with the complexity of the social system and, often, with its very efficiency. Though I was referring only to energies, emotional attachments, and gratifications, I would hold that they come ultimately from innate drives canalized into particular desires. However this may be, we have psychological 'forces' provoked as well as blocked, and led towards self-realizations which prove to be barred. We usually speak of a clash of loyalties or of conflicts of values, which is only another way of saying the same thing.

The innate drives will be blocked, further, by the rational nexus between social tasks and by the regularities or 'invariant relations' that seem to govern them. Consider that every social task is carried by mental energies and that at least many forms of this energy derive from innate action potentials. It is clear that the different action potentials do not indiscriminately fit all social tasks. Certain modes of behaviour are adequately carried only by the strong tensions of love, hate or fear, or by an intense desire for conformity reinforced by the threat of shame; think of wars, blood revenge, or a group loyalty which is to survive under pressure. Technological tasks, on the other hand, or everyday routine, are carried most efficiently by habitual manipulations of little emotional weight, by rhythmical and ordered repetition, or by the slight 'function pleasure' that goes with craftsmanship. If innate drives of this kind characterize the group engaging in such tasks, these simply become congenial cultural occasions for the expression of the drives. But we can hardly assume that this will always be so; for we hold that social tasks such as these are present in a society in virtue of some regularly recurrent and rationally intelligible nexus with other social facts. We cannot therefore assume that the innate drive will be opportunely available in just the required strength among all groups or all individuals in a group where the rational nexus happens to come into play. In other words, a society will undertake wars because it needs to expand its resources; it will institutionalize blood revenge because it possesses no effective centralized authority; it will specialize in craftsmanship because its distribution of wealth leads to a demand for 'luxuries'; and this 'invariant' interdependence may well materialize irrespective of the energy pattern the people innately possess. Perhaps this energy pattern will fail altogether to sustain the rationally required tasks. These will be executed—wars will be fought, blood revenge carried out, craftsmanship pursued—but in an uncertain and inadequate fashion. There are undoubtedly instances of this.[1] Yet if the group effectively executes the tasks, this may mean that, say, too strong a tension drive has been suppressed or one too weak over-stimulated, that is, that the innate action potentials have been constrained in some fashion.

[1] To quote two examples from anthropological literature. Of the Arapesh we are told that their utterly tension-free life gives them 'no discipline of hand or eye', so that their efforts of craftsmanship are tentative, clumsy, and readily abandoned (Margaret Mead, 1935, p. 49). The Alorese, while recognizing blood revenge as a group responsibility, yet shrink from its full implications by trying to reduce its scope and leaving its execution to the irregular initiative of individuals (C. Du Bois, 1944, pp. 126–8).

In a sense even the congenial cultural expression of the innate action potentials bears within itself some element of constraint. For this expression is once more a stable expression; and once it emerges into the sphere of social things, crystallizing in a standardized behaviour pattern, all subsequent impulses of this nature are bound as by a model that must be followed. Mostly, this is merely a matter of pathways into which the drives will readily flow, much as any style of art, once it evolves, absorbs the creative desires of artists and constrains them only imperceptibly. Yet as styles of art harden and are felt to fetter imagination, so the culturally standardized expressions of innate drives may become inadequate vehicles; for the drives fluctuate as do the creative desires of artists, and by the same laws—they fluctuate with changing events and, above all, with the amplitude of exhaustion and satiation.

Here we have turned to the debit side of our balance sheet. Our knowledge of the innate action potentials only tells us what happens when these are blocked or deflected; in order to understand why they are blocked, or why the effects of the blockage are neutralized and in a sense spirited away by culture, we must invoke such non-psychological factors as the permanence of things social and the rational requirements of social existence. Nor indeed does our knowledge of the nature of action potentials account fully for their cultural expression. The compulsion of culture to create occasions for their expression does not extend to the specific forms this genesis takes. What sort of experiences become the objects of pleasure and displeasure; when and how balance is enjoyed rather than tension; and with regard to what kinds of behaviour everyone wants to be like the next man—these questions are at least often unanswerable from the knowledge of action potentials alone. In cultural life the innate action potentials always appear harnessed to specific tasks and invested with specific references to 'objects', so that, in defining them, we must use 'object language'; yet their psychological analysis yields, with few exceptions, only broad ('generic') potentialities of acting, definable only in 'function language'—in such terms as pressures, tensions, release, balance, directions. Perhaps even 'directions' is saying too much; what we discern is directedness rather than direction, movement towards or away from goals, not the goals themselves. The directions and goals seem to be given in the form of conventions about things and rules about behaving, that is, they seem to come from an environment of objects which is always already there, with its given 'demand character'. Are we, then, back at the conception of a 'social field' in which the properties of the environment completely over-shadow the innate drives and the latter acquire their aim direction only through operating in a given social environment?[1]

Nothing in the situation warrants such a conclusion. The fact that there are conventions about the pleasing or displeasing quali-ties of things or forms of behaviour, or that groups are habituated to find excitement or serenity in different experiences, does not imply that the cultural aims are placed in random fashion into the innate drives. Rather, there is a definite 'fit' between the two, which no convention can obscure or override. It has been emphasized, in more general terms, that such a fitness obtains between all psycho-logical 'functions' and their 'material'.[2] This concept is, I think, legitimately applied to the present context, where the aims and tasks given in the culture represent the 'material' (or 'objects') of mental events, and the action potentials the psychological 'functions'. When we spoke before of 'congenial' expressions or outlets for mental energy we were referring to this 'fit' which limits random connections and combinations. Thus the drive towards peaceful enjoyment cannot be adequately expressed in hectic dances, in a bloodthirsty mythology, in the admiration for a rugged landscape, or in initiation cults prescribing a vigil in the bush, which modes of acting answer, rather, the desire for tension-fraught experiences. If I have here stated the obvious I have done so in order to point out that all conventions and cultural habits must conform to these basic and stable connections between psychological 'functions' and their 'objects'. Even so, this conformity is a broad one, and can be realized in varying ways. At any given moment the human environ-ment, physical or social, offers a vast variety of such potentialities, that is, a vast variety of congenial objects or aims upon which the innate drive might fasten. Our problem, then, is to understand their actual selection. And this we can picture only as the result of pro-cesses of 'emergence' whereby the specific experiences and satis-factions of individuals come to crystallize, for whatever reason, in the sphere of things social.

Now, 'for whatever reason' can only mean two things. It may mean, first, sheer accident—a purely fortuitous attachment of the action potentials to some 'fitting' object and to the modes of be-

---

[1] See above, pp. 308–9.   [2] F. C. Bartlett (1932), p. 290.

haviour concerned; vicissitudes of tastes and fashions certainly seem to exemplify this kind of process. But the reasons for this attachment may lie, secondly, in the fact that a particular self-expression of the action potential fits in a different sense into the framework of social things. Let me make this clear by these examples. The drive towards excitement can be expressed congenially both in hectic mass rituals and in the private ecstasies of visionary cults; in a romantic art and in age-grade life entailing strenuous competition. Now, in a society scattered geographically and internally segmented, group unity can often be maintained only through periodical gatherings of strong emotional appeal; this social necessity, then, would seem to preclude the adoption of individualistic visionary cults, which might divide the group even further, and to dictate instead the alternative of mass rituals. Again, in a tribe organized for war or some other exploits demanding physical prowess, discipline, and the selection of capable leaders, the pursuit of a romantic art would further these ends less advantageously than would an age-grade organization of the kind outlined. We therefore understand the presence in a culture of a particular mode of action— the mass ritual or the age-grade system—partly because it appears to follow from social 'necessities' or 'advantages', that is, from a nexus of means and ends; and partly because it follows from psychological requirements, namely, the self-expression of innate action potentials. If the genus of the latter circumscribes the range of possible congenial expressions in behaviour, social necessities or advantages narrow down this range. In other words, the selection of the mode of behaviour as it finally emerges into culture rests on a *convergence* between the two demands and on an *assimilation* (as I previously put it) of aim-directed drives to the aims existing in the society.

This process does not stop here. For any object and mode of action serving the self-expression of innate drives is built into a network of other objects and modes of action, bearing upon this self-expression as conditions, safeguards, or prerequisites of some kind. These may well exist in virtue of other social requirements— as do, for example, the economic factors which always enter into aesthetic or religious activities; intrinsically, these conditions or prerequisites would be neutral with regard to the innate action potentials, neither 'fitting' nor 'ill-fitting' them. But they lose their neutrality once their bearing upon the self expression of the drives is experienced and understood. This is the range of *manipulanda*—objects which are useful or not for the approach to desired satisfactions—and of modes of acting (the 'manipulations') which acquire a reflected demand character according to the way in which they help or hinder the approach.[1] They are, therefore, involved in the same process of emergence, if only as by-products, intermediate steps, and aids rationally assessed.

But consider, further, that if any innate drive is made to converge with social necessities or advantages, it is also made to 'do work' which no longer serves its intrinsic aim of self-expression alone. The mass ritual, besides offering the thrill and excitement for which the tension drive is pressing, also impresses upon the individuals the awareness of belonging together and the demands of group loyalty and morality; and these are meant to bind the individuals in all their actions, on all occasions, often against their desires of the moment. The age-grade association, besides offering chances for experiencing the desired tension in competition or in the 'function pleasure' of physical exertion, inculcates a discipline which must hold good in many other contexts and may create tensions neither desired nor anticipated. The convergence of innate desires and social requirements thus means the convergence also of self-expression and constraint; once more, then, the cultural expression of innate drives bears within itself the elements of inhibition.

I would hold that the same convergence or assimilation also enables us to understand the genesis of certain, perhaps of all, universal features of culture. Their universality comes both from the innate action potentials, ubiquitous as is man, and from the social necessities of a similarly ubiquitous order, that is, from the necessities entailed in group existence everywhere. Religion (and not only mass rituals); art and recreation of all kinds; the realm of mythology—all these are modes of action 'emerged' from the spontaneous innate demands for pleasure, tension, quiescence, catharsis, or conformity. Equally, the standardized form they assume, the way in which they become at once channels for the innate drives and occasions for their consummation, depends on the operation of social necessities.

In speaking of 'social necessities' I am anticipating, but let the phrase pass for the moment. We can now see that the environment

[1] See above, pp. 304, 308, n. 2.

of demand-invested objects in which all action takes place is not a fully alien structure, nor one that alone lends direction to the innate energies. Rather is the aim-structure of the environment a reflection of the innate drives and emerges from them. The two are correlates—and not only in the sense of directionless forces moving in the paths furnished by the 'topography' of their environment (as Lewin and Köhler would say).[1] For the 'forces' *have* directedness, which can fasten upon certain 'objects' in the environment but not upon others; and its 'topography' is such that it *fits* the directedness of the forces operating within it. Let me use a different simile. We have, not a matrix arbitrarily constructed to take the pressure of liquids, but one so shaped as to conform to the nature of the liquids, and indeed one partly shaped by them, as it were, through successive stages of hardening. Yet at any given moment there *is* the matrix; there *are* the given pathways, whose constraining character rests upon social purposes, advantages or necessities. The environment of given social tasks is thus not fully reducible to the innate drives; nor yet is it fully independent of them. It exhibits some subservience to the innate demands, as it also exhibits some autonomy.

4. DRIVES AND RATIONALITY

The 'autonomy' just referred to is that of the given rational requirements of social life and of the necessities of group existence. It represents something like the business side of culture, as against that other side made up of the expressions of the innate action potentials. The relationship between the two appears as one of concessions and surrender—concessions exacted from society by the human organism, and some surrender of self-expression exacted from the organism by society. We know that in one or the other sphere of culture the 'concessions' may amount to full acknowledgment, and that the 'surrender' may be equally complete, amounting to full suppression. Some such dualistic view seems to me inescapable, whether we speak of 'topography' and 'forces' or of the 'business side' of culture as against the 'self-expression' of

[1] I am referring to the paradigm of Gestalt Psychology, from which the Social Field Theory essentially derives. This paradigm is the nature of physical systems, in which two factors are always at work: the 'dynamic' factor, i.e. the forces existing in the system, and the 'topographical' factor, i.e. the structuring of the system, which prescribes the pathways in which the forces will move (see W. Köhler, 1947, pp. 107, 108).

action potentials. But the dichotomy is far from clear-cut and can easily be overdrawn. For one thing, it is not the dichotomy of rationality *versus* non-rationality. Although the 'business side' of culture is governed by rational requirements, these pervade also the self-expression of drives; for there we have the rational choice and assessment of *manipulanda*—of the ways and means to attain or safeguard the self-expression. Nor yet does the dichotomy refer to distinct classes of behaviour. Such a distinction is drawn by Kardiner when he contrasts 'primary' and 'secondary' institutions, the former acting as means of constraint and 'disciplines', and hence creating the 'basic and inescapable problems of adaptation', while the latter are calculated to satisfy the 'needs and tensions' so created.[1] I would speak, rather, of two 'sides' of culture and of their 'convergence'; for as I have tried to show, 'disciplines' and 'satisfactions' may often be evenly weighted in the same institutional task. But even where a social task is fully constraining, it may yet promise some gratification within its behaviour cycle or at least in one closely allied to it. The school or age grade offers pleasurable excitement and other enjoyments besides discipline; war offers adventure, some licence granted to the soldiers, and of course the prospect of peace, besides frustrations; manual labour, the thrill of craftsmanship or at least the prospect of some compensation, besides the boredom of routine. Also, what is constraint for one person may well be a gratification for another; so that there will always be those who love school life, enjoy wars, are satisfied with unvaried routine, and hence sustain these modes of behaviour by their congenial desires.

In a sense this interpenetration of two aspects is true of any single rational task. Psychological analysis shows that task consciousness starts with some felt discomfort, pressure or tension, and that the completion of the task has a distinct pleasure quality.[2] Every task, then, has some element, however weak, of self-propulsion—the attainment of that final pleasure—which becomes effective once the task can be set in motion. And this will depend on the balance between the initial discomfort and tension, from which we might merely withdraw, and the final gratification. We probably do not act like the man in the joke who runs his head into a wall to enjoy the ebbing-away of the pain. But we do undertake tasks because the

---

[1] A. Kardiner (1939), pp. 345, 474, 476.
[2] See H. Driesch (1925), pp. 35 ff.; W. Köhler (1947), p. 302.

pleasure to be gained outweighs the discomfort; or if this end-pleasure is too remote, because there is some intermediate satis-faction to be gained—reward, praise, the feeling of conformity—or a greater discomfort to be avoided—punishment, frustration, shame. Or perhaps we undertake the task because we are oppor-tunely moved by the very desire for the tension and 'function pleasure' involved in grappling with difficulties. Culture and society, which set most of the human tasks, must also solve the problem of this additional impetus; and they solve the problem in precisely this fashion.

Yet surely, this additional impetus may also come from the very rationality of the task if this is sufficiently clear to the actor? Cer-tainly, a great many rational tasks are performed upon mere verbal instruction, upon being explained and understood; and this understanding seems to command some drive quality of its own, perhaps summoned up out of an amorphous 'will' or some other store of indeterminate energies. In speaking as we were of a 'con-vergence' between rational requirements and innate action potentials we appear to have ignored or at least minimized this possibility. I will not venture to discuss its implications. If this peculiar drive quality of rationality exists, it is extremely difficult to isolate. For in a vast number of cases we act rationally (or logically) in pursuit of some innately desired satisfaction, ultimate or intermediate, so that the impetus carrying our actions would be accounted for by this innate impulse; reason and logic perhaps merely guide our search for *manipulanda* and act as 'limiting and directing agents'.[1] The elusive drive quality of rational and logical understanding would reveal its true nature only where this under-standing is sought for its own sake, that is, in the realm of idea systems ordering the universe and philosophies of some kind. Perhaps this drive does exist in its own right, over and above the action potential similarly pressing for order, consistency (or 'equilibrium'). But to account for philosophies is itself philosophy.

Only this much may be said. Where society operates with idea systems and philosophies valid, not only as theories and specula-tions, but as ethical codes and maxims for action, it does not trust to their intellectual appeal alone. For these ideas about right and wrong, good and evil, tend to be announced in the context of cere-monials and dramas, of stirring events or of words whose imagery

[1] H. Driesch (1925), p. 55.

is suggestive of such events, so that the ideas may fuse with the awareness stimulated by these contexts and occasions. In simple language, society 'advertises', with all the psychological refinement of up-to-date methods. It catches your attention through some appeal to deeply seated demands, and then presents its own demands. It does not seem to matter whether ideas so announced fall upon a phase of tension produced by repressions and inhibitions or upon one of felt satisfaction. What matters is that the maxims for action should fall upon a consciousness heightened by the play of an innate drive; the impetus which is to carry the actions is thus somehow fashioned out of that other impetus. This is not a direct conversion of energy into behaviour, as when the tensions stimulated by the beating of drums and the blaring of trumpets simply overflow into some excited way of acting. Instead, the forces at play in the act of experiencing have a more indirect and long-range effectiveness; for they seem to summon up or at least to strengthen some other force capable of turning the ideas announced into demands accepted. Perhaps we may compare this effectiveness with that of a catalyst which, by its mere presence, liberates other energies and sets other processes in motion, which would constitute a final aspect of that pervasive 'convergence'.

However this may be, there always is the 'announcement'— some form of verbal instruction or pantomimic demonstration intelligible in a rational or logical way. Without it, the energies brought into play would simply run their course and be dissipated in random fashion. Also, there must be some cognitive 'fit' between the occasion and the import of the announcement. A crowd watching an exciting game will hardly respond to the preaching of the Decalogue; but it will respond admirably to patriotic exhortations. Rational and logical understanding thus appear to act essentially as 'limiting and directing agents'; as I would say— they provide the fitting 'objects' upon which the dynamic 'functions' of the mind may fasten.

CHAPTER XIII

Function and Pattern

We had no warrant to speak of 'necessities of group existence' or of 'social advantages' in an absolute sense. For so far our approach has been essentially relativistic. We have taken Explanation to mean the search for 'invariant relations' *between* facts; we viewed society and culture essentially as systems built out of interdependent parts; we were describing something in the nature of a vast machine where, could we only fully understand it, cogwheels drive cogwheels and levers press upon levers. Now precisely this simile has been used in criticism of all approaches to culture which similarly aim at the discovery of interdependences and 'functional' relations. Thus Linton blames anthropologists of this persuasion for seeing culture only as 'a mass of gears all turning and grinding each other'—endlessly, confusingly, and presumably to no purpose.[1]

This criticism is neither quite sound nor quite fair. For one thing, such machine-like regularities are at least closely akin to the kind of knowledge natural science—and indeed all science—looks for. And, for another, no anthropologist, however much he may be wedded to the methods of natural science, is content with defining these machine-like regularities alone. Briefly, he also attempts to say what the machine is for. Nor can he do otherwise. Consider that all explanations in terms of interdependence lead from one combination of data to other, 'anterior' ones; they present us with an infinitely moving system without beginning or end, even without conspicuous centres or pivots upon which the interconnected parts revolve. This infinite interaction can be given a beginning and end only through introducing at some point or points the impetus or goal of an ulterior *purpose*, coming from without the system.[2] Physical science has no warrant to take this step; for it

[1] R. Linton, in A. Kardiner (1939), p. viii.
[2] L. T. Hobhouse (1927), p. 411.

367

would imply the mystic assumption of an intelligence behind the machine which is the universe, and a Great Engineer who conceived its design. In the study of human society such a step is neither unwarranted nor mystic. Society and culture are made and worked by man. May we not assume that they are made and operate for man? The Great Engineer is merely Man in the abstract, and the Intelligence at the back of all things social, the Human Mind writ large. These are, of course, logical constructions which we, the observers, form out of our data. This Intelligence is not in the intentions of which the actors are aware nor in the narrow-range rationality which makes them link action with action and move from event to event; at least, this Intelligence enters into their actions only in an irregular and fragmentary fashion. It is *we* who feel impelled to piece the design together, to guess at the Intelligence, and construe an ulterior Purpose. Our attempts will be successful if we can read into the social phenomena some subservience to things or states that *must* be, in other words, if we can say that social phenomena fulfil a necessary *function*. I have introduced this term since it is expedient to distinguish this ulterior purpose, construed by the observer, from the proximal purposes of intention and rationality which move the actors. We can at once see where this ulterior purpose from 'without the system' must reside. Since our subject matter is man-acting-in-society, this ulterior purpose can refer only to one of two things: to the nature of the human organism and its requirements (or 'needs'); and to the nature of society and its requirements (the 'necessities of group existence'). A few words, however, must first be said about the concept of 'function'.

1. THE FUNCTION CONCEPT

The word is as familiar as it is ambiguous. Indeed, it has been used with such varied meanings that certain scholars would discard it altogether. I do not think that this is either practicable or desirable, for we need a concept of this kind, and no better word is available. Also, a certain ambiguity in the concept is not accidental but expresses a relevant aspect of our whole enquiry. Let me, then, try and save or vindicate the term.

It seems to me that it is applied in four different ways. First, having a 'function' is used as a synonym for 'operating', 'playing a part,' or 'being active', the 'functioning' culture being contrasted with the sort of culture archaeologists or diffusionists reconstruct. This is an indifferent and redundant use, which can be disregarded. Secondly, function is made to mean non-randomness. Malinowski, especially, argued with much vigour that all social facts 'have a function' (whatever its nature) and that in culture there are no 'functionless' survivals, relics of diffusion, or other purely fortuitous accretions. Unless we take this for a philosophical axiom holding that, what is, is for a reason, we have here simply an assertion which stands or falls with its verification. For things that have a function, that is, play a part, must have consequences; more precisely, any variation in these things must be accompanied by variations in others. Now in the case of unique cultural features, at least, we cannot demonstrate co-variations, and hence cannot prove their 'functions', though we could presumably guess at them. For my part, I have seen cultural facts which are thus unique and unconnected even with imaginable consequences. So that I would discard this meaning of 'function' also. Thirdly, 'function' can be given the sense it has in physics, where it denotes an interdependence of elements which is complex, intermediate, and reciprocal, as against the simple, direct, and irreversible dependence implied in classical causality.[1] Finally, 'function' may be taken to mean the specific effectiveness of any element whereby it fulfils the requirements of the situation, that is, answers a purpose objectively defined; this is the equation of function with purpose which, since Spencer, has dominated biological thought. Both these meanings of 'function' are important, though they are again ambiguously employed.[2] Yet there is more in this usage than merely a terminological laxity which could with care be avoided; rather will one meaning tend to lead to the other.

Any statement on invariant relations between social facts is a 'functional' statement in the sense of physics; but once the invariant relations are conceptualized and defined in terms of a rational nexus, the 'reciprocal' interdependence turns into the irreversible relation between means and ends, between things having a certain utility and the conditions requiring it. This purposive relation, however, remains limited in several ways. If, for example, we discover the familiar correlation linking age-grade

---

[1] E. Mach (1920), pp. 278–9. See also above, p. 287.
[2] This was pointed out by v. Wiese (1924), p. 49.

organizations in primitive societies with a political system based on military efficiency, we interpret the former as a 'means' and the latter as an 'end' because this 'end' is present as an intentional task of the people we observe; it is present in this sense through being fitted into various other purposive chains in which military efficiency appears both as a means for further ends (e.g. war) and as an end upon which various other means converge (e.g. political leadership, the norms of morality, the themes of art and religion). The very intelligibility of the correlation depends upon this intermediate position in a network of rational relationships. Equally, the particular relation is only one in a series of possible co-variations; in other situations there might be no design for war or for military efficiency, and hence no design for the age-grade training of adolescents. The particular correlation, then, indicates a state of affairs which has a 'subjective' and contingent utility—for the actors, and in a specific situation. Here the words aim, intention, purpose state all we wish to state.

Hold against this the following 'function' formulated by Malinowski: incest taboos, and equally exogamy, have the function of eliminating the 'open working of sex' from a 'typical cooperative group'.[1] Again, at first sight, this formula may seem to bear only upon an observable interdependence and co-variation; remove exogamy (*ceteris paribus*), and the cooperative group ceases to work efficiently; strengthen exogamy, and cooperation becomes smoother and more efficient. But this correlation no longer depends upon its intermediate position in a network of interdependences. It does not link two action patterns which are themselves linked with further action patterns, but links one such pattern with a state of affairs of a general and pervasive kind, namely, social existence as such. Clearly, if the 'typical cooperative group' no longer works efficiently it ceases to be a 'cooperative' group, or indeed a group at all. Such a change can no longer be regarded as one possible variation among others; nor can the conjunction exogamy-smooth cooperation be regarded as one chosen for reasons of its utility in a particular situation. Wherever there are groups, that is, wherever there is society, a conjunction of conditions leading to smooth cooperation is the only possible variation; without it, the group would simply not be effective as a group. The 'end' of smooth cooperation must always be there, and if the observed 'means', exogamy, is absent,

[1] (1931), p. 630.

some other mode of action must be expected to take its place. The observed correlation, then, indicates an 'objective' and absolute utility, valid in all contexts and for any observer who thinks in terms of 'groups' or 'social existence'. It is here that we need the new word 'function'.

It is true that the need for fostering smooth cooperation and protecting the unity of the group may be clearly realized and expressed by the actors themselves—not perhaps by just any actors, but by those in command and those responsible for government and group organization in general. But this only means that the actor is also the observer and can judge the importance of these integrative effects. Many instances will remain where no conscious motives of this kind can be traced. Whether they are one thing or the other, the integrative effects appear conspicuously as ulterior and ubiquitous purposes. Modes of action realizing them also realize an aim which Society writ large seems to set itself—towards the full integration of groups, their stability and frictionless operation, and their undisturbed continuity. This is the 'function' concept formulated by Radcliffe-Brown. He speaks of social fact as exercising 'remote effects upon social cohesion and continuity'. The 'social function' of any cultural mode of action refers to these effects, that is, it lies in 'the relation [of the mode of action] to the existence and continuity' of social structures and in the 'contribution it makes to creating or maintaining the equilibrium of the [social] system'.[1]

2. INTEGRATION AND SURVIVAL

The phraseology referring to this aimed-at state is profuse and fluid. Cohesion, continuity, equilibrium, solidarity, integration—each of these terms is employed at one time or another. We spoke of these states as of 'necessities' of group existence; others would speak of 'forces' of integration, as though there existed something in society actively pressing for greater unity. Whichever phrase is used, it means the same thing, namely, observed processes leading to smooth and full co-adaptation of behaviour; control of frictions and conflicts; the preservation of unity. Now these are all *attributes of society as we can alone conceive it*. In calling them 'forces' or 'necessities' or 'functions' we merely translate state-

[1] (1933 a), p. x; (1940 a), p. 10; (1946), p. 40.

ments about just-so existence into statements about a goal or purpose in this existence. For society *means* cohesion, integration, and the rest, in some form or degree; inasmuch as it is not fully coherent and integrated it is society disturbed or in a 'pathological state' (which may well be overcome); and if it had no permanence and cohesion, it would not be society at all. If anyone defined anarchy in the full sense of the word as the ultimate design of human existence, this design could not be expressed in terms of society but only in terms of its negation. Thus the cultural facts said to subserve social 'necessities' or to possess an integrative 'function' are merely said to have the purpose of making society what *ex hypothesi* it must be, or making it so to a fuller degree. Society, in other words, *is* a certain thing, and *shall* be that thing, which seems to be little more than a 'glorified tautology'. Indeed this could have been predicted; for since all these statements bear on an absolute desirability, on a 'must' valid for social phenomena, they can only indicate a logical compulsion, resting ultimately on the implication of concepts and hence on tautologies of some kind.

There is no need to go over the same ground again.[1] Nor perhaps is the present tautology irreducible. To begin with, social integration is not the only absolute and ubiquitous purpose we can name, and the social facts leading towards it not the only ones which fulfil a 'function'. What we have called the innate action potentials, specific or generic, and what other writers call the 'needs' of man, equally pose purposes of such absolute validity. For if the action potentials are indeed given in the nature of the human organism so that their demands must everywhere be satisfied in one way or another, then we can say of the appropriate modes of behaviour that they have this *raison d'être* and fulfil this 'function' in the design of human culture. But we can name this 'function' more precisely. For these innate demands must be satisfied if man is to *survive*, as individual or species. Applied to certain of the specific action potentials—hunger, sex, sleep, withdrawal from noxious stimuli (the 'biological' or 'primary needs' of other writers)—this is a mere truism. But the same argument holds in the case of the more plastic, generic action potentials. The suppression of pleasure, the inability of avoiding pain, the absence of exciting stimulations or of quiescence and equilibrium, the mounting pressure of tensions which are offered no catharsis—all these states at least impair

[1] See above, pp. 251–3.

health, well-being, and normality. 'Normality' is probably always an arbitrary standard, though we cannot do without it. But in a broad sense it can be based upon the same argument of survival; for normality, whatever else it may mean, clearly also means the conditions which aid survival.

We have, then, two sets of 'functions'—the fulfilment of the necessities of group existence, and the fulfilment of biological and psycho-physical necessities. Their compulsion is logically not of the same order. In the first case we argue—there is society; and in forming that concept we posit the presence of group integration. In the second case we argue—there is the human organism; and we know empirically (more or less accurately) that it requires the satisfaction of certain needs. But for the purpose of this discussion we may take the two sets of functions to be evenly matched. Equally, they hang together. For it can be argued, and has frequently been argued, that the satisfaction of the given needs of any human being is facilitated or rendered possible by his existence in that ordered togetherness we call society. Society, then, has a survival value; man improves his chances of survival through living in society. Indeed, it is tempting to say that society must be if man in the collectivity is to survive.

There is a certain speciousness in this argument. If ordered group existence aids survival, it also presupposes it; for we cannot conceive of groups existing here and now save as a result of continued human reproduction and hence survival. Nor can we deny that existence in society also leads to constraint, inhibitions, and deprivations, that is, to states impairing the chances of survival, and even to the outright denial of these chances—as in conquests, wars, and mutual destruction. 'Survival' represents only an ultimate balance drawn from the narrow viewpoint in time and space which we happen to occupy. All we can say is that man has survived up to this moment and probably will survive for another span of time, living in society and perhaps because of that. But we have no empirical test to prove this last point, for this would mean showing that man living in ordered togetherness managed to survive while man living in unordered multitudes (which simply do not occur) has not survived. Yet this much can be said. Every society implies in its conscious and intentional self-organization the prospect of survival. People, groups, societies do not merely survive in fact, but *wish* and *plan* to survive, whether this design is expressed in principles of grouping based on the biological continuity of descent, in practical efforts at self-preservation, or in speculations about existence in the beyond. In this sense, I think, we may legitimately say that societies are designed for human survival and guarantee it—in the only manner in which we can judge such a guarantee.

We have thus resolved our original tautology by pushing the ultimate datum of social existence a stage further back. Instead of saying: Certain human activities have the purpose or 'function' of making society possible, we now say: Society has the purpose or 'function' of making human survival possible. In taking this step we simplify the whole picture of culture and society. We reduce the two classes of 'function'—social integration, and satisfaction of innate 'needs'—to a common denominator. And we also subsume the two dimensions of social existence from which we started under one principle. The dimension of action and culture, ordered in the sense of purpose, and the dimension of relationships and society, ordered in the sense of 'positional qualities' (or 'structure'), can now be seen to belong to a unitary universe, ordered in the sense of that ultimate purpose—survival.

I take survival to be such an ultimate, given purpose. Its import of course extends beyond the province of social existence, to living matter of all forms. For life, wherever it occurs, occurs also with the tendency of continuing. Biology can demonstrate the mechanisms —adaptation, selection, evolution—through which that tendency operates, so that survival must be understood to be inherent in life itself. Society, as an organization of human beings, is one road to survival. That it rather than another (which we cannot picture) was taken at some point of evolution is a final fact not further reducible. But once society exists, it exists teleologically, orientated towards that end.

Clearly, the concept of 'function' has radically altered the picture of an infinitely moving social universe, without beginning and end, and filled with a vast, shapeless aggregate of interconnected parts—the 'gears grinding gears' of our quotation. The social universe as we now perceive it has a beginning and end, or better, it possesses conspicuous foci upon which all the interconnected parts are oriented and where all movement ultimately converges. The interrelations which fill the social universe appear no longer unordered and of equal relevance; for as they can be seen to subserve more or less fully one or the other function, so they are seen to be more or less directly or importantly involved in the vital movements of this universe. The functions, then, serve as criteria of order and relevance. But this order and relevance bears on the social universe and not on any narrower province of social enquiry. The subservience of social facts to these ulterior purposes or 'functions' belongs to the most general concepts we can form. In knowing the functions we reach the limits of our understanding. Yet it is mostly upon a lesser plane and within these limits that all the really important and interesting things happen. Cultures are much richer and more complex than can be shown by exhibiting them merely as realizations of functions. Thus, to invoke in the analysis of a concrete culture only these limits; to pronounce at once upon the ultimate functions subserved by social facts, is to short-circuit explanation and to reduce it to generalities which, so prematurely stated, have little significance. The bare statements that, say, exogamy aids cooperation; that myths provide a charter for conduct; or that religion contributes towards maintaining the social equilibrium, make sense only if we wish to speak about human society writ large; otherwise they are about as informative as the description of a steam engine as an instance of the conservation of energy.

The function concept, predicating certain absolute requirements —the integration of societies and the survival of populations— permits us to assess concrete social facts against these requirements. Without it, we could not legitimately speak of adjustment or mal-adjustment, that is, invoke a criterion of adequacy. But there is mal-adjustment as well as adjustment; the function concept only poses the question of adequacy but does not settle it beforehand. Only of society in the abstract can we say that it is integrated, and only of culture at large, that it leads to survival. Concrete societies weaken, disintegrate, or show symptoms of 'social pathology'; and concrete cultures may be full of frustrations and threats to survival. In their analysis, then, subservience to function means an attempted, varying, and often problematic adequacy. 'Functionalist' anthropology is apt to lose sight of this corollary and to speak about social facts 'having' such-and-such 'functions' as though these were self-sufficient truths. Yet if we simply aimed to show that exogamy facilitates cooperation, myths buttress codes of behaviour, and religion helps towards social equilibrium, we should be implying that these modes of behaviour fulfil the given necessities (under the given conditions) in the most adequate manner possible, and that any society having exogamy and the rest is to that extent an ideal society. Clearly, such a presumption of adequacy cannot be defended.

It might, however, be asked if the ascription even of an attempted and blundering adequacy must not sometimes fail, so that certain social modes of behaviour would appear to subserve no function at all and to be purely negative if not destructive. I doubt if this is often true, although modes of behaviour thrown up by psycho-physical mechanisms, such as reactions to frustration, may give that impression. Waves of suicide are certainly an exception; but witchcraft beliefs, for example, or exaggerated aggressiveness, while expressing fears and frustrations also relieve these tensions in a cathartic manner (through witch-hunts and the like), and so satisfy a 'need'. Let us emphasize that they do so inadequately, securing no lasting relief as well as disturbing social unity and stability.

I am speaking with some hesitation; for I am not certain how far our methodological standpoint does not prejudge the issue. Since we hold that the ulterior purposes of social integration and physical survival represent principles of explanation, we shall clearly search for evidence of this nature, if only in the form of that attempted and blundering adequacy with which peoples and cultures may endeavour to realize these purposes. If we found that a wide range of social phenomena could not be seen in this light, that is, that numerous modes of behaviour come into being and are maintained in mere futility and destructiveness, this would mean that these states of affairs are beyond the kind of understanding we aim at. Thus, in doubting the frequency of such negative instances I might merely be expressing my feeling or faith that we can indeed understand and explain. There is no reason why this should be so. But since we set out to understand, in whatever manner, I suspect that we should·not be content with merely accepting our failure; rather should we attempt to revise our categories of explanation. Yet there are no others—unless indeed we make this very futility and negativeness sound convincing and take them to indicate some self-destructive force or goal, such as Freud's 'death instinct' or Schopenhauer's cosmic Will. And if our own view savours of some tacit optimism, these other views betray the opposite presumption.

To be sure, 'from a scientific point of view, optimism and pessimism are alike objectionable: optimism assumes, or attempts to prove, that the universe exists to please us, and pessimism that it exists to displease us. Scientifically, there is no evidence that it is concerned with us either one way or the other.'[1] But though this is true of the physical universe, it cannot apply to the realm of human behaviour and creation, which, it seems to me, cannot be conceived of without some such 'concern'. So that in this realm there is no middle path.

Now, when I referred to the 'inadequate' realization of functions I meant two things: first, simple unsuccess, for whatever reason, in achieving the required task; and secondly, success in the given task, which would yet cause failures or frustrations in others. (The examples of witchcraft and aggressiveness quoted above imply both kinds of inadequacy.) In other words, the fulfilment of one function may interfere with that of another. Think of a society preoccupied with the acquisition of titles and the wasteful display of wealth for the sake of prestige, even at the risk of insecure subsistence. If we spoke of 'functions' pure and simple we could only draw some such picture as this: Here the people derive pleasurable excitement from intensive competition and perhaps achieve social integration by the same means; and there they till the soil and expend efforts for the sake of such subsistence as they can secure. But surely we wish to say more than merely that each mode of behaviour has its utility; we wish to say that the people buy their pleasures and integration *at a price*.

Here, however, we meet with a further difficulty. We are now implying that the importance which particular modes of behaviour assume in concrete societies can be all wrong; that certain pleasures are indulged in and certain effects achieved at the expense of more vital things; and that the various functions have a graded urgency which may be belied by actual behaviour. But can we really construct such an objective scale of urgency? In extreme cases, when a particular requirement of social or biological existence remains conspicuously unfulfilled, we can argue in this manner. For we always operate with a standard of normality, however arbitrary, by which famines, neuroses, internal conflicts, and the like, amount to instances of such failures. Yet beyond this *ad hoc* assessment of extremes we have no criterion whereby to judge the relative

[1] Bertrand Russell (1946), pp. 786–7.

relevance which the various functions ought to assume in an ideal or 'normal' society. We may occasionally think, though we should not venture to say it in so many words, that subsistence needs are the most important; the needs of sex less so; and pleasure or the other 'psychological' needs less important still; while social integration belongs to a different scale altogether. Clearly, the relevance of the various functions is of an indiscriminate kind; they simply should all be fulfilled in some balanced manner. But 'balanced' suggests some such concept as the *sophrosyne* of Greek ethics; while 'should' is once more a word meaningful only for an enquirer viewing human culture and society from the widest philosophical perspective. For the people themselves, who in any given society overweight (as we should say) their desires, the game is probably worth the candle; or they may have no conception of a price paid and a loss incurred.

We are, it seems, between the devil and the deep sea. If we do not employ the function concept we cannot speak of adjustment; yet if we employ it, we must be prepared to judge by ultimate values. My point is that we always do judge cultures and societies in some such fashion; let us at least be clear that we philosophize and dabble in ethics, and admit where we do so.

The question of the primacy of particular needs or functions can, however, be attacked from a different angle; for it might be argued that certain needs are more basic than others in a genetic or causal sense. Culture, crudely speaking, would begin there, and grow and change from these centres. Such is Malinowski's hierarchy of needs, in which the satisfaction of the 'primary', biological, needs sets the foundation of culture, while all other social aims correspond to 'derived needs' or 'imperatives'. The biological needs (of which there seem to be seven) thus cause certain modes of behaviour to arise which are concerned with 'solving the primary problems of human beings'; and the manner of this solution, that is, the 'cultural satisfaction of biological needs', creates new needs, now concerned with maintaining the efficiency of this solution or correcting its shortcomings. So that 'these new needs impose upon man and society a secondary determinism', accounting for law, political control, 'social contract', education, religion, and so forth.[1]

---

[1] B. Malinowski (1944), pp. 73–8 et passim. The seven biological needs, which I will quote without comment, are: metabolism, reproduction, bodily comforts, safety, movement, growth, and health (p. 90).

Surely, this sweeping schema is only another, though non-ethical, philosophy of culture; at least, only as a philosophy—and with certain corrections—is it defensible: as a frame of reference applicable to concrete societies, it must fail. The corrections, incidentally, are weighty ones. They would apply to the equation of the 'basic' needs with biological necessities to the exclusion of the other psycho-physical drives; to the meaningless assumption that existence in groups (which is simply given) is only one of the means for solving the 'primary problems', and social organization one of the 'derived needs'; and finally, to the presumption of adequacy which pervades Malinowski's system.

More convincingly, the primacy of subsistence needs is upheld in the materialist theory of history. For here there is no presumption of adequacy; rather are conflict and maladjustment regarded as the moving impulses in human history. And the subsistence needs are understood to operate, not *in vacuo*, but always already in a particular type of society and through its organization. Thus material production and the control of resources are marked off as of basic relevance in the make-up of societies; they are the *fons et origo* of all cultural developments—the 'basis' acting upon and determining a 'superstructure' which embraces all other modes of thought and action. To understand the latter is to understand their dependence upon the given methods of production and hence, ultimately, upon social activities bearing on that crucial purpose—subsistence. I would not venture to deny the truth, or the great measure of truth, in this conception. But it is valid, once more, only in a general sense and for an all-embracing perspective. Bertrand Russell seems to mean the same when he says that 'social causation [as implicit in the Marxian doctrine] ceases to apply as soon as a problem becomes detailed and technical'.[1] Perhaps we may put it this way. The truth of the materialist conception of history cannot readily be translated into the specific grading of relevance characterizing this or that society; for in any given society the network of determinants is much more complicated and the scale of urgency more varied; and in this or that society it is simply not true that the 'productive forces' are the only 'real' or 'final' causes, or that —more crudely expressed—'men must first of all eat, drink, dress, and find shelter before they can embrace politics, science, art, religion, and anything else. . . .'[2]

[1] Bertrand Russell (1946), p. 813.   [2] From Engels' funeral oration for Marx.

If I am right, we are left with a multiple polarity—with a number of ultimate purposes or functions upon which, as we know in the abstract, all modes of behaviour must converge, but whose relative relevance in concrete societies we cannot predict. This relative relevance is visible in the graded emphases which a culture assigns to its various aims and tasks. And this relief map of aims is in turn only visible if we view cultures as wholes. The concept of functions shows us the foci of society and culture writ large; in order to define the foci in any given society or culture we need a new concept—that of a cultural (or social) totality.

With this concept we are as yet unequipped to deal. We have so far been concerned only with regularities and forms of inter-dependence between social facts wherever they occur, without considering the total forms or shapes of cultures. We have, as it were, practised social anatomy rather than social morphology. If we now turn to the latter we do so also for another reason. It is clearly important to know whether the combinations into which these regularities and interrelations may enter in diverse cultures are of an infinite variety, or limited and repetitive, falling into distinct types. In other words, we now ask whether the regularities or laws holding for the component facts of culture are not subject to further laws—laws of combination, as it were. A social morpho-logy or typology need not, of course, concern itself with such total combinations alone; we could, for example, search for the different types of political organizations, legal systems, kinship structures, religions, and so forth. Indeed, at the moment the attempt to construct a morphology of total cultures may well be incapable of achievement. But it is legitimate to examine the problems involved in such attempts; and this I propose to do in the sections that follow.

3. THE TOTALITY OF CULTURE

Let me say by way of introduction that in speaking of a totality of culture I include to some extent the phenomena which should, more accurately, be assigned to the dimension of Society. Only where these require special recognition shall I refer to them speci-fically as 'social structure' or as 'organizing principles' pervading a social system.

Now, at the very start of our enquiry we come upon a question which it is extremely difficult to answer; I am referring to the meaning that should be given to such phrases as 'a culture', or 'total culture', or 'culture as a whole'.[1] We hardly know how to begin if we are asked to point to an assembly of modes of action forming an unequivocal totality, neither more nor less, and clearly separated from other totalities of this kind. In a sense the concept of a cultural totality can have no precise meaning at all; we cannot observe absolutely everything, but only what, by the criteria of relevance we bring to bear (tacitly or overtly), we believe to be 'everything'. But let this pass; even with this precaution considerable difficulties remain. For there seem to be two different ways of arriving at such totalities, which do not lead to the same results. Obviously, when speaking of any total assembly of facts which is separable from other such assemblies we visualize a situation in which we can put a ring round the data in question. There must be boundaries: either the boundaries constituted by some extraneous enclosure—as when frames separate (identical or dissimilar) pictures; or the boundaries resulting from the patterned arrangement of the data, that is, from its intrinsic closure and wholeness— as when a geometrical figure is set off against a background. We commonly employ both criteria at once. We speak of the culture of a people or society, taking the extent of the group to be the 'frame' enclosing our assembly of cultural data; and we also hold that such cultures are not amorphous or random arrays of items, but unitary patterns of some kind, internally ordered and externally 'whole'.

Unhappily neither 'people' nor 'pattern' has an unequivocal meaning. About the former concept we need say little. We have discussed the criteria for defining a 'people' or 'society', which proved to be ambiguous and to some extent arbitrary. Only in the case of small homogeneous groups, sharply segregated from others by barriers to intercourse of some kind, shall we find it easy to link a 'total culture' with a clear-cut 'society' or 'people'. Elsewhere we shall find groups of varying span co-existing within a widest group, and 'quasi-groups' extending beyond that boundary. Not all will be 'peoples' by the criteria we normally apply; they may only be social classes, strata, sub-tribes, populations of districts, and so forth.

---

[1] 'Although the term *a culture* has been used for many years to designate the way of life of a particular society, its exact meaning in terms of content is still vague at certain points' (R. Linton, 1947, p. 20). Many of the arguments put forth in this discussion correspond closely to Linton's masterly analysis.

2 B

But they may exhibit diverse assemblies of modes of behaviour, that is, appear as the carriers of varying cultures, and hence provide the 'frames' we are looking for. Each assembly of modes of behaviour can clearly serve as a starting point in our search for forms or types of culture. In other words, there will be a peasant culture and the culture of the aristocracy in a stratified society; the cultures of provinces, towns, or ethnic segments in a heterogeneous State. And we could compare each of these component cultures with other similar ones, though we may note that the respective groups need not be of equivalent span. For example, we could compare the peasant culture of the subject population in a conquest State with the similar culture of an autonomous peasant community. Furthermore, the very heterogeneity of a culture found in a group of widest span, say, in a stratified society, constitutes itself a particular kind of totality, which we can again classify as a type and compare with others. To sum up, we have, not one clearly marked off 'totality' of culture, but a hierarchy of relatively 'total' cultures, corresponding to the hierarchy in the span of groupings.

We turn to the second definition of a 'total' culture, in terms of its unitary pattern and wholeness. There has been much talk in certain schools of psychology, biology, and sociology about 'wholes' which are 'more than the sum-total of their parts'.[1] About a decade ago this theme was taken up by anthropologists, who saw in the search for the total 'configuration' of cultures a problem in its own right and a new approach to social understanding.[2] Let me begin at the beginning, that is, with the psychological proposition that the whole is more than its parts. Shorn of its metaphysical fringes this statement means, in brief, that certain perceptual arrangements of elements are as such productive of a novel, unitary quality, not found in the elements considered apart or grouped differently. The particular character of this unity or wholeness thus comes from the interrelation of the parts and not from anything they singly contribute. To quote a familiar paradigm, a succession of tones is per-

---

[1] The psychology in question is the Gestalt school of Köhler, Wertheimer, Koffka and others. Among sociologists Talcott Parsons speaks in the same sense of the 'organicism of action systems' (1937), p. 749.

[2] See Ruth Benedict (1935); Margaret Mead (1935); G. Bateson (1936). Cf. this statement by Linton: '. . . cultures and societies are all configurations in which the patterning and organization of the whole is more important than any of the component parts' (1947), p. 3. For a critique of this 'configurational' approach to culture see my article (1937 a).

ceived as a coherent melody, and a combination of dots as a square or a circle; that is, we register a 'pattern' or *gestalt*, not an aggregate of added-up sensations; we register a 'whole' closed and segregated from its environment. When we apprehend a figure against a background, see a coherent movement or gesture, are aware of the style of a work of art, or understand the meaning of a set of signs, visual or auditory, the same process is at work. Undoubtedly, society and culture as we understand the terms seem to exhibit something like this wholeness, or to exhibit it to some degree. Indeed, when we think of societies, this is merely a tautology; for unless there is some embracing co-activity, that is, some perceptible 'organization of the whole' to which the 'component parts' are subordinated, we could not speak of a society. But there is some danger in simply adopting the concept of a pattern or *gestalt* in the study of cultures. I can see two difficulties.

The first refers to a verbal confusion. If I speak of 'culture', or 'one culture', I may be tempted to believe that, to the simple noun, must correspond a simple thing. I should then equate a culture, *ex definitione*, with a *gestalt* or some unitary entity of this kind. Many anthropologists seem to proceed in this manner. It is useless to argue about matters of definition, which cannot be proved true or false. If I remonstrated that I know of cultures which do not exhibit a unitary pattern, those who accept the other definition would simply say, with Sapir, that these were not 'genuine' cultures at all (see below, p. 391); and if I were to point out that a modern European society, say, England, though surely possessing a culture, does not possess it in the form of a unitary whole, my opponents might say that here we are dealing, not with a single culture, but with a mixture of several cultures.

Let me, then, repeat that when I speak of a total culture I merely mean the assembly of modes of action occurring within a group of given span, and such a relative definition cannot predicate anything about a single unitary pattern that must be found. On the contrary, since we are thinking of a hierarchy of relatively total cultures, we imply that at least the cultures of wider and widest span may show some looseness and lack of unity. True it is that we think of the component parts of any culture—that is, of the various modes of behaviour—as hanging together and being interrelated; so far as these interrelations extend, something in the nature of a pattern will extend also, since by 'pattern' we mean such interrelations. But whether or not they fill the whole of a culture (of any span) cannot be decided beforehand. Nor must we lose sight of the condition óf social understanding laying down that relations between modes of behaviour are meaningful only if the latter can be shown to 'come into contact through minds'.[1] At least in large and complex societies the 'total culture' will often fail to satisfy this condition. Such societies may well include certain aggregates of individuals which are not involved in the same activities, do not influence each other, or do not stand under the same influence. More precisely, they need be involved only in one embracing co-activity, namely, that which makes the society a society (and which is mostly political). But in other sectors of cultural life these aggregates may represent separate, disconnected groups, and to construe some 'pattern' or 'wholeness' uniting them all will simply make no sense. An aloof and self-recruiting ruling class which cultivates polite ideals and a serene philosophy of life, and a *misera plebs* given to hectic enjoyments or religious beliefs fraught with tensions and fears, do not add up even to a 'disoriented pattern' or 'ethos' (if I may anticipate these terms); they constitute two disparate 'patterns' or 'ethoses' co-existing in the same culture.

The second difficulty concerns the particular method of social enquiry. In psychology the novel quality of 'wholeness' is entailed in the process of perception, or apprehension in general, and indicates a spontaneous organization of the perceptual field. The *gestalt* is not built up out of primarily given elements; rather does it come before analysis, and is in fact destroyed by it. In the social field precisely the opposite is true. If the unitary character of cultures and societies means anything at all, and more than an impressionist picture gained by the observer, it means the outcome of understanding. It is not simply entailed in our apprehension of the given material; the unitary character emerges from our search for an organization existing in the material and from our discovery of significant relations between the component parts. In other words, we analyze first, and build up the 'whole' as a result.

Yet if the unitary character of societies and cultures is the outcome of analysis and understanding, it must conform to the rules governing social understanding. This rests, as we remember, on three kinds of categories—rational purpose, psycho-physical causality, and logical connection. The 'unitary character' can thus

[1] See above, pp. 256, 320.

be named the integration of purposes; a pattern of psychological nature; and a pattern of logical consistency. This is, to begin with, a heuristic division; for it is clear that the three 'unities' will prove to be interrelated. But their interrelation is complicated and partly ambiguous, and follows no simple formula.

4. PATTERN FORMATIONS

The phrase 'integration of purposes' stands for the widest interlocking of means-to-end relations traceable in any given culture. In tracing it we should be describing the multiple interrelation of institutions which we discussed in an earlier context; we should view modes of behaviour as 'operative' and 'regulative' respectively, buttressing and controlling each other, serving as 'instrumentalities', facilitating each other's effectiveness, or reflecting each other's aim contents. The smaller a society and the less differentiated its culture, the more compact and comprehensive will be this network. In a small, homogeneous primitive community the whole culture may well come near to being 'uni-focal' and to converging upon one dominant aim. Think of a primitive hunting community living close to the subsistence level. The method of livelihood will clearly determine the division of labour and hence to some extent the whole group organization; there will be a machinery to provide and renew the team of primary producers; this will be reflected in the training of adolescents and in the standards of morality extolling virility, skill, and courage. Legal rules will govern access to the corporate resources or the distribution of the game secured by communal enterprise. Political mechanisms, kinship obligations, or other rules of mutual assistance will aim at safeguarding co-operation. Religious beliefs will reflect the all-pervading interest and anxiety of the people; there may be special rituals to provoke the tension that is to flow into readiness for adventure or to promise certainty of success, and myths or quasi-rational constructions may build up a congenial picture of the universe. Finally, the concern with hunting will be dramatized in dances and feasts, and the same theme will assume aesthetic value and pervade stories and legends. We might, with John Dewey, speak of a 'hunting psychosis as a mental pattern', and conclude, more generally: 'So fundamental and pervasive is the group of occupational activities that it affords the schema or pattern of the structural organization of mental traits. Occupation integrates special elements into a functional whole.'[1]

Much the same outline could be drawn for peasant communities, warlike tribes, cattle-owning peoples, and the rest, though, as we have stressed, a similar compactness would be true only of relatively simple societies. Yet even there such a general description will have to include many 'may's' and 'either-or's'; clearly, the embracing unity of purpose admits of certain alternative solutions, and there is some latitude in the way in which the nexus of means-and-ends is formed. Equally, as we know, there will be shortcomings in this interlocking of purposes—the choice of inadequate means, the choice of ends which conflict with each other, and the consequences of such failures, above all, correctives and the buttressing of weak points. All this, of course, is true only from the viewpoint of the observer who, from general knowledge or from the comparison of different societies, will regard solutions other than those adopted in a particular culture as equally feasible or as more adequate. For the people themselves, the particular solutions are often just there, as part of a heritage not normally questioned.

These given solutions might be traced further if we could sufficiently widen our scope of enquiry. For they may be determined by extraneous conditions, such as the presence of neighbouring groups with which relationships of one kind or other have to be established; by the rise or fall in the size of populations, and hence by the problems of social integration; by accidents of success or failure which cause one mode of action rather than another to harden into an institution; and by other 'historical accidents'. Equally, the given solutions will reflect the 'convergence' of rational requirements and psychological mechanisms, which point we may for the moment disregard.

Viewed genetically, the 'integration of purposes' must mean the successive emergence of modes of behaviour bearing upon each other as means and ends. A particular activity entails another as its (more or less) adequate means, and this becomes in turn an end for a further instrumental, or in some other way prerequisite, activity. Also, any effect achieved by one activity will add to the pre-existing means-to-end relations or modify them; thus success in a new enterprise may add to or change the pre-existing interests and values, and failure of a customary enterprise will entail some re-

---

[1] J. Dewey (1931), p. 176.

organization of efforts, if only to buttress the old values. This is, in essence, Wilhelm Wundt's Heterogony of Ends, which seems to me a still useful concept if we disregard its evolutionary implications.[1] For it corrects the slight presumption of adequacy which goes with the word 'integration'. And it also emphasizes the fluidity and the dynamic character of this integration of purposes, which is constantly 'becoming' and never final.

At any given moment, however, the visible interlocking of purposes exhibits a structure, a given order of importance. We constantly speak of 'dominant purposes' and 'paramount interests' typical of a culture or society. By which we mean that a great many of the activities existing in the society converge upon a particular aim and are linked with its realization by firm co-variations. And if its importance is correctly assessed, then, whichever point we start from, most roads will lead to Rome. In a society like our paradigm, which lives close to the subsistence level, the methods of production may well prove to be Rome. In others, there will be other focal points and perhaps several of them.

Even so, the heterogony of ends does not pervade or account for the total culture. The interlocking of means and ends stops somewhere; and though indeed we may have started from some basic group of activities, it will not lead us to all others. The 'hunting psychosis' of our example has no bearing, say, upon belief in a High God rather than in a multitude of deities; upon the methods of reckoning descent through the father, mother, or both; upon the permanence of marriage; or upon the styles of dances or music. And if, conversely, we started from these other sectors of culture, we should not necessarily be led towards the paramount occupational interests. How far the unity of purpose will be found to extend cannot be decided on general grounds. But always there will be some looseness and some separateness between the sectors of culture.

To turn to the other forms of unity—the psychological and logical 'patterns'. I take the former to be defined by the levels of energy and by the efficacy of action potentials; the latter, by the reduplication of 'motifs' and ideas, and by the diffusion of organizing principles. Now it is upon these two aspects that the anthropological theories of 'culture patterns' essentially revolve, though they imply more than the schematic kind of unity that can alone be derived from

[1] W. Wundt (1902), pp. 370–1.

energy patterns or the play of logical consistency. But if these theories draw a richer and less abstract picture they also, it seems to me, overstate the wholeness of culture or misread its nature.

The theory of Culture Patterns has a mixed ancestry. It subscribes to the tenet of Gestalt psychology that the 'whole is more than its parts'; it draws on such popular conceptions as the 'spirit of the times' or the 'genius' of a people or civilization; it also harks back to Nietzsche's early philosophy and the German 'verstehend Psychologie'; and it claims some kinship with the theories of personality. The key concepts of the theory are 'configuration' and 'dominant trends'. Cultures exhibit configuration through integrating their various modes of action in a firm and coherent manner. For the observer, this is visible in the 'characteristic purposes' which exist in a culture and in the typical attitudes evinced by the people, their leanings and ideals, their preferences and idiosyncrasies. These differ widely from culture to culture. But in each they constitute a limited number of motives, consistent among themselves, to which all behaviour is subordinated. The numerous standardized tasks, then, which make up a culture hang together in this way: their nature is such that they express, or fit, certain 'unconscious canons of choice' and not others, and hence some pervasive dominant trend. For it is argued that any culture, in order to be adequate to the ordinary and universal problems of life, has a wide variety of possible courses of action to choose from, as a language may operate with all manners of sounds or principles of word formation. But as any given language utilizes only a selection of these, and operates consistently with this solution, so cultures select; they utilize only a few of the possible courses of action, making them into 'themes' for consistent 'elaboration', and disregard others. It is thus that any culture comes to form, not a miscellany of ways of acting, but a 'more or less consistent pattern of thought and action'.[1]

This search for dominant trends can be carried to varying lengths. One might, for example, stop at the mere selectiveness of cultures and link their varying collections of 'themes' directly with so many tendencies governing the minds of individuals. Thus Bartlett sees in the particular interests exhibited by a group the expression of 'tendencies ... which give the group a bias in its dealings with external circumstances'. Take mythology, one such

[1] Ruth Benedict, op. cit., pp. 16–17, 33–4, 171.

way of dealing with external circumstances. In one group myth centres upon the theme of greed, in another upon sex, in a third upon boasting. Each theme selected is thus a bias expressed; and to the selectiveness of the culture corresponds, psychologically, an 'organized cluster of preferred persistent tendencies'.[1]

But we could also, with Dr. Benedict, press our analysis further, through the whole field of culture and to some more fundamental motive behind this seeming arbitrariness. Obviously, the mere selectiveness of cultures has limits. A people may conceivably adopt boasting, democracy, or war, or reject these ways of acting, as its 'dominant trend' demands. But certain modes of action are not merely available for acceptance or rejection; they occur always, as do productive techniques, or the control of resources, or religious observances of some kind. Here, then, the culture no longer selects its themes, but varies their treatment; or, if we still speak of selection, this concerns, not the action complexes as such, but their modality. And this may be seen to extend through the entire range of actions, each being given a uniform emphasis or orientation. In other words, we are led beyond the cluster of 'biases', towards one all-pervading bias. Thus production may be fiercely competitive; the protection of resources rigorous and aggressive; religious observances, intense, ecstatic, and violent. Alternatively, production may be leisurely and cooperative; the protection of resources amiable and lenient; religious observances, mild and peaceful. This juxtaposition is not accidental; for Benedict's patterns essentially reduce themselves to two, corresponding to the dichotomy which Nietzsche saw in the genius of Greece. Culture, like the Greek tragedy, is either Dionysian or Apollonian. Human civilization, it seems, has only these two ways of self-fulfilment.

This appears to be only another way of describing the two even levels of energy which we have formulated—excitement and tension, against serenity and quiescence. But let me note these points of divergence between the pattern theory and my approach. First, I have regarded the energy levels as 'ideal types' which, in the concrete case, are met with only in approximations. And by this I meant more than the existence of 'deviant' individuals (which the exponents of the pattern theory fully admit), namely, an incompleteness in the 'pattern' itself—which view is argued elsewhere.[2]

[1] F. C. Bartlett (1932), pp. 255, 257.
[2] See above, p. 321.

Secondly, the students of culture patterns tend to regard them as just-so existing, and on the whole as permanent and unalterable. Indeed, the basic mental orientations and the dichotomous tenor of life are said to show their persistence in the reaction of groups to extraneous changes and contrasts, when the unitary pattern is maintained and new cultural items are adopted selectively or remodelled. This cannot, I think, be accepted as a general principle. There are too many instances of groups changing their whole tenor of life either through accepting a new religion or morality, expressive of a diverse 'genius', or through some change from within. Think of the spread of Buddhism or Christianity; of the fervent mysticism of Islam taking root in the Sudan, in tribes which had nothing of the kind before, and culminating in the frenzy of Mahdism; or of the spreading of political systems based on intense ambition and class consciousness to homogeneous peasant communities in West Africa, whose social life had been governed by smooth cooperation. As regards the change from within, I have suggested that the ambivalent drive towards equilibrium and tension may operate as a pendulum swing set in motion by exhaustion or satiation; so that the tenor of life visible at any stage in the cultural history of a people would only represent one phase in a cyclical process. Perhaps the two kinds of change hang together, the reaction to external events being determined by some inner 'readiness'. Yet equally such changes may reflect the process of 'syntonization'. The disappearance of a spirit of adventure among people who grow accustomed to wealth and comfort is one example; another, the sudden destruction of economic or political security, which causes tensions and violent reactions to spread throughout the modes of behaviour.[1]

The exponents of the pattern theory do not deny that cultures may change, especially in response to extraneous influences, in a manner contradicting their dominant trends. But this means cultures 'disoriented', marginal cases, cultures that are not truly cultures.[2] This brings me to my third point. We need not again

---

[1] Linton-Kardiner describe a change of this kind among the Tanala of Madagascar (1939), pp. 251–90; (1945), pp. 42, 418.

[2] Ruth Benedict (1935), pp. 161–3. Dr. Benedict, however, considers that this disorientation may only be a passing phase, or, indeed, that it may be 'the description of the culture which is disoriented rather than the culture itself' (p. 164). I feel that the opposite danger, too strong a pattern-consciousness of the observer, is at least as real.

argue the fallacy of identifying 'culture' with 'integrated whole' in this preemptive manner. But let me point out that the uneven levels of energy and the whole interplay of frustrations and compensation from which they may result have no place in the pattern theory. At least, they have no legitimate place; for situations of this kind are taken to mean, not another kind of pattern, but a true pattern disrupted. This view is expressed most sharply in Sapir's distinction of 'genuine' and 'spurious' cultures. In the former the complex of attitudes, views of life, and values, which make up the 'national genius' is 'inherently harmonious, balanced, self-satisfactory'; while this genius cannot express itself as happily in the 'spurious' cultures, which are full of 'spiritual frustration'.[1] The refusal to speak of the 'genius' of a culture unless its dominant trends are 'harmonious' and 'self-satisfactory' may be arguable; but it is unprofitable, and introduces an unwarranted criterion of value. The very choice of the term seems an unhappy one; for it makes you think of missions in life and gifts divinely bestowed. Surely if the concept of 'patterns' (or 'genius') is to be applied at all, it must also be applied to cultures showing disorientation and frustration. Any primitive community licensing violence on certain occasions while suppressing it on others equally exhibits a pattern, a coherent totality, whose character lies in the very contradiction; the frustrations and disorientations of the present-day European middle-class *are* the pattern of its culture or the spirit of the age, and their acceptance or the struggle against them, the genius of the people—or such genius as we are able to discover.[2] If societies also possess a genius which is as such frustrated, and hence invisible, then it is invisible and it seems futile to worry about it. To talk about a frustrated genius of a culture is like trying to answer the question in Lessing's *Laokoön*—whether Rafael would have been a painter had he been born without arms.

Finally, even with all these corrections I find the dominant trends and cultural patterns something of a miscellany. They are made up of 'unconscious choices', of tacit impulses and diffuse emotional motives, of 'purposes', of formulated thoughts and ideals, of

---

[1] E. Sapir (1925), p. 405.

[2] To some extent this view is expressed in Dr. Benedict's later work; for the contradictory traits in the Japanese character are said to be 'as deeply based in their view of life as our uniformities in ours'; so that the spirit, genius, or pattern of Japanese culture would seem to rest upon its very disunity (1946, p. 197 et passim).

rational judgments, and of moral values planfully upheld. For more system and order we may turn to Bateson's approach. It rests, briefly, on the distinction between the *ethos* and *eidos* of cultures. The 'ethos' is the total orientation of a culture so far as it rests on the emotional and impulse side of the mind; that is, it expresses the standardized 'emotional emphases of the culture as a whole'. The 'eidos' is the total orientation of a culture so far as it rests on the cognitive aspects of the mind; it thus gives us a 'general picture of the cognitive processes' operating in the cultural make-up.[1] 'Total' in these statements does not necessarily mean 'unitary'; but it does mean some perceptible integration and coherence—some 'general patterning' to which individual items are subordinated. These two orientations do not yet make up the total 'configuration' of a culture; they do so *plus* something else, namely, '*plus* such general characteristics of a culture as may be due to other types of standardization.'[2] It is not clear what these other characteristics are supposed to be. Yet if we take them to mean the integration of rational purposes—the 'heterogony of ends'—we come close to the threefold schema outlined at the beginning of this discussion.

Of the eidos concept I need say little; it corresponds very closely to our 'logical consistency'. The eidos is visible wherever group behaviour is characterized by intellectual efforts of a similar kind, say, by such features as a marked bias for pseudo-historical explanations or intricate abstract problems and sophisms; a proneness to dualistic arrangements or a predilection for complexity in all spheres of life. The reduplication and diffusion of 'motifs' of which we spoke, and the pervasiveness of organizing principles, conspicuous, above all, in kinship organization and social structure in general, are clearly implicit in the eidos; so are the idea systems logically spun out, both in the sphere of speculative constructions and in that of pragmatic values. Let us note, however, these two aspects of logical consistency—its measure and extent, and the qualitative material upon which it operates. The 'eidos' seems to refer essentially to the latter, that is, to the *contents* of thought which are so consistently organized, rather than to the strength or extent of this organization.

The same is true of the concept of ethos as it is commonly understood. It refers once more to the qualitative contents of

[1] G. Bateson (1936), pp. 29, 32.
[2] Ibid., p. 33.

ideals, desires, impulses, emotional states, and so forth. Greed, boasting, fear of witches, aggressiveness against rivals, or love of peace and domesticity, avoidance of open feuds, a gentlemanly code of behaviour, these and more are such qualitative contents. So understood, the ethos is much richer and more concrete than the energy patterns with which we operate. But I take it to represent only a preliminary result, only a first inventory of data still requiring to be ordered and harmonized. It gives us a 'cluster'—not yet a pattern, at least not one that can be used for the classification of types. For on that basis we should arrive at an infinite variety of cultural configurations, each possessed of its own irreducible individuality.

Now, you may not be concerned with classifications and types. Dr. Benedict explicitly denies such an interest. 'Nor are these configurations we have discussed "types" in the sense that they represent a fixed constellation of traits. Each one is an empirical generalization, and probably is not duplicated in its entirety anywhere else in the world. ... There is no "law", but several different characteristic courses which a dominant attitude may take.'[1] Bateson, more cautiously, considers 'that it might ... be expected that ethoses would be infinitely various from culture to culture. ... Actually, however, it is possible that ... it is the *content* of affective life which alters from culture to culture, while the underlying systems ... are continually repeating themselves', so that we may 'ultimately be able to classify the types of ethos'.[2] Yet if the pattern or ethos is so infinitely various, what do we gain by defining it? It is claimed that this approach affords the right kind of understanding and has explanatory value; the 'parts' are shown to have a *raison d'être* in the existence of the whole, the items of behaviour are explained by their subordination to dominant trends. But these, if I may quote from myself, 'seem to spring, fully grown, from history, like Minerva from Jupiter's head'.[3] It is a curious kind of explanation which takes so much uniqueness for granted; as it is a curious kind of 'empirical generalization' which must not be mistaken for 'laws'. How can we generalize about coherent 'wholes' or even talk about them unless we can demonstrate that they hang together? And this means co-variations, comparison, and the demonstration of relations (or 'laws') holding

[1] Ruth Benedict (1935), pp. 171–2.
[2] G. Bateson (1936), p. 118.　　[3] (1937 a), p. 272.

uniformly. Uniqueness and understanding simply do not go together; nor do infinite variety and explanation. The rejection of 'types', 'laws', or uniformities in general, is tantamount to rejecting all that science stands for. Such an approach leads, at best, to a preliminary survey, and at worst, to some 'general picture' based on nothing firmer than the impressions of the observer.

If then, we wish to go beyond such preliminary surveys and to arrive at material classifiable and reducible to types we must also go beyond the qualitative contents of the actions and modes of thought visible in any culture, that is, we must search for the regularities and mechanisms behind them. In the psychological sphere (or the 'ethos') this means, as we know, translating from 'object language' into 'function language', whatever the loss in descriptive fullness; so that the 'patterns of culture' are reduced to energy patterns. Yet in the sphere of logical consistency (or 'eidos') the same approach would empty this very concept of half its meaning. The types we could construct on this basis would refer merely to degrees of consistency and to the extent to which (unspecified) ideas or motifs are diffused through the various sectors of a culture. We can clearly not speak intelligently about logical consistency without specifying the contents upon which it works. Still, we must find a way to deal with the contents of thoughts and idea systems without presenting them merely as so many illustrations of the uniqueness of cultures. This, it seems to me, can be done in one way only: we must view the ideas elaborated in any culture as instances of cardinal possibilities of thought—of cognitive schemata, or of basic philosophies of life, if you like. We may suggest some of these—a trend towards simplicity and order as against complexity and intricacy; preoccupation with what is settled and past as against preoccupation with the future, hopefully or anxiously; and emphasis of different planes of reality, say, in realistic as against idealistic and mystic philosophies. As will be seen, the cognitive schemata correspond to the 'accents' typical of all mental events; nor can it be otherwise since they can only spring from the common source of all forms of experiencing. But not much more can be said with any definiteness; the categories here suggested can be neither exhaustive nor final; our philosophies and histories are full of attempts to fix such cardinal possibilities of thought.

5. CONFIGURATIONS

As I have emphasized, the three 'unities' are merely heuristic divisions. Our final problem, then, concerns their interrelations and the overlap that might exist between them. Some overlapping there must be. It is clearly not so that we can put a ring around certain modes of action which give us the integration of purposes, and other rings around other actions, which constitute the ethos or eidos. The desires and impulses which we examine for the evidence of energy levels may be the same desires and impulses which we discover when constructing the integration of purposes; logical consistency may work upon ideas or values occurring within that integration; and the basic 'philosophies of life' may merely give expression to the psychological tenor of quiescence or tension. Thus the same modes of thought or action will belong, with different sides of their make-up, to different 'rings'. We are dealing only with diverse alignments, implying a particular frame of reference—purposive, psychological, or logical. Our final question, then, concerns the coincidence and interrelation of the three alignments in any culture, and thus the possible existence of an over-all pattern or unity. And as we need a word for this super-integration (such as it is), I propose to call it, with Bateson, the 'configuration' of culture.

Now, each alignment can be shown to overlap with the others in a definite manner; more precisely, each alignment in some measure *implies* the others; so that some kind of configuration will emerge from this threefold implicitness. Let me discuss each in turn.

(i) *Purpose-Ethos*

As the modes of action directed towards their varying purposes imply a 'fitting' form of energy to sustain them, and their inter-relation an appropriate linkage, so the integration of purposes implies a concomitant energy pattern. Such is (somewhat re-interpreted) the 'hunting psychosis' of our earlier example; the tense tenor of a society dominated by political ambition or econo-mic rivalry; or the quiet, serene, 'Apollonian' mood which Dr. Benedict ascribes to the Zuñi—to a society enjoying wealth and security, without external enemies, and based upon a stable, frictionless internal order. I envisage, then, an analysis which starts with the rational purposes obtaining in any society; in understanding these we also gain some purely psychological know-ledge as well, namely, of the 'fitting' mood or energy pattern. We gain this knowledge by implication, though we may name it specifically by speaking of 'dominant trends', 'persistent tenden-cies', or of the 'ethos' or 'spirit' of a people. We have, in fact, a con-venient word for this implicit ethos; when we speak of the *morale* required of a group acting in a particular task or of social persons acting in their respective roles (soldiers, citizens, workmen, and so forth) we mean precisely this.

It is meaningless to speak here of a 'genius' creating its con-genial culture; nor does it make sense to ask whether the 'morale' is the antecedent or consequent of the rationally required ways of acting. The two simply operate together; they 'fit', and no more can be said. This question can only be asked (up to a point) if we go outside the network of actions where this implicitness obtains. We know that there is such an 'outside', for the network of rational relations does not fill the whole culture. Moreover, many social tasks, though shaped to the rational requirements, do not rigidly determine their 'fitting' energy but permit of 'alternative solutions'. You can have markets where trading is done with excited haggling and intense rivalry or, as efficiently, in a calm, business-like fashion; and you can have public gatherings, feasts, funerals, court meet-ings, and so forth, held in an atmosphere of deep excitement or in one of calm and restraint. If the economic structure of the society requires some form of market organization, it yet leaves it open in what mood the market shall be run; and if a society composed of locally scattered sections requires for its integration periodical public gatherings, it cannot be understood to require also their particular temper or emotional tone. These are, of course, argu-ments from ends to means; and they rest on the assumption that, given the ends, such-and-such means (the 'alternative solutions') are all equally adequate. It is because the alternative solutions are all 'good' solutions that we can take any concrete instance of one or the other to express, not an implicit morale, but a mood or energy pattern of more independent status, that is, an ethos effective, in some measure, as an antecedent of the concrete ways of behaving.

This evidence is more convincing still if the 'solution' observed in the concrete case is less adequate than some other we can think of. We know of situations of this kind. Consider an intricate tech-nology carried out without concentration and perseverance; wars and blood revenge executed without the impetus of strong passions; or perhaps a training of adolescents based on shock experiences and severe tests, and occurring in a society where there are no wars (or no longer any wars) nor any other tasks demanding such a tense and excited mood.[1] Such societies are clearly served by an inadequate 'morale', that is, they allow some uncongenial energy pattern to 'break through', and an ethos to be effective independently of the rational requirements. Finally, in certain sectors of culture all solutions would appear to be equally good, since the rational requirements do not reach there at all. This is true of religion, art, mythology, and recreations of all kind. For here rational requirements and mental trends only *converge*; what nexus there is refers only to the contents handled by religion, art, and the rest, and perhaps to the way in which the respective activities are organized; it does not, or not fully, imply their mood, temper, or style. It is here that the ethos of a culture will become complete, being now visible 'outside' the provinces where the requirements of morale might hold.

This completion of the ethos may take two forms. The first corresponds to the paradigm of the culture pattern theory; that is, the ethos visible within and without the network of rational requirements will be of the same kind. Now, the understanding of the former will not lead us to the total ethos; and to that extent the pattern theory is vindicated. We rationally understand that the life of a tribe revolving upon hunting and warfare should include such features as a severe, tension-fraught training of the young; rewards for individual bravery; ceremonials having war or blood revenge for their theme; belief in a universe peopled with animal spirits. But that this tribe should also possess an ecstatic visionary cult; carry the same tense tenor into all ceremonials and dances; cultivate secret societies; and practise trance possession by animal spirits—these features cannot conceivably be related to the integration of rational purposes.[2] This uniform level of high tension indicates some novel, additional factor, something like an autonomous tenor of life. Yet, as we know, it need not spring from a given tension drive which fashions its congenial cultural expressions;

[1] We need not consider the converse case, where the solution adopted is the 'better' solution; for here we should be dealing with rationally intelligible and adequate ways of behaving, and so with a 'required' morale.

[2] I am thinking of the Crow Indians described by Lowie (1935).

2 C

the uniform tenor may also be the result of syntonization (though we cannot point to the crucial initial stimulus), so that its autonomy may only be that of level mechanisms effective in response to some mode or occasion of experiencing. And this may well arise within the implicit ethos and the rational purposes it fits. In other words, the 'dominant trend' may only be a trend towards unifying the ethos but not the prime mover behind all purposes. Indeed, the question of a prime mover is insoluble, as we might suspect.

Again, the completion of the ethos may lead to a heterogeneous picture, that is, to moods, attitudes, desires, conflicting with those making up the 'morale' and sustaining the rational tasks. Here we shall discover the efficacy of repressions and of compensatory mechanisms, the curbing and deflecting of drives, and the spontaneous operation of the 'inner economy'. We have, once more, an additional, novel, factor—a tenor of life, though this is now uneven and often only relatively autonomous, being shaped by constraint; which aspect has been sufficiently discussed. We need only add that this heterogeneity of the ethos may also be carried within the field of rationally required tasks, which means that certain of these will be without the 'fitting' energy and hence executed in an inadequate or ill-adjusted manner. Of this, too, we have spoken. If we previously called this a case of inadequate morale, we may now speak of a tenor of life which fails to provide the 'implicit ethos'.

(ii) *Purpose-Eidos*

At first sight, the sphere of logical consistency appears to contain a close counterpart to the implicit ethos. When we speak of the 'ideology' of a society we seem to mean precisely this, namely, ideas and values, more or less widely' diffused and logically spun out, which express and buttress the principles of acting implicit in the rational requirements. Let me make my examples as varied as possible so as to include all the different kinds of logical consistency. Think of a primitive hunting tribe whose preoccupation with game and the success or failure of its mode of subsistence is reflected in its morality, mythology, or art; of a community where succession to kinship status is governed by primogeniture, and where the same 'organizing principle' is employed in the political field, in access to priestly offices, or is illustrated in myths and cosmology; of a heterogeneous society which must maintain its integration in the presence of sharp cleavages of wealth, and whose philosophy or religion persuasively illustrates how man is called to his estate by God or destiny; or of a State based on conquest, so that its justification lies in historical happenings, which carries historical viewpoints and reasoning into a wide range of social contexts. Ideas, values, and organizing principles, then, which emerge somewhere within the network of rational requirements, are also made into material for consistent elaboration outside this network.

Yet this viewpoint is neither generally applicable nor quite correct. To begin with, there are ideologies which are not implicit in this sense; or at least, the crucial intellectual efforts which we find so consistently elaborated may not be intelligible as an expression of rationally required principles of acting. We are often struck, for example, by the intricacies of primitive kinship systems, the same complicated arrangements pervading the whole of the culture. This is clearly such a crucial intellectual orientation; and once we accept its appearance within a network of rational purposes we might say that the intellectual orientation visible in the kinship system spreads outward to other sectors of culture. But this appearance itself cannot be taken to be implicit in any rationally intelligible requirements, or to be more implicit than, say, a simple and uncomplicated system of reckoning descent and organizing the descent group. Nor can we say that the preoccupation with a mythical past and with adventures ascribed to ancestors is more implicit in the life of a primitive hunting community than concern with the future or some code of living for the moment. Here then, we must accept an irreducible 'cognitive schema', an ideology which is simply given and intelligible only as a choice from alternative solutions. Perhaps these are not equally 'good'. The complicated kinship division into clans, sub-clans, moieties, and numerous marriage classes, might well make the social system difficult to operate; the emphasis on past events and 'mythical charters' might well impede development and hinder adjustment to urgent needs and contingencies. If so, the cognitive schema would reveal its autonomy even more convincingly: we have a 'philosophy of life', and nothing less fundamental.

Whatever the contents of the ideology which we find so consistently elaborated, the extent or measure of this elaboration seems fully to evade our criteria of implicitness. Paradoxically, where ideas or motifs are not themselves 'implicit' in the network of rational requirements, their spinning-out appears to be so implicit; and where we find an implicit ideology spun out in this consistent fashion, there seem to be no limits to its implicitness. If these existed, we should be able to point to some portion in the consistent elaboration of ideas or motifs which occurs outside the integration of purposes, as it were, in a supererogatory manner. Now there seem to be a few, banal examples of this. We might mention a society like that of the Crow Indians, where the social system consistently operates with fourfold divisions (in clan organization, in the grouping of 'clubs') and where the same numerical motif also appears in unexpected quarters—as a sacred number, as the number laid down for the sponsors of neophytes, or in the arrangement of songs and dances. Again, among the Nupe the paramount concern with political ranks and titles has penetrated into a context which stands in no relation to political life, namely, the award offered to the best farmer of the year, which takes once more the form of a title. Yet can we even here speak of a supererogatory consistency spun out for no rational advantage and implying a choice from alternative solutions all equally 'good'?

Surely the very fact that a certain mode of behaviour is elevated to a value and a principle of acting must imply some such spinning-out, since a solitary presentation of the principle would be ineffective. If the importance of the division into four or of the acquisition of titles, or whatever the case may be, is to be impressed upon a people, it would seem that the reduplication of these motifs even in unexpected quarters yet subserves the rational requirements of the situation. In other words, any such principle of acting cannot be stated or demonstrated often enough. Indeed when we acknowledge a certain principle of acting as *important* we implicitly suggest that it is employed, not only in one particular context, but in as many contexts as possible. Furthermore, when a society consistently spins out its organizing principles (a division into four, primogeniture, recruitment by descent) it would merely seem to employ adequate means for maintaining social integration and cohesion; so that the logical consistency, however far it is carried, would fully coincide with the integration of purposes. Now, as regards the first point, anthropological evidence shows that such an extensive spinning-out, although it seems to represent a 'good' alternative, is not always employed; often, important principles for acting are only perfunctorily stated and left without consistent elaboration, even in the sphere best adapted for the announcement of values and ideals—cosmology and myth.[1] As regards the second point, this much may be said. The purpose of social integration, too, admits of alternative solutions, of which the spinning-out of the same organizing principles is only one, and not necessarily the only 'good' one. For the same purpose may be achieved through employing several different organizing principles at the same time (say, recruitment by descent and by achievement, a numerically symmetrical segmentation and an irregular one), or through relying on a coercive machinery rather than on the homogeneity of the social structure. The situation, then, seems to be this. Wherever we find the same ideas or organizing principles diffused through a culture we can understand their consistency as being implicit in the integration of purposes; yet the measure of this diffusion also represents an independent variable, expressing such trends towards logical consistency as the people possess. Social 'importance' and the consistent elaboration of the things that are important do not necessarily go together; where they do, we understand this to mean, not only that here rational requirements are effectively sustained, but that logical consistency is as such desired and gratifying.

(iii) *Ethos-Eidos*

It is clear that the 'philosophies of life' imply definite psychological trends and energy patterns, and this is probably true also of certain of the cognitive schemata. The preoccupation with the past, with things bearing the accents 'certain' and 'settled', would seem to reflect the striving after equilibrium, and concern with the moment or the future, greater tension and the search for stimulation and uncertainty. The emphasis on complexity rather than simplicity, might be similarly interpreted. However this may be, the contents of these 'philosophies', the particular ideas and motifs which are consistently spun out, will decide the issue. More importantly, the measure of consistency visible in any culture appears to have clear psychological implications.

---

[1] Though statements on norms of conduct 'sometimes [find] rich expression in myth', they are also 'sometimes pared down to a minimum'; in fact, 'primitive cosmologies are often elaborated in direct contradiction to this theme' (Ruth Benedict, 1938, pp. 661, 663).

We understood the equilibrium drive to be consummated in the perception and appreciation of ordered arrangements, clarity, symmetry, and consistency, and the tension drive to imply the opposite kinds of experience. An even low level of energy, expressing the efficacy of the equilibrium drive, would thus seem bound up with logical consistency, while inconsistency, at least of a strongly noticeable kind, would correspond to the opposite energy pattern. It can in fact be shown experimentally that a low expenditure of energy goes together with the perception of arrangements exhibiting order, clarity, and symmetry, while the perception of disordered, obscure, and asymmetrical arrangements evokes tensions and assumes a dynamic character. We can, I believe, apply the same viewpoint to arrangements of a cognitive kind, so that logical consistency and inconsistency would correspond to similarly opposed levels of mental energy. If I am right, logical consistency has its 'implicit ethos' in that an even and serene tenor of life can only exist in a culture or society offering a wide scope for logical consistency. Conversely, if you have a society where, say, kinship organization rests on one organizing principle and political organization on a different one, or where religion teaches one thing and the mundane ideology another, then the tenor of life, it would seem, must be of a tense and dynamic kind. But no other 'fit' of this kind can be predicated. A widely consistent social structure, for example, may yet co-exist with an uneven level of energy, since the unevenness may be introduced by some other highly excited modes of action. Also, the consistency may itself be of a dynamic, tense kind, as when the motif of severe competition is consistently employed throughout the culture. Perhaps other permutations are equally possible. But I am speaking tentatively, and would merely suggest that logical consistency and energy patterns are to some extent independent variables, though we can hardly define this extent on general grounds alone.

6. CONCLUSIONS: CULTURE AND PERSONALITY

Let me summarize. Culture and society exhibit three pattern formations—purposive, psychological, and logical. None can be absent, and there is some overlapping and 'fit' between them; yet equally, there is the latitude of alternative solutions and some measure of independent variability. In brief, we have, not a conspicuous coherent configuration, but a composite picture with blurred contours and many gaps. We can speak only of pattern trends extending a certain way, and only of an incipient wholeness. Nor are the pattern trends ready-made or unequivocal in the manner of a perceptual *gestalt*. The integration of purposes must be constructed from calculations of means and ends; and the existence of the psychological 'pattern', from our knowledge of level mechanisms, that is, of some 'hidden machine' intervening between diverse impulses and attitudes. In either construction we may err.

The question, however, arises whether the independence of the three pattern trends is not limited so that we might yet enumerate and classify their regular combinations for the whole field of human culture. In the present state of our knowledge, with the field of social morphology in this widest sense yet uncharted, this question cannot be answered. I have attempted elsewhere to define a few cultural types from this threefold viewpoint. My approach was based on the method of co-variations, without which any statements about such regularities would only amount to suspicions. Thus I compared groups of cultures among the Nuba tribes which shared certain rational action patterns and organizing principles while differing in others; and I compared also the strength of their impulses and the attitudes indicative of energy patterns. I could, I believe, define within this limited field certain apparently fixed correlations between the three pattern trends.[1]

Perhaps, then, such configurational types exist. If so, this 'super-integration' can come from one source only—from the human personality, which is ultimately the carrier of all integrated modes of action and thought. The problem of 'personality structures' underlying in some way the cultural totality figures prominently in modern anthropological literature. Indeed, we are told that 'the anthropologist's studies of culture process and culture integration have now reached a point where further progress necessitates the use of the findings of Personality Psychology'.[2] But let me make it clear in what sense I for one am here speaking of 'personality'. I take the principle of personality formation *as such* to be an ex-

---

[1] See (1947), especially the sections entitled Conclusions. Let me stress that my 'morphological' studies are far from complete, not only because in that book certain important sectors of culture are only touched upon (e.g. religion, mythology), but also because at the time of writing I did not clearly see the methodological issues involved.

[2] R. Linton (1947), p. x.

planatory principle; I am referring only to the *existence* of this psychological mechanism, and to nothing more specific. In other words, I argue that, inasmuch as it seems to be a fact that the predispositions and ways of behaving of individuals occur in firm, limited combinations (or 'personality types'), this fact will also account for the firm, limited combinations of ways of behaving that occur throughout human culture (assuming this repetitiveness of cultural configurations to be in fact true). I am *not* suggesting that any one cultural configuration need be reducible to a corresponding personality type; rather may the former correspond only to some scatter or frequency distribution of diverse personality types; in complex societies, at any rate, where the modes of action pertain in some measure to separate human aggregates, we could not predicate more than such a frequency distribution. Above all, I do *not* predicate anything about the particular types of personality we should discover.

Indeed, personality psychology is at the moment in too confused a state to permit any precise statements or predications of this kind. I feel that what Spearman said in 1937 still holds: 'One cannot but be discouraged to find that almost everywhere the method adopted is that of general impression . . . "Typology" has become a word with which to conjure', and its field of study the playground for 'vagueness and lack of agreement'.[1] We cannot therefore hope that our own presentation of a cultural make-up, exhibiting such-and-such conjunctions of traits, would be capable of being at once diagnosed and placed on some reliable map of personality types.

Nor yet are we, as anthropologists, in a position to extract the personalities that might be concealed in our picture of cultures and societies. This view might seem to take little account of the recent work of anthropologists who, with great determination and even greater optimism, have made personality structure their motto. But my view is not pessimistic, only guarded. For consider what it is that anthropologists of that persuasion are really doing. They try to infer the personality types bound up with a particular culture directly from the modes of behaviour visible in it. They are thus relying on the uncontrolled observation of behaviour, which method in itself is bound to be inadequate and often misleading.[2]

---

[1] C. Spearman (1937), vol. II, pp. 204, 276.

[2] Even professional psychologists have amply subscribed to this approach. In either case the following criticism seems to me fully justified: 'On the whole,

More importantly, in adopting this method of inference, anthropologists are misreading, and indeed by-passing, the real problem.

We may take it for granted that there is some connection between the make-up of a culture and the particular personality (or personalities) of its human carriers. Yet in taking this connection to be a simple and obvious one, so simple and obvious that one can be inferred from the other, we run the risk of arguing in a circle and of using the word 'personality' in an ambiguous sense. For by 'personality' we can mean two things. We can mean, first, the sum-total of the overt modes of behaviour of an individual, in which we discern some integration and consistency, and which we thus understand to be facets or 'traits' of that total, patterned entity. Or secondly, we can mean some basic mental make-up *underlying* the pattern of overt behaviour and accounting for it in the sense of a 'hidden machine' or a causally effective set of factors. With Cattell, we may call the personality traits of the former kind 'surface traits', which give us 'clusters' of intrinsically related characteristics of behaviour observable in everyday life, while 'personality' in the latter sense is made up of 'source traits' or 'factors', which are extricated by analysis and have a causal significance, being 'possible explanations of how the actually existing cluster forms may have originated'.[1] It seems to me that the anthropologist who operates with the personality concept always aims at the discovery of 'source traits' and 'factors', and that he must do so if this concept is to be of any use. Yet while he approaches the personality merely from cultural observation, by means of direct inference, he can only reach the 'surface traits'. It might seem that he goes beyond or beneath them; for the anthropologist will also infer the desires, motivations, leanings, or predispositions prompting the overt behaviour. Yet he penetrates, as it were, only a short distance beneath the surface; for the desires, motivations, and so forth, are simply implicit in the cultural mode of behaviour; in our terminology, they are merely its sustaining energies, and have no causal and explanatory significance.

Now, whenever we define a culture, we imply that the population in question behaves uniformly in many ways. If, then, we find

and considering the amount of writing and discussion devoted to the method, the observational approach cannot but be judged disappointing' (R. B. Cattell, 1946, p. 4).

[1] op. cit., pp, 78–9.

the 'personality' in ways of behaving, the individuals making up the population must, *ex hypothesi*, exhibit common personality traits. In saying, 'Here is a personality,' we are merely repeating, 'Here is a culture,' and nothing more. In some African peasant community, for example, you will find that the average male individual is a farmer, a good father, a loyal clansman (that is, on occasion, a determined avenger), a believer in magic and witch-craft, perhaps an excited dancer and participant in some frenzied secret ritual, and so forth. There will be certain variations in ac-cordance with sex, age, and status, but these we may ignore. This is of course a thumbnail sketch of the culture and social organiza-tion of the people; but you may, if you like, regard these uniform leanings and modes of behaviour as the traits of a typical person-ality. And you may conclude, more generally, that 'the members of any society will always be found to have a long series of personality elements in common. These elements may be of any degree of specificity, ranging from simple overt responses of the sort in-volved in table manners to highly generalized attitudes. . . . To-gether [they] form a well-integrated configuration which may be called the *Basic Personality Type* for the society as a whole.'[1] But surely, the word 'basic' ought not to be there; for it suggests a more deep-seated mental make-up, *underlying* and *conditioning* the observable modes of behaviour and not simply implicit in them—precisely the sort of thing this personality is not.

For all the latter amounts to is a *social personality*, that is, that series of social 'persons' which, in a given culture, appears com-bined in the average individual (see above, p. 97). In outlining this personality we only repeat, purely descriptively, what we know of the society and of the roles it assigns to its members. Admittedly, we use a slightly different language. Instead of saying that in this or that group there exist clans and an institution of bloodfeud, the institution of a family implying a loving attitude of parents towards their children, religious rituals performed with intense excitement, and so forth, we now say that such-and-such people are on the average revengeful, good parents, frenzied worshippers. Even so, the construction of the personality is nothing but a duplication of our construction of the culture. This duplication has a certain heuristic value since it enables us to show the variety of social tasks and attitudes loaded upon the individual in a particular culture.

[1] R. Linton (1947), p. 83.

But to speak of this personality as though it had been extricated from cultural behaviour, and to treat it as something that can be opposed to culture and examined for its illuminating relations with culture, is entirely unwarranted. This kind of personality simply *is* the culture, and apart from its heuristic usefulness in description the concept is both redundant, since it adds no novel knowledge, and misleading, if it is suggested that it does.

Yet there is another approach which does lead to the 'source traits' and 'factors' and, perhaps, to causal explanations. I am thinking of the study of the personality types occurring in any culture by the set techniques of experimental and clinical psychology. Indeed, it seems to me the most obvious thing in the world that, if I wish to be certain about the mental make-up of a group possessing a certain culture, I must test it by means of the techniques evolved by psychology; and that, if I wish to define the cultural patterns of behaviour in terms of 'basic' psychological agencies, I must examine them where they are ultimately rooted— in the individual. Unhappily, this kind of study is still in its infancy; nor does it follow any uniform, accepted technique that would allow us to compare and treat as equivalent the data obtained in different societies.[1] It would lead far beyond the scope of this book to examine the methodological implications of this approach or to evaluate the results so far obtained. At the moment I would not venture to say how far it does all it promises to do and is indeed capable of furnishing that 'novel knowledge' we are after.

As long as we are inferring personality types from cultural observation we cannot legitimately claim any explanatory value for the personality concept; if we did, we should be committing the cardinal sin in science, namely, of pronouncing upon invariant relations between facts which are not 'demonstrably separate'. Now if we attack personality by means of *ad hoc* psychological experiments and the like, and relate the findings so obtained with our observation of cultural facts, we seem to be dealing with sets of facts 'separate' in some respect. At least, the relations we discover are between facts *independently established* (another condition of true explanations). But this separation might only be on the surface

[1] I am here referring to the use of the Rorschach test by Kardiner and others; to the psychiatric case studies of Laubscher; and to my own experiments in 'racial psychology'. See C. Du Bois (1944); A. Kardiner (1945); A. I. Hallowell (1945); B. J. F. Laubscher (1937); S. F. Nadel (1937b, 1937c, 1939).

and the facts might be 'independently established' only in the super-ficial sense of the techniques applied. Perhaps we shall even so only be describing the same thing, and explain nothing. Whatever else we may expect the study of personality-in-culture to do for us, we surely expect it to lead some way 'behind the screen of culture' (as Linton once put it). How far it does so, and how far it will ultimately 'explain' all that we wish to see explained, I will, once more, not venture to predict.

Bibliography

Adams, D. K., 1937, 'Note on Method' (*Psychological Review*, vol. xliv).
Allport, F. H., 1924, *Social Psychology*; 1933, *Institutionalised Behaviour*.
Aveling, F., 1931, *Personality and Will*.

Bartlett, F. C., 1932, *Remembering*; 1937, 'Psychological Methods and Anthropological Problems' (*Africa*, vol. x).
Bartlett, F. C., and others (ed.), 1939, *The Study of Society*.
Bateson, G., 1936, *Naven*.
Becker, H. and L. von Wiese, 1932, *Systematic Sociology*.
Benedict, Ruth, 1935, *Patterns of Culture*; 1938, 'Religion' (in *General Anthropology*, ed. F. Boas); 1946, *The Chrysanthemum and the Sword*.
Bentley, A. F., 1926, *Relativity in Man and Society*; 1935, *Behaviour, Knowledge, Fact*.
Bernal, J. D., 1939, *The Social Function of Science*.
Bernard, L. L., 1924, *Instincts*.
Blackburn, J., 1945, *Psychology and the Social Pattern*.
Boas, F., 1920, 'Method of Ethnology' (*American Anthropologist*, vol. xxii); 1928, *Anthropology and Modern Life*; 1940, *Race, Language and Culture* (collected Essays).
Bogardus, E. S., 1939, *The Fields and Methods of Sociology* (ed. L. L. Bernard).
Bridgman, P. W., 1927, *The Logic of Modern Physics*; 1938, *The Intelligent Individual and Society*.
Britton, K., 1939, *Communication: A Philosophical Study of Language*.
Broad, C. D., 1937, *The Mind and its Place in Nature*.
Brown, A. R. Radcliffe, *see* Radcliffe-Brown.
Brown, J. F., 1936, *Psychology and the Social Order*.
Bühler, K., 1928, 'Displeasure and Pleasure in Relation to Activity' (*The Wittenberg Symposium*, ed. M. L. Reymert); 1930, *The Mental Development of the Child*.

Carnap, R., 1934, 'The Unity of Science' (*Psyche*, vol. xiv).
Cattell, R. B., 1944, *General Psychology*; 1946, *Description and Measurement of Personality*.
Chapple, E. D., and Coon, C. S., 1942, *Principles of Anthropology*.
Claparède, E., 1946, *Le Développement mental*.
Cohen, Morris, 1946, *A Preface to Logic*.
Cohen, M., and Nagel, E., 1939, *An Introduction to Logic and Scientific Method*; 1947, The same—abridged edition.
Collingwood, R. G., 1946, *The Idea of History*.

Dewey, John, 1925, *Experience and Nature*; 1931, *Philosophy and Civilisation*; 1938, *Logic: The Theory of Enquiry*.
Diamond, A. S., 1935, *Primitive Law*.
Dollard, J., *see* Miller and Dollard.
Driesch, Hans, 1925, *The Crisis in Psychology*.
Du Bois, C., 1944, *The People of Alor*.
Dunlap, Knight, 1922, 'Identity of Instinct and Habit' (*Journal of Philosophy*, vol. xix).
Durkheim, É., 1897, *Le Suicide*; 1902, *De la Division du Travail Sociale*; 1927, *Les Règles de la Méthode Sociologique*.

Eddington, Sir Arthur, 1928, *The Nature of the Physical World*; 1935, *New Pathways of Science*; 1939, *The Philosophy of Physical Science*.

Farmer, E., 1939, 'The Study of Social Groups in Industry' (*The Study of Society*, ed. F. C. Bartlett).
Farris, Ellsworth, 1929, 'Current Trends in Social Psychology' (*Essays in Philosophy*, ed. T. V. Smith and W. K. Wright).
Firth, R. W., 1938, *Human Types*; 1939, *Primitive Polynesian Economy*.
Forde, D., 1947, 'The Anthropological Approach in Social Science' (British Association for the Advancement of Science).
Freud, S., 1933, *New Introductory Lectures on Psychoanalysis*; 1936, *Inhibitions, Symptoms, and Anxiety*.
Fromm, E., 1942, *The Fear of Freedom*.

Gennep, A. van, 1909, *Les Rites de Passage*.
Ginsberg, M., 1934, *Sociology*; 1947, 'Reason and Unreason in Society' (Essays in Sociology and Social Philosophy).
Goldenweiser, A., 1933, *History, Psychology, Culture*; 1937, *Anthropology*.
Goodfellow, D. M., 1939, *Principles of Economic Sociology*.
Griaule, M., 1948, 'L'Alliance Cathartique' (*Africa*, vol. xviii).
Gumplovicz, L., 1899, *The Outline of Sociology*.

Hallowell, A. I., 1945, 'The Rorschach Technique in the Study of Personality and Culture' (*American Anthropologist*, vol. xlvii).
Herskovits, M. J., 1940, *The Economic Life of Primitive Peoples*; 1948, *Man and his Works*.
Hilgard, E. R., and Marquis, D. G., 1940, *Conditioning and Learning*.
Hobhouse, L. T., 1924, *Social Development*; 1927, *Development and Purpose*.
Hogben, L., 1938, *Political Arithmetic*; 1940, *Science for the Citizen*.
Holt, K. B., 1931, *Animal Drive and the Learning Process*.
Horney, K., 1939, *New Ways in Psychoanalysis*.
Hull, Clark L., 1934, 'Learning—The Factor of Conditioned Reflex' (in C. Murchinson, *Handbook of General and Experimental Psychology*); 1937, 'Mind, Mechanism, and Adaptive Behaviour' (*Psychological Review*, vol. xliv).
Humphrey, G., 1933, *The Nature of Learning in Relation to the Living System*.

Janet, P., 1925, *Principles of Psychotherapy*; 1926, 'L'Excitation sociale dans les Sentiments Réligieux' (International Psychol. Congress, Groningen); 1935, *Les Débuts de l'Intelligence*.

Kardiner, A., 1939, *The Individual and his Society*; 1945, *The Psychological Frontiers of Society*.
Klineberg, O., 1935, *Race Differences*; 1938, 'Emotional Expression in Chinese Literature' (*Journal of Abnormal and Social Psychology*, vol. xxxiii).
Kluckhohn, C., 1944, *The Navaho*.
Koffka, K., 1935, *Principles of Gestalt Psychology*.
Köhler, W., 1938, *The Place of Value in a World of Facts*; 1947, *Gestalt Psychology*.
Kroeber, A. L., 1915, 'Eighteen Professions' (*American Anthropologist*, vol. xvii); 1923, *Anthropology*; 1944, *Configurations of Culture Growth*.

Lashley, K. S., 1934, 'Nervous Mechanisms in Learning' (in C. Murchinson, *Handbook of General and Experimental Psychology*); 1938, 'Experimental Analysis of Instinctive Behaviour' (*Psychological Review*, vol. xlv).
Laubscher, B. J. F., 1937, *Sex, Culture, and Psychology: A Study of South African Pagan Natives*.
Lewin, K., 1935, *A Dynamic Theory of Personality*; 1936, *Principles of Topological Psychology*; 1938, *The Conceptual Representation and the Measurement of Psychological Forces*.
Linton, R., 1936, *The Study of Man*; ed. 1946, *The Science of Man in the World Crisis*; 1947, *The Cultural Background of Personality*.
Lips, J. E., 1938, 'Government' (in *General Anthropology*, ed. F. Boas).
Lowie, R., 1935, *The Crow Indians*; 1936, 'Cultural Anthropology: A Science' (*American Journal of Sociology*, vol. xlii); 1937, *The History of Ethnological Theory*.
Lundberg, G. A., 1939, *Foundations of Sociology*.
Lynd, R. S., 1939, *Knowledge for What?*

MacCurdy, J. T., 1928, *Common Principles in Psychology and Physiology*.
McDougall, W., 1912, *An Introduction to Social Psychology*; 1923, *An Outline of Psychology*; 1934, *Modern Materialism and Emergent Evolution;* 1935, *The Energies of Man*.
Mach, Ernst, 1920, *Erkenntnis und Irrtum*.
MacIver, R. M., 1924, *Community*; 1931, *Society*.
Maine, Sir Henry, 1888, *Ancient Law*.
Malinowski, B., 1926, *Crime and Custom in Savage Society*; 1931, 'Culture', in *Encyclopædia of the Social Sciences*; 1932, *Argonauts of the Western Pacific*; 1934, Preface to I. Hogbin, *Law and Order in Polynesia*; 1944, *A Scientific Theory of Culture*.
Mandelbaum, M., 1939, *The Problem of Historical Knowledge*.
Mead, G. H., 1934, *Mind, Self, and Society*.

Mead, Margaret, 1929, *Coming of Age in Samoa*; 1935, *Sex and Tempera-
ment in Three Primitive Societies*; 1939, 'Native Languages as a
Fieldwork Tool' (*American Anthropologist*, vol. xli).
Meyer, Ed., 1902, *Zur Theorie and Methodik der Geschichte*.
Mill, J. S., 1875, *A System of Logic*.
Miller, N. E., and Dollard, John, 1941, *Social Learning and Imitation*.
Morgan, Lewis, 1877, *Ancient Society* (ed. 1910).
Morgan, Lloyd, 1923, *Emergent Evolution*.
Morris, Charles, 1946, *Signs, Language and Behaviour*.
Murchinson, C., 1929, *Social Psychology*.
Murdock, G. P., 1945, 'The Common Denominator of Cultures' (in
The Science of Man in the World Crisis, ed. R. Linton).
Murphy, G. and L. B., and Newcomb, T. M., 1937, *Experimental
Social Psychology*.

Nadel, S. F., 1937 a, 'The Typological Approach to Culture' (*Character
and Personality*, vol. v); 1937 b, 'Experiments on Culture Psychology'
(*Africa*, vol. x); 1937 c, 'A Field Experiment in Racial Psychology'
(*British Journal of Psychology*, vol. xxviii); 1937 d, '*Gunnu*, a Fertility
Cult of the Nupe in Northern Nigeria' (*Journal of the Royal Anthro-
pological Institute*, vol. lxvii, Part I); 1938, 'Social Symbiosis and
Tribal Organization' (*Man*, vol. xxxviii); 1939, 'The Application of
Intelligence Tests in the Anthropological Field' (in *The Study of
Society*, ed. F. C. Bartlett); 1942, *A Black Byzantium*; 1947, *The Nuba*;
1949, 'The *Gani* Ritual of Nupe: A Study in Social Symbiosis'
(*Africa*, vol. xix); 1950, 'Dual Descent in the Nuba Hills' (in *African
Systems of Kinship and Marriage*, ed. R. A. Radcliffe-Brown).

Oakeshott, M., 1933, *Experience and its Modes*.
Oppenheimer, F., 1922, *System der Soziologie*, vol. i.

Park and Burgess, 1924, *Introduction to the Science of Sociology*.
Parsons, Talcott, 1937, *The Structure of Social Action*.
Pavlov, J. P., 1927, *Conditioned Reflexes*; 1938, *Lectures on Conditioned
Reflexes*, vol. i; 1941, *Lectures on Conditioned Reflexes*, vol. ii.
Peters, H. N., 1935, 'The Judgement Theory of Pleasantness and

Unpleasantness' (*Psychological Review*, vol. xlii).
Poincaré, H., 1914, *Science and Method*; 1935, *La Valeur de la Science*.
Pratt, C. C., 1939, *The Logic of Modern Psychology*.
Prince, Morton, 1928, 'Feelings and Emotions' (*The Wittenberg Sym-
posium*, ed. M. L. Reymert).

Radcliffe-Brown, A. R., 1931, 'The Present Position of Anthropological
Studies' (British Association for the Advancement of Science); 1933 a,
The Andaman Islanders; 1933 b, 'Primitive Law,' in *Encyclopædia of the
Social Sciences*; 1935, 'Patrilineal and Matrilineal Succession' (*Iowa
Law Review*, vol. xx); 1940 a, 'On Social Structure' (*Journal of the
Royal Anthropological Institute*, vol. lxx, Part I); 1940 b, 'On Joking

Relationships' (*Africa*, vol. xiii); 1941, 'The Study of Kinship Systems' (*Journal of the Royal Anthropological Institute*, vol. lxxi); 1945, 'Religion and Society' (Henry Myers Lecture, Royal Anthropological Institute); 1946, 'A Note on Functional Anthropology' (*Man*, vol. xlvi).

Radin, P., 1933, *The Method and Theory of Ethnology*.

Ribot, Th., 1897, *The Psychology of the Emotions*.

Rickert, H., 1910, *Kulturwissenschaft und Naturwissenschaft*.

Ritchie, A. D., 1936, *The Natural History of the Mind*.

Rivers, F. W. H., 1914, *Kinship and Social Organization*; 1926, *Psychology and Ethnology*.

Roback, A. A., 1927, *The Psychology of Character*.

Robbins, L., 1935, *An Essay on the Nature and Significance of Economic Science*.

Ross, E. A., 1901, *Social Control*.

Russell, Bertrand, 1926, *Our Knowledge of the External World*; 1931, *The Scientific Outlook*; 1946, *History of Western Philosophy*; 1948, *Human Knowledge: Its Scope and Limits*.

Sapir, E., 1925, 'Spurious and Genuine Cultures' (*American Journal of Sociology*, vol. xxix).

Schilder, P., 1942, *Goals and Desires of Man*.

Schiller, F. C. S., 1921, 'Value,' in Hastings' *Encyclopædia of Religion and Ethics*.

Smith, Edwin W., 1946, 'Plans and People: A Dynamic Science in the Service of Africa' (Frazer Lecture, University of Liverpool).

Spearman, C., 1937, *Psychology down the Ages*, vols. i and ii.

Stebbing, L. S., 1930, *Modern Introduction to Logic*.

Sumner, W. G., 1907, *Folkways*.

Sumner W. G., and Keller, A. G., 1927, *The Study of Society*, vol. i.

Tawney, R. H., 1936, *Religion and the Rise of Capitalism*.

Thomson, G. H., 1924, *Instinct, Intelligence and Character* (1946 edition).

Thorndike, E. L., 1911, *Animal Intelligence*.

Thouless, R. H., 1937, *General and Social Psychology*.

Toennies, F., 1926, *Gemeinschaft und Gesellschaft*.

Tolman, E. C., 1937, 'Demands and Conflicts' (*Psychological Review* vol. xliv); 1938 a, 'The Determinants of Behaviour at a Choice Point, (*Psychological Review*, vol. xlv); 1938 b, 'Physiology, Psychology, and Sociology' (*Psychological Review*, vol. xlv).

Toynbee, A. J., 1935, *A Study of History*, vol. i.

Tylor, Edward, 1871, *Primitive Culture* (5th ed.); 1881, *Anthropology* (1930 edition) vol. i.

Watson, J. B., 1930, *Behaviourism*.

Weber, Max, 1904, 'Die Objektivität sozialwissenschaftlicher und sozialpolitischer Erkenntnis' (*Archiv f. Sozialwissenschaft und*

2 D

Sozialpolitik, vol. xix); 1913, 'Über einige Kategorien der Verstehenden Soziologie' (*Logos*, vol. B4); 1947, *The Theory of Social and Economic Organisation*; 1948, *Essays in Sociology* (ed. H. H. Gerth and C. Wright Mills).

Wheeler, W. M., 1928, *Emergent Evolution and the Development of Society*.

White, Leslie A., 1943, 'Energy and Evolution in Culture' (*American Anthropologist*, vol. xlv); 1947 a, 'The Expansion of the Scope of Science' (*Journal of the Washington Academy of Science*, vol. xxxvii, no. 6); 1947 b, 'Culturological vs Psychological Interpretation of Human Behaviour' (*American Sociological Review*, vol. xii, no. 6).

Whitehead, A. N., 1919, *An Enquiry concerning the Principles of Natural Knowledge*; 1933, *Adventures of Ideas*; 1937, *Science in the Modern World*; 1938, *Modes of Thought*

Wickstead, P. H., 1933, *The Common Sense of Political Economy*, vol. i.

Wiese, L. von, 1924, *Allgemeine Soziologie*, vol. i; 1929, *Allgemeine Soziologie*, vol. ii.

Wilson, G. and M., 1945, *The Analysis of Social Change*.

Wisdom, J., 1934, *Problems of Mind and Matter*.

Wittgenstein, L., 1922, *Tractatus Logico-Philosophicus*.

Wolf, V., 1928, *Essentials of Scientific Method*.

Wundt, W., 1902, *Outline of Psychology*.

Young, Kimball, 1946, *Handbook of Social Psychology*.

Index

Abnormal behaviour, 117–18, 143
Abnormality, 269, 270, 292, 315
Abreaction, 344
Abstraction, 24, 60, 95, 99, 123, 131, 234; in constructing relationships, 81–2; in concepts of 'society', 'culture', 80, 82
'Accents' of experience, 302–3, 394, 401
Accident, historical, 13 ff., 17, 386; in scientific enquiry, 193, 237–8, 255, 360; v. chance
Action, as against behaviour, 30; affectually orientated, 31; purposive-rational, 31; value-orientated, 31
Action potentials, 305 ff., 311; analysis of, 328 ff.; functional, 339, 343, 351, 356; generic, 311, 333 ff., 336; specific, 312, 332–3, 336
Adams, D. K., 61 n.
Adaptation, of individuals to social tasks, 96; to constraints, 364; of societies to contingencies, 326–7
Adjustment, maladjustment, 270, 375–6, 378, 379; mutual, of purposes, 268–9
Administrative machinery, staff, 119–20, 154, 160
Adrenalin, 209
Advance, evolutionary, 104 n., 105
Adventure, striving for, 355, 385, 390
Aesthetic experiences, 339, 343, 350
Affective states, 65
Age, 38, 99, 152
Age grades, sets, 38, 178 n., 231, 269, 286, 361–2, 364, 370
Aggregates, human, 77, 82, 90, 145, 155
Aggression, aggressiveness, 62–3, 90, 278, 323, 335, 376; and frustration, 197, 281, 325
Aim, as constituent of action 31–2; -contents, 76, 78, 90, 107 ff.; -control of behaviour, 30 ff., 307, 309; -direction of mental energy, 303–4, 305, 360, 363
Aims, illegitimate, 117, 173; proximal, 31; ulterior, 32
Allegiance, 99, 184
Alliances, 181 n., 186

Allport, F. H., 108, 109, 111, 220, 329, 332 n.
Alorese, 358 n.
Alternative possibilities, in choice of means, 268–9; in conduct, 69–70, 72; in sociological explanation, 254–5
Alternative solutions, 386, 396, 400
Analogies in explanation, 196, 197, 199, 205–6
Anamnesis, in psycho-analysis, 324
Andaman Islanders, 66
Animal experiments, 57, 63, 64, 349
Animal spirits, 397
Animism, 130
Antecedents and consequents in explanation, 283 ff., 396
Anticipation, 28, 31, 33, 62, 69, 71, 123, 302; in motivation, 343; of pleasure, satisfaction, 337, 365
Anxiety neurosis, 303–4
Apollonian and Dionysian cultures, 346 n., 389, 395
Applied anthropology, 52 ff.
Apportionment of tasks, 122, 157, 178, 179, 180
Apprehension of consistency, order, 343, 365, 402
Approach-avoidance, -withdrawal, 56, 303, 307, 309, 337, 338 n., 359
Approval, disapproval, 69, 110, 117–18, 137, 138
A priori certainty, knowledge, 251, 284
Aptitudes, 152
Arabic, Arabs, 39, 42, 47, 207
Arapesh, 358 n.
Archaeology, 4, 369
Architecture, 88
Arctic, 239
Aristocracy, 382
Art, 13, 17, 28, 88, 143, 324, 346, 361, 362, 398
Ascription, of dynamic characteristics, 344–5
Ashanti, 147
Assemblage of facts, 22, 23, 27
Assimilation, to indigenous culture, 18–19; to other persons, 96, 350–1; of repressed impulses, 315, 327, 361

Association, 145, 152, 158, 167; open, closed, 158; multi-purposive, 159–60; single-purpose, 158
Associations of words, 41
Atomism, in social enquiry, 75
Australian aborigines, 154 *n.*, 164
Authority, 169, 244
Aveling, F., 305 *n.*
Awareness, 74, 244 *n.*, 302, 303

Bacon, Francis, 22, 25
Balanced experiences, 338, 339
Barriers, social, 167–8, 188
Bartlett, F. C., 50 *n.*, 292 *n.*, 293 *n.*, 360 *n.*, 388–9
Bateson, G., 382 *n.*, 392, 393, 395
Becker-Wiese, 108, 136, 142 *n.*
Behaviour, as against action, 30
Behaviourism, 33, 57 ff.
Behaviour cycle, 76, 78, 331
Behavioural environment, 296
Benedict, Ruth, 27, 309 *n.*, 382 *n.*, 388–9, 391, 393, 395, 401 *n.*
Bentley, A. F., 29 *n.*, 95, 96 *n.*, 206 *n.*, 220 *n.*, 290 *n.*
Bernal, J. D., 55 *n.*
Bernard, L. L., 328 *n.*, 329
Bias, in experience, memory, 293, 398; cultural, 388–9, 392
Biochemistry, 209, 210 *n.*
Biographical aspect, of behaviour cycles, 75; of institutions, 75, 124
Biography, 30
Biology, biological, 1, 193, 200, 209 *n.*, 248, 369, 374
Birth rate, 33, 239; and standards of living, 256–7, 258, 286
Blackburn, J., 329 *n.*
Blockage of drives, impulses, 312, 314, 318–9, 323, 325–6, 333, 351, 355–7, 359
Blood brothership, 189
Bloodfeud, revenge, 86, 111 ff., 124, 155, 159, 161, 162, 166, 297, 298, 357, 358, 397
Blood sports, 315–6
Boas, F., 11 *n.*, 12 *n.*, 27, 254 *n.*
Bogardus, E. S., 330
Brentano, F., 291, 292 *n.*
Brideprice, 124, 127, 130, 137, 241, 245–6
Bridgman, P. W., 74 *n.*, 134 *n.*, 208 *n.*
Britton, K., 43 *n.*, 245 *n.*
Broad, C. D., 64 *n.*, 74 *n.*, 83 *n.*, 216 *n.*
Brown, J. F., 168 *n.*, 307 *n.*
Buddhism, 390
Bühler, K., 331 *n.*, 340, 341 *n.*, 348 *n.*

Calvinism, 237, 265
Canalization of impulses, 327, 357, 362

Capitalism, 237, 265
Carnap, R., 191 *n.*
Caste, 174, 175 *n.*, 177, 178–9
Catharsis, 343–4, 362, 376
Cattell, R. B., 328, 405
Causality, *a tergo*, 258, 283; general, 257, 267, 280; historical, 10–11, 15; psycho-physical, 256–8, 276–8, 280, 281, 383–5; and purpose, 257–8, 280, 285, 286; in social enquiry, 207 ff., 232
Causal nexus, awareness of, 303; social-psychological, 213 ff.
Celibacy, 269, 270
Ceremonials, 36, 138, 140, 234, 365
Ceremonial weeping, 66
Ceteris paribus, condition of, 230, 234, 247
Chance, 193–4, 255; *v.* Accident
Change, cultural, social, 52, 101 ff.; laws of, 102; and social equilibrium, 102; psychological effects of, 103; in 'tenor of life', 390
Chapple and Coon, 27, 62 *n.*, 192 *n.*, 239, 343 *n.*
Charismatic authority, 190
Charter, of groups, institutions, 108, 109, 116–17, 260, 375; mythical, 140, 399
Chieftainship, 68–9, 127, 244
Child psychology, 334, 348, 349
Chinese, anthropologists, 7; culture, 66, 270
Choice, in behaviour, 68 ff., 270, 388, 391; 'unconscious', 388, 391
Christianity, 184, 390
Church, 108, 120, 162, 177, 180
Circumcision, female, 39
Clan, 69, 86, 165, 177, 179, 231, 357, 399, 400
Claparède, E., 300 *n.*, 302, 348 *n.*
Class, social, defined, 174 ff.; -division, -stratification, 13, 168, 177, 180–1, 182, 183, 188 *n.*, 381, 382, 384
Classification, 23–4, 129–30, 145–6, 393; of institutions, 130 ff., 163 *n.*; of social purposes, 132–3
Cleavages in groups, 168, 180
Climatic events, 15
Closed shop, 152
Co-activity, defined, 28; co-actors, 118, 120
Co-adaptation, 28, 32, 123
Code, of groups, 85, 147, 158, 167, 178, 190
Coercion, 180, 401
Cognitive, aspects of culture, 392; processes, 301, 303, 305, 313, 337, 340, 343; schemata, 394, 399; summaries, 44
Cohen, Morris, 22, 53 *n.*, 54 *n.*, 229,

249 *n.*, 251, 254 *n.*, and Nagel E., 134 *n.*, 208, 224 *n.*, 253 *n.*
Cohesion, social, 165 ff., 189, 204, 205–6, 252, 377
Collingwood, R. G., 9, 10
Common sense, 24–5, 194 ff.
Communication, 29, 47–8, 143, 155, 188, 335
Community, 78, 90–1, 145, 153; -character of groups, 153, 154–5, 164
Comparative method, 193 ff., 222 ff.
Compensation, compensatory effects, in psychology, 314, 318, 319, 322, 398
Competition, 171, 180, 190, 244, 361, 377
'Complete description', 199, 201–2
Conation, conative, 301, 306
Concentration, physical, of groups, 155–6
Concepts, basic, 253; explanatory, 32, 106, 110, 203 ff., 252–3; in language, 45; operational use of, 134; conceptualizing, 107, 203, 234
Concomitant variations, 222 ff.; *v.* Co-variations
Conditioning, 32, 56, 57, 58 ff., 70
Configurations of culture, 382, 388, 395, 403–4
Conformity, of behaviour, 90; drive towards, 348 ff.
Conquest, 188, 373, 399; -State, 15, 382
Consciousness, 32, 33, 56 ff., 70, 72, 74, 147, 148, 185, 291 ff.; dynamic components of, 301, 303; heightening of, 333, 366; group-c., 91 *n.*, 291 *n.*
Consociation, 168, 181, 182
Constitutional factors, 356
Constraint, social, 324, 326, 373, 398; and mental energy, 325, 332, 333; and gratifications, 364; and over-expenditure of energy, 323; in psychological explanation, 323 ff., 326; implicit in drives, 359
Contact-groups, 145
Context, in social enquiry, 228
Contingent, qualifications, 152; genesis of social facts, 354; institutions, 119
Continuity, 19, 164, 371, 374
Conventions, *v.* Customs
Convergence, social-psychological, 361, 362, 366, 386, 397
Conversion, of energies, 300, 314 ff., 322, 327, 332, 333, 366
Correlations, multiple, 231–2, 234, 255
Cosmology, 89, 398, 401

'Cost', in social choice, 272, 377–8
Co-variations, 101, 259, 271, 387, 393; as attribute of social behaviour, 242; internal, 240–2; technique of study, 229 ff.
Craftsmanship, 31, 358, 364
Crime, criminal, 117, 143, 149, 172–3, 269, 271
Crow Indians, 397 *n.*, 400
Crowd, 90–1, 231, 349, 351
Crusades, 143, 190
Culture, as subject matter of anthropology, 21, 29; defined, 29, 79–80; as against Society, 79 ff., 85; -contact, 101; dualism of, 363–4; 'genuine' and 'spurious', 383; heterogeneous, 382, 384; -pattern, 83, 211 *n.*, 320–1, 346, 381 ff., 385 ff., 388 ff.; sectors of, 132, 346, 384
Cultural, 'adhesions', 204; 'lag', 102
Culturology, 21
Cures, magic, 213, 274
Custom, customary, 65, 68, 117, 142, 185
Cyclical processes, 89, 103–4, 346

Dance, 31, 213, 385
Darwinism, 26, 197
Death-instinct, 376
Defecation, 332
Definitions, in science, 244–5; and scientific laws, 245; minimum, 246; operational, 134, 225
Deflection, of energy, impulses, 312, 316, 327, 356
Density, of contacts, 94; material, 156 *n.*; of population, 154; social, 13, 150, 156 *n.*
Demand, character of objects, 306, 310, 311, 318, 325, 360; functional, 308 *n.*; d. upon Self, 303. 305
Deprivations, 137, 325, 373
Descent, 149, 152, 163, 167, 185, 238–9, 400
Description, as against explanation, 20 ff., 194–5, 201–2; methods of, 20, 22, 23, 24, 34, 101
Determinants, social, 231–2, 283 ff.
Deviants, 95, 389
Dewey, J., 29 *n.*, 44 *n.*, 67 *n.*, 143 *n.*, 196 *n.*, 197 *n.*, 201 *n.*, 204–5, 385–6
Diachronic approach, 100
Diacritical, characteristics, 67, 95, 109, 157, 179; use of names, signs, 45, 47, 262–3
Diagnosis, in scientific enquiry, 196, 197, 213; in psycho-analysis, 314–5, 324–5
Diamond, A. S., 133 *n.*
Diffusion of culture, 4, 13, 87; diffusionist approach, 4, 21, 198, 369

Diffusion of interests, motifs, 260, 263, 285, 394
Dimensions, social, 21, 78 ff., 146, 374, 380
Direct experience, 74
Disciplines, social, 325, 326, 364
Disintegration, of cultures, 300
Disoriented, behaviour, 326; culture, 384, 390–1
Displacement, 314, 319
Division, of labour, 160, 178, 239; of social tasks, 122, 160, 179, 181
'Dominant trends', 388–9, 396, 397
Doctrines, religious, 265
Documentary evidence, 3–4, 36
Dogma, religious, 85; dogmatic aspect of institutions, 116
Dramatizations, 31, 138, 262–3, 344, 365
Dreams, 30, 71
Driesch, H., 64, 292 n., 302 n., 364 n., 365 n.
Drives, 305, 306, 312, 330 n., 331, 358; and cultural occasions, 360 ff., 363; v. Action potentials.
Drugs, use of, 67
Du Bois, C., 358 n., 407 n.
Duels, 157
Dunlop, K., 329
Durkheim, E., 8, 26, 80, 91 n., 150, 156 n., 178, 205, 220, 222, 226, 278
Dynamic psychology, 305, 314

'Economic man', 197; e. motives, 133 n
Economics, 14, 37, 46, 51, 130–1, 133, 134, 135, 137, 159, 193, 241, 271
Eddington, Sir Arthur, 73, 202 n., 212 n., 248 n., 253 n., 299 n., 347 n.
Ego-relatedness, 302
Eidos of culture, 392, 394, 395, 398 ff., 401 ff.
Élan vital, 348
Élite, social, 38, 181, 268
Emergence, 216 ff., 354, 360, 362 ; emergent evolution, 216; group character, 153
Emotions, emotional, 31, 49, 56, 66, 68–9, 72, 167, 261, 297, 298, 301, 303, 304, 312, 349, 361, 391
Empathy, 18, 19, 344, 349, 350
Endogamy, 175 n., 179
Endurance, physical, 332
Energy, mental, 69, 73, 297, 298 ff.; analogy with physical e., 299–300; constant quantity of, 319; deficit of, 319; determinate, indeterminate, 301, 305, 307, 311, 312, 313; explo-ive discharge of, 319, 343, 344, 347; 'free', 326–7, 356; laws of, 316 ff., 322; organic sources of, 300, 305;

over-expenditure of, 319, 324–5; -patterns, 316, 318, 403, 320–1, 403; and personality, 318; reservoir of, 309, 313
Entropy, 300
Environment, physical, 111, 150, 200, 252, 282
Epistemology, 64, 253 n.
Equilibrium, dynamic, 343; in phy-sics, 299, 341–2, 343; psychological, 316, 317 n., 320, 341, 342, 365, 390, 402; social, 165, 204, 205–6, 371, 375
Ergs, 329
Eskimos, 270
Esprit de corps, 147, 230
Estate, 161, 187
État du vide, 303
Ethics, ethical, 26, 51, 85, 365, 378–9
Ethnography, 20, 21, 27
Ethnology, 1, 21, 26, 87
Ethos, of culture, 320, 384, 392 ff., 394, 395; implicit, 396, 398
Etiquette, 18, 88, 124, 142, 157
Euclidean geometry, 85
Evans-Pritchard, E. E., 27, 51
Evolution, 3, 13, 26, 104–6, 197, 204, 374
Excitability, 65
Executive, of groups, 160; legal, 137; of organism, 305
Exhaustion, 325, 359, 390
Exogamy, 69, 116, 121, 155, 159, 179, 244, 370, 375
Expectation, chances of, 115–16, 117, 120, 121, 125; in psychology, 60
Experiment, in social enquiry, 25, 34, 221–2, 228, 348
Explanation, analytical, 198, 199, 205; constructive, 201; deductive, 196, 205; descriptive, 201; extraneous, 282; inductive, 199; methods of, 20, 21–2, 101, 191 ff.; rules of preced-ence in, 279, 281
Expressive behaviour, 65 ff., 261, 316, 344; expressiveness of objects, 261

Face-to-face relations, 153
Family, 77, 78, 120, 130, 141, 183, 235, 357
Farmer, E., 348 n.
Fatigue, 331, 332
Feeling, f.-tone, 211, 302, 303, 305, 337
Fieldwork, 6, 18, 20, 25, 26, 27, 35 ff., 39, 51
Firth, R. W., 52 n., 55, 133
Fission, of groups, 155
Fitness, in observed regularities, 202–3, 206–7, 219, 256, 279, 283; betw. psychol. functions and material,

360; betw. social tasks and mental energies, 358, 360, 361, 396, 398
Force, in political systems, 131–2, 180, 187
Forces, in explanation, 204, 206; field of, 204, 304, 308, 363; psychological, 204, 206, 299 n., 310, 317, 347, 357
Forde, D., 228 n.
Fortes, M., 51
Frazer, Sir James, 193 n.
Freud, S., 294, 304, 306 n., 313 n., 314, 315, 319, 329, 348, 376
Friendship, 91, 189
Fromm, E., 294, 351 n., 353
Frustration, 61 n., 195, 281, 314, 319, 375, 376, 391; v. Aggression
Fulani, 66
Function, as against content, 83; concept of, 368 ff.; in biology, 369; 'latent' and 'manifest'. 275 n.; in physics, 287, 369; social, 253 n., 275, 370–1; -language, 314, 316, 359, 394; -pleasure, 340, 358, 362
Functionalist anthropology, 375
Funeral ceremonial, 32, 66, 166

Gbari, 235
Generalization, 27, 60, 193, 202, 247, 'Genesis' of social facts, 312, 327, 354, 362
Genius, of a people, 320, 391, 396
Gestalt, in interpretation of culture, 383–4, 388 ff.; in perception, 382–3, 403; -psychology, 64, 363 n., 382 n., 388
Ghost dance, 15, 143, 327
Ginsberg, M., 104 n., 105 n., 108, 110, 185
Goals in behaviour, 61 n., 71, 303, 304, 310, 340, 359
'Golden age', 38, 117
Goldenweiser, A., 15 n., 91 n., 218 n., 346 n.
Goodfellow, D., 133 n.
Grammar, 88
Gregarious instinct, 366
Griaulle, M., 181 n.
Grimm's Law, 89
Groups, groupings, 78, 82, 84, 88, 92, 98, 111, 144; analysis of, 151 ff.; compulsory, 120, 151; corporate, 95, 160–1, 183, 187; definition of, 78, 90, 145–6; ideological, 186; internal division of, 150, 176, 178 ff., 182, 247; local, 154, 164; naming of, 147–8, 163–4; open and closed, 98, 151–2, 158, 160; overlap of, 176–7; potential, 154, 186, 188; group-barriers, 168; -loyalty, 166–7, 300; -mind, 291 n.
Gumplovicz, L., 188 n.

Habit, habitual, 59, 71, 109, 137, 329, 331, 353–4
Hallowell, A. I., 407 n.
Hegel, 187
Heredity, 282
Herskovits, M. J., 21 n., 80 n., 105 n., 117 n., 189 n., 228 n.
Heterogony of Ends, 387, 392
Hierarchy, in group structure, 177; of levels of analysis, 209 ff.; of needs, 378
Hilgard and Marquis, 58 n., 60 n.
History, 1, 3–5, 7, 9 ff., 21, 26, 30, 37, 90, 103, 104, 142, 185, 192–3, 394; ideological, 37
Hobhouse, L. T., 8, 108, 200 n., 367 n.
Hogben, L., 2, 55 n.
Holt, K. B., 338 n.
Homicide, 86, 113, 162, 163 n.
Homonyms, 45
Homosexual, 315, 355
Horney, K., 322 n., 329 n.
Hospitality, 124, 297
Hull, Clark L., 57 n., 59 n., 61
Human geography, 1
Humphrey's Law, 341 n.
Hunger, 61 n., 308, 331, 332, 338, 372
'Hunting-psychosis', 385, 387; -society, 385–6, 397, 398
Huxley, T. A., 22
Hypothesis, in behaviourism, 62; in scientific enquiry, 22, 199, 230, 247–7; and scientific laws, 248
Hysteria, 30, 213

Ibo, 143
Idea systems, 83, 84 ff., 116, 154, 167, 343
Ideal types of behaviour, 114, 389; ideals, 388, 391, 401
Identity, judgments of, 224–5
Ideology, ideological, 28, 85, 143, 185, 398–9
If-situation, 111 ff., 158, 162
Imagination, 302, 337; imaginary experiments, 238 ff., 251; objects, 304, 307
Imitation, 348 ff.
Implicitness, psychological in social facts, 294
Incentives, 305
Incest, 42, 69, 71–2, 370; -dreams, 71
Incompatibility of purposes, 269, 271
Indeterminacy, 193, 255
Indian, American, 66; Plains-, 15; Pueblo-, 179; anthropologists, 7
Individual and society, 91 ff.
Individu désagrégé, 95
Inducement, 137
Infantile experiences, 195, 322, 326, 353

Informants, use of, 35 ff.
Initiation, 38, 66
Innateness, 306, 312–4, 334
'Inner economy', 319, 322, 398
Insight, 59; social, 38, 181; into situation, 271, 273
'Inspection', 60
Instincts, 71, 209, 301, 306, 310 ff., 349
Institutions, 78, 82, 89, 143, 146, 156 ff.; analysis of, Chap. VI.; alternative, 120; associative, 120–1; 158; compulsory, 120, 151; definitions of, 107–9; elements of, 124 ff.; naming of, 107, 123, 130 ff.; operative, 135, 136–7, 385; 'primary' and 'secondary', 314; regulative, 130, 135, 136–7, 167, 180, 181, 385; theory and practice of, 117; types of, 119 ff.
Institutionalization, 143, 147, 154, 189, 190; institutionalized occasions for expression of impulses, 354–5, 361–2; outlets, 327, 360
Instrumental nexus, 77; instrumentalities, 385
Integration, social, 164, 165 ff., 181, 182–3, 234, 371, 374, 377, 399, 400
Intent, 61 n., 62, 213; intentional character of action, 31–2, 297
Interaction, psycho-physical, 214; psychological-social, 211, 213 ff.
Interdependence of sub-groups, 179
Interests, 123, 145, 260, 303, 305; 'common' and 'like', 186
Intermittent generations, 235 ff.
Interpreters, use of, 39 ff.
Interstimulation, 189, 190
Intervening concepts, variables, 203, 205, 207, 311, 312
Introspection, 57 ff., 73, 304
Intuition, 17
Invariant relations, 199, 201, 251, 357, 367, 369
Invasion, 13, 14, 15
I-reference, 302
Irrationality in behaviour, 271, 273, 279, 313
Islam, 41, 143, 184, 390
Isolates in social enquiry, 75

James, William, 352
Janet, P., 292, 299 n., 314, 316 ff., 322, 336 n., 347, 393
Japanese, 66, 391 n.
Joking relationship, 180–1, 235
Jurisprudence, comparative, 26

Kardiner, A., 98 n., 109, 110, 279 n., 294, 324, 326, 355 n., 364, 390 n., 407 n.
Kikuyu, 178 n.

Kingship, 140
Kinship, 13, 18, 46, 137, 141, 169, 182, 392, 399; -terminology, classificatory, 154, 262, 264
Kirchhoff, G., 22
Klineberg, O., 65 n.
Kluckhohn, C., 80 n., 275 n.
Koffka, K., vi, 59, 64 n., 261 n., 296 n., 297 n., 298 n., 301 n., 302, 304, 305, 306, 308 n., 326 n., 341 n., 382 n.
Köhler, W., vi, 59, 64 n., 74, 261 n., 298 n., 302 n., 304 n., 339 n., 344 n., 347 n., 363, 364 n., 382 n.
Kroeber, A. L., 5 n., 12 n., 75, 91 n.
Kula, 131, 134
Kulturkreis theory, 4
Kwakiutl, 172

Labour organization, 13
Land tenure, 13, 162–3
Language, vi, 6, 28, 35, 39 ff., 72 ff., 83–4, 85, 88–9, 143, 185, 262, 366; formal parts of, 43 n.; nature of, 43–5; operational aspects of, 88; pragmatic aspects of, 43 n., 83, 84; psychological aspects of, 40, 45
Lashley, K. S., 330 n.
Latency, of innate drives, 334, 336; of institutions, 122, 199
Laubscher, B. J. F., 407 n.
Law, legal, 5, 86, 94, 95, 108, 110, 116, 130, 131 ff., 141, 159; courts of, 120, 135
Law of Effect, 58 n.; of Parsimony, 280, 281
Laws, scientific, 10, 11–12, 191, 192–3, 201 ff., 245, 248, 253–4; sociological, 10, 16, 247, 254, 380, 393
Learning, 58 ff., 70, 328, 334, 349–50
Legends, 324, 385
Lessing, 391
Levels, of analysis, 294 ff.; of mental energy, 316 ff., 320–1, 327, 346, 355, 387, 389, 402; level-formation, spontaneous, 318, 322; through repression, 319, 322
Lewin, K., vi, 73 n., 203, 294, 298 n., 305 n., 306, 307–9, 317 n., 341 n., 345 n., 347, 363
Libido, 313 n., 314, 322
Lineage, 149, 150
Lingua franca, 47
Linguists, 46, 85 n.
Linkage of social facts, 219, 311, 327
Linton, R., 14, 21 n., 27, 80 n., 82 n., 93 n., 98 n., 122 n., 135 n., 152 n., 171 n., 349, 352, 367, 381 n., 390 n., 403 n., 406 n., 408
Lips, J. E., 133 n.
Locale, 150, 154, 155–6

Logic, vi *n.*, 44, 134 *n.*, 253, 365; logical, classes of behaviour, 77; consistency, 256–7, 258 ff., 279, 316, 394, 398–9, 401–2; demonstrations in social enquiry, 252–3; necessity, 252; nexus, 77, 78, 207, 223 *n.*, 244; positivism, 242 *n.*; understanding, and drives, 365
Loneliness, 95, 353
Lowie, R., 11 *n.*, 21 *n.*, 23, 26 *n.*, 91 *n.*, 247, 397 *n.*
Loyalties, 67, 68–9, 166, 167, 168, 182–3; clash of, 357
Lundberg, G. A., 102 *n.*, 202 *n.*, 206 *n.*, 300 *n.*
Lynd, R. S., 234 *n.*

MacCurdy, J. T., 302
Mach, E., 23 *n.*, 202 *n.*, 208, 287 *n.*, 369 *n.*
'Machines' in explanation, 198, 199, 205, 277, 280, 281, 403
MacIver, R. M., 90, 106 *n.*, 108, 142, 145, 146 *n.*, 158 *n.*, 186
Magic, 18, 130, 273
Mahdism, 390
Maine, Sir Henry, 5
Maintenance schedules, 330
Malinowski, B., vi, 1, 17–18, 27, 34, 37, 39 *n.*, 80, 91 *n.*, 109, 110, 116, 131, 132, 133 *n.*, 135, 252 *n.*, 275 *n.*, 370, 378–9
Mana, 49
Mandelbaum, M., 10 *n.*, 11 *n.*
Manipulanda, 304, 362, 365
Marriage, 99, 121, 124, 126, 159, 162, 210, 241, 271
Marx, Karl, 379
Materialist conception of history, 379
'Mathematical psychology', 73; m. symbolism, 82, 204
Maturation, 334, 336
McDougall, W., 216 *n.*, 298 *n.*, 306 *n.*, 328, 334, 336, 339, 394
Mead, George H., 63 *n.*
Mead, Margaret, 27, 39, 46, 50, 95, 358 *n.*, 382 *n.*
Means-to-end relations, 31, 76, 207, 266 ff., 361, 386, 403; and causality, 286–7; chain effects of, 271
Memory, 292, 301
Mental events, 244, 302; processes, 35, 213; states, 65, 67, 68
Metabolism, 211, 300, 378 *n.*
Method, v; of anthropology, 6 ff.
Meyer, Ed., 10 *n.*
Migrations, 13, 15
Military, exploits, 139; organization, 159, 161, 182, 190, 370
Mill, J. S., 208, 222, 224 *n.*

Miller and Dollard, 60 *n.*, 62 *n.*, 63 *n.*, 349, 350
Mind, concept of, 57, 62, 63, 210–11, 301; 'connection in the m.', as condition of social understanding, 256–7, 320 *n.*, 384
Miracle cults, 327
Misfit, social, 95
Mobility, social, 98, 152, 171, 190
Mobilization, of energies, 305 ff., 309, 317 *n.*, 326; of groups, 78, 79 *n.*, 158, 161–3, 168
Mommsen, F., 4
Morale, 173, 277, 396–7
Morality, 84, 278, 281, 332, 398
Morgan, Lewis, 5, 106
Morgan, Lloyd, 216 *n.*, 292 *n.*
Morris, Charles, 29 *n.*, 142, 261 *n.*
Motifs, in cultural patterns, 260, 263, 387, 392, 394, 400
Motivations, 37, 68, 297, 304, 305; anticipatory, 343; 'subjective', 33
Multiple polarity of purposes, 380
Murchinson, C., 188 *n.*
Murdock, G. P., 59 *n.*
Murphy and Newcomb, 293 *n.*, 338 *n.*
Music, 51, 88, 261, 276, 387
Mutual aid, 160, 163
Mysticism, 390
Myth, 89, 167, 324, 335, 362, 375, 388, 398, 400

Names, naming, 83, 107, 128, 147–8, 185, 186, 213; *v.* Groups, Institutions
Nation, 149, 182, 184, 187; national character, 183
Necessity, in scientific laws, 254; necessities, biological, 373; of group existence, 361, 362, 363, 370, 372, 273; believed-in n., 179, 181; *v.* Logical *n.*
Needs, organic, psycho-physical, 32, 54, 109, 123, 137, 198, 204–5, 278, 282, 305, 308, 330 *n.*, 331, 333, 354, 372, 373–4; 'primary' and 'derived', 378–9; 'pseudo-n.', 198, 205; social, 205
Nerve processes, 210, 212, 213, 214
Neurosis, 327, 356
Ngoni, 147
Niche, social, 95, 96
Nietzsche, 346 *n.*, 388, 389
'Noble falsehood', 268, 276
Nomadism, 156
Nomenclature, of anthropology, 47–8; of dynamic psychology, 72 ff.; of science, vi, of social enquiry, 132–3, 163, 225
Normal curve of error, 113–15, 226 *n.*, 250 *n.*

Normality, of behaviour, 116, 126, 272, 354, 373, 377; of drives, 354; judgments on, 270, 272

Norms, social, 31, 70, 94, 108, 109, 110, 215, 334, 401 n.; implicit in institutions, 107–8, 117–18; believed-in n., 116–17

Nuba, 38, 46 n., 47, 66, 71, 111, 143, 165, 179, 235, 269, 387, 403

Numbers, sacred, 400

Nupe, 38, 42, 46 n., 97, 149, 178 n., 235, 355, 400

Nutrition, 52

Oakeshott, M., 193, 194 n., 195 n., 242 n., 243 n.

Object-language, 314, 316, 359, 394; -reference, 213 n., 291–3, 302, 312, 359; objects, 'intellectual', 'social', 213 n., 292, 294–5; 'natural', 292, 296 n.; of drives, 360

Observation, 20, 23, 24, 25, 28 ff., 34, Chap. III

Oceania, 7

Offence or defence, organization for, 187 n., 188 n.

Operations, intellectual, in language, 44, 225

Oppenheimer, F., 188 n.

Optimism in science, 228, 376–7

Optimum size of groups, 150, 155, 164, 234, 247

Organism and environment, 252

Organizing principles, 260, 264 n., 269, 380, 387, 392, 398, 400–1

Orgasm, 339

Origins, study of, 16

Oscillation of drives, 311, 312, 322

Ostracism, 172, 353

Outcast, 95

Pain-rejection, 332

Parentage, 141

Pareto, W., 267, 273, 279

Park and Burgess, 135 n., 145

Parsons, Talcott, vi, 8, 30 n., 33 n., 109, 216 n., 222 n., 267 n., 382 n.

Paternity, knowledge of, 164

Pathic states, 291

Pathological states, 303–4

Patriotism, 62, 168, 180, 355, 366

Pavlov, T. P., 26, 57, 62 n., 74 n., 234 n.

Peasant-culture, 382, 390

Pendulum-swing in culture, 104, 345, 346, 390

Perception, 292, 301, 302, 307, 309, 312, 339, 344, 384; of 'wholes', 339, 381, 383, 384

Persecution, racial, 237, 281

Person, in dynamic psychology, 302–3,

316–17; 'social', 92 ff., 98 ff., 119, 147, 171 n., 182, 190, 350

Personal equation, 35

Personality, 'basic' 406; psychological, 320, 388; social, 97–8, 406; of the anthropologist, 49 ff.

Personnel, of institutions, 109, 111, 118 ff., 189

Peters, H. N., 338 n.

Phantasy, 322, 328; -gratification, 324

Phenomenal regression, 211–12

Philosophy, vi, 24, 53, 103, 104, 106, 242 n., 342, 346, 365, 378, 394; social, 8, 9; philosophies, 'of life', 401–2; personal, 49, 51

Physics, 55, 75, 191, 193, 204, 205, 208, 219, 367, 369; analogy with, 79, 85, 206, 298–9, 341–2

Physiognomic character, 261, 344, 350

Physiology, 200, 204, 209, 210–11, 213, 214, 219, 234 n.

Phonology, 88

Plato, 181, 268, 276

Play, 324, 332, 343, 345

Pleasure, 31, 32, 36; -drive, 337 ff.; and consummation, 338–9; -quality of tension, 339–40

Poetry, 41

Poincaré, H., v, 202, 203, 243 n., 245 n., 255

Pointer-readings, 211; -relations, -events, 98 ff., 151

Policy, colonial, 52–3, 54, 55

Political, activities, system, 85, 131, 132, 134–5, 163, 188 n., 385; group, 77, 147, 187–8; institutions, 135, 141; planning, 54

Polygyny, 239

Positional formulae, qualities, 77, 81, 82, 83, 90 n., 169, 374

Potlach, 48, 131

Power, 169–70; -state, 180

Pragmatic nexus of behaviour, 77, 78, 107, 125

Pratt, C. C., 196 n., 211 n.

Predictability, of social behaviour, 113, 115 ff.

Prestige, 170 ff.; -suggestion, 349, 350

Presumption of adequacy, 376–7, 379

Price, 133

Priest, priesthood, 13, 41, 68, 69, 138, 353, 398

Primitive societies, attitude towards, 52; as subject matter, 2, 3–4, 7, 233 n.

Primogeniture, 398

Prince, M., 298 n.

Principle, explanatory, 203

Probability, 194, 248, 251, 254; 'objective', 113; statistical, 115, 246, 248 n.

Problem-solving, 89
Processes, social, 100 ff.
Procreation, 99, 141
Production, 35, 52, 244, 379, 381
Profit, 133, 135
Progress, 52, 105
Projection, 260, 314, 344
Propensities, 306
Property, 120, 130
Protestantism, 265
Proximity, physical, 90–1, 154, 189, 348
'Psychic economy', 323
Psycho-analysis, 26, 50, 197, 277, 278, 281, 314 ff., 322, 332
Psychology, 1, 26, 30, 51, Chap. IV, 195, 200, 204, 210–11, 219, 230 ff., Chaps. XI, XII; clinical, 296, 321, 334; experimental, 292, 296, 321, 334, 335; 'individual', 290–3; 'social' 220, 290 ff., in sociological explanations, 219–20, 278
Psychological, functions and material, 295, 302, 360; mechanisms, 13, 257, 295, 296, 297, 314, 326, 330 n.; 'silent', 313; processes, 210, 212, 213, 215–6; space, 296; tests for anthropologists, 49, 50; training, 50, 299
Psycho-pathology, 30, 59, 60, 313, 314, 323–4
Psycho-physical, level of analysis, 218, 219; mechanisms, processes, v. Psychological
Punishment, 112, 173; v. Reward and p.
Purpose, 31, 32, 33, 108, 109, 126–7, 145–6, 168, 207, 374; absolute, 237; social, 32, 53; subjective and objective, 266, 271; ulterior, 287 n., 321; 367–8, 372, 375, 380; purposes, characteristic of culture, 387, 388, 391; integration of, 385 7, 395, 397, 400, 403

Quantitative and qualitative methods, 114, 128–9, 192
Quasi-groups, 185, 186 n., 188, 381
Quiescence, 342, 343, 362

Race, 65, 282; racial minorities, 237, 315; psychology, 407 n.
Radcliffe-Browne, A. R., vi, 11 n., 16 n., 21, 27, 28, 37, 66, 80, 88 n., 92, 109, 118 n., 132 n., 133, 138, 139–40, 154, 160 n., 181 n., 220, 227, 235, 239 n., 240 n., 247, 275 n., 371
Radin, P., 2, 12 n., 25 n., 36 n., 49 n.
Randomness, 45, 58, 91, 105, 124, 218, 243, 310, 360, 366, 369; random sampling, 233, 249

Rank, 171, 238, 355, 400
Rational, choice, 270–1; nexus, 357–8; requirements, 392, 398, 400; requirements and drives, 363–4; understanding, drive quality of, 365
Rationality, defined, 266–7; in behaviour, 267–8, 271–2, 279, 313, 315, 353, 357, 363, 364, 384, 397; 'incorrect' r., 271 n., 273; 'subjective' and 'objective'. 273–4
Rationalizations, 196
Reality, degrees of, 302–3, 324
Reciprocity, 82
Recruitment, 100, 119, 122, 151 ff., 167–8, 171, 177, 180, 182, 188 n., 189
Recurrence in behaviour, 29 ff., 32–3
Reduplications, 260, 344, 382, 392, 400
Reflexes, conditioned, v. Responses; psycho-physical, 331, 348, 350; prepotent, 321; in expressive behaviour, 65
Reincarnation, belief in, 236
Reinforcement, of conditioned reflexes, 58
Regularities, search for, 10, 191, 196, 198 ff., 206, 246, 255; v. Laws, scientific
Relationships, social, 77, 78, 79 n., 81 ff., 84, 88, 90, 92, 93, 98 ff., 374; dynamic, betw. sub-groups, 180, 182; symmetrical, asymmetrical, 82, 169
Religion, religious, 5, 26, 30, 89, 182, 185, 273, 275, 315, 321, 324, 335 n., 346, 362, 375
Repetitiveness, of events, phenomena, 10, 14, 191–2, 193, 246; of cultural types, 393, 404; of sub-groups, 178; 'repetitive emergence', 219
Repression, 314, 319, 356–7, 398; and release, 323; neutralizing factors of, 327
Requiredness, empirical and logical, 244–5
Residence, 58, 92, 99, 100, 125, 152–3, 163
Responses, conditioned, 58 ff., 71, 209; hierarchy of, 62
Reward-and-punishment, 58, 70, 137, 349–50
Rhythm, 332, 338, 343
Ribot, Th., 339 n.
Richards, A. I., 26 n.
Rickert, H., 10 n.
Rights and duties, obligations, 85, 92 ff., 146 ff., 157, 166, 185
Ritchie, A. D., 63 n., 74 n., 342 n.
Rites de passage, 262

Ritual, 138, 140, 158, 167, 189, 343, 361–2
Rivers, F. W. H., 57, 211 *n.*, 229, 298, 311 *n.*
Road accidents, 33
Roback, A. A., 322 *n.*
Robbins, L., 133 *n.*
Robinson Crusoe, 29
Role, social, 93 ff., 97, 119, 151, 396
Rome, ancient, 10–11, 41, 93 *n.*
Rorschach test, 407 *n.*
Ross, E. A., 136
Routine, in behaviour, 70, 71, 76; and relaxation, 280, 285–6, 324; technological, 321, 332, 364
Russell, Bertrand, 27 *n.*, 192, 195, 201 *n.*, 208 *n.*, 248 *n.*, 377 *n.*, 379
Russia, 4

Safety, desire for, 278 *n.*, 343, 351
Sanctions, 110–11, 112, 117, 137, 353
Sapir, E., 383, 391
Satiation, 333, 340, 345, 359, 390
Satisfaction, 305, 339–40, 364, 365
Scale of urgency, in needs, 377–9
Scapegoat-motive, 281
Schilder, P., 340 *n.*
Schiller, F. C. S., 53 *n.*
Schopenhauer, 376
Science, aims of, 10; field of, 88–9; natural, vi, 10, 12, 23, 25, 191 ff., 201; pure and applied, 2–3, 52; scientist, as citizen, 55
Secret societies, 152, 262
Sections, segments, 121, 157 *n.*, 168, 178, 179
Security, collapse of, 326–7, 390
Selectiveness of culture, 388 ff.
Self, concept of, 302, 303, 307, 351; self-analysis, 74; -assertion, 334; -instruction, 58, 62; -knowledge, 197, 204, 207, 259, 278; -preservation, 374; -propulsion in tasks, 325, 364–5
Semantic economy, 43
Sensations, sensory, 301, 302, 338, 340, 343; sense-perception, 49
Sentiments, 56, 67, 68, 69, 71, 72, 297, 298, 305
Separateness of phenomena, 243 ff., 297, 407
Settlement, 13, 14, 36, 237
Sex differences, 38, 152, 264, 352; -drive, 278, 308, 314, 331, 332, 333, 338, 339, 370, 372, 378, -ratio, 239; -relations, 124–5; sexual shame, 352
Shock experiences, 103, 314, 347
'Shorthand', in scientific analysis, 209–10, 214; in construction of relationships, 77, 81; -symbols, 81; of words, 44, 148

Signs, 28, 29, 65, 66 *n.*, 344; in expressive behaviour, 65–6; s.-nexus, 303
Simmel, G., 8, 220
Simulation, 66
Sleep, 332, 333, 372
Smith, E. W., 58 *n.*
Sociability, 94–5
Social, anatomy, 380; morphology, 380, 403; pathology, 117, 271, 375; field theory, 192 *n.*, 307 ff., 360, 363 *n.*
Society, defined, 79–80, 95 ff., 183 ff.; teleological aspect of, 374
Sociology, 3, 5–6, 8–9; comparative, 20, 26, 227, 228; 'pure',. 20, 220, 280, 281
Solidarity, 'mechanical' and 'organic', 178, 204; social, 165, 177
Solidity, apparent, of groups, 82, 84
Solitude, 94, 95, 353
Sophrosyne, 378
Source traits, of personality, 405–6
South America, 7
Sovereignty, territorial, 188 *n.*
Spearman, C., 292 *n.*, 293, 302, 317 *n.*, 404
Specialization, 239
Spencer, H., 8, 106, 206, 369
Stability, social, 54, 165, 174, 180, 204, 205–6, 234, 356, 376
Standardization, of behaviour, 29, 65, 69, 136, 190, 392; alternative, 115 *n.*, 120; of catharsis, 344; of drive-expression, 326, 332, 345, 359, 362; of institutions, 111 ff., 142, 144
State, 78, 159, 160, 180, 187–8, 382, 399; analogy with family, 183
Statistics, 6, 114–15, 115 *n.*, 242 *n.*, 248 ff.; statistical nature, of institutions, 114; of scientific laws, 246, 251, 254
Status, 18, 38, 45, 82, 93 *n.*, 138, 169 ff. 188 *n.*
Statutes of groups, *v.* Codes
Steady states, in physics, 341
Stebbing, L. S., 201, 208 *n.*
'Steering' of mental energies, 307, 308, 310
Stimulus, internal, external, 311 *n.*, 330; and response, *v.* Responses, conditioned
'Strangeness' of primitive culture, 5–6
Strangers, attitude towards, 155, 281, 352
Striving, 61 *n.*, 305 *n.*, 306
Structure, concept of, 83; logical, 89; of groups, 150, 177; of institutions, 108; of language, 88; of society, 51, 190; segmentary, 123, 178; social, 182, 374, 380, 392, 402; aim-s., 363

Style, 88; of art, 265, 359
Subjective and objective aspect of social behaviour, 32 *n.*, 33, 185 *n.*, 189, 203, 273
Subjectivity, 32, 48, 54, 57, 63, 74 *n.*, 203, 253 *n.*, 321
Sublimation, 314, 322
Submissiveness and dominance, 334–5, 336
Subsistence, 139, 337, 377, 378–9, 398
Sudan, 390
Suicide, 30, 33, 117, 143, 278, 376
Summaries, implicit in concepts, 77, 80, 107, 203; in formulation of laws, 201; in words, 32; *v.* Cognitive s.
Sumner, W. G., 108; and Keller, A. G., 135 *n.*, 142 *n.*
Super-ego, 315, 319
Surface traits, of personality, 405
Survival, 54, 104, 168, 187, 330 *n.*, 372–3; -value of society, 373–4, 375
Symbiosis, social, 168, 179, 180, 182
Symbols, 28–9, 43, 58, 67, 67 *n.*, 261 ff., 344; artificial, 262; iconic, 261; 'natural', 261; s.-system, 43, 262, 264; symbolic, behaviour, 261 ff.; benefits, satisfactions, 170, 324
Symmetry, in perception, 338–9, 402
Sympathy groups, 189
Sympathetic emotion, 349
Synchronic approach, 100, 102
Syncretic rights and obligations, 157, 179 n.
Syntonization, 317, 320, 322, 327, 390, 398
System, closed, 218; isolated, 299–300, 342; physical, 299, 300, 341–2, 363 *n.*; tension-s., in organism, 307, 308, 317 *n.*, 341; in scientific enquiry, 49, 134, 254 *n.*
Systematization, 22–3, 27, 49

Taboos, 179; *tabu,* 48
Talion, 111
Tanala, 390 *n.*
Task character, of social behaviour, 32, 33, 67, 75, 84, 86, 93, 122, 297, 310, 358; of institutions, 123; t.-consciousness, 303, 313, 364–5; uncompleted t., 326 *n.*
Tautologies in explanation, 21, 251 ff., 259, 372, 374, 375
Tawney, R. H., 265 *n.*
Teamwork in anthropology, 37, 51
Technology, 35, 87, 88, 155, 327, 358
Tenor, of life, 397–8, 402; psychological, 395
Tension, in psychology, 303 ff., 305 *n.*, 313, 319, 321, 326, 339, 359, 364;

and expenditure of energy, 318; and generation of energy, 319, 347; -less states, 339, 393; *v.* Systems
Terence, 9
Territory, 153 ff., 166, 187
Thomson, G. H., 328, 329
Thorndike, E. L., 58 *n.*
Thouless, R. H., 301 *n.*
'Thread of meaning', in repressions, 324, 325, 355, 391
Ticopia, 143
Time-dimension, 100; -perspective, 17, 118, 284
Toennies, F., 145
Tolman, E. C., 61, 62, 64 *n.*, 73 *n.*, 203, 210 *n.*, 330
Tolstoi, 276
Topography, in Gestalt psychology, 363
Total culture, concept of, 320, 321, 380 ff.; t. society, 183 ff., 381
Totem, totemism, 48, 130, 263
Toynbee, A. J., 10 *n.*
Trance possession, 397
Transference, of aims, 138 ff., 265; of loyalties, 168, 182–3; in psychoanalysis, 314; of values, 265
Translation, difficulties of, 41 ff.
Traumatic experiences, 314
Tribe, 184
Trobriands, 68, 143, 164
Tsoro, 66
Tylor, Edward, 106, 193 *n.*, 198 *n.*, 204
Types, of action, actors, 81; type-concept, 92; typical behaviour, 113 ff., 116, 250
Typology, social, 380, 393, 404; psychological, 404

Unconscious, 60, 71; collective, 291 *n.*
Undefinables, 74
Unemployment, 38, 117, 271
Uniform culture, 185–6
Uniqueness, of behaviour, 29, 30; of events, 10, 12–13, 16, 17, 142, 193, 237, 369, 394
Universals of culture, 237, 333, 335, 352, 362

Valences, in psychology, 61, 306, 307 ff., 310
Validity of institutions, 118 ff., 157–8
Value judgments, 53, 54–5, 272–3
Values, clash of, 117, 357; ethical, moral, 51–2, 117, 272, 295–6, 401; in psychology, 305; social, 31, 138, 139 ff., 264–5, 392, 398
Variability of behaviour, 113 ff., 125–6, 226, 240–2
Vectors, in psychology, 61, 73 *n.*, 192 *n*
Verification, 27, 63, 200, 334, 336

Vernacular, use of, 18, 39 ff.; words, terms, 48
Verstehende Psychologie, 296, 388
Vested qualifications, 151–2
Visionaries, visionary cults, 15, 325, 353, 361, 397

Wages, 348
War, 190, 210, 231, 325, 326, 358, 361, 364, 370, 397; Holy, 143, 190
Watson, J. B., 57 *n.*, 59 *n.*, 62
Wealth, 122, 152, 226 *n.*, 264; wasteful display of, 377
Weber, Alfred, 105 *n.*
Weber, Max, vi, 8, 31, 92 *n.*, 115 *n.*, 151 *n.*, 190, 215 *n.*, 226, 238, 265 *n.*, 271 *n.*, 279
West Africa, 15, 143, 153
Westermarck, E., 8, 71, 298
Wheeler, W. M., 261 *n.*
White, Leslie A., 21, 91 *n.*, 105 *n.*, 106 *n.*
Whitehead, A. N., vi *n.*, 22, 23 *n.*, 24 *n.*, 25 *n.*, 49 *n.*, 80 *n.*, 106 *n.*, 146, 211

'Wholes', in cultural analysis, 75, 382 ff., 393
Wickstead, P. H., 131 *n.*, 137 *n.*
Wiese, L. von, 8, 143 *n.*, 145, 369 *n.*
Will, 301, 305, 306, 313, 365; 'w. to live', 300
Wilson, G. and M., 102 *n.*
Wisdom, J., 10 *n.*, 11 *n.*
'Wishes', in social inquiry, 145
Wish-fulfilment, 197, 324, 327
Witchcraft, 18, 52, 244–5, 275, 376
Wittgenstein, L., 252 *n.*, 253 *n.*
Wolf, A., 201 *n.*
Wolf-children, 21
Wundt, A., 387

You-awareness, -certainty, 64, 261 *n.*, 350
Young, Kimball, 65 *n.*, 349
Youth-movements, 315

Zulu, 153
Zuñi, 395